Squadron of Deception

Stephen McKenzie Hutton

DEDICATION

This book is dedicated to my father, Iredell Hutton, and to the men of the 36th Bomb Squadron RCM both air and ground who were the Gremlins

Squadron of Deception

The 36th Bomb Squadron in World War II

Stephen McKenzie Hutton

Schiffer Military History
Atglen, PA

In Memory

Airmen of Lt. Joseph Hornsby's crew who died in the crash of Liberator #42-51226, R4-L near Boucly, France on November 10, 1944.
2nd Lt. Frederick G. Grey (navigator)
Sgt. Raymond G. Mears (gunner)
Sgt. Frank A. Bartho (gunner)

Airmen of Lt. Norman Landberg's crew who died in the take-off crash of Liberator #42-51219, R4-I near Cheddington, England on November 15, 1944.
2nd Lt. Walter S. Lamson (navigator)
Pfc. Leonard Smith (gunner)

Eight men of Lt. Harold Boehm's crew who were lost to the Irish Sea after parachuting from Liberator #42-51232, R4-J nicknamed *The Jig's Up* near Valley, Wales on December 22, 1944.
2nd Lt. William H. Lehner (navigator)
S/Sgt. Arthur R. Clemens (engineer)
S/Sgt. Harvey N. Nystrom (radio operator)
S/Sgt. Francis J. Lynch (radio operator)
S/Sgt. Andrew Zapotocky (gunner)
Sgt. Roger F. Gagne (gunner)
S/Sgt. Jaime Fonseca (gunner)
Sgt. Charles H. Dautel (gunner)

S/Sgt. Herman J. Wolters, (radio operator) who died as a result of electrical shock while on detached service and performing his duties at Namur, Belgium on January 19, 1945.

Lt. John W. McKibben's crew of ten in Liberator #42-51239, R4-C nicknamed *The Uninvited* who failed to return from their assigned operational mission on February 5, 1945. Those lost were:
2d Lt. John W. McKibben (pilot)
2d Lt. Gaylord Moulton (co-pilot)
2d Lt. Eugene H. Junkin (navigator)
S/Sgt. Raymond P. Brecht (engineer)
Sgt. Bruce E. Gist (radio operator)
S/Sgt. Galen A. Brooke (radar operator)
Sgt. Robert G. Brass (gunner)
Sgt. Max W. Oettle (gunner)
Sgt. Harold E. Eckert (gunner)
Sgt. Paul W. Frantz (gunner)

Airmen of Lt. Louis McCarthy's crew in Liberator #42-50385, R4-H nicknamed *Beast of Bourbon* who died in a tak-off crash near Cheddington, England, on February 19, 1945.
S/Sgt. Carl E. Lindquist (gunner)
Pvt. Fred K. Becker (gunner)
Pvt. Howard F. Haley (gunner)

Book Design by Ian Robertson.

Copyright © 1999 by Stephen M. Hutton.
Library of Congress Catalog Number: 99-60321

Printed in China.
ISBN: 0-7643-0796-7

We are interested in hearing from authors with book ideas on related topics.

Published by Schiffer Publishing Ltd.
4880 Lower Valley Road
Atglen, PA 19310
Phone: (610) 593-1777
FAX: (610) 593-2002
E-mail: Schifferbk@aol.com.
Visit our web site at: www.schifferbooks.com
Please write for a free catalog.
This book may be purchased from the publisher.
Please include $3.95 postage.
Try your bookstore first.

In Europe, Schiffer books are distributed by:
Bushwood Books
6 Marksbury Road
Kew Gardens
Surrey TW9 4JF
England
Phone: 44 (0)181 392-8585
FAX: 44 (0)181 392-9876
E-mail: Bushwd@aol.com.

Try your bookstore first.

Contents

Preface

The research and development for this book has truly been one of my life's most meaningful experiences. Allow me to explain what led me to this endeavor.

Not unlike my many friends that I played with as a young boy, I was naturally curious about my father's service during the Second World War. I recall when I was about ten years old (circa 1960), he told me that he had served in the Eigth Air Force. He said his outfit performed radar countermeasures (RCM), dropped tin foil, and electronically jammed German radar. He had served in a B24 Liberator, flying 54 missions over Europe with the U.S. Eighth Air Force and British Royal Air Force. He also told me that one day another crew had taken his plane, nicknamed *The Jigs Up*, and never came back. Of course, this story piqued my interest to find out the how, when, where, and why. So my quest began.

In time I saw Dad's wartime photographs and naturally sought more information about his special outfit. I learned that Dad had served in the 803rd and 36th Bomb Squadrons, but unfortunately, after extensive research, I discovered very little had been written about this radar countermeasure squadron.

Now it seems that I may have been indeed destined to undertake this mission to produce this unit history book. In 1990, forty-five years after the end of the war, I read the book titled, *Secret Squadrons of the Eighth*, by Pat Carty. His fine work revealed to me much sought after information and wonderful photographs of Dad's old outfit. Before long, I had spoken with Pat on the telephone and soon we were corresponding. Pat told me that the squadron was a secret outfit whose combat records had not been declassified until the late 1970s. To satisfy my desire to learn more of Dad's squadron, he informed me of the archives in England and the U.S. and where to write. Within two years, my wife Pam and I traveled to England to meet Pat. He lived near Cheddington, one of Dad's bases, and during our visit he gave us the grand tour, pointing out the functions of the airfield buildings, and the location of the runways and taxiways. Our visit was marvelous.

Wishing to finally uncover the complete story and facts surrounding the loss of Dad's Liberator, I immediately started my re-search upon returning home to the U.S. I contacted the archival offices about receiving microfilm copies of historical records concerning the 803rd and 36th Bomb Squadrons, and the U.S. RCM program. Before long I was gleaning over the official records—eight rolls of microfilm from the U.S. Air Force Historical Research Agency at Maxwell Air Force Base, Alabama. This data, now public domain, gave me my answer concerning the loss of *The Jigs Up*. It was then that I decided to prepare a unit history in order to properly recognize not only the men of the 803rd/36th BS, the first secret 8th Air Force Radar Countermeasure combat unit, but also the men and women involved in the U.S. radar countermeasure program. I quickly developed a passion to learn more, but time was to be my greatest enemy.

The official records not only revealed other squadron crashes and mission data, but more importantly, provided many names and hometown addresses of squadron participants. In time I traveled to Maxwell to view the original document files. To capture and to copy the historical file photographs, my good friend, author, and gifted photographer, Sam Sox, Jr., accompanied me. At this time I should have bought stock in my telephone company, because soon I began running up my telephone bill in an unrelenting effort to locate these "old brave eagles," to hear their story and learn of their experiences with the RCM program. Of the 43 air crews assigned to the 803rd/36th Squadron, I was successful in locating one or more members of each crew or a family relative. I was elated to locate and speak with so many of those attached to the squadron, well over two hundred in all. However, I was also saddened that I had started late. To my dismay, I found many men had died. The men and the families I contacted heard me out and patiently listened to my quest, my "labor of love." Even with the passage of a half a century, all the men kindly told me what they could of this last great air war. Shortly after our conversation, which most often included a recorded interview, I mailed each member a package of material, telling them what I had learned about their secret outfit and its unique support function, and I asked for their input. Their response was tremendous. Many wrote of their war time experiences, and sent their personal records, memorabilia, and their old photographs for me to copy.

In summation, this book is meant only to present a chronological account detailing the work of the 803rd and 36th Bomb Squadrons. Omissions certainly exist after such a passage of time. I realize there are many squadron members that I failed to locate, and quite naturally I would love to hear from them as well. There is no attempt here to fully define the entire field of radar countermeasures in Europe. However, much important information has now been collected to rightly recognize and to honor the men of this support squadron. I felt from the start that this important story must be told by its participants. Therefore, I have tried to use as much of the original information as possible from the diaries, orders, letters, and the historical documents written by the squadron adjutants. Not every participant's story or recorded interview was transcribed and printed here. I found that a few stories might have embarrassed some people; a few might have offended some readers, but just to read or listen to their stories was my greatest thrill. I have tried to use the best stories, illustrations, and photographs for this book. Some of the photographs were creased, torn, or naturally faded over the many years. And there were times where many different people sent the same photo.

With the publication of this history many thanks are in order. First, my greatest thanks go to the men of the Eighth Air Force, especially those of the 803rd and 36th Bomb Squadrons and their families for their most valuable time and assistance in this worthwhile project. It is much to ask of individuals to stoop down on their not-so-young knees, to look into their nooks and crannies, dig out and pick through old family albums, rummage through many drawers, or sometimes hot scorching or freezing cold and dusty attics for old photos, records, or documents to send to someone they don't know from Adam. Generous thanks go to the former members of the American-British Laboratory Division 15, the Radio Research Laboratory, personnel of the U.S.A.F. Historical Research Agency, the U.S.A.F. Safety Center, the National Archives, the Veterans Administration, the 8th Air Force Historical Society, the Mighty Eighth Air Force Heritage Museum, and the Association of Old Crows for aiding me in my search for original historical material. Additionally, special thanks go to Pat Carty, who got me started, to my friend, advisor, and fine photographer Sam Sox, Jr., to Dr. Dan Kuehl for his suggestions with the manuscript, and to my Welsh friend Brendan Maguire who retrieved *The Jigs Up* propeller blades from the Irish Sea. For the great artistic help with the D-Day illustration and airfield maps, I thank Tim Trudgeon and Deborah Wright. Also, many thanks go to my mother and father who encouraged me to see this project reach its rightful end. And lastly, to my wonderful wife, Pam, go my deepest thanks. Pam not only patiently endured my time away from her side, but also my time away from family, friends, and the usual demanding household chores.

During these past eight years I have endeavored to write a book that is historically correct. Because the 803rd/36th Bomb Squadron was so much involved in testing and utilizing the various countermeasure equipment, I believed it was most important to recognize the work of the training, engineering, and communications sections. Hence the lengthy appendices. This side of the story was a must to be told as it goes behind the scenes and illustrates their service to the airmen in the aircraft on the missions. It was my goal that the book be comprehensive, thorough, and enlightening to the former squadron members and their families. May it show value to them and also to future generations. The men of this pioneering electronic warfare squadron having waited more than half a century, may now view more of the whole of their work to better understand their special contribution toward victory in Europe during World War II.

Stephen M. Hutton

Abbreviations

AAF - Army Air Force (U.S.)

ABL-15 - American British Laboratory, Division 15

AI - Airborne intercept

AOC - Air Officer Commanding (British)

BG - Bomb Group

BS - Bomb Squadron

CBI - China, Burma, India Theater of Operations

CHAFF - American term for aluminum tinsel cut in widths and lengths to jam enemy radar

D-Day - June 6, 1944 - the day of the Allied invasion of France

Det. - Detachment

DS - Detached service

DG - Directional Gyro

ELINT - Electronic intelligence

ETO - European Theater of Operations

FERRET - electronic intelligence reconnaissance aircraft used in enemy frequency searches

GCI - Ground-controlled intercept

GI - Government issue (American soldier)

GL - Gun-laying

H - Heavy

MIA - Missing in action

MIT - Massachusetts Institute of Technology

NDRC - National Defense Research Committee

NLS - Night Leaflet Squadron

ORS - Operation Research Section

OSRD - Office of Scientific Research and Development

OTU - Operational Training Unit (RAF)

PGEU - First Proving Ground Electronic Unit at Florosa Field, Florida

PROV - Provisional

RAF - Royal Air Force

RCM - Radar/Radio countermeasure

RRL - Radio Research Laboratory

R/T - Radio/telephone

SEAD - Suppression of enemy air defenses

SHAEF - Supreme Headquarters Allied Expeditionary Forces

TRE - Telecommunications Research Establishment (England)

USAAF - United States Army Air Forces

USAFI - United States Armed Forces Institute

USAAFUK - United States Army Air Force in the United Kingdom

USSTAF - United States Strategic Air Forces in Europe at High Wycombe and code name Pinetree

W/T - Wireless/telegraphy

WINDOW - British term for aluminum tinsel cut in widths and lengths to jam enemy radar

1

Beginnings

The story of the 36th Bomb Squadron Radar Countermeasure (RCM) unit is a tale quite unlike and very different from any other American heavy bomber squadron that served during World War II. They dropped not a single bomb, but nonetheless performed a very important function, supporting both the Royal Air Force (RAF) and the Eighth Air Force (8AF). Their missions came under the category of "special operations." The bomb squadron name was designed to mislead the enemy and Allied personnel with no "need to know" into believing this was just another American bomber squadron. In fact, this special squadron was truly one of a kind and was charged with a very secret mission—to jam German radar and to deceive and confuse the enemy.

Dr. R.V. Jones, who as the Assistant Director of Science Intelligence for the British Air Staff, and one of the most important aides to Winston Churchill, placed great emphasis on this important support program. Dr. Jones wrote in his book *Most Secret War* , "The war can be lost without a good, clear thinking, countermeasure policy."[1] Today, more than fifty years after the 36th Bomb Squadron completed its last mission, Dr. Daniel Kuehl, author of *The Radar Eye Blinded,* and Professor at the National Defense University, School of Information Warfare in Washington, DC, wrote: "They were the leading edge of a transformation in warfare. They were completing the extension of warfare into the third dimension—the air, that was begun only three decades earlier during World War I. They were also beginning the extension of warfare into what I call the fourth dimension, the electronic arena, what some today call cyberspace."[2] Their missions during 1944-45 are what is termed today as "suppression of enemy air defenses," or SEAD.

The Birth of RCM

The first recorded use of radio countermeasures by the military dates back to the turn of the twentieth century. In 1902, the British Royal Navy, while conducting maneuvers in the Mediterranean, attempted to smother or jam "on top" of other radio signals. The U.S. Navy applied this same method of jamming to their exercises off the Atlantic coast the next year. During the 1904 Russo-Japanese War the first real combat application occurred. When the Japanese bombarded Port Arthur, a Russian naval radio operator, using a spark transmitter, successfully jammed the Japanese radio signals which were being used to provide the shellfire corrections to the Japanese armored cruisers *Kasuga* and *Nisshin*. As a result, only a few casualties and little damage was sustained.[3]

Later, during the opening of World War I, radio jamming and signals intelligence played a valuable role in naval engagements. In August of 1914 British cruisers jammed wireless communications when the German cruisers *Goeben* and *Breslau* fled across the Mediterranean Sea. Even though it was radio and not radar transmissions that were being jammed during this event, the military learned the value and practical applications of the "fourth dimension." The Germans would have the opportunity to reverse this scenario in the next great war.

In the 1930s research scientists in Britain, the U.S., Germany, Japan, the Soviet Union, France, and Holland were all working independently to produce operational radars. In Great Britain, Robert Watson-Watt led the radar development program. In 1936, with storm clouds gathering over Europe, the British first tested their operational defensive radar and erected their first early warning radar station, or "Chain Home" radar. The Bawdsey radar site was the first of many along England's coast. It could detect aircraft up to 100 miles away. Two years later, with Germany now posturing for war, in order to test its vulnerability, the British jammed their own radar using a ground spark transmitter on board a Sunderland aircraft flying offshore Felixstowe. After these tests, the Chain Home stations along the south and east coasts of Great Britain began having anti-jamming systems built into their radar equipment.

Defensively, the British gave a large measure of credit for their victory in the Battle of Britain to their Chain Home radar early warning capability, but offensively their real actions had not yet begun. In fact, hard lessons were still to be learned by the British, and these did not come easily. One case in point, for example, occurred when in 1942 on 11 and 12 February, the German battle cruisers *Scharnhorst* and *Gneisenau*, along with the heavy cruiser

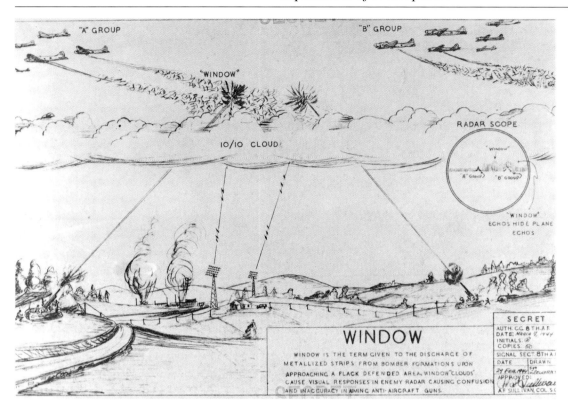

WINDOW utilization cartoon. WINDOW was a form of passive jamming. *Courtesy of USAF Historical Research Agency.*

Prinz Eugen, made a surprise sortie toward friendly waters and home by sailing through the English Channel and narrow Straits of Dover in broad daylight. The British were startled and most embarrassed by this bold event which came to be known as the "Channel Dash." The German success in this significant wartime feat was in a large part due to the successful jamming of the British radar chain. All doubts as to Germany's ability to jam British radar defenses were now removed. The first great steps in Britain's radar countermeasure offensive would soon begin.

During the fall and winter of 1942 the British initiated countermeasures against German radar and communications systems. RAF Bomber Command learned that as their countermeasure program improved, their bomber losses decreased. The British soon realized great success by utilizing an effective countermeasure program. Bomber Command discovered RAF aircraft losses were 50% less than before the employment of such countermeasures.[4]

Great Britain's offensive radar jamming took two different forms—active and passive. When Britain's Sir Henry Tizard created the Cavity Magnetron (with significant American assistance), his invention led to the first production of various complicated active radar jamming transmitters. These functioned by actively transmitting signals to mislead or obscure the enemy radar signals. Joint British and American scientific cooperation into this new electronic arena was later to become the most important factor in the rapid development of their combined electronic warfare technology. The second technique—passive jamming—was a simple form of jamming, known as WINDOW by the British or CHAFF by the Ameri-

cans. (See WINDOW cartoon illustration.) These were metallized strips dropped from bomber formations upon approaching enemy searchlight areas and anti-aircraft or flak (from the German word Fliegerabwehrkanon) batteries. WINDOW would confuse the enemy radar responses and cause inaccuracy in the aiming of the radars by generating literally thousands of radar returns, of which only a few represented real aircraft. The Germans also saw the po-

German radar site. *Courtesy of the Mighty Eighth Air Force Heritage Museum.*

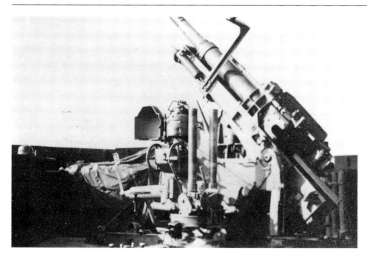

German flak battery. *Author's collection.*

Men of a German flak battery. *Author's collection.*

tential of these metallic strips, but forbid work on it, fearing the British would learn of it and use it against them. So for a time both Britain and Germany opted to wait.

Sir Arthur Harris, Marshal of the RAF, felt the pressure to use WINDOW, the tinsel gremlin. Even though he believed that it would not have been wise to use WINDOW over Germany in August of 1940, by 1942 he felt the time had come to take the risk. During the summer of 1942 he continually pressed for the development and use of WINDOW along with other available radio and radar countermeasure equipment.

History has recorded that the British were the first to use the metallic strips, and use it they did with stunning success. The British first employed WINDOW in combat during July 1943, when the RAF made a stunning raid on the German port city of Hamburg. In the first raid forty tons of tin foil were dropped and scattered by British airmen, thus confusing the German ground controllers, who began misdirecting the Luftwaffe's night defenses. The deceived controllers believed thousands of bombers were being displayed on their radar screens, when actually only 791 bombers took part. One horrified German radar operator exclaimed, "The planes are doubling themselves!"[5] The RAF raiders lost only 12 planes. Protected by WINDOW during this opening success, the RAF continued bombing Hamburg four more times over the next nine nights. During the raid on the evening of 27 July, Hamburg became the world's first victim to a raging firestorm. Over 50,000 people perished, and half of the harbor city's buildings were either destroyed or damaged.[6]

Having forseen the great potential for the use of WINDOW, Harris had actually desired to employ it earlier in 1943. He felt convinced that had they been able and allowed to use WINDOW in the first months of that year, hundreds of aircraft and thousands of lives would have been saved and the accuracy of their bombing would have increased.

For the United States the countermeasures program started late, since the need for it was not realized until after heavy bombardment groups began operating from England. Even after American bombers went into operation, there were no countermeasure officers in the 8AF, so it was quite natural for the U.S. that at first the role the German radio and radar system played in the enemy defenses was not well understood.

The first countermeasures institutions in America were formed in the latter months of 1942. Influenced considerably by British design and brainwork, the first U.S. countermeasures equipment became available during the spring of 1943. More equipment would eventually be ready, and consequently a plan was drawn up to provide the ETO—the European Theater of Operations—with a suitable organization to utilize this material as soon as it became available.

In June of 1940 the National Defense Research Committee (NDRC) was formed under the guidance of Dr. Vannevar Bush, who reported directly to President Roosevelt. This new committee was chartered to marshal the U.S. scientific community and to sup-

One of the huts where the men and women of ABL-15 worked. *Courtesy of Shirley C. Merrill.*

The ABL-15 laboratory was on the grounds of the British research institution Telecommunications Research Establishment (TRE). John Dyer, the Director of ABL-15 (American British Laboratory Division 15), is seen sitting on the wall in shirt and tie with his hair on his forehead. In the background the large building housed TRE, and the smaller building in the foreground is one of the temporary huts where ABL engineers and technicians worked. *Courtesy of Shirley C. Merrill.*

port the national defense. Within a few months NDRC created the Radiation Laboratory located at the Massachusetts Institute of Technology (MIT) to concentrate the U.S. radar research effort. Although not much thought was given toward radar countermeasures at this time, the surprise attack on Pearl Harbor soon changed that. Four

days after the infamous attack, NDRC, Radiation Lab, the Office of Scientific Research and Development, and the Navy, established Division 15. Dr. C. Guy Suits was placed in charge. Division 15's primary responsibility was for design, research, and development of radar countermeasure equipment. Before long Division 15 began its own lab called the Radio Research Laboratory (RRL). Dr. Fred Terman, who had been in charge of Stanford University's Electrical Engineering department, was selected as head. RRL was located at Harvard University in July of 1942. Dr. Terman recruited 150 men and women, many of whom were his former students, for this specialized work. RRL would provide the U.S. military with the necessary RCM equipment for the duration of the war.[7]

Professor of Electronics Donald Reynolds was one of the first Americans asked by Dr. Terman to work on RCM and travel to the UK. In 1982, during an interview with the Association of Old Crows, he elaborated:

Dr. Terman had been invited to set up the laboratory [Radio Research Laboratory]. Of course it was extremely secret at that time, and so we didn't know what he was really doing, but we knew he was on some important mission. So, I was just one of the early recruits for RRL.

The first week of November of '42, we put ourselves in the hands of the RAF. They had us go up to Montreal to take the flight over to Scotland in one of these B24s sold to the RAF, which they were using just for transporting people. Perhaps the same plane that Terman went over on earlier. We had to sit in the rear section on the floor. It wasn't configured for passenger seats and no pressurization, so we had to wear oxygen masks, so sort of an exciting trip.

CARPET utilization cartoon. CARPET was a U.S. made active jammer. *Courtesy of USAF Historical Research Agency.*

The Allied Air Warfare decision makers — Air Marshal A. T. "Bomber" Harris and Lt. Gen. Ira Eaker. *Courtesy of the Mighty Eighth Air Force Heritage Museum.*

Later, we were in London for a few days before we were distributed to these other research establishments. They took very good care of us. All of us had the chance to meet Sir Robert Watson-Watt, who is considered to be the father of radar, at least as far as England is concerned.

We were on a loan to the British, but with our salary continued to be supported from Cambridge, Mass., and Harvard. We would just make arrangements with local banks to have portions of our salary transferred for local expenses. We were also put up simply in local housing. There were many RAF officers at this establishment. TRE, the Telecommunications Research Establishment, was their principal radar development place. It also had the section on electronic countermeasures, which was called "House 7."

My first boss there was Dr. Martin Ryle, who later on became world famous as a radio astronomer at Cambridge. We were simply mixed right into a group of British electrical and electronic engineers. TRE had already been moved a couple of places around England. The previous location had been a coastal location where it was vulnerable for attacks by fighter bombers coming across the channel, so they finally moved it inland to Great Malvern, Worsetshire, where it was far enough away that it was never attacked again.

Those of us that went were allowed to read some of the documents that were the results of Terman's trip, including the details of the Bruneval raid where the first Wurzburg electronics were brought back to England and details of the radar and so forth. I was talking to one of the British fellow colleagues about this and the fact that I was aware of the story of that and I said, "What happens to equipment of that sort that's brought back?" And he said, "Oh, you want to see it? It's in the back room, right over there." Right across the hall from me all this time, after I had been there for about six months. He had studied it in fine detail, taking everything apart and traced all the circuit diagrams. They knew that thing cold. Well, once they had all the information, from then on, then it was a museum piece.

George Klemm, who would later head Division 15's Antennae Group in England remembered the beginnings of this elite group of scientists and researchers:

I was donated by a general radio company in Cambridge. I was doing my co-op work from Northeastern at that time and was just about ready to graduate. They hired me in the spring of 1942. Well, Terman assembled this group and our assignment was to investigate radar, what the enemy had, and what could be done about it. We were to design investigative equipment. We made all kinds of receivers, some of them you just twiddled the dial, others were automatic you could put aboard planes. These flew over enemy territory and we searched out the location of the various enemy radar.

The men of the 8AF gave training to the RAF in the operation and maintenance of B17 aircraft. *Courtesy of William R. Hoagland.*

L-R RAF Wing Commander Desmond John McGlinn, CO 803BS Capt George E. Paris, and Squadron Leader RCAF, William S. Day. *Courtesy of George E. Paris, Lt. Col. USAF (Ret).*

RAF Squadron Leader Bradshaw. *Courtesy of William R. Hoagland.*

George Wright was a RAF liaison officer to the 8AF. *Courtesy of George E. Paris, Lt. Col. USAF (Ret).*

Then with that information we knew where to go and use our countermeasure equipment.

ABL, which is American-British Laboratory Division 15 of our Radio Research Laboratory, was set up in Great Britain in order to introduce the American forces to radar countermeasures. Since it was too late to get radar countermeasures in the table of organization of the Army and Navy, we as civilians worked with all of the services in applying the various pieces of equipment which had been designed back here in the United States. At the latter part of August 1943, ABL was set up and we arrived on scene over there in

Great Malvern, which is about eight miles southwest of Worcester, England. We were associated with the Telecommunications Research Establishment, which was the British development and research organization for radar and radar countermeasures.

Our technical director was Peter C. Goldmark. He was the technical director of Columbia Broadcasting System and was assigned to come over to Britain. He actually brought not only his engineers from CBS laboratories, but [also] his complete machine shop and all the electronic measuring equipment and stockroom supplies at the same time. I was one of the few people who initially

Capt. George Paris, the first 803BS CO, warming up his B17 at Oulton. *Courtesy of George E. Paris, Lt. Col. USAF (Ret).*

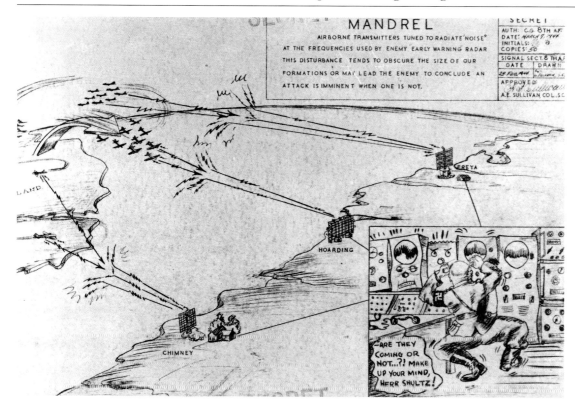

MANDREL utilization cartoon. MANDREL was a British made active jammer. *Courtesy of USAF Historical Research Agency.*

arrived from Radio Research Laboratory. (Goldmark, incidentally, post World War II was President of the Columbia Broadcasting System Laboratories, and it was during that time that they developed the 33 &1/3rpm records. He also worked on the development of the Columbia Broadcasting System post war color television system.) Goldmark was our technical director over there for about a year and a half, then he came back to the United States. Our new technical director was John N. Dyer. He was originally from CBS. John was quite a colorful fellow in that he was the Boy Scout radio operator on the [1933] Admiral Byrd expedition to the South Pole. Every evening CBS had a broadcast from Antarctica, and John was involved in that. After World War II, he became president of Airborne Instrument Laboratories in Mineola, Long Island.

Shirley Clark Merrill, a secretary for Division 15 at Great Malvern, remembered their reason for being at this time:

The purpose of the laboratory to begin with was to work with the 8th Air Force in the field, because whenever there were problems with the equipment, there were 23 engineers there and they could go directly from the laboratory to the field and check out any bugs in the equipment. The secretarial people were from CBS in New York, most of us were from Harvard University. The reason for that was the British girls were subject to the draft, so in order to support this engineering establishment, they needed the secretarial help. That was why we were over there. We lived in British hotels and were on British rations.

The 8AF advanced its electronic warfare capability near the end of 1942 by forming the Operations Research Section (ORS). The following spring, Kenneth A. Norton was chosen to lead the section on radar countermeasures. Norton had the keen foresight to recognize the necessity for reducing the 8AF vulnerability to German radar, even though at the time the greatest threat to U.S. bombers during the daylight attacks was not the enemy flak, but fighter aircraft of the German Luftwaffe. Norton soon recommended the 8AF undertake a program to equip every bomber with radar jammers and radar warning receivers.[9]

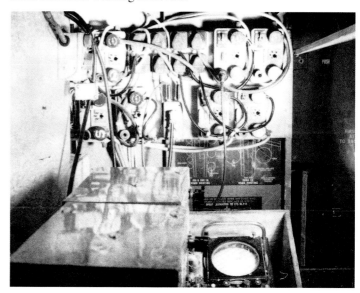

MANDREL equipment in B24 bomb bay. *Courtesy of USAF Historical Research Agency.*

The B17 Flying Fortress #42-3438 "F" from the 96BG was one of 803rd's first aircraft and equipped with six MANDREL. This B17 was lost during Project Aphrodite on 10/30/44. Aphrodite was the secret ill-fated project that also claimed the life of Lt. Joseph P. Kennedy Jr., brother to President John F. Kennedy. *Courtesy of V. Glendening.*

By September 1943, in order for the 8AF to gain technical countermeasures assistance, Division 15 joined Great Britain's scientists at Telecommunications Research Establishment (TRE) located at Great Malvern, to form the American-British Laboratory of Division 15, or ABL-15. ABL-15's first director was Victor Fraenckel. America and Great Britain would gain much by this association. U.S. countermeasure experts would learn from the knowledge already gained by the British. Great Britain in turn would receive an enthusiastic breath of fresh air and therefore prosper by no longer having to work on a limited budget.[10]

Back in the states RRL set up a RCM training school in Boca Raton, Florida. Here a highly classified training course was given to military officers. The reason for the high security classification was due to the special equipment with its potential capabilities. The school's graduates were nicknamed "Ravens," codeword for RCM. Over the course of the war approximately six hundred officers were trained. These select officers served in a variety of capacities. They served not only as operators, but also as planners. They also maintained equipment and served in other related functions. Unfortunately, this led to their becoming an isolated group.

RCM equipment field testing took place at the First Proving Ground Electronic Unit (PGEU) in Florosa Field, Florida (now Eglin AFB), and was conducted along with evaluation specialists from Wright Field in Dayton, Ohio. Enlisted men were used to train the enlisted radar operators and mechanics. One such instructor for the enlisted men at Boca Raton was Sgt. James Sloan. He remembered:

They [the Army] sent me to Radio Operator and Mechanic (ROM) school at Sioux Falls, SD, in the fall of 1942. Before I shipped out of there it got to be 20 degrees below zero. In January 1943 I

was shipped from ROM school to Boca Raton, FL, where it was 85 degrees. There I spent 1943, 1944, and until April of 1945 as a RCM instructor, shift chief, and finally as the non-commissioned officer of the RCM school.

The air base was divided into the north and south areas. We were in the north area. Most of the schools were tar paper barracks. They were not in a row, but scattered like they had been thrown there by hand. They told us that was to keep us from getting strafed in case of air attack. We were on the east edge of the Everglades. A chain link fence with barbed wire on top enclosed the building. In 1943 we had an armed guard on the gate 24 hours a day.

Capt. Robinson and crew. L-R Lt. Walter L. Slade, Capt. Raymond A. Robinson, Lt. William R. Hoagland... others unknown. *Courtesy of William F. Flagler.*

At the RCM school we took our job very serious. Someone's life might depend on it. Each class would spend approximately half of the eight hours in the lab and half in theory. The RCM transmitters and receivers were displayed on tables for the students to operate and trouble shoot. Each class contained from 15 to 30 students. The instructor had a rostrum and black board to work from. The theory was laid out each day, including electrical schematics of the sets, how they operated, etc. A troubleshooting and operating test was given sometimes each day, but always each week.

We had a schedule to follow each eight hours. So much time on the power section of a certain set, then so much time on the RF section or antennas, etc. We worked from schematics explaining the electron flow, the voltage at a certain point, what would happen if this condenser opened up or this resistor shorted to ground, etc. After theory, the student went to the lab for four hours of "hands on" experience in operation and trouble shooting. The regular instructor had assistance in the lab by two or three lab instructors. We kept getting new equipment, mostly new transmitters. Even the instructors went through instruction on the new stuff so they could teach it. But the old basic search receiver, the SCR-587, stayed with us forever. It was a good, solid receiver.

The Nazi Threat

German radar technology and its air defense program were among the world's best at the outbreak of World War II. The radar which directed the German fighters and flak batteries presented a most formidable technological threat. Indeed, Allied airmen braved a very hazardous situation in the skies over Central Europe by the time America began large scale bombing operations in 1943. The problem the Luftwaffe faced against the Royal Air Force's nighttime attacks was altogether different from that of the American daylight precision bombing campaign. At night the Luftwaffe was required to find the individual bombers in the loose formations of the RAF's bomber stream.

The Germans developed several techniques, all of which depended on using radar to locate and destroy the RAF night bombers. First, an early warning radar called Freya was used to give warning notice that a raid was coming. Next, radar-guided searchlights were directed to spotlight the RAF night bombers so that the German flak guns and Luftwaffe fighters could repel the attack. The searchlight control relied on radar called the Wurzburg. The Germans also used the Wurzburg as a gun-laying (GL) radar. It provided more accurate guidance to flak batteries than could be obtained through visual aiming. The Wurzburg was unhindered by weather elements such as clouds, haze, and smoke. German fighter controllers used ground-controlled intercept (GCI) radar as an aid to direct their fighters to the attacking bombers. The GCI radars greatly assisted the ground controller's ability to inform the German fighters of the enemy bombers' position. This information was delivered in the form of running commentaries. In addition to GCI, some Luftwaffe fighters were further equipped with their own air-

Lt. Travis and crew June 1944. L-R unknown, Navigator - Lt. Gruelich, Sgt. Rutkowski, Sgt. Lovelace, Sgt. Baldwin, Sgt. Reynolds, Pilot - Lt. Travis is kneeling 3rd from left. *Courtesy of William R. Hoagland.*

borne intercept (AI) radars, such as the Lichtenstein, to home in their attack to destroy the RAF invaders.

With the Americans and the British now attacking Germany in the air over Europe during the spring of 1943, it was not surprising that German defensive radar played the same role for the Germans as the Chain Home radars did for the British. The German defensive radar program expanded rapidly both in number and type. At least 300 early warning radar installations were operational. Upward of 1,300 equipments were known to be available to use in vectoring fighters and controlling searchlights and flak anti-aircraft guns.

German flak batteries were placed in rings bordering important cities, vital industries, and military installations. By 1944 the Reich employed some 900,000 men and women to operate the nearly 50,000 flak guns, 6,700 searchlights, and 1,500 barrage balloons. When the flak guns were radar-aimed, the center of the bomber formation was the target. At its height, the flak defenses could blast 5,000 tons of shells per minute into the bomber infested skies threatening Germany. The German flak was so effective that half of the American combat losses would be due to flak. Unfortunately for the 8AF, Army intelligence consistently underestimated the threat of German flak.[11] Of the feared flak guns, one of which was the mighty German 88mm, British ace J.E. "Johnnie" Johnson, in his book *Wing Leader*, wrote:

That outstanding gun of the war, the deadly 88mm., hampered the progress of the bombers when they crossed the coast and stained the clearness of the high sky with innumerable bursts of flak, like foul, bursting sacks of black soot.[12]

The 8AF believed the Wurzburg radar was being used as a gunfire control radar during the 15 May bombing raid against Wilhelmshaven, Germany, and the 17 May raid against St. Nazaire in France. To verify this belief, 8AF Headquarters ordered tests using a jammer nicknamed CARPET (APT-2) to counter the

Lt. Gen. James H. "Jimmy" Doolittle inspecting the troops. *Courtesy of Frank J. Trovato.*

Wurzburg. (See CARPET cartoon illustration.) Fortunately for the U.S., CARPET jamming equipment was already under production to counter the Wurzburg. By October of 1943 the 8AF was ready to test its first RCM operational capability. Aircraft of the 96th and 388th Bomb Groups were equipped to use the new jammer. Bombers of these groups carried the CARPET jammers during missions against Bremen, Gdynia, Munster, and Schweinfurt. Although the threat during this time was primarily due to German fighters, the CARPET jammers definitely helped. The analysis of operations indicated bomber aircraft loses were 5% less among aircraft equipped with CARPET than aircraft in other unprotected units without such equipment. Results indicated that 14 aircraft were lost out of 186 sorties, or 7.5% vs 134 aircraft lost out of 1,066 sorties, or 12.6% of the unprotected force.[13]

Professor of Electronics Donald Reynolds of Dr. Terman's team recalled his work on CARPET equipment. In the same 1982 interview with the Association of Old Crows, he recalled:

At the very first what I did was simply get some of the U.S. built CARPET transmitters (one of the early jammers for the Wurzburg frequency range) ready for some flight tests in England. RRL sent a few over as sort of candidates for evaluations. They were going to test it against a British radar that was the closest relative operating at a frequency nearby to the Wurzburg. We had to check it out to see if it was working properly after it had arrived.

George Klemm of the ABL-15 remembered the work toward countering the Wurzburg:

We were trying to find out where the various German radar sites were. If you're going to do anything about them, first you've got to know where they are. It's characteristic of the radars that they are electronically noisy, and each of them has a so-called voice which is characteristic of that [radar]. As a result of that, we more or less mapped the location of every or most (we hoped every) German radar throughout the European continent. If they moved them from one site to another, we knew that, too! Then when we wanted to do countermeasures against them, what we did was concentrate on that area and we knew what frequencies to use. These were the German Wurzburg, the so-called gun-laying radars, where they could actually direct the gunfire automatically once they had locked onto a plane.

What we did was develop jamming transmitters. CARPET was one, which operated over a band of frequencies that were in their radars. We flew planes over their areas and just fouled them up in general, we hoped.

One of the great mistakes that the Germans made in their Wurzburg design (the Wurzburg radar was a wonderful piece of

A postcard showing Aylsham Market Place near Oulton. *Courtesy of Charles W. Sanders.*

equipment) was that they die cast everything, and when we started to jam it, they couldn't change frequency. That was their great mistake.

Undoubtedly, because of such favorable results the 8AF wanted to continue to expand its RCM capability. On December 3, 1943, in a letter from the Headquarters 8AF Office of the Signal Officer, the "Proposal of an American RCM Unit for the United States Army Air Force in the United Kingdom" was delivered to Lt. Gen. Ira Eaker, the 8AF Commanding General. The proposal recommended that an American radio and radar countermeasures unit be established and under the control of Headquarters United States Army Air Force in the United Kingdom (USAAFUK). This unit would cooperate to the fullest extent with the central countermeasures organization the British had established under the Air Ministry. It was not intended that a large organization be formed at that time, but was essential that the organization be flexible to meet the future requirements in the fast moving science of countermeasures.

The 8AF Headquarters Signal Office proposal summarized the reasons for recommending that an American RCM unit be established. And the reasons were very good. First, the British RCM organization already had a few American aircraft, even though they were primarily interested in problems of the RAF. The RAF problems included radar-guided searchlights and radar-equipped night fighters. It was expected that enemy use of radio and radar against the 8AF daylight formations would differ from that used against the RAF at night. The U.S. countermeasures, therefore, would be different. The establishment of the RCM unit under the Headquarters USAAFUK would avoid duplication of effort in the RCM field. Secondly, through the RCM unit, the 8AF would have a means of utilizing the talents of ABL-15 and ORS to the fullest extent. Also, aircraft and aircrews would be available for experimental and test flights. Operational commands would not be called on to do this type of work. Since investigation of enemy radio and radar activity was a highly technical job and beyond the scope of average aircrews and technicians in operational commands, selected aircrews would be of an exceptionally high type, specially trained and briefed on this work. The recommended aircrews would have operational experience and an interest in the work. It was expected that by the organization of a central RCM unit personnel problems would be simplified. Technical Orders would be authorized to include RCM mechanics capable for the necessary repairs in the groups using RCM equipment, but RCM mechanics of higher qualifications necessary for more special work would be assigned to the central RCM unit.

Lastly, it was believed that by this sincere offer to cooperate with the British on RCM, not only regarding equipment, but with personnel matters as well, much information and aid would be gained from the RAF. Close cooperation with the British RCM organization would not only enable the American RCM unit to get full information on their activities, but also many additional facilities would be opened to it.[14]

By 5 December Ira Eaker received authorization for the creation of the 8th Air Force's Radio Countermeasures Unit from Gen. George Marshall, the Army Chief of Staff. On January 4, 1944, just two days before being relieved of command and being ordered to report for duty as the head of the new Allied Air Forces in the Mediterranean, Eaker made official the equipment and personnel requirements for an 8AF RCM unit. Within this document he stated:

A central RCM unit is being organized to deal with RCM requirements which require special handling. This central unit will be equipped with aircraft and air crews, plus necessary maintenance and technical personnel, and will provide channels though which the talents of American civilian scientists may be utilized. It is intended that this central unit will cooperate with British radio and radar countermeasures organizations and considerable additional information and facilities will be available to this Air Force. Operational Research personnel will collaborate with this unit and assist in the analysis of Information gathered and in the recommendation of operational tactics to counter enemy radio and radar activity."[15]

Leading Great Britain's Royal Air Force secret RCM outfit— the RAF 100 Group (Special Duty)—at this time was Air Vice Marshall E. B. Addison. RAF 100 Group's motto was "Confound and Destroy," and Addison was its Air Officer Commanding (AOC). With him at Bylaugh Hall, located 20 miles from Norwich, were the necessary staff officers for planning group operations. Air Vice Marshall Addison wanted American officers to join the 100 Group

RAF Oulton Officer Staff. Back row L-R: Bulmer, Milledge, Pims, Jennings, Jock Bowie (the Met Officer) Salew, Curtis and Roberts. Centre row: Fletcher, May, Brown, Squadron Leader Bradshaw (Senior Flying Control Officer), Section Officer Woodman, (WAAF) Mastin, Gaffney, Uphill, Conway, Burns C/W. Front row L-R: Squadron Leader (Doc) Vyse, (Station Medical Officer) Major Butler, Section Officer Horrocks (WASAF) Flight Lieutenant Hawarth, Group Captain T.C. Dickens (Station Commander) F/L Sownay, Flight Officer Madeline Wareham (WAAF "G" Officer, a.k.a. the Queen Bee) Howard and Sutton. *Courtesy of Murray Peden.*

staff who were now greatly overworked. Quite naturally he believed U.S. personnel would be a most useful addition. On 17 January air and ground crewmen from various organizations in the 8AF were placed on detached service (DS) at RAF Station Sculthorpe. These men of the 8AF gave training to RAF personnel in the operation and maintenance of B17 aircraft, which were serving as the jamming platform. The British held the B17 in highest regard; as RAF ace Johnnie Johnson said, "They made a most impressive sight when they pounded their stately way through the skies in battle array. Flak and fighters could not stop them."[16]

The first U.S. personnel formed what was to be termed the "American Detachment" at Sculthorpe. They were placed under the command of Capt. George E. Paris, who had completed an operational tour, as had other flying personnel in the detachment. The RAF air and ground personnel were "checked off" in the operation and maintenance of B17 aircraft which were to be used in connection with various RAF Bomber Command radar countermeasure equipment. The RCM equipment included MANDREL, JOSTLE, CARPET (active electronic jamming forms), WINDOW (passive jamming form), and other ramifications. (See MANDREL cartoon illustration.)

This work continued until 21 March when it was decided that U.S. crews and aircraft would fly joint missions with RAF aircraft. Six crews and six B17 aircraft were transferred from the 96th Bomb Group (H) at Snetterton Heath, AAF (Army Air Force) Station 138 for these missions. These crews had been engaged in radar countermeasure work with the AAF since the second week of February at Snetterton Heath and were the first crews to be used for these operations in the ETO. The aircraft brought in were equipped with the special equipment required.

The crews placed on detached service from the 96th Bomb Group (H) were those piloted by Captains Robert Stutzman, Raymond Robinson, and Lts. Richard Obenschain, William Overstreet, Howard Klimetz, and Charles Travis. Aircraft were

Bomb's away. The RAF 100 Group and 803BS' reason for being— Bomber support. Effective jamming could mean fewer bomber losses and in return more bombs on the target. *Courtesy of Frank J. Trovato.*

modified for night flying, and the aircrews were checked off for operations, although no operational missions were flown. Further necessary installations were made to the aircraft, and additional technical facilities for maintenance were constructed. During this period training operations were conducted in conjunction with the RAF 100 Group, 214 Squadron.

On 28 March the 803rd Bomb Squadron Heavy (H) Provisional (Prov) was formed by General Order #5 from Headquarters VIII Air Force Composite Command. In the same order the personnel assigned to the squadron were placed on duty at RAF Station Sculthorpe. The operational program at Sculthorpe was concerned with the training of combat and ground crews in radar countermeasure flights and related procedures. Nine crews and six B17 aircraft were then assigned to the squadron.[17]

As stated before, Capt. George E. Paris, the first commanding officer of the 803rd Bomb Squadron, had already completed his operational tour. Paris had previously served as the Assistant Operations Officer for the 368th Bomb Squadron, 306th Bomb Group (Heavy) where he had flown B17 Flying Fortresses. By that time he had already distinguished himself in combat, sometimes as lead pilot. He had been awarded the Silver Star, Distinguished Flying Cross, Air Medal with 3 Oak Leaf Clusters, plus other medals. Paris recalled:

I finished my missions in December and was invited to go down to 1st Division Headquarters and interview. They had a certain number of jobs available. Subsequently, they needed people to do other things, like this 803rd.

I was assigned and took the Detachment up there [to Sculthorpe]. We were the first contingent of the 803rd to go up to the base. The British commander was Group Captain Dickens, the base commander. He had an assortment of crew members there from all over. They had Icelanders, Indians, Canadians, all the Allied forces, pilots and other grades, navigators and radio people. I liked the British and the Canadians very much. We got along splendidly. Also, it was a chance to continue flying. We knew that we were going to win over there. We just didn't know when, so all of us wanted to stay there.

We had some technical people there that knew the aspects of radar countermeasures. They had experience in this and worked with the British. The base was kind of low key. They had training in the morning and some flying in the afternoon. Our job was to check out the guys in the B17, which could fly higher than their ships. The end objective was to use the B17 flown by the British flyers to do diversionary tactical flights; to try and divert the German fighters from the place that they [the British] were actually going to bomb. The ships that would drop the chaff, the tin foil would go up to the North Sea on a diversionary tactic. Then, of course, the bombers would go in lower south of there to another target and bomb it. Supposedly they [the Germans] would have less prior notice of the incoming bombers, and therefore [the bombers] might run into less flak, and certainly less fighters. At that time the German forces were becoming limited as far as the fuel goes and also aircraft and crew members, too. We had at that time very good support in P51s with extended range tanks on them and also P47s. It was getting to be that there was hardly any opposition.

Another airman of the original "American Detachment" was flight engineer and gunner Sgt. Vane Glendening. Glendening, who would log 53 jamming missions, remembered:

In January 1944, I along with other Americans became attached to the RAF 100 Group, 214 Squadron for the purpose of assisting and training RAF personnel in the maintenance and operation of these [RCM] aircraft. And in March of 1944 we went out on our first mission as an integrated crew to accompany a RAF bomber force to attack an enemy facility near the Hague in Holland. The flak over the target was heavy. We didn't really understand what we had accomplished until the next morning at briefing. We were told that the night before we accompanied the force the RAF lost over 100 airplanes. This night no aircraft were lost to enemy action. At this point I realized that this was something that would change air warfare.

One of my tasks on these countermeasure flights was to ensure the proper amount of electricity was generated by each of the generators on all four engines. Sometimes we would turn off the gun turrets to save power for the jammers. On one particular flight I smelled electrical smoke in the bomb bay where the voltage regulators were attached to the bulkhead. Upon inspection I found one regulator on fire. I immediately opened the bomb bay doors. I then ripped the burning regulator off the wall and tossed it out the bomb bay. I received a slight burn on my hand even though I had gloves on. I realigned the other generators and we continued on our way. The able ground crew repaired the damage when we returned to base.

We continued to fly these integrated missions until more U.S. personnel were brought in. In May we were officially assigned to the 803rd Bomb Squadron. We continued to operate under RAF Bomber Command.

Cpl. Kent MacGillivray, a squadron mechanic with the first detachment, recalled:

We were on detached service to the RAF for a good bit of the time. I came back [to the U.S.] in July of '45 and had been over there two years. When I first went over there I went to the repair depot at Honington. A guy came around one day and wanted to know if our crew wanted to go on thirty days detached service. That we did. When we came back two years later, I was still on that thirty days detached service. We never did go back to our own outfit—the 90th Repair Squadron.

Lt. James Warner was co-pilot in Lt. Richard Obenschain's crew, one of the first six RCM crews. Lt. Warner spoke of his new assignment:

Our crew with the 388th BG, Obenschain and myself and the rest of the crew completed our twenty-five missions in February of 1944. Everybody else went home after their twenty-fifth mission, but we hung around for about six weeks or so until this 803rd RCM squadron came into being. Sometime in April 1944 we moved to RAF Sculthorpe and the training and our missions began to take shape. Sculthorpe was not an active RAF combat base at that time. We were assigned an additional airman, Sgt. Wilson, to complete our crew. Capt. George Paris was already in place at Sculthorpe as Operations Officer. Some night training missions were flown in conjunction with the RAF where evasive action/reaction to possible Luftwaffe night fighters was stressed. Our aircraft were stripped of identification except serial numbers.

We were flying stripped down B17s. The British had some older model B17s which had been stripped down. They were also flying Lancasters and Sterlings. We were initially at Sculthorpe, and then we moved to Oulton with Group Captain Dickens as the commander of the entire unit. Our immediate commander for the American portion was Lt. Col. Scott. We flew a number of night missions in the support of the British bomber stream. We would be given certain coordinates, then we would go over the North Sea and orbit a five mile orbit with all this jamming equipment on. The British really flew a bomber stream because sometimes you'd find yourself right in the middle of it.

On one night training mission we were to orbit a set of coordinates within a five mile radius. After about one hour we received anti-aircraft fire and immediately got out of the area. As it turned out we apparently hit a jet stream and Jim Ostler, our navigator, estimated our ground speed between 475-500 kts., which placed us over the enemy held coast in a hurry.

Night flying involved flying without clearance lights of any kind, and engine exhausts were equipped with flame suppressors. The aircraft instrument lights consisted of small ultra-violet lamps which normally were left on and directed toward the instruments, which activated the radium coating, causing the instruments to glow. However, the recommended procedure at that time was to turn on the lamps just long enough to energize and incite the instrument radium, then turn them off. The instruments would glow for some time. The lack of clearance lights, complete blackout, and minimum instrument lighting was responsible for my first encounter with vertigo.

Returning to Sculthorpe after a night training mission we were introduced to a directional and landing procedure completely new to me, and one I thought was great and a compliment to British ingenuity. If you needed assistance (and who didn't in a complete blackout) you proceeded to call by radio and say "Hello Darky, where am I?" Codes were used to identify your aircraft and the airfield you wanted. Searchlights would come on vertically, then lay down in the direction you were to fly. This continued until suddenly there appeared a circle of lights (about 3 miles in diameter) at your destination. The procedure was to make a left turn around

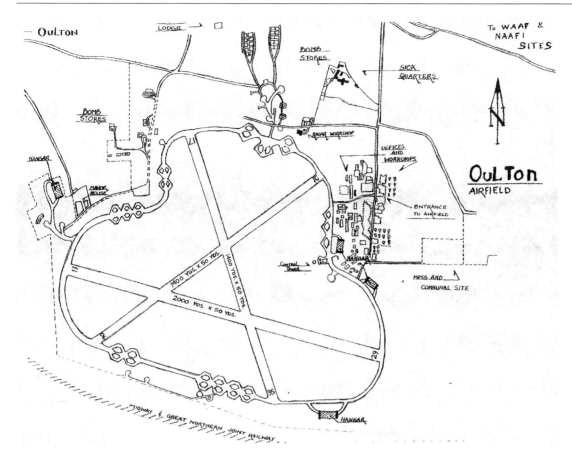

RAF Oulton aerodrome map.

through the circle of lights until you came to a funnel configuration in the circle. You turned into the funnel, and after completing the turn and leveling out, the runway lights appeared. You would fly in and land with no aircraft landing lights, and immediately all the runway lights went off. Leaving the lights on for even a short period made it possible for Luftwaffe night fighters to follow bombers on landing and destroy them on the ground. Hence the caution!

We had a good crew. Dick Obenschain [later to become Assistant Operations Officer] was an excellent pilot, aircraft commander, gentleman, and friend. Jim Ostler [later to become Squadron Navigation Officer] was an excellent navigator, officer, gentleman, and friend. Our airmen were top notch. This crew made the disappointment of not returning to home and family after our 25th mission a lot easier to take.

Another of the first 803BS airman, S/Sgt. James Wooden, B17 tail gunner for Capt. Ray Robinson, remembered:

We all had finished our bombing missions with the 385th BG. We were assigned to this 803rd BS. I flew with a different crew on my bombing missions than I flew with at the 803rd, because part of my crew—two of them were shot down on their last mission over Berlin. The co-pilot was shot down, and one of the waist gunners was shot down with him on the same mission. Then the radio operator on our crew was shot down. So there were three of them on

the crew that were shot down, before the 803rd BS ever became an entity.

Some of us were to volunteer for this 803rd Bomb Squadron flying off of a RAF field. We would go up at night most of the time. We would set up what we'd call a screen for the night bombers going out.

Co-pilot Bill Flagler of Lt. William Overstreet's crew kept a record of his new assignment to the 803BS, what he called: *"My Second Tour"*

After my missions with the 385th Bomb Group I sat around in a fog waiting for my orders to come in. When they did, I was sent to the 96th Bomb Group on temporary duty. Capt. R.A. "Robbie" Robinson, Lt. Hoagland, and Lt. Slade were on similar orders. We were stationed at Snetterton Heath for about four weeks. We were assigned on special duty as MANDREL crews. Robbie's [Capt. Robinson] crew stayed together, but I was flying and sharing first pilot time with Lt. W.P. Overstreet, nicknamed "Red." Outside of flying a few local hours and getting two passes to London, we didn't do a thing at the 96th.

Our next move was to a RAF base at Sculthorpe on the Wash. We had six crews at the 96th, and we all moved to our new outfit. Shortly after our arrival we received a seven day pass and Red, Robbie, and Klem [Lt. Klimetz] and I spent it in London. We took in all the shows and even the zoo. As usual I spent too much money and came home broke. Things have been SNAFU [term of the time meaning Situation Normal—All Fouled Up} here since no one knows what we are here for or when we will be relieved. There are six crews that completed tours, but three others have had from zero to four missions. Our squadron is now known as the 803rd Bomb Squadron and we call ourselves RCM-DSR—translated as Radio countermeasures—Detached Service Radar. Today we had a visit from a Bomb Group and a Colonel from General Doolittle's staff who briefed us on this RCM business. We still don't know any more, except that it looks as though we'll be here for a while.

April 25

Tonight we started flying with circuits and bumps [familiarization flights]. Our new CO, Lt. Col. Scott, replaces Capt. Paris, who is now Operations Officer. You can tell that Scott is all military, but he has a bunch of ideas of his own.

April 28

We flew again last night, but we aborted after an hour of the cross country because of GEE [navigational equipment] failure On the landing we ran off the runway because our brakes gave out. The Colonel was quite browned off, so we had to fly again tonight. Capt. Robbie took off ahead of us, and we beat him back home, but where did we pass him? That's why I don't care much for this night flying with most of our windows blacked out with paint. As a RAF squadron leader said the other night, "Only birds and damn fools fly, and the birds don't fly at night!

Capt. George Paris and crew of a B17 which participated on a special daylight mission to Brussels with fighter escort on 6/3/44. L-R: Lt. Latvaitis, Lt. Zatlin, Sgt. Lewis, Sgt. Simkins, Sgt. Long, Sgt. Roberts, Sgt. Bogart, & unknown Kneeling left to right: Lt. Gilzinger, Sgt. Pratt, Capt. Paris, Capt. Robinson, Lt. Solveson. *Courtesy of George E. Paris, Lt. Col, USAF (Ret).*

By 30 April a radio countermeasures functional plan for the new 803BS had been developed. The plan as designed called for the 803BS to deny the Germans effective utilization of their radar and radio equipment. The enemy equipment the 803BS would attempt to counter generally fell into three categories:

1. Small Wurzburg radar, which had a range of twenty miles and most frequently used in the direction of gunfire control of flak batteries against aircraft.

2. Giant Wurzburg radar, which had a range of forty miles and normally employed in fighter control, but could occasionally be used in the direction of gunfire control of flak batteries against aircraft.

3. Freya radar, a long distance early warning radar with a range up to 125 miles used in conjunction with Giant Wurzburg for fighter control. Various types and models of Freya were employed for various tasks.[18]

Thus, on 2 May a secret RCM directive to the Commanding Officer, USAAF Detachment, RAF Station Sculthorpe stated that the 803rd Bomb Squadron (H) (Prov) was to conduct the 8AF RCM activity as a counterpart to RAF 100 Group's RCM squadrons—214 and 199 Squadrons. The 803BS, together with the RAF 100 Group RCM squadrons, would carry on radio countermeasures activities of the RAF and the 8AF, operating separately or jointly to best serve the separate and/or combined requirements of either or both in the RCM field.

Initially the 803BS was to perform experimental and developmental operations only. Another objective of the 803BS was to effect the maximum cooperation and coordination between the RAF 100 Group and the Eighth Air Force regarding the planning, engineering, prototyping, testing, and research functions of this activity. Operational control of the USAAF RCM activity was to be exercised by Lt. General James H. "Jimmy" Doolittle, Commanding General, Eighth Air Force through Headquarters RAF 100 Group in coordination with RAF Bomber Command.[19]

The 803BS continued to function at Sculthorpe until 16 May when it was transferred to RAF Station Oulton, Norfolk. (See aerodrome map.) The 214 Squadron of RAF 100 Group also transferred to Oulton at the same time. Lt. Col. Clayton A. Scott, then on temporary duty, assumed command of the squadron. Capt. Paris was appointed Executive Officer, with Capt. Stutzman serving as Operations Officer.[20]

Co-pilot James Warner wrote:

Upon our arrival at RAF Oulton, the RAF Commander issued all members of the 803rd new bicycles. I thought it was wonderful and practical for all of us on a new base without the transportation facilities we were used to. Oulton was Ann Boleyn's home. It was a place for visitors to go to until the time of the war, then the RAF took it over and the house itself was the officer's club. The bar and main club activities were in the great room of the home. At one end of the great room was a huge fireplace. Up one wall across the high ceiling and down the opposite wall was a set of boot prints. We were told that the RAF people at a rousing party took their smallest member, a Scotsman and navigator, blacked the soles of his flight boots and held him as he walked up the wall. His boots were rimcoated with soot from the fireplace, put back on him, tables were stacked as the height increased, and the steps continued until the entire track was completed. It seemed to me at the time it would have been simpler to just use the boots for the prints, but the RAF fellows felt it was more meaningful to have a man in the boots, even though he had to be held upside down to make the prints. They flew hard without any thought of a completed tour and lived it up when they could. A truly remarkable group of people.

Co-pilot Bill Flagler continued in his record:
May 23

Still keep getting busier with the new jobs. The Colonel had a rush call to Composite Command and from now on every man in the 803rd will carry firearms. According to HQ, last night 20 paratroopers were dropped by Jerry only six miles from here, so we're going to be ready just in case. The boys of the 803 and the 214 [RAF] are out on a combined "Bullseye" [training] operation tonight.

May 30

We still haven't started operations, but indications are that it won't be long now. We are still carrying the .45s everywhere, and we are restricted to base. The weather has just been beautiful the past few days. Red, Travis, Birmingham, Paul, Klimetz, Smith, and I went over to Blickling Hall this afternoon and spent the day swimming and soaking up the sun and played ball in undershorts and bare feet. I never thought this could happen in England. The RAF men are living in Blickling, which was built in 1637 and was originally the place that Anne Boleyn stayed when she was chasing around with old Henry the VIII. The gardens are still beautiful, and I have taken many color and black and white pictures.

Flight and ground training peculiar to RCM operations continued at Oulton. The personnel changed considerably at Oulton, where most of the flying personnel who had completed an operational tour prior to coming into the 803BS were transferred out and returned to the United States. They were replaced by crews who had not completed an operational tour, which proved more satisfactory from a morale standpoint. Previously the personnel were selected from crews which had completed an operational tour of 25 missions. This created the poor morale because only part of the crew was selected, and the rest of the crew was allowed to return to the U.S. Personnel from various crews were thereby formed into new crews, necessitating the development of new crew "teams."

Two important test flights were made during this time. The first flight was on 27 May in B17 #42-37743, piloted by Capt. Robert Stutzman with Lt. Franklin Zatlin in charge of recording instru-

ments. This test flight made possible the field diagram of the Bawdsey antenna ray on England's east coast by the North Sea. The second flight took place on 3 June in B17 #42-3518 and piloted by Capt. George Paris, with Lt. Zatlin again in charge of recording instruments. It was made with fighter protection and proceeded to a point near Brussels, Belgium. No opposition was met. The purpose of this flight was to measure over enemy territory the operational height and relative field strength of radio transmitters located at both Bawdsey and Sizewell on the east coast of Britain. An enemy FuGe-16Z radio receiver modified by ABL-15 to indicate relative signal strength was mounted in the nose of the aircraft. Both flights were completed successfully, and their results contributed to the research being accomplished on countering German fighter control.[21]

Capt. Paris said of one flight during this time:
Around May we were authorized to make a flight over France by ourselves, solo. I remember Lt Col. Scott went with me. All of the guys that had been there at that time had finished their missions. We were free to go home, but we all wanted to stay there until D-Day. We made a flight penetrating into France. I don't really remember how far in we went. We were really apprehensive because we had no fighter cover. We went into our destination and then came back. That was it. Fortunately, we didn't see any enemy fighters. This was an authorized mission for British purposes. We had some of their men on board. They eventually got checked out, and I presume that they started making the flights in conjunction with the invasion.

George Klemm spoke of ABL-15 and his efforts to equip the RCM aircraft :
As far as ABL is concerned, my first function in life over there was to put together our laboratory's physical facilities working under Peter Goldmark. Then I graduated from there and went into the antennae field, working with antennae, prototyping, actually designing some of them and putting them on some of the various aircraft. This is how I got into going to the various airfields.

A couple of times we needed a B17 for our work, and Defford airfield, a British development field, was within fourteen miles of us. I went out to the field one day to get a plane, a B17 that was sent in for some tests. They flew in two planes, they landed them on the field and the crew got out of one plane and got back into the other. The fellow came out and he said, "Are you from ABL?" I said,"Yes." He said, "Sign here." So I signed there. So he says, "Good-bye." I said, "Where are you going?" He said, "Well, you wanted a plane, you've got one!" I said, "But what am I going to do? Where's the crew? He said, "You didn't ask for a crew, you just asked for the plane." They got in the other plane and flew off. I went back over to the control tower and the British CO was tearing his hair out. The plane was at a hardstand it couldn't stay at. I said, "I can't fly the plane. What in the world am I to do with it? Somebody fouled up.

They gave us a plane but no crew." He said that I'm going to have to get somebody back at the lab to get a crew. He said, "Well, it's gotta be moved." Just then a fellow in an American Air Force uniform said, "What's the matter?" I said,"You see that B17 out there? The Officer of the Day, the Control Officer in the tower says I can't leave that plane there and I can't move it." He said, "I'll move it! Come on." So, we got out and got one of these follow-me trucks to take us to it. We got the motors going and moved the thing over to a hardstand and got it stopped and left it there. I said, "That's good. I'm glad you know something about this." He said, "I'm glad we made it." I said,"What do you mean?" He said, "Well I'm a fighter pilot. I've never been in one of these things before." If he had wrecked the plane, what would have happened?

Back in the United States, S/Sgt. Iredell Hutton, the tail gunner for Lt. William M. "Mac" McCrory's crew, a new crew for the 803BS, was preparing to go overseas. Hutton began a war diary to his wife Caroline in High Point, North Carolina. Hutton wrote:

On the 29th of May we were told to pack our bags. We were out and ready to go, but we had to wait until 11 o'clock. We pulled out at 11:30 and proceeded to Jersey City. We arrived there at 1 a.m., where we boarded a ferry and headed over to 51st St. in New York where we were supposed to get our boat. As we got off the ferry, a band was playing "Idaho." All of the boys joined in and sang with them. When we were on the pier the Red Cross gave us coffee and do-nuts. After we finished eating we were given mess tickets and our bunk numbers.

We walked up the gang plank of the "Queen Elizabeth." It was the largest boat I had ever seen. Our bunks were on the main deck in the Winter Garden. We were really crowded in our sleeping quarters. We shared them with an anti-tank division. I got busy looking for Norwood [his older brother who was a paratrooper in the 502nd Parachute Infantry, 101st Airborne—the outfit nicknamed The Screaming Eagles. Iredell, being the youngest, had two more brothers, James and Marion, both older than Norwood]. Looked all over A deck and also the Promenade. Looked until it was about time for me to go to chow. Just as I started to leave, I saw Norwood coming on the deck. He didn't see me, so I ran up and put my arms around him. It was the happiest we both had been in many a moon. We both sat down on the end of a bunk and just about cried. In fact we did.

After chow we messed around the deck until 1 o'clock p.m., and then we felt the boat beginning to move. It pulled out into the harbor and it was there that we saw the Statue of Liberty. Norwood and I put our arms around each other and wished each other luck and said that we wanted to come back and see the same sight together. The sooner the better. I'm sure that every one of the soldiers on the boat felt an empty feeling as we passed out of view of New York. Some among us may never see those shores again. It is an awful feeling to go off to war when you know you are young and have so much to live for.

This "Little Friend" P51 escort was #3106447, C5-L from the 357th Fighter Group, 364th Fighter Squadron. The Mustang was nicknamed *Shoo Shoo Baby* **and piloted by John C. Howell.** *Courtesy of George E. Paris, Lt. Col. USAF (Ret).*

2

First Missions - The RAF

June 1944

RAF Bomber Command planned to support D-Day Operation Overlord by the use of radar countermeasures. RCM operations would also be carried out by the British Royal Navy. The RAF RCM operations would involve the RAF 100 Group which included the 803rd Bomb Squadron. On 30 May a requirement was placed upon the 803BS to support the RAF in the upcoming invasion by providing MANDREL cover. Its airborne MANDREL transmitters would target a whole range of enemy coastal early warning frequencies. This was known as barrage jamming. The MANDREL barrage jamming by design would form a screen behind which Allied aircraft could operate unseen. The MANDREL transmitters radiated noise, thus obscuring the attacking Allied formations. This electronic curtain completely blocked the probing beams of the enemy radars, such as the Freyas, causing their control monitors to illustrate nothing but a deluge of "snow."

Prior to D-Day the 803BS only had three MANDREL equipped B17s, however, arrangements had been made to pick up additional transmitters and have them flown directly to the Oulton air base. A special team was to be there to immediately install the sets. To insure that four planes would be in operating condition for D-Day, five planes would be equipped with MANDREL, and a request had been made for an additional plane.[22]

Total RAF RCM operations in the air would involve over 100 aircraft. The planning and responsibility was carried out entirely by Headquarters RAF Bomber Command. The plan called for RCM cover for the entry of the airborne forces who were to land in two distinct areas, east and west of the main invasion assault beaches.[23]

Within a few days the necessary equipment was installed and the new squadron was now ready for its first operational mission. For electronic intelligence, or ELINT, the Fortresses carried special intercept receivers which were used to keep check on frequencies of new radar sets the Germans were developing. The stage was now set. The 803BS would help protect the first of nearly 12,000 Allied aircraft that would fly on the morning of D-Day.

RAF Bomber Command actually planned many different and unique RCM operations for D-Day. The operations were code named TAXABLE and GLIMMER for naval and air diversions against Cap d'Antifer and Boulogne; MANDREL for barrage jamming of enemy radar frequencies to cover the Allied airborne forces; operation A.B.C., which provided VHF jamming support to cover the airborne forces; and lastly operation TITANIC to simulate or feint the attacks of large Allied airborne forces.

Because of new long range German radar installations located on the westerly tip of the Cherbourg Peninsula, plus a number of coast watchers in the Channel Islands area, twenty MANDREL equipped aircraft were necessary for the barrage jamming operations. Sixteen Short Stirling bomber aircraft of RAF 100 Group's 199 Squadron would be deployed in positions 1-8, along with four B17s from the 8AF's 803rd Bomb Squadron in positions 9-12, orbiting specific latitude/longitude positions. All of the jamming aircraft were to conduct their special operations for 5 1/4 hours.[24] (See Overlord MANDREL illustration.)

One squadron adjutant expressed his strong sentiments about this truly historic day:

B17 Flying Fortress. At rest before the battle. *Courtesy of Leonard N. Backer.*

Getting ready for D-Day. Capt. Robert Stutzman warms up his B17.

Invasion Day—From the dark, chilled, early hours of the morning, well into the night, all officers and enlisted men were at their post of duty, eager to perform any order of the day with complete disregard for the size of the task. Every job was important. Every man was important. No man shirked his duty. No man allowed fatigue to overcome the complete performance of his duty. This was the long awaited day. We were making our first thrust across the English Channel, to free an enslaved country, France, from the fiendish rule of a ruthless group and their fanatical followers, whose beliefs in every phase and form of life are completely opposite to all that we, Americans, hold close to our hearts. France was the pathway to the destruction of Hitler and Company. Nothing must stop us. Nothing will stop us.

Four war weary MANDREL outfitted B17 Flying Fortresses of the 803BS left the darkened runways of Oulton, England, on 5 June, at 2200 hours to fly in support of the airborne operations for Operation Overlord. The four B-17s, piloted by Capt. Stutzman and Lts. Klimetz, Obenschain, and Overstreet, were in position from 2235 hours on 5 June to 0450 hours on 6 June.[25] Flying "Forts" and Stirlings orbited their specific locations offshore southern England south of Portland Bill and Littlehampton and jammed virtually all of the radars between Cherbourg and LeHavre. The mission proved very effective in countering the enemy warning system and contributed materially to the success of the landings on the Normandy beachhead.[26] Thus began the combat operations of the only American radar countermeasure squadron to fly from England during the Second World War.

Sgt. Charles Sanders, an 803BS ground mechanic, recalled D-Day:

They had told us for some time that the first maximum effort we would have would be the invasion of Europe. We had gotten a new B17 and supplies to equip for night flying. Capt. Preuss [the Engineering Officer] told us that the Colonel said many lives depended on us getting these planes in the air as soon as we can. That

night we did almost the impossible. We put the flame suppressors on all four engines in about three hours. We had four planes that took off. We all figured this was the big night. I can assure you that it was a long night.

Our planes were flying an assigned area. If a German fighter should see them, they would be a sure target. This was the first time I had sweated out the planes since leaving the 92nd Bomb Group. It was that suspense of hoping everybody would get back with no enemy contact.

June 6, 1944, was the big day. I don't think I have ever heard as many planes as I did that night. They just kept on coming over. We did not know when to look for our planes back. Sometime in the real early morning we had four planes come in pretty close together. I had been up about twenty-six hours.

On June 7 the Colonel told us the 803rd and the RAF squadrons had saved hundreds of lives. He said we would never know just how many. He also told us that the top army men had expected about a forty percent loss of men in paratroopers and airborne troops. Due to the radar screen, they had less than a two percent loss. He said the surprise was the difference. The MANDREL would stop the German radar from picking up activities in England. They told us it was like having a solid fence between us and the Germans.

D-Day B17 pilot Capt. Robert Stutzman, who served as the Squadron Operations Officer for the 803BS and later as the same in the 36th Bomb Squadron RCM said:

Late in the afternoon or early evening of June 5 our squadron was alerted that the long awaited invasion was on. I received a copy of General Eisenhower's letter to the troops thanking them for the noble adventure they were about to undertake. I recall get-

Lt. Klimetz and crew - June 1944. Kneeling L-R S/Sgt. Hagan, Lt. Gilzinger, Lt. Klimetz, and Lt. Smith. Standing L-R S/Sgt. Duff, S/Sgt. Belcher, S/Sgt. Markley, S/Sgt. Popadyn, and S/Sgt. Zuckerman. *Courtesy of William R. Hoagland.

ting the flight crews together and briefing them for the mission that was laid on by RAF 100 Group. We did jamming and led groups of paratroopers and gliders that were flying. We were ahead of them jamming. We saw gliders being towed by C-47 aircraft, many flights of C-47s with paratroopers. We did jamming so that the C47s carrying paratroopers and gliders wouldn't be sitting ducks. While we were in our orbiting position we could see the flashes of the guns from the Naval bombardment. We could see the firing, the softening up of the beaches there. We hoped our jamming would conceal the presence of the airborne troops from the Germans.

Lt. Wade Birmingham, navigator for Capt. Stutzman, wrote this account of the events on June the 6th:

For the last 8 or 10 days our squadron has been alerted—an air of mystery was hovering over our entire base. We knew deep down that the mighty invasion was just a matter of days off; and when the time came, the 803rd Squadron was to play an important role. In fact, the importance of our work gave us all quite a start. We could hardly believe that at last, our 4 months of waiting was to bring a rich reward. We had all been waiting for this moment, and now that we were to be back in operations we all felt 100% better. Morale was at its highest peak.

Early in the afternoon, the 5th of June, our C.O. alerted 4 of our trained crews; myself having the privilege of being on one of these choice few. Of course we did not know that this, at long last, was the real thing. We had an idea that it was just another night practice flight—or perhaps a Bullseye, practice for search lights. The navigators were called for immediately after supper, and with an air of question surrounding our being, we entered the British Intelligence briefing room. There on the map we found the answer to our questions—we were to cover the airborne and seaborne in-

Lt. Overstreet and crew - June 1944 Standing L-R in front Sgt.'s O'Malley, Janeczko, Muse, Dinicola, unknown. Kneeling L-R Engineer - Sgt. Hoover, Co-pilot - Lt. Flagler, Pilot - Lt. William Overstreet, Navigator - Lt. Bevan, Sgt. Jack Kings. *Courtesy of William R. Hoagland.*

vasion with our special MANDREL equipment. Our ships were equipped to put out a screen, a screen that rendered the Jerry's radar receiving equipment useless. They could not tell what was going on behind the screen, nor could they use radar for aiming their coastal installation guns. In other words, our "sets" would play havoc with the entire radar system and communication system of our enemy.

To make our job a success, we, the navigators, were entirely indispensable. Our duty was to patrol within 5 miles of a certain point near mid-channel, and this 5 miles had to be stayed within. Each aircraft had an individual point, and the points were so set that the screens would blend together without an opening. Our take-off was set for 10:05, and landing the morning of the 6th was supposed to be near 6:30—8 hours of flying in a small area, in the dark—quite a job. However, we knew we must make good. The success or failure of the invasion, the amount of losses, both naval and aircraft; these were all piled upon the shoulders of the 803rd.

[After] take off we proceeded to Portland Bill, and made good our time—now to Point 11 and on went our sets at 11:35—that time had to be made to the minute, and luckily our GEE set (See GEE illustration) was working fine; no jamming interference, therefore my navigation was very precision like. We began our orbiting 8 minutes one leg, 2 1/2 the other. We had one helluva wind, blowing from the Northwest and a velocity of near 80 mph. In other words, if we weren't careful, we would be blown too far to the south and over enemy territory. Also, our screen would be broken—our whole task would be a failure. I began to sweat now, are we right? Did I judge this wind correctly? Will they send night fighters after us? Will our engines hold out? Two were running rough now. Would our oxygen hold out? Our gasoline? Hundreds of petty thoughts

Lt. Obenschain and crew June 1944. Standing L-R Lt. Obenschain, Lt. Ostler, unknown, Lt. Warner. Others unknown. *Courtesy of William R. Hoagland.*

were running through my mind as we continued circling at Point 11.

At about 12:00 we watched the fireworks begin. As we were over an overcast, we could not see what was going on beneath the clouds, however, we could see huge flashes beneath the stuff. This no doubt was the fleet's pounding of the coast, the prelude to the airborne fleet. All during the night these flashes kept going at a mighty pace; I felt a surge of pride within me—this is truly it, and my part is being carried out! About 01:30 we could see the marker flares of the RAF ships. These boys were now doing their part— precision bombing at night. We watched great flashes as the bombs found their targets. Truly it was; this is where the invasion took its first step. The remainder of the night was just a repetition of this— flashes, gunfire we could see but not hear. Flak bursts at night are horrible sights. Again I was thankful I was sitting up here at 20,000 ft. away from enemy fire.

As time passed we all began to get tired, the gunners began to see planes that did not exist, stars looked like lights of planes. I had taken so many GEE fixes that I could do it without even thinking, almost with my eyes closed. About 4 o'clock the daylight began to come into being—and what a spectacle it brought into sight. We watched the fighters and the bombers going over to take part, hundreds of planes—all kinds. How we wished the cloud cover was gone, so we could see the sea power at work—the 4,000 landing craft and ships that took part. All were beneath us, but not one could we see.

At 4:50 we cut off our sets and started for the base. 6:15 our wheels set down and 10 very tired young men went into interrogation. Tonight we were told that our part was played to perfection, the screening was perfect. Also we were told that our job had caused the slight losses of the first blow—15 transport planes and just 3 ships. We felt wonderful! We had a job to do and we had done it.

Another D-Day pilot, Lt. Richard "Dick" Obenschain, spoke of his mission in a most nonchalant way:

We went up at about 18 thousand feet and were to make a ten mile circle out over the channel and turn the MANDRELS on. What we tried to do was to jam the radar, and I guess we did. I heard some reports later that we were credited with saving quite a few lives because the Germans couldn't see. We just kept on flying in our circle until we got all through and we went back to base and landed. So it wasn't very exciting then. Airplanes were flying below us, above us, and all around us. All the running lights were off, and how we escaped getting run over by somebody, I'll never know, because it was dark, and you couldn't tell who was where. You couldn't see well enough. We were up over when the Navy opened up the guns—started firing on the French coast. It was quite a show!

Obenschain's co-pilot Lt. James Warner remembered:

Our mission, beginning the night of 5 June 1944 was to orbit around specific geographical coordinates over the English Channel. We were not informed officially that D-Day was coming up. Our time on station was about 6 1/2 hours. My personal flight records show a total time of 8:15 hours. Shortly after arrival at our assigned station, we lost #3 engine and completed the remainder of the flight on three engines. It had begun to be light enough on our return to base to see fantastic activity on the ground along the coast and in the air.

Lt. James Ostler, Lt. Obenschain's navigator and later to become the 36th Bomb Squadron Navigation Officer, reflected:

My main memory of that night is coming back to England on the morning of D-Day. You probably have no idea now how many airfields there were in southern England. It was like one large aircraft carrier. There was not a plane on the ground anywhere in

Airmen at D-Day briefing. Dwight D. Eisenhour's letter to the soldiers, sailors, and airmen said, "You are about to embark upon the Great Crusade." *Courtesy of Joseph A. Bartus.*

Airmen at prayer D-Day at briefing. "The hopes and prayers of liberty-loving people everywhere march with you." *Courtesy of Joseph A. Bartus.*

Airmen at prayer before D-Day mission. "Let us all beseech the blessing of Almighty God upon this great and noble undertaking." *Courtesy of Joseph A. Bartus.*

England. The emptiness of the airfields was just absolutely astonishing. Much of the territory over which we flew coming back was strange to us because it wasn't on a normal bomber track from the heavy bombers we had been used to flying from east Anglia out over the North Sea. That baby went directly south over the southern part of England and to the English channel. And just the emptiness of the airfields. That's the most significant impression that that flight left with me.

Lt. Bill Flagler, co-pilot for Capt. Overstreet, wrote of the restless anticipation in his diary:

This is it. The day we have all been waiting for. This is the part we played. On the morning of the 5th, four crews were alerted for a "BULLSEYE" [training mission]. Our crew, Capt. Stutzman, Lt. Obenschain, and Lt. Klimetz. We knew something big was in the air, and an hour before briefing our navigator, Lt. Bevan, was bursting with what he knew. Our four B-17s, carrying MANDREL were to take off at 2200 hours and orbit our position. It was a beautiful moonlit night, but flying in circles at an assigned altitude at night in range of their fighters and flak made us uncomfortable. Our MANDREL equipment made the invasion by paratroopers possible. A report by S-2 [the Intelligence Officer] said that only 15 planes out of 1000 odd carrier ships were lost, along with 2 personnel and 2 landing vessels lost. From our position we could see the shelling by the Navy, and the explosions lit up the entire night sky. It was a very tiresome flight just flying in circles, but I wouldn't have missed it for anything.

S/Sgt. James Wooden, tail gunner for Capt. Robinson, spoke of the historic mission:

We went up at about 11 o'clock that night. We could see ships as far as we could see across the horizon. I mean it was as far as the eye could see, clear from horizon to the end of the horizon. Underneath us were these gliders with the C47s pulling. You could see them going underneath us as we were flying around up there in a circle. We didn't even move out of the circle, about a fifteen mile circle. As soon as it got daylight, we came back.

Our main purpose on D-Day was to be up and set up this screen, and when we did, nothing could work. You couldn't use radar or radio. We weren't even allowed in the bomb bay. The whole bomb bay was filled with radar and jamming equipment. It was what they

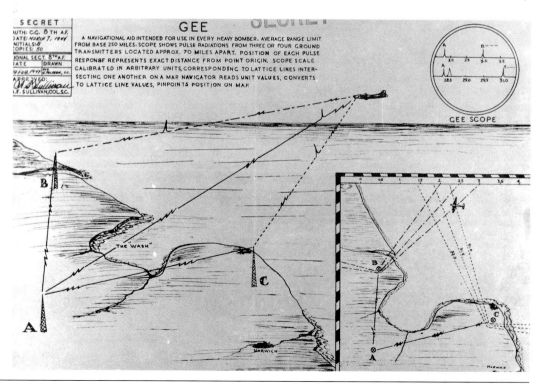

Illustration of GEE equipment utilization. *Courtesy of the USAF Historical Research Agency.*

called a MANDREL ship at the time. It had antennas sticking out all over it, up on the fuselage and out on the wings, everywhere.

Almost as soon as the British and American crews returned from their operation their commanding officers forwarded letters of congratulation on the success of their historic mission. Here is the first from Air Vice Marshal E. B. Addison, the Air Officer Commanding RAF 100 Group (AOC), to the men of the 803BS:

6TH JUNE

FROM AOC 100 GROUP TO LT. COL. SCOTT PLEASE CONVEY TO YOUR UNIT MY CONGRATULATIONS ON THE EFFICIENT MANNER IN WHICH THEY CARRIED OUT LAST NIGHT THEIR FIRST SPECIAL OPERATION. THE OPERATION APPEARS TO HAVE BEEN CARRIED THROUGH WITHOUT A HITCH, DESPITE ITS INTRICACY, A FACT WHICH AUGURS WELL FOR THE CONTINUED SUCCESS OF YOUR UNIT.[27]

More recognition followed, on 8 June. Both Air Vice Marshal Addison and Group Captain T.C. Dickens, Commanding RAF Station Oulton, forwarded their explicit congratulations to the officers commanding RAF 214 Squadron and the U.S. 803BS on their combined success of the D-Day mission. Their message read:

The results achieved on the night preceding invasion day were highly successful, this has already been established. It may be found that your achievement was of even greater importance than can be known at present. I appreciate that the culmination of your effort can only have been achieved by careful training and attention to detail, this is reflected by the results of the crews concerned. Great appreciation has been expressed by Naval Commanders of the support from the Squadrons, and it can now be disclosed that the work of 101, 214, and 803 Squadrons succeeded most effectually in confusing the enemy as to the point of landing, thus permitting the tactical surprise which we gained.[28]

L-R The second 803BS CO, Lt. Col. Clayton Scott and Station Commander G.C. Dickens, June 1944. The 803BS found its relationship working alongside RAF personnel amiable and very satisfactory. *Courtesy of William R. Hoagland.*

Shortly before the main Overlord operation commenced, even though the enemy coastal radar activity was checked and found to be much less than usual, due no doubt to the number of installations which had previously been destroyed by air attack, the MANDREL screen nevertheless jammed effectively the stations which were active. As stated in *Most Secret War* by Dr. R.V. Jones:...*Reviewing the results, Sir Trafford Leigh Mallory, the Allied Expeditionary Air Force Commander, said in his Official Dispatch (London Gazette, 2 January 1947):*

The application of radio countermeasures immediately preceding the assault proved to be extraordinarily successful. These results may be summarized as follows: The enemy did not obtain the early warning of our approach that his radar coverage should have made possible; there is every reason to suppose that radar controlled gunfire was interfered with; no fighter aircraft hindered our airborne operations; the enemy was confused and his troop movements were delayed.

Both RCM squadrons, RAF 199 Squadron and the 803rd Bomb Squadron, saw no fighters and suffered no casualties.

So began the Allied attack on Hitler's mighty "Festung Europa." To the coast of Normandy came the greatest airborne and sea invasion in the history of modern warfare 12,000 Allied aircraft and over 5,000 ships and landing craft. The 803rd Bomb Squadron (H) (Prov) had flown its first operational mission. It had contributed to the initial deception by successfully jamming the Nazi coastal early warning radar. It would follow with other ingenious ways to fool the enemy through its deceptions.

This was to be one of many Allied surprises planned for D-Day. Britain's Prime Minister Winston Churchill said on that most historical day, "There are already hopes that actual tactical surprise has been attained, and we hope to furnish the enemy with a succession of surprises, during the course of the fighting."[29]

Four days after D-Day a top secret memorandum from Allied Expeditionary Air Force for the British 21st Army Group and the American 1st Army Group requested that JACKAL jammer airborne sets be installed in aircraft of the 803BS for the jamming enemy tank and vehicular radio communications. The JACKAL equipment—an active electronic jammer—although not used on D-Day, would later be used during the Battle of the Bulge counteroffensive. Dr. Donald Reynolds of Dr. Terman's team at ABL-15 remembered during a 1982 interview with the Association of Old Crows what his contribution to invasion day was supposed to have been:

What my support of D-Day was to have been was getting the JACKALs operational. We were directed to prepare to jam German tanks on the ground from aircraft in support of the D-Day invasion. This was February. No one knew when D-Day was going to come. Just a few months in advance we got word that we would be wanted to support the D-Day invasion. We were to take a number of transmitters which had been crash produced in the U.S. to be ready for

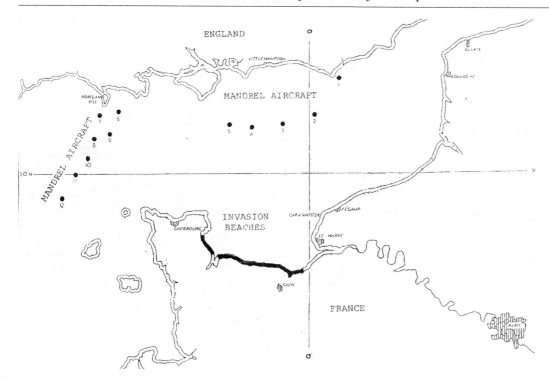

D-Day MANDREL operations had sixteen Stirlings from RAF 199 Squadron deployed in positions 1-8 along with four B17's from the 803BS in positions 9-12, orbiting specific latitude/longitude positions.

this operation and had to get them ready to fly. Well, they didn't come and they didn't come and they didn't come. We couldn't find where they had gone. They had been lost. One of those things. This was a German tank [radio frequency] band which was something like 28-34 mhz. It overlaps the U.S. tank band. The German was AM and the Americans were FM. Our sets could operate right through that jamming. But they didn't appear. We finally found the sets in a depot in Southern England at D+25 of June. They never appeared until then. Then a big crash program started getting them ready for future use.

We flew those and made some field tests over England using captured German tank receivers and transmitters because we were terribly afraid that they would interfere with the U.S. communications. We found that the U.S. communications between two tanks on the ground in rolling country was almost completely unaffected. They could get maybe 10-15 mile range between two tanks while at the same time the German tank receivers were essentially knocked out down to 1/4 mile range. So, it was effective.

One airplane flying one of these around the tank battles could play havoc on the whole area. The pressure was off. D-Day had been accomplished and the foothold had been obtained on the continent. They used that above the tank battle finally in that Battle of the Bulge. It was used finally operationally. They didn't get immediate information back on the effectiveness. It's very very difficult to assess the effectiveness of what one measure of this sort will do to the overall success of the campaign. It's hard until later. Historically you could find out and talk to people to find out whether the jamming that was experienced interfered with their operations.

Apparently it did, and it was highly worthwhile. There were no U.S. planes lost in the process.

The next operational mission was flown the night of 16/17 June 1944. Six 803BS B17s were operated as part of the MANDREL screen over the North Sea in a semi-circle from Orfordness to a point at sea 5320N-0300E. Sixteen aircraft from 199 Squadron operating in pairs furnished the other eight equally spaced positions. The screen was in support of an attack into Holland by Bomber Command. RAF 100 Group's assessment of its effectiveness stated: "MANDREL screen operating 16/17 June, 1944, covering bombers attacking Sterkrade. 803BS Fortresses began jamming at 2240 hours. Leading elements of the bomber formation were due to cross enemy coast north of Frisian Islands at 0045 hours. Enemy warn-

The bloody beaches of Normandy. Aerial photograph of the invasion beachhead. *Courtesy of Richard H. Brunell.*

ing systems plotted some aircraft 15-20 miles off Garleston at 0030 hours. A few plots were made of aircraft 30-40 miles off the coast, but until it was crossed the number was meager until the bomber formation was actually over enemy occupied territory."

The next night five Fortresses of the 803BS, along with aircraft from RAF 199 Squadron, again flew a protective screen in support of a RAF Bomber Command attack on Aulnoye, France. The mission was completed successfully.

S/Sgt. James Wooden remembered these first missions:

We had RAF counterparts that flew with us on these missions. We were stationed on their field, and we would go up at night together and fly. A lot of times we would get up over Ipswich or somewhere like that and they would throw a spot light on us. Of course, we had flares of the day that we'd shoot into the air to inform them on the ground that we were friendly, hoping they wouldn't shoot at us. Of course a couple of times we'd get caught in a raid coming over from Germany. Well, they'd be shooting up anti-aircraft fire all around the place. We'd be right in the middle of it. Most of the time we evaded that.

We would go up at night and we'd fly in a circle just in sight of the enemy coast, all up and down the whole length of the English coast with this equipment on. We would cover a certain area, other aircraft south of us would cover another area, and to the north of us were other aircraft. Usually there were about eight to fifteen aircraft up at a time on a night mission.

Lt. Bill Flagler recalled:

Primarily, we were screening the RAF bomb force which took off every night. We would go ahead of them with our three or four ship formation with this jamming equipment to jam the radar that the Germans were using to determine where the landfall was going to be from the RAF bombers. We would screen them all the way to the target and then turn around and go home. We never were hit, we never lost an airplane, and we never dropped a bomb.

The Normandy coast on 7 June, the day after D-Day. *Courtesy of John Madero.*

Major General George S. Patton at the microphone addressing the troops. Patton was also part of the D-Day deception. His performance convinced the Germans that he would lead the main invasion force on the Pas-de-Calais. *Courtesy of Earl R. Siler.*

The night mission of 22/23 June had five B17 aircraft of 803BS operating in a protective screen, together with ten aircraft from 199 Squadron. From 0045 to 0100 hours, 100 OTU (Operational Training Unit, RAF) aircraft passed through the MANDREL screen to a point eastward over the North Sea as decoys to draw the attention of the German Air Force warning system.

The day of 22 June was an important date for the 803BS when the squadron gradually began to transfer from B17s to B24 Liberators. The B24 would provide greater electrical power necessary for the high voltage jamming and search equipment. The squadron designation assigned to the new aircraft was R4, which was painted on each side of the fuselage by the waist gunner's window.

Lt. Charles Travis spoke of the changeover:

I remember several B24s arriving before their crews. I also remember taking one up with my crew chief reading from the tech orders as we went along. All went well.

Mechanic Cpl. Kent MacGillivary recalled the arrival of one new B24:

We were with the RAF on their bases and we would get new airplanes in occasionally. They would sit around there for quite a while before they got ready with all this radar equipment and what not for service. One just sat there on the ramp for a long time. Finally they got it all equipped and assigned a crew to it. They named it the "RAMP ROOSTER." It had been just roosting on the ramp for quite a while. Several different crews, of course, came through there that used the plane.

The first of new B24 aircraft assigned to the 803BS arrived in June 1944. B24 #42-50665, R4-K nicknamed *Lady in the Dark*. This Liberator was soon to be equipped with both MANDREL and JACKAL for jamming operations. *Courtesy of Dr. Robert F. Hambaugh Jr.*

Like many of the thousands of young American GIs entering the British Isles daily, Iredell Hutton from North Carolina arrived on June the 5th, just before D-Day, with heightened excitement and anticipation. From the decks of the "Queen Elizabeth" he first sighted land—the high mountains in the distance. The land was Ireland. The ship sailed on and docked at Greenock, Scotland.

He wrote about beginning his new adventure in a new land:

It was about 2pm when we pulled in. Never in my life have I seen such beautiful country. It looked so peaceful, and one would never know that they were at war here if there hadn't been so many battleships around. It was around 4pm when Norwood was told that he was leaving the boat in just a few hours. He and I went down and got his bags together. Around 6pm he put his pack on and was getting ready to leave. We put our arms around each other and said goodbye. He then picked up his duffel bag and got into a small ship which had come along side.

After a short while we began to move towards shore. When we docked we were near the railroad station. We saw some pretty girls in a tower who were sending messages to the battleships and flat-tops that were stationed all around the "Queen Elizabeth".

Once on the train, Hutton elaborated about what he saw:

When we had pulled out of the station, we headed for England. As we rode along people would be standing along the railroad, houses, and gardens waving V for victory at us. They were happy because the invasion which they had waited for so long had just come off. The country was a lot different from that which we have back in the states. Each hill where the water ran down was all covered with grass. We didn't see any soil erosion. From the window we could see castles way up on the distant hills. All of the hills were barren of trees. All that was growing on it was grass and a few crops. The soil was too rocky for very much farming. Each farm

was separated by high rock walls. It took years and years to build these walls.

It was around 10:45 pm when we pulled into the station. We put on our musette [canvas] bags and gas masks and proceeded to get off the train. The officers were first marched away, and then we were loaded into trucks. The name of the station was Stone. The new camp is a reception center for air crews called Nelson Hall.

On Friday afternoon the 9th of June we were told that we were shipping out the next morning for Northern Ireland. We were loaded on a train and headed for Manchester. We got off at Worthington and took a truck out to the air base. The base was a repair depot for the British and American planes. There were all kinds of planes. We ate chow and then put into a B17 and were flown over to Kilkeel, Ireland. There were around 30 men put into the plane and it kinda got bumpy at times. As we flew over the camp which was right on the ocean, I saw the country and it was really lovely.

When we landed the weather was the nicest I have seen since being on this side. There were few clouds, and the sun was shining. We were marshaled from the field to our new tin huts which we are to live in while we are in school here. They are oval huts with 15 men in each one.

There are a lot of Irish people living and working on the post here. They seem friendly, but you can tell that they have had dealings with the GIs before. The theaters on this side are all free. They are 16 mm and have to stop the show after each reel.

We have 3 days of Intelligence school and after that we have 6 of gunnery. Just a refresher on what we had in gunnery school [Tyndall Field, FL]. Intelligence is what to do and what not to do if captured by the enemy [and] how to escape from enemy territory. This is going to be much tougher than I ever expected.

B24 #42-51226 R4-L. Crew Chief Dick Holman in pilot's seat. *Courtesy of Jack W. Charlton.*

Hutton continued:

June 18, 1944

Today was our first class in gunnery. The first thing they did to us was give us a test to see what we had remembered from gunnery school. To tell you the truth, I remembered very little. After the exam two ex-combat men, fresh back from combat, have been made instructors here, awaiting furlough back home, gave us lectures on medals and some of the experiences which they had had. One had been wounded in action and had been awarded the "Purple Heart." It is a beautiful medal, but I don't ever care to receive it.

The task of gunnery isn't as easy as I had once thought. There are only a few percent of these men that come back. From what they say the enemy fighters and ack ack [flak] is really something. All we can do is put our trust in God and hope that he sees us through OK.

June 23, 1944

Today was our last day of school. I'm glad we took it because it enlightened the tail turret to me a lot. I think that I can operate it OK now. I made a better grade on the test than some who have had it for six months.

We leave for England tomorrow. More than likely they will rush us right into combat because the British are getting a little shaky over the jet propelled rocket [the V1s] which has been hitting the south coast of England for the last couple of weeks.

June 24, 1944

Today we left Kilkeel, North Ireland. We were loaded on trucks and crated away to a boat. The boat took us to Stranraer, Scotland. There we got on the train and traveled all night. We got into London about 12:30. We were told that we had a layover until 6pm that night.

Andrew [nicknamed Sack, Lt. McCrory's radio operator] and I took a walk around London. The first place we went was to see the bomb damage that the new jet propelled bombs had done. We saw whole blocks where the windows were knocked out, and some where the buildings were torn all to hell. These British have really taken a beating during this war.

We were talking to an Englishman and he said that he could hear the bombs coming at night while in bed, but he just lay there hoping that it wouldn't hit him. He said he just figured that if his time had come, he was due to go.

We got back to the train about 6 and got our compartment. All enlisted men had the same car. We had a stateroom all to ourselves.

We came to a place called Huntingdon. I tried to call Marion [the next older brother] then, but the operator was busy so I had to wait until I got to camp, which was four miles from Huntingdon at a town called Alconbury.

June 27, 1944

We had to get up about 8 o'clock to pack our bags to get ready to leave on the trucks. We were going on detached service to our new camp but would still be assigned to Alconbury or rather the 482nd Bomb Group. We didn't stop till we got to the base [Oulton]. On the way here we passed through Cambridge to Norwich. As we drove down to the field we saw more British airmen, WAAFs [Woman Army Air Forces], RCAF [Royal Canadian Army Air Forces], and RAF. We went into the mess hall and an officer told us what the setup was here. It seems like a pretty good deal, but I think that I had rather get into combat and get the missions over with. We may be here for the duration. Doing this you still have a chance of getting killed.

The barracks are very nice. There is room enough in them for about 24 men. They are all new and haven't been lived in before.

B24 #42-50622, R4-N nicknamed *This is it Men* and later *Bama Bound*. Courtesy of Earl R. Siler.

B24 #42-51232 R4-J (later nicknamed "The Jigs Up") joined the 803rd in June. *Courtesy of Roy W. Stroud.*

Our crew sleeps right beside each other. Herbert [a waist gunner on McCrory's crew] on one side and Sack on the other. There are two ex-combat men in the barracks who have completed their missions and are waiting to be replaced here and sent back to the states. As soon as enough '24 crews come in, they will be on their way to see their loved ones. The beds are OK except for the mattress. It is divided into three parts. These are called biscuits. You do good if you don't have a space between each one when you go to bed. The toilets, showers, and wash room is about a half a mile away. You really need a bath by the time you make that hike.

Hutton's buddy on their aircraft, waist gunner S/Sgt. John Shamp, had also started a diary to his sweetheart. On 27 June Shamp wrote about their new airbase and about their special work:

The new base here is a RAF field. I wish I could tell you in my letter what our job is but the secrecy of it makes it impossible for me to write of it or even hint. We just have to keep our mouths shut and our pens quiet. So far we have been told that we are the luckiest men in the 8th Air Force because the flying will be short and not very dangerous. The planes are equipped with some new type of equipment that counteracts radar. Most of the flying is done at night helping the RAF heavy bombers. We fly out over the channel and just cruise around with the "stuff" turned on. The enemy then cannot tell if any aircraft are coming their way or what. The whole set up is new. They just started it the first of the month, but they claim that over 10,000 lives were saved on D-Day alone. So, they are going to continue using it.

S/Sgt. Hutton continued in his diary:
June 29, 1944
Today we all had a meeting in the briefing room and the Colonel told us that we were going into operations immediately. It won't

B24 tail turret interior. *Courtesy of George F. Lechner Sr.*

The men of the 803BS worked side by side with the RAF. Here a British Halifax under maintenance. *Courtesy of Stanley Harris.*

be too long now. We had a test flight this afternoon and I got back in the turret and tried to operate it. It operated good in azimuth, but not in elevation. I still seem to get a little sick when I fly. Sure hope it wears off soon.

June 30, 1944

Today we had a cross country flight. We flew over Ipswich and a few other towns that I have forgotten the names of. The countryside is really beautiful from the air. Each strip of land is marked off by a hedge or a high wall. There are more cattle, goats, sheep, horses, and pigs here than I have seen in my life. All the land has something growing on it. As we flew over the country you could see airfields everywhere you looked. I can't see how in the heck Germany stands a chance with the air fleet that we and the British have. I was back in the tail today and the turret operated perfectly. I think that I can take care of anything that comes my way now. Didn't even get the slightest urge to get sick. Maybe it is wearing off of me. I pray that it is. I don't want to get sick when everyone else is OK.

803BS pilot, Capt. Richard C. "Dick" Sackett remembered those first days settling in and finding a home at Oulton:

When we were in Oulton we were close by the RAF mess, which we were entitled to use anytime we wished. It was located at Blickling Hall, about a mile or two from the base. The story was that at one time Blickling Hall had been residence of Ann Boleyn. Anyway, we all had bicycles of course, and the road from Oulton to Blickling Hall was narrow as all the roads seemed to be in the country in England. We'd go over there, officers, pilots, navigators, and so forth and enjoy an evening at Blickling Hall. On the way home back to the base it was dark, and at sometime or another somebody had discovered there was a shortcut on that road which cut off probably a quarter to one half of a mile. It led down a country road which was nothing but a lane. It was quite a precipitous descent down at the bottom of it where it came out on the other road. What

usually happened was that there would be five or six of them in a big pile up at the end of that steep drop off on that hill when they were taking that short cut. Usually after an evening at Blickling Hall there would be at least a half a dozen in most cases, pilots and navigators checking in with the flight surgeon in the morning, and some of them weren't able to fly. This came to the attention of the powers that be what was going on. Finally they were told that if you want to go to Blickling Hall and want to turn yourself in unfit to fly the next day that's too bad, because you're going to fly.

Pilot Joseph Brookshire said of his first meeting with the RAF:
I remember the first day I went to the British Officer's bar and I was standing there at the bar and this Limey comes up and starts cutting the buttons off my blouse. So, I just stood there and let him cut them all off. Then they got a greasy old overseas cap and filled it full of beer and handed it to me to drink. I reached for it and deliberately let it drop on the floor. I wasn't going to drink. Then I got my knife out and I went around there and cut off enough Limey buttons to take the place of mine. That was my introduction to the RAF.

Another Yank, radar mechanic Sgt. Aristide Blais, expressed his impressions of England in his poem titled:
A YANK'S LIFE IN ENGLAND

WHERE THE HEAVY DEW WHIPS THROUGH THE BREEZE,
AND YOU WADE THROUGH MUD UP TO YOUR KNEES,
WHERE THE SUN DOESN'T SHINE AND THE RAIN BLOWS FREE,
AND THE FOG'S SO THICK YOU CAN HARDLY SEE.

WHERE WE LIVE ON BRUSSEL SPROUTS AND SPAM,
AND THOSE POWDERED EGGS WHICH AREN'T WORTH A DAMN.

Blickling Hall. The off-duty playground for airmen of RAF 100 Group and the USAF's 803rd Bomb Squadron. *Courtesy of William F. Flagler.*

IN TOWN YOU EAT THEIR FISH AND SPUDS,
AND DOWN THE TASTE WITH A MUG OF SUDS.

YOU HOLD YOUR NOSE WHEN YOU GULP IT DOWN.
IT BITES YOUR STOMACH, THEN YOU HAVE TO FROWN.
FOR IT BURNS YOUR TONGUE, MAKES YOUR THROAT FEEL QUEER.
IT'S RIGHTLY CALLED BITTERS—IT SURE AIN'T BEER.

WHERE THE PRICES ARE HIGH AND ITS QUEUES ARE LONG,
AND THOSE YANK "GI'S" ARE ALWAYS WRONG.
WHERE YOU GET WATERED SCOTCH FOR FOUR BITS A SNORT,
AND THOSE LIMEY CABBIES NEVER STANK SHORT.

AND THOSE PITCH-BLACK NIGHTS WHEN YOU STAY OUT LATE,
IT'S SO BLOODY DARK YOU CAN'T NAVIGATE.
THERE'S NO TRANSPORTATION—SO YOU HAVE TO HIKE,
AND YOU GET YOUR CAN KNOCKED OFF BY A GAWD-DAMN BIKE.

WHERE MOST OF THE GIRLS ARE BLONDE AND BOLD,
AND THEY THINK EVERY YANK'S POCKET IS LINED WITH GOLD.
AND THERE'S THE PICCADILLY COMMANDOS WITH PAINTED ALLURE.
STEER CLEAR OF THEM OR YOU'RE BURNT FOR SURE.

THIS ISLE ISN'T WORTH SAVING, I DON'T THINK.
CUT LOOSE THOSE BALLOONS—LET THE DAMN THING SINK.
I'M NOT COMPLAINING, BUT I'LL HAVE YOU KNOW,
LIFE'S ROUGHER 'N HELL IN THE E.T.O.[30]

Five aircraft were dispatched on the next mission, the evening of 27 June. This mission was flown at 19,000 feet as compared with 15,000 in previous operations. One aircraft on station, No. 10 at 5155N-0100E, was in the RAF bomber stream, narrowly escaping collision on several occasions. Two aircraft failed to complete the mission due to mechanical failures. Lt. James Warner recalled one such mission:

On one particular jamming mission to cover the RAF bomber stream, we were to fly at 16,000 ft., well above the RAF aircraft. After a few orbits we began to receive severe turbulence during part of our circle, and on one turn toward the west in the faint horizon we saw a RAF Lancaster at our altitude. Apparently RAF aircraft in the bomber stream also encountered turbulence from aircraft in front of them and climbed to avoid it. As a result they wound up at our assigned altitude. My personal observation is that even in the beginning when the jamming missions got underway, the RAF losses began to decrease.

The last mission of the month was flown the next evening when five squadron aircraft effectively provided the protective MANDREL screen.

By the end of June support for a permanent RCM unit had grown. The 803rd Bomb Squadron was still a provisional unit, but to effectively prosecute the RCM program a permanent organization was needed. A permanent organization would be able to secure additional intelligence information, which combined with British

Most beautiful surroundings. Post card photo of Aylsham and Blickling Hall. *Courtesy of Melvin A. Remus.*

intelligence would enable the 8AF to plan the most effective countermeasures and predict future trends in the enemy's developing use of electronic defensive systems. It would also be available to act on RCM problems requiring prompt action on a relatively small scale, such as special search missions and countermeasures against radio-controlled missiles—Hitler's secret V1 and V2—Vergeltungswaffe, or revenge weapons. [31]

On 29 June, Major Robert F. Hambaugh, the Commanding Officer of the 858th Bomb Squadron, 492nd Bomb Group, was relieved of duty and placed on detached service with the 803BS. Hambaugh would later be placed in command of the new 36th Bomb Squadron (H) RCM.

June had indeed been a historic month with the successful Allied invasion at Normandy. By D-Day, the Luftwaffe had ceased to be a major threat to Allied bombers. Air superiority had been achieved earlier during "Big Week" (Feb. 19-26). Germany found itself unable to replace its lost aircraft, but more importantly, unable to replace so many of its trained veteran pilots.[32] Another advantage for the 8th Air Force was the growth in U.S. fighter escorts, which carried extra fuel in drop tanks for extended range. The fighters now provided bomber protection to the target and back. After D-Day flak became the primary threat faced by the Americans. Hitler's first V1 flying bombs were now hitting England. June also marked the first full month of operations for the new elite 803rd Bomb Squadron flying MANDREL night missions with the RAF.

Since its beginning at Sculthorpe and then later at Oulton, the 803BS had found its relationship with RAF personnel amiable and very satisfactory. Excellent cooperation was enjoyed with the RAF, and operations had gone smoothly. The 803BS had begun to prove its military worth.

3

Lady in the Dark

July 1944

The new 803rd Bomb Squadron, working with the RAF 100 Group at Oulton, now began seeing its fair share of support operations. More crews were reporting on board, conducting their training, and getting checked off on both night and day navigational and cross country flights. Here the new airmen practiced, refined, and learned more about their flying machines, individual job functions, responsibilities, and equipment. They also saw more of the beautiful summer patchwork of this new land, the Norfolk broads, as well as the vast array of airfields in East Anglia. They learned about flying control, navigational aids, potential problems with terrain, weather, and "friendly" hazards.

The new 803BS B24 pilot, Capt. Dick Sackett, spoke of his first missions:

My first mission was with Capt. Robinson, he was of the 803rd, as were Captains Obenschain and Stutzman and J.P. Ostler. They had all finished their tours and were filling in until we could get the 36th organized with B24s rather than the 17s. The reason being, I was told that the B24 had a higher power output. We had a very very roomy bomb bay. These MANDREL sets and jammers were bolted into the bomb bay permanently.

We were briefed on the missions by intelligence. That entailed advising the crews of any areas that they were aware of [and] where there might be any flak or fighters. The navigators were briefed by the navigation officer of the squadron. That was for their business, of course. There was always the big important thing of a time hack. Time being of the essence in this operation. It was always important for all the aircraft to arrive at their orbiting position pretty much at the same time. The equipment was always turned on at the same time and off at the same time.

The first mission with Capt. Robinson, I flew co-pilot with him in a B17. At the conclusion of the mission we came then up over the coast to our base, and at Ipswich we were immediately coned by British searchlights and we fired all of our recognition flares. They still kept us coned, like pinned to a board, but we finally escaped that and headed back to base. As we approached the base our radio operator was in touch with them by telegraph key. We used no voice transmission for obvious reasons. We were told that there were Intruders [enemy fighters that were known to have sought the bombers from their airfields and to and from the target] in the area and to stay clear of the base for a while, which we did; and eventually we were allowed to return and went in and landed.

B24 #42-7607, R4-A. *Courtesy of Roy W. Stroud.*

803BS B17 pilot Capt. Dick Obenschain flying the B24 Liberator.

The next time we went out, we went out with my crew. We started on our own. Things went along a pace quite nicely. We didn't have too much difficulty. Of course, we were flying nights, screening the RAF, alone, and no lights, which was somewhat hairy to begin with. The lighting arrangements that they had on the fields was a light circle, a circular ring of lights around the aerodrome, and a lead-in string of lights which led into the active runway. Well we didn't use any lights on our aircraft. Procedure was that you would get down to traffic [pattern] altitude, follow the light line around the aerodrome, and turn in on the approach light line. There were no runway lights visible until you got down to around 200 feet, then you had the standard runway lighting ahead of you on each side. We didn't use any landing lights. It took a little bit of getting used to until you were really comfortable to do those things, but we did it.

As I think back on it I wonder if I were asked to do something like that today, like for instance, taxi out onto the runway in the fog and set your directional gyro on the heading of the runway, and with one runway light visible ahead—no more, just maybe one, maybe 200 feet ahead of you, take off on that DG [directional gyro] knowing that you had 6,000 feet of runway, and you'd better get something done or you're going off the end. It was quite a thrill to say the least. I think back on it now, we must have been crazy, but we were ordered to do it, so we did it!

Another airman, Sgt. Lester Jones, gunner for Lt. Norman Landberg's crew, remembered his arrival in the British Isles:

They sent us up to Ireland for training for several weeks before we started flying. We flew the radar planes. It was a different radar from what we were trained in. We turned it on to run interference for the RAF. It took the place of chaff that we dropped. Sometimes we flew with the RAF, sometimes they sent us out alone, to confuse the Germans. Sometimes we'd go with the RAF in front of them. They'd go out in on the south and we'd be up north, just to confuse

them. It was my job to turn that thing on and off. Just flip the switch to the equipment in the bomb bay section.

Sgt. Jones spoke of one particularly hazardous night mission:

I remember one night we were flying over the North Sea, next to Norway, somewhere in that territory and the plane starts to sucking gas out of the wing tanks and flowing back over the window just like it's pouring down rain. Of course you could smell the gas. The first thing we did was to cut the electrical off, the radar, afraid a spark would come from that and blow us up. The pilot was diving, and we had to turn around and come back. He dived that thing to stop the suction out of the wing tank. He dived and did a little of everything. We were flying at a pretty high altitude, had to cut the booster pumps on. After we got down below to where we didn't need the booster pumps, it stopped. It didn't suck any more out of there. We barely made it back to the field. I understood that they cussed out the pilot who had made the decision, but we were glad he did. We thought a lot of him. He was a good fellow.

He recalled another one over France:

One time we were flying over France, they told us we could fly at 20,000 feet and we could get over the [weather] front. We got up to around 25,000 and we still did not get over that thing. We were picking up ice over the wing. The plane wouldn't stay up there.

The tail dropped down, mushing along. The pilot tried everything, [such as] kicking the ice off the wings with the deicer. [But] they froze up and we couldn't do anything with it, so he made the decision to come back. In fact, he asked us about it. So, we said yes. We didn't want to stay up there and take a chance of killing ourselves. The B24 just wouldn't stay up there where it belonged, because it was loaded with ice. So we came back. We were fussed at again, but I think we would have done the same thing again if we had to.

Newly assigned Liberator #42-51188, R4-O nicknamed *Lady Jane* arrived in July 1944. Courtesy of *Charles M. Todaro.*

S/Sgt. Iredell Hutton recorded in his diary on 2 July:

Today while we were in the mess hall seeing a VD [venereal disease] film, Mac [Hutton's pilot, William "Mac" McCrory] came in and called for his crew. We went out and loaded into a jeep and went down to the briefing room. Colonel Scott was there to tell us about the mission. We were to test some new equipment which they had. We got our flying clothes and loaded in a truck. We then went down to the armament shop and got our guns. Herb [a waist gunner on McCrory's crew] and I both had trouble getting our guns in. The armorer gave me the wrong bolt studs for mine. The Colonel was pissing and moaning around Herb.

While we were putting our guns in, an oxygen bottle blew out and it had to be fixed. It was fixed in a little while and we took off. Went to 18,000, and there the oxygen got low in the nose and we had to return to the field.

The next day Hutton played a waiting game. He wrote:

At the 1 o'clock briefing the Colonel told us that we were going to fly down to Defford to test some equipment at 7:30 tomorrow morning. At 8 o'clock tonight he told us what was to be expected and everything. At 9 he received a call and told us that the mission was scrubbed.

On the 4th of July 1944, Major Robert F. Hambaugh assumed duties as liaison officer with RAF 100 Group. That night, the first mission of July was flown. Five aircraft of the 803BS, along with fourteen Sterlings of the RAF 199 Squadron, carried out a protective MANDREL jamming patrol in twelve equally spaced positions from 5147N-0200E to 5308N-0255E. All aircraft completed the mission without incident. The patrol was in support of RAF Bomber Command attacks on targets in northern France. One hundred aircraft of the RAF OTU feinted an attack through the screen at 0001 hours on an easterly course at 5220N-0200E, then out to

John Shamp on his bicycle poses alongside *Lady Jane. Courtesy of Iredell Hutton.*

sea for twelve minutes and returned through the screen at 0024 hours at 5231N-0225E.

On the 4th of July—America's Birthday, S/Sgt. Hutton wrote:

As I got up this morning we heard planes going over to bomb Germany and France. They were above the clouds, but we could see them every once in a while. They continued to go over for about 2 hours.

We flew formation around the countryside this morning. It is a very beautiful country. You can see bomb craters and damage just about everywhere you look.

After dinner we went back to the briefing room where they gave us 20 minutes of drill and then dismissed us. While we were walking back to the barracks the planes started returning from their missions. You could tell that there were some missing. I would have given anything to have gone on a raid today. It looks as though we will be here doing work that no one else will know about until the war is over. It is very essential, but is also highly secret. Our chances of coming back are very good, but you can never tell how things will turn out. As yet only Mac, Calisch [the navigator], Krueger [the co-pilot], and Sack [the radio operator] have been on a mission. They flew in '17s then. As soon as they get the equipment in the '24s we will get our chance. Lt. Dodgen [the bombardier] left us today, since we won't be needing him anymore. We carry no bombs on our missions, so they had to find another place for him.

The next evening he noted:

Tonight we went on a practice mission. We had to make 8 landings. The Colonel came in and briefed us from 8pm until about 9:15. He warned us about Intruders and how to look out for them. We put our guns in, but didn't have to use them.

MANDREL jamming was carried out successfully by five 803BS aircraft on the night of 7/8 July. Fourteen aircraft of the RAF 199 Squadron also operated in the patrol.

B24 #42-50385, R4-H nicknamed *Beast of Bourbon* also arrived in July. *Courtesy of Donald Burch.*

RAF targets. A bombed airfield in Holland. *Courtesy of Dr. Robert F. Hambaugh, Jr..*

In his diary entry of 8 July, Hutton longed for a different jam:

Today the crew with the exception of Herbert and Shamp took some baggage of Colonel Scott down to Cheddington. We ate dinner down there. The meal wasn't so hot. When the officers told us what they had for dinner it made our mouths water. Ice cream and strawberries. It has been a long time since I have even tasted a strawberry.

Two nights later five 803BS aircraft were dispatched along with fourteen aircraft of the RAF 199 Squadron. One 803BS aircraft was forced to return to base early when an engine caught fire. Aside from this incident the mission was completed successfully.

On 9 July, Hutton described his first B17 mission.

I flew a mission in a B17 tonight. The only boy I knew that was flying with us was the radio operator. After we had been briefed, we got our equipment and went out to the ship. While we were standing around waiting for take off time, the flight surgeon Capt. Jere Johnson brought us some coffee and sandwiches. The coffee came in good. When it was about time to take off I put my heated suit on and climbed in the tail. The tail of a '17 works different from a '24 since it has the guns just mounted in there and not in a turret. When we got to 10,000 ft. the pilot told us to put on our oxygen. From there we went on up to 19,000 ft. It wasn't too cold there, but I had to cut the rheostat up on the suit a little.

It was really beautiful flying over the North Sea. The moon was shining down, and I looked in the dark part of the sky for enemy fighters. The mission lasted around three hours. As we were landing we saw a big flash and later on learned that a flying bomb had landed about 30 miles away. The Jerries are really sending them over in numbers these days. When we came down we got into the truck and drove back to where we were interrogated. They asked all sorts of questions, if we saw any fighters, flares, flak, or shipping. We saw one convoy, but it was ours.

Hutton's buddy, waist gunner John Shamp, wrote of the same mission in his diary:

The only way we have of knowing whether or not we fly a mission is by the bulletin board in the mess hall. At chow time I look at the bull board. I'm scheduled to fly with another crew in a B17—briefing at 20:00. We go to the briefing—we are told where the RAF are going to and what our job will be. Over to the chute room to pick up our flying clothes, etc., then out to the ship. The guns are brought out and we install them, then sit around outside smoking, talking, and eating sandwiches and drinking coffee that the flight Doc [the Flight Surgeon, Capt. Jere Johnson] has brought out to us.

At 11:00 the engines are started and we take off at 11:20. As we climb the full moon is coming up and oh how beautiful it is peeking through the broken clouds. At 10,000 feet we put on our oxygen masks. Everyone is at their post and a sharp lookout is kept in all directions. One half of the heavens are light while the other is dark and hazy. At 11:45 the "stuff" is turned on. At about 12:30 there is a call from the radio operator, "fire in the radio room." Everyone gets their chute on and ready to leave in a few seconds. The radio man has the fire out, but the equipment won't operate, so we abort our mission. As we start descending a vapor trail is noticed right above us. We are kept more alert because it may be an enemy fighter. We get permission to land, but overshoot the field and go around for another approach. It's good this time and we come on in. After the ship is parked and all flight clothing removed we go by truck back to the briefing room for interrogation, which is given after we all have a big shot of Scotch whiskey.

The next day, S/Sgt. Hutton spoke of the tight security and secrecy within the outfit.

We now have to give our mail to one of our officers to censor it. We don't like this a darn bit. This is the first base I have ever seen where you just lay around if you are not flying. What a life. As yet they haven't decided how they are going to count our missions. Some say by combat hours, others say by missions. The Colonel said we should continue what we are doing for the duration.

At the present time you are not hearing anything about what this outfit is doing, but after the war you will find that it has been a deciding factor and has saved many thousands of lives since we began to use it. I am talking about Allied lives.

Tonight we have another mission. All of us rode over to the briefing room on our bikes. We were taken into the British war room and there each officer got up and told us about our mission for tonight. We were to cover the RAF as they flew deep into France and hit oil dumps and marshaling yards. We were to fly up over the North Sea as we did the previous night. After the briefing was over we went over to the drying room to get our equipment. While we were putting that on an officer came in and told us that the mission was scrubbed.

Five 803BS aircraft and twelve from the RAF 199 Squadron supported Bomber Command operations with a MANDREL jamming screen from eleven equally distributed stations on the night of 12/13 July. The mission was completed successfully without incident. S/Sgt. Hutton wrote about this mission:

About 8pm went to chow and then to the briefing room. We got our flying equipment and went out to the plane, a new '17. Morin and I were to fly as waist gunners. Herbert was to fly in the ball. We took off at 10:20pm climbing to 10,000 ft and then proceeded on our course. There was a thick layer of clouds up to 10,000 ft., and on the ground you couldn't even see through it. After we were up there it was really beautiful. Under us was a solid layer of clouds. It looked as though you could get out and walk on them. It looked safe, but I would have certainly hated to jump.

While we were flying someone in the forward part of the plane called back and said look at 4 o'clock high at the parachute. At first I saw the moon, but to the right of it I saw the chute. As we flew down the channel, I saw convoys coming and going to Cherbourg. Some had balloon barrages on top of them. Every once and a while I saw formations of bombers returning from raids over Germany and France. As we flew through the Straits of Dover I saw the white cliffs all along the channel with high walls which looked like cement, but were only white because the sea had washed up against them for so many years. We flew down to Lands End which is the most southern part of England. While flying we would take a deep breath of oxygen every once in a while since we didn't need our masks. The reason for the mission was to test some new equipment. It was the longest mission that I have yet flown in the air. It was a little over six hours.

While we were flying Herb asked me if I wanted to fly in the ball [turret] for a while. After getting strapped into it, I started operating it. You are really cramped in that thing. You are under the plane, and it looks as though you are flying alone.

Crossbow target — a V1 storage depot at Pas-de-Calais. *Courtesy of Richard H. Brunell.*

Two days later he continued :

This morning all four B24 crews had to get up at 5:30 to take our planes down to Defford. We took off around eight and got there about nine. When we landed and the officers had taken off somewhere, Sack and I took some gasoline out of the plane and put it into a can and washed our clothes in it. It took all the dirt out.

The RAF there tried their best to treat us as good as possible. We stayed there until three and then we were told that we were not going to fly the mission there. We had to come back to the base because the Colonel wanted our crew to fly a mission tonight. When we came back we were told that the mission was scrubbed.

Missions continued, and on the night of 14/15 July five aircraft of the 803BS and twelve from 199 Squadron, RAF 100 Group again operated a MANDREL jamming screen. One aircraft had to abort due to failure of its GEE equipment. Sterlings of 199 Squadron and Forts of 214 Squadron from RAF 100 Group operated a special WINDOW mission through the MANDREL screen. A group of RAF OTU aircraft passed through the screen, feinting toward the Ruhr, turned over the North Sea and reentered the MANDREL screen. Analysis of German night fighter defense indicated that these operations confused the enemy. Enemy forces were airborne in the area of the Frisian Islands to intercept this suspected force. In the southern area, enemy night fighters were airborne, believing British Intruders were a main force. No serious interception of the bomber stream was accomplished.

Lt. James Snoddy, the co-pilot for Lt. Louis McCarthy's crew, remembered:

We flew a variety of missions. I remember the early ones where we went out over the North Sea and orbited for hours. I especially remember orbiting over the Frisian Islands because there was a

Belgium target. *Courtesy of Dr. Robert F. Hambaugh, Jr.*

flak boat just off the coast and every time we got close they would open fire. We stayed just outside their range.

Iredell Hutton witnessed Britain's illuminating searchlights on the night of 16 July:

Tonight about 12 o'clock while I was outside, I heard an airplane and all of a sudden bright arc lights sprung up all around it. From every direction the lights seemed to come. The plane remained in the light until he shot colors of the day. It reminded me of the newsreels that I had seen back in the states about the Battle of Britain.

On the night of 17/18 July, four 803BS aircraft, along with thirteen Sterlings of the RAF 199 Squadron, operated a "creeping" MANDREL screen—a moving one in support of Bomber Command operations. Fourteen aircraft of various RAF 100 Group squadrons effected a WINDOW mission through the screen and to the Dutch Coast. One hundred RAF OTU aircraft feinted through the screen toward the Dutch Coast, turned over the North Sea, and re-entered the screen. Analysis of enemy night fighter defense operations and intercepted signals clearly indicated that these operations confused and misled the enemy night fighter controllers. Bomber Command attacked a number of targets in France and Germany. This night mission was successful.

S/Sgt. Hutton recorded the mission:

Tonight we flew within 8-10 miles of the coast of Holland. We saw heavy guns being fired down in the channel. It was the first time I had seen flying bombs in the air. They would streak across the sky with a ray of spark following in the wake. There was plenty of flak, but it was not directed at us. We met no fighter opposition. At one time we were over the English coast and the searchlights picked us up. Sack shot a flare so they immediately turned them off.

Crewmate John Shamp added:

We had a mission tonight. This is the first time we've ever flown as a crew. Norm [Morin] was on sick call so we had to have a

replacement for him and one for the left waist. So far I've taken care of both waist guns myself. The person who replaced Norm in the nose turret was our radar director. We took off at 11:17, two minutes behind schedule, because the bomb bay doors wouldn't close or open. Then #1 [engine] wouldn't start. Herb had trouble with the ball. I was plenty worried, but nothing went wrong after we got into the air. We had to be in position "A" at 12:15, there at 150 mph, over the Holland coast. The RAF had forty training bombers go under us spreading WINDOW. Once we reached position "B," we circled for two minutes, then came back at 160 mph. We saw flak from a barrage, and Hut says he saw a couple of buzz bombs.*

The next day Shamp wrote of the squadron's effectiveness:

S-2 told us today that the mission was very successful last night. The Huns pulled all of his fighters out of France to repulse what he thought was going to be a major attack.

The next night, that of 18/19 July, four aircraft of the 803BS and sixteen Sterlings of 199 Squadron operated a MANDREL screen in support of Bomber Command forces attacking targets in France and Germany. The MANDREL screen was a creeping one from positions near the coast of Belgium and Holland. Aircraft of RAF 100 Group operated a WINDOW screen. RAF OTU aircraft emerged from the screen and flew in the general direction of northwest Germany. Enemy reaction to these activities was optimum. As if their radar equipment had been invaded by an army of electronic gremlins, the Germans failed to plot the bomber stream until it was across the enemy occupied coast. They reacted strongly to short penetrations in the north of France.

S/Sgt. Hutton noted on 19 July:

We learned today that the mission which we flew night before last was a preclude to the big assault which followed this morning. Biggest air blow that has fallen on the enemy since D-Day. The Yanks captured St. Lo this morning.

Crossbow target — a V1 site at Siracourt . *Courtesy of Richard H. Brunell.*

S/Sgt. Douglas McComb, the nose gunner for F/O (Flight Officer) Bert Young's crew, recalled one of the missions near Belgium:

One night while flying just south and west of Belgium we saw a sight that none of us will ever forget. Well below our pattern we saw a plane coming from the south with all of its running lights on. As our plane reached our northeastern flight pattern and turned around, then either the tail gunner or myself, the nosegunner, would give reports of what was going on. This was given several times. All of a sudden we saw the searchlights picking this plane up with one or two lights, and what seemed two or three seconds, about six or eight more lights joining in, keeping the plane in the cross arc of lights. All of a sudden the explosion of bombs hitting the target or ground lit up the night sky. Watching this plane and in the cross arc of lights and all the bullets and tracers going up, we expected to see the plane blow up in the air. But none of this happened. It flew back to wherever it came from and disappeared into the night.

Two nights later, four 803BS aircraft along with fourteen Sterlings of the RAF 199 Squadron, operated a MANDREL screen in support of Bomber Command. A WINDOW patrol by aircraft of various RAF 100 Group squadrons was carried out. Bomber Command targets included Hamburg and targets in France.

S/Sgt. Iredell Hutton wrote of a near-miss in the night skies on this mission :

Tonight we went out on another mission. We flew out over the North Sea. After we were up for about an hour, planes came by us in every direction. One passed within 50 feet of us with the lights off. Would hate like heck to run into one of those things. From where we were we could see shell fire coming from Hague and also some fire coming from a boat in the sea. It looked as if it was coming straight for us, and you can bet your boots that I had my chute close at hand all the time. The guns were loaded from the beginning. It was the roughest one yet. They will probably get worse every time we go out.

His buddy John Shamp remembered three close calls:

While on our mission we got in the bomber stream and had two close calls and another one after we got into the traffic pattern. Took off at 10:45 and landed at 2:30. Saw plenty of flak.

The mission of 21/22 July called for three aircraft of 803BS and eight of 199 Squadron, together with twelve aircraft of various RAF 100 Group effecting a WINDOW screen. German night fighter reaction was all that could have been desired. The tinsel gremlins were active against the enemy radar again. Various control points in occupied Holland reported formations of enemy (RAF) bombers approaching the coast. German night fighters were airborne from 2329 hours to 2356 hours searching in vain for the "ghost" squadrons in the bomber stream before they appreciated the situation.

George Klemm of ABL-15 spoke of WINDOW in another light:

As far as the passive equipment was concerned, CHAFF or WINDOW was dropped [from the aircraft]. The British called it one name and we called it the other. We had it, the British had it, and the Germans had it. We discovered that in dropping some of our stuff over the continent, that in addition to fouling up some of their radar—the cows were eating it and dying of indigestion. That was the side effect of it.

Terror continued to fall from the skies of the British Isles in the form of Hitler's Vengeance weapons—the V1s, as Hutton wrote on 22 July:

The Germans are still sending their buzz bombs to London. From what I hear that place is a wreck. The Allies are blasting the launching sites, but without much success. Hitler is still executing his high generals for his attempted assassination.

It didn't take Bomber Command long to retaliate and target the V1 launch sites. It did so with its program called Operation

Murray Peden, pilot RAF 100 Group, 214 Squadron. *Courtesy of Murray Peden.*

Crossbow. On the night of 23/24 July, five 803BS aircraft, along with twelve from RAF 199 and 214 Squadrons supported Bomber Command operations with a protective MANDREL screen. A force of RAF OTU aircraft penetrated the screen preceded by WINDOW dropping aircraft. Aircraft from various squadrons of RAF 100 Group laid down a WINDOW screen in support of the same operations. Targets also included Kiel, Berlin, and targets in France. Six hundred twenty-nine aircraft attacked enemy submarine pens at Kiel. Only four were lost. One hundred fifty bombers attacked other targets. Two RAF aircraft were lost. Enemy reaction to these supporting operations appears to have been all that could have been expected. The mission proved to be most successful for 100 Group and the 803BS.

The OTU and WINDOW dropping aircraft inclined the enemy to marshal its night fighters to protect the Ruhr and Crossbow targets in northern France. The main bomber stream flying at minimum altitudes and passing behind the MANDREL screen was not plotted until 0500W, too late to permit concentration of night fighters in the Kiel area.

Bomber Command had sought to disperse enemy defenses as well as avoid heavy losses. Denis Richards, author of *The Hardest Victory*, wrote of this mission:

On 23/24 July 612 aircraft, with the help of a MANDREL jamming screen, took the defenses of Kiel by surprise, and in the space of 25 minutes cascaded nearly 3,000 tons of bombs into the town and port. They did enormous damage, to the U-boat yards and to many other areas, and lost only four of their number—0.6 per cent.[33]

Iredell Hutton wrote of this mission's fiery aftermath:

Tonight we had another mission, one of the longest night missions yet. We left at 11 pm and got back at 4 am. Never have I been as tired and sleepy as I was. All the other boys were the same way. The RAF struck at Kiel, the German naval base, with great success. Without us they would have lost ten times as many planes as they did—lost 6 planes out of 600. We also learned tonight that within the next week or two, we will be flying into France with our equipment. After we start that, it shouldn't take long before we get our 300 hours in and then we can go back home. Just before we landed number four engine caught on fire. When we landed it continued to burn. I had come out of the tail up into the waist when I saw the flames. Herbie already had the back hatch open and was going to jump out. I had to hold him back, if I hadn't, he would have hurt himself on the runway. Also, before we landed the GEE box and the whole electrical system went out. Mac and Krueger had no lights except a flashlight to see by.

The Americans were learning much from the RAF about the employment of RCM in air warfare operations and the "Battle of the Beams." By far the most accurate description found of the WINDOW and MANDREL jamming during this time comes from veteran Canadian pilot Murray Peden. Peden, of RAF 100 Group, 214 Squadron, who would be completing his missions within a month, wrote in his book *A Thousand Shall Fall* :

Through experimentation it had been discovered that a handful of aircraft "WINDOWing" with precision and at a high rate— one bundle every two or three seconds—could simulate the approach of a bomber force of 500 aircraft. We were told that six of our Fortresses, with two men industriously WINDOWing from the waist gun positions, could produce the same effect on the German radar screens as a force of 200 to 300 bombers. Thus the stage was being set for a new era in bomber tactics, and to capitalize on the situation some of our old weapons were being vastly improved.

Using the MANDREL for jamming, Peden said:

When the target to be bombed lay in Southern Germany, for example, the plot might shape up like this: Just before dusk, a dozen or 14 MANDREL aircraft would fly out and take up their stations off the enemy coast, strung out in pairs in a great line so as to shield our bases completely from observation. At the appointed moment the operator in each aircraft would switch on MANDREL, blanketing all the Freyas' screens with snow. The central German fighter controller would thus have no early information on which to base his preliminary concentrations, and in fact would be unable to tell whether there were operations pending. After some considerable time, however, an attacking British force would suddenly come thrusting through the northern portion of the MANDREL screen and begin to be discernible on the Freyas. It would take several minutes before the size of the force, its altitude and its course, became apparent, precious minutes to the controller concerned; but it was essential for him to ascertain these facts in order to make a valid assessment of the threat. Even if no other factors had been introduced into the situation, the MANDREL screen itself would have delayed his reactions, to the point where fewer fighters could have been maneuvered into position for injection into the bomber stream. But, as the controller well knew, at least after the first time Bomber Command did it, an important new factor had been introduced. The powerful bomber stream reported to be heading for the Frisians, and potentially threatening such targets as Kiel, Cuxhaven, Wilhelmshaven, Bremerhaven, or Bremen, while it certainly appeared to be a force capable of wreaking terrible damage on a target city, might only be a handful of Fortresses dropping WINDOW. The controller, therefore, delayed longer on that account, watching to see if anything further materialized through the MANDREL screen; then, when he could afford to delay no longer, began scrambling fighters from more remote aerodromes and moving them north to meet the approaching threat. Three-quarters of an hour later, this northern "attack" evaporated in a settling cloud of tinfoil, while at the same time, the Main Force, which had gone into France at low level over territory held by the Allied armies, suddenly appeared on the German radar screens far to the south, and began climbing for bombing height—already well on its way to the chosen target. Local fighter controllers along their route then had to contend with powerful jamming of their communications as they attempted to vector remaining fighters into the bomber stream.[34]

When not flying missions, the aircraft's navigation equipment had to be tested and checked. Time was also taken for fun and mischief. Pilot Mac McCrory, being a Southern fellow from Jacksonville, Florida, had "Raunchy Rebel" painted on his A2 jacket and lived by those very words. He and his crew raised a little hell as Hutton related on 24 July:

Today we had to take a plane up and check the GEE box in it. Mac asked the navigator that went along where he wanted to go and he said anywhere. He took us over the King's summer home. What a beautiful palace it is. Big and spacious. It had one of the biggest flower gardens I have ever seen. Beautiful flowers, too. He then took us out on a stretch of wasteland and it was there that we did a little buzzing. First time I had ever flown that close to the ground. The farmers thought that we were going to hit them we were so low. We then flew up a small canal, and if we were a few feet lower we would have hit the trees—only thrill that I have got out of flying.

And the next day they went buzzing again. Hutton said:

This afternoon five officers, Sack and I went buzzing in a '17. I'll bet we weren't five feet from the ground. Birds came in the front turrets and radiators. Some made big dents in the wing. I never knew a plane as big as that could maneuver so easy. What we need is to fly more like that. The officers will probably hear about that.

S/Sgt. Frank Church was the flight engineer for Lt. George Sandberg's crew, and would fly 55 jamming missions. S/Sgt. Church remembered the missions and McCrory's crew:

In between missions we went out on what they called search training missions out over the North Sea, keeping our eyes peeled and report what we saw, if anything. Our crew and McCrory's crew were out on such a search mission. We were flying over an area in East Anglia on the coast in an area called the Wash. It was a swamp area—marshes. We were flying along and we couldn't find McCrory's airplane. He had been right with us. We were right down on the deck—real low. And son-of-a-gun, we discovered he was under us. We were right down there probably not more than 50 feet off the cattails and he was under us.

Our plane "Lady in the Dark" was a B24J, #665, call sign K-Krug. It was assigned to us when it was new and we completed 55 missions in it on Feb. 7, 1945. Stan Walsh was the one who painted her picture on the side of it. It was an outstanding piece of art work for that type of thing. It was a picture of Ginger Rogers with Donald Duck peering out from around her leg. The reason that plane was given that name was a popular movie at that time was named "Lady in the Dark." Ginger Rogers and Ray Milland starred in it.

The next mission on the night of 24/25 July three 803BS aircraft and eight Sterlings and Forts from various RAF 100 Group squadrons operated a protective MANDREL screen in support of Bomber Command operations. Twelve aircraft of various RAF 100 Group units emerged from and reentered the screen. Their destination for the evening was Stuttgart and various other targets in France and Germany. Enemy reaction to the MANDREL screen, OTU and WINDOW patrol appeared to have drawn some night fighters into the Ruhr area and prevented them from being dispatched to intercept the main bomber stream. The electronic and tinsel gremlins had struck again.

The next night another protective MANDREL screen was provided. The MANDREL force was comprised of three aircraft from 803BS and fifteen aircraft from RAF squadrons. The screen moved eastward from its initial positions and returned to its point of origin. Seven aircraft of various RAF 100 Group squadrons operated a WINDOW patrol through the MANDREL screen eastward to the vicinity of the enemy coast and returned. Appraisal of enemy reaction to the protective measures indicated that it denied information regarding the impending attack on the Ruhr until after the bombers were well over enemy territory, thus allowing the enemy insufficient time to organize or press home an attack.

But success was not always to be found in the joint Allied effort. The deception tricks did not always work as evidenced on the night of 28/29 July when three aircraft from the 803BS and fourteen RAF aircraft operated the MANDREL patrol. Nine aircraft of various RAF 100 Group squadrons furnished a WINDOW patrol which passed through the MANDREL screen eastward to the area of the enemy coast and returned. Bomber targets included Hamburg, Stuttgart, Frankfurt, and other objectives in France and Germany. Monitorial reports indicated that enemy controllers did not react to the MANDREL and WINDOW patrols on this date, but marshaled their forces to intercept the bomber stream.

Death it seemed was always around the corner, seen in the eyes of many airmen, and certainly on the minds of most men. The aircrews prayed and dreamed of safely completing their operational tours. Missions and Allied losses were on Iredell Hutton's mind when he noted in his diary on 28 July:

Tonight we had another mission. This time we were up for five hours. If we had five hours a night it wouldn't take so very long before we would have our tour completed. The sooner the better for me. Didn't see any activity at all tonight. Bomber Command struck at Stuttgart and Kiel. 62 out of 1000 planes were shot down. Not so good.

The next night three 803BS aircraft were dispatched and successfully completed a MANDREL screening mission. This mission completed the RCM operations for the month. Airmen were not always comfortable being put with other crews in other aircraft. S/Sgt. Hutton wrote:

Ready for operations — A new Liberator and a new crew for the 803rd Bomb Squadron Provisional. Lt. Sandberg and crew with *Lady in the Dark*. L-R S/Sgt. Frank R. Church, S/Sgt. Stanley L. Walsh, S/Sgt. Paul L. Amanti, 2d Lt. Arthur D. Bennett, 1st Lt. George G. Sandberg, 1st Lt. Talbott B. Clapp, S/Sgt. Joseph Melita, S/Sgt. Howard A. Nolan, S/Sgt. Anthony P. Vaccaro. *Courtesy of Frank R. Church.*

Our crew was a spare tonight. Another tail gunner on another crew's uncle came to see him, so I had to fly in his place. Don't like flying with other crews. Tonight we struck at Germany's oil supply.

Later that day he continued:*Today I saw the largest formation of planes I've ever seen coming back from a mission. About four of them had to make an emergency landing here. One prop was shot completely off. They struck at Ploesti oil fields and a synthetic oil plant in Merseberg.*

Naturally, most airmen preferred to stick with flying with their own crew, men with whom they had trained and developed trust and friendship. Another tail gunner, S/Sgt. Tony Vaccaro of Lt. Sandberg's crew, remembered flying with another crew:

The one time I flew with another crew, we were at 20 or 25 thousand feet high, and apparently the co-pilot hit the master switch with his right knee and shut off all four engines. We went into a dive. It's fortunate the propellers were still rotating, and when he put the master switch back on the four engines started. I think that was a miracle.

The airmen were also not always comfortable with the squadron aircraft, either, as many of the older planes had seen a lot of battle and were war weary. However, still the aircraft mechanics and ground crews delivered their best in the worst of times to keep the planes in the air.

At this time it was indeed a small world for Iredell Hutton, for on the last day of July, he was surprised and elated to see a hometown friend. He wrote:

The plane which we used today was an old crate which had done 51 missions. Stanley Harris, who worked for me at the Paramount theater, is crew chief on it. He has only been at this field for a few days.

July had given the 803BS another full month of missions working alongside RAF 100 Bomb Group, primarily 199 Squadron. The 803BS B17 and B24 aircraft were flying with RAF Sterlings on night jamming missions and also participating with the RAF OTUs. Strategies were being refined as the squadron missions supported RAF Bomber Command's main bombing operations against such targets as the German submarine pens at Kiel, Operation Crossbow against Hitler's V1 launch pads, and Berlin. Nearly all of the MANDREL and WINDOW jamming operations were effective and successful. Enemy defenses were most often deceived and confused. The squadron also received more men and new Liberators. More changes would occur in August. The squadron would receive a new designation, a new commanding officer, and a new home base for its special operations. The 803BS now had a strong purpose and was finding good results.

4

RAFU - Radar All Fouled Up

August 1944

Having achieved favorable results in the missions during the previous two months, the 803rd Bomb Squadron began to solidify its position within the RAF Bomber Command support campaign structure. The Eighth Air Force also began thinking ahead for a permanent RCM squadron. The 803BS was still only a provisional unit and not fully organized. It realized that there was much to be gained in intelligence information through close association with the scientists and related technical engineers in Great Britain.

An internal letter dated 1 August from the 8AF Office of Director of Operations at Headquarters of U.S. Strategic Air Forces in Europe (USSTAF) at High Wycombe—code named Pinetree—attests to this and states in part:

It is believed that any American RCM air unit which is formed in this theater to perform experimental and development operations, radio search and intelligence operations, or special small scale radio countermeasures should be directly controlled by the highest USAAF Headquarters in the theater. This practice would accomplish maximum utilization of RCM intelligence and experimental information, maximum utilization of specialized RCM airplanes and equipment, a more straight forward and efficient means of utilizing the British for RCM Intelligence organization (we now depend practically 100% on the British for RCM Intelligence), and a more organized means of cooperating with and utilizing our American civilian scientific and experimental organizations in the theater. In addition, this practice will provide a definite nucleus of experienced RCM personnel which may be expanded, if necessary, when redeployment of our forces occurs.[35]

With the friendly invasion of the Yanks to the British Isles, lighter forms of association and entertainment were quite naturally to be enjoyed with the Brits. Iredell Hutton recalled on 3 August:

Sack and I got off flying today so we could go down to Aylsham to meet Marion when he came in on the bus. We waited in a little radio shop there. We needed a #75 tube for our radio, so we asked the girl there if she had one. She looked everywhere for one, but no luck. A man that worked there found one for us. It was an old one, but after I gave him a package of cigarettes he came across with a new one.

B24 #42-51239, R4-C was assigned to the 36BS in August 1944. This Liberator and its entire crew of ten would later be lost on February 5, 1945. *Courtesy of Antoinette Marchello.*

B24 #42-51308, R4-M nicknamed *Modest Maid* was also assigned. *Courtesy of Arthur J. Eschbach.*

Hutton had his wife's name "Caroline" painted on the tail turret of *The JIGS UP. Courtesy of Iredell Hutton.*

Later the fun continued. Hutton wrote:

Marion, Sack, and myself went down to Blickling Hall and had a few beers. It was really drunk out tonight. We came back after they clocked and listened to the radio.

August operations continued in a manner similar to July. 803BS aircraft occupied positions in the protective MANDREL screens put up in support of RAF Bomber Command operations. The first mission occurred on the night of 6/7 August when four squadron aircraft successfully completed their MANDREL jamming operation. One aircraft aborted due to mechanical problems and was replaced by a reserve B24. Upon completion of the mission all returning aircraft landed away from base. The Immediate Analysis of Enemy Reaction Report from RAF 100 Group indicated that the enemy was again confused as to the approaching RAF force.

As the missions continued S/Sgt. Hutton, like most GIs, followed the war news. He noted in his diary on 6 August:

This war can't last too much longer. Our men are fighting close to the Brest peninsula now so it will soon be ours. Some of our men are in the suburbs of Florence. We are only 100 miles from Paris. Tonight we had another mission. As we rode up above the clouds the moon shone through the tail turret. We were up from 9:40 until 2:30. The field radioed in and said that fog had covered the field so much that we had to land at another field.

The next mission on the evening of 7/8 August had five squadron aircraft dispatched. One aircraft was forced to return early due to mechanical difficulties. The rest of the squadron aircraft completed their assigned mission, but were again forced to land away from base due to weather conditions. The Immediate Analysis of Enemy Reaction Report on the night of 7/8 August made the following comment: "From the evidence available at this time, it is obvious that the MANDREL screen, strengthened by ground [jamming] stations at Hastings and Dover, was again instrumental in

depriving enemy ground controllers of information which would have allowed them to estimate the direction and size of the large-scale bomber attack in the Caen area."

On this night mission Sgt. Leo Hoffman, a gunner for Lt. Ralph Angstadt and who would fly 55 jamming missions, faced an unexpected hazard and entered in his record:

Almost hit by Sterling inflight.

Real or perceived problems with the aircraft or equipment were all too common as described in Iredell Hutton's diary on 7 August:

Tonight we had another mission. We no sooner took off when the tail began jumping around so much that we had to return to base. The Colonel was really pissed off.

The next day Colonel Scott took a look-see into the aircraft problem. Hutton wrote:

This afternoon the Colonel went with us up in the plane which we had last night. It didn't act up at all. Rode as good as a new one. From the way things look, we will have another mission tonight.

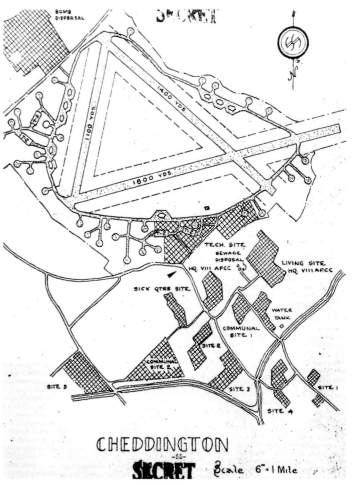

SECRET Station 113 Cheddington map. *Courtesy of the USAF Historical Research Agency.*

Birds-eye view of Cheddington, AAF Station 113. Note South End Hill at top right corner of photograph. Radio operator, Sgt. Joseph Danahy remembered: "About all I remember of Cheddington is the hill. That hill was a great hazard. We lost a crew to it." *Courtesy of John Madero.*

Indeed, equipment problems and hazards in night flying occasionally plagued the missions. On the night of 8/9 August four squadron aircraft were dispatched. One aircraft returned early due to a gas leak, but was immediately replaced. There were reports on this mission that aircraft of RAF 3 Group were flying a good deal higher than was originally planned, possibly due to cloud cover. This situation caused some interference to the MANDREL aircraft. In spite of this fact the monitorial reports still indicated that the enemy night fighter controllers were somewhat muddled, undoubtedly due to the MANDREL screen.

Iredell Hutton was evidently feeling the effects of operational stress when he wrote on 9 August:

Tonight we had the toughest one yet. We went to the Frisian Islands off the coast of Holland. We were just about caught in the searchlights. We would have [been] if Mac hadn't told Duke [navigator Lt. Merril Calisch] to alter his course so as not to go through them. The flak was coming up all around us. Was sure glad to get back on the ground after this one.

Four aircraft from the 803rd were dispatched on the night of 9/10 August. Here the weather presented problems. Severe icing was experienced above 10,000 ft., but all aircraft completed their mission successfully. To quote from the Immediate Analysis of Enemy Reaction Report, published by RAF 100 Group: "Study of the plots broadcast by the enemy on the bomber forces demonstrates the effectiveness of the screen in denying the ground controllers of raid information." The next night, four squadron aircraft were again dispatched and were successful in their mission. The next Immediate Analysis of Enemy Reaction Report from RAF 100 Group had this

to say; "The success of Bomber Command operations the night of 10/11 August together with countermeasures and bomber support activities in connection with same can, from a preliminary survey of the evidence available, be classified as one of the major successes achieved in defeating the enemy night fighter organizations."

Again on the night of 11/12 August four aircraft from the 803rd were launched, successfully completing their mission. The next night, of the five aircraft dispatched, one had to return early due to the malfunction of its GEE equipment. The rest of the flight completed their mission without snafus. The monitorial report again gave evidence of the effectiveness of the screen. The last mission for the 803rd Bomb Squadron (H) (Prov) occurred on the night of 13/14 August when three aircraft were dispatched with all successfully completing their mission.

The papermill at Pinetree had been flowing and a reorganization was ordered. On 8 August the strength of the 803rd was reduced to seven Field Officers and Captains, eight 1st. Lieutenants, sixteen 2nd Lieutenants, one Warrant Officer, and twenty-seven enlisted men. Personnel from Det. "A" of the 858th Bomb Squadron, 8AF Composite Command, which had joined the 803rd a month earlier, became the nucleus of the new 36th Bomb Squadron. It consisted of four Field Officers and Captains, six 1st Lieutenants, fourteen 2nd Lieutenants, two Warrant Officers, and two hundred and eleven enlisted men. On 13 August both the 803rd Squadron and Det. "A" 858th Squadron were officially terminated. That same day personnel from the 856th Bomb Squadron (H) 492nd Bomb Group formerly at AAF Station 143, North Pickenham, Norfolk, joined with personnel formerly from the 803rd and Det. "A" to form the new 36th Bomb Squadron (H) RCM—Radar Countermeasures organization. Most of the personnel transferred into the 36th Bomb Squadron RCM on 14 August. Simultaneous with this event, the new unit moved from Oulton to AAF Station 113 at Cheddington. (See aerodrome map.)

The British "Mossie" — the RAF Mosquito built mostly of plywood. The RAF 26th OTU initially flew from Cheddington. *Courtesy of Stanley Harris.*

Crashed RAF Mosquito. *Courtesy of Frank J. Trovato.*

Picture postcard of nearby Cheddington.

Cheddington had been one of hundreds of aerodromes constructed which dotted the face of the British Isles. Prior to August 1943 the Royal Air Force used the base for training personnel of the 26th Operational Training Unit (OTU) to fly the British Wellington bomber aircraft. After about a year, it became apparent that the airfield was unsuitable for the operational purposes and the particular requirements of RAF OTU. This was partly due to the runways and surrounding hills. Its runways were not suitable for heavy aircraft; however, by the end of 1943 all airfield perimeter taxiways and runways were resurfaced so that heavy aircraft could be accommodated. The aerodrome also lacked servicing facilities—it had only one hangar, and it was only partially completed.

American personnel had been based at the airfield for varying but brief periods prior to the 36th Bomb Squadron's arrival. These U.S. outfits included officers and men of the 12th Combat Crew Replacement Center, the 44th Bomb Group, the 20th Bomb Wing [which was to later become the 4th Combat Crew Replacement Center], the 8th Photo Reconnaissance Wing, the 8AF Composite Command, and also two squadrons of the 801st Bomb Group.

The small village of Marsworth nearby Cheddington was billeted by the Headquarters Squadron. Almost a thousand years before, the inhabitants of this community experienced the effects of an invasion of a different sort to the one they were now undergoing. The evidences of the Roman occupation of England some ten centuries before could still be seen on the South side of Marsworth. There at Ickeild Way, one of the few Roman roads still to be found in Britain was still being used as the main thoroughfare that the soldier's Liberty Run trucks took on their way to Luton and Dunstable. In the village of Marsworth stood a 13th century church, one of the earliest known to date (circa 1213). Some two hundred yards down the road and over the Grand Union Canal bridge was the small 15th century "Ship Inn." It was used in the days of horse drawn barges by the bargemen as a stopping off place for staying over night and to rest their horses in the stable under the inn while on their way to Birmingham.[36]

One of the early American arrivals at the airbase was Henry Woolf, Sergeant Major in the Station Headquarters Adjutant's Office. He wrote of his tour:

I was at AAF Station 113, Cheddington, from 10 June 1943 to 21 June 1945 as a member of Headquarters and Headquarters Squadron, and from 1 July 1943 on served as Sergeant-Major at base headquarters with the rank of master sergeant. My duties were those of all the hundreds of Sergeant-Majors on duty at USAAF bases throughout the world. I was the ranking enlisted man at base headquarters and worked directly under the base adjutant. All correspondence to and from headquarters passed over my desk; the daily bulletin, special orders, and various reports were prepared at my direction; and I supervised the base message center and the central files. About a dozen enlisted men worked under me.

The name Cheddington was taken from the village in Buckinghamshire, northeast of the base that is located on the main line of the railroad that runs from Euston Station in London to Glasgow. It was the scene of the Great Train Robbery in 1963. Within the base was the village of Marsworth, with a pub, a parish church and vicarage, and some other residences. Through it also wound

Quaint English thatched roof house by the canal near Station 113. *Courtesy of Frank J. Trovato.*

the Grand Union Canal, which runs from London into the Midlands and which was used to transport goods on conventional canal boats. A mile or two south of the base was the town of Tring, in Hertsfordshire. The county line separating Bucks and Herts ran through the base. And it was Tring Station, the first stop south of Cheddington, that we traveled to London, 30 or 40 minutes away, on days off.

Cheddington was originally an RAF base that was taken over by the USAAF in May of 1943, and I was a member of the holding party when it was returned to the RAF in June of 1945. Thus, save for several weeks at the start, I was stationed at Cheddington for nearly all the time that it was an American installation.

During its first eight months AAF Station 113 was a combat crew reception center. B24 crews—those who flew the Liberators—came directly to the base from the States, received a week's instruction and orientation, and then were sent on to their bomb squadrons. There were no operational planes at Cheddington until late in 1943, when a weather squadron was transferred, for a short while, from the nearby AAF Station 112, Bovingdon.

In February 1944 Cheddington underwent a marked change, with the arrival from Northern Ireland of the Eighth Air Force Composite Command Headquarters. They brought their WACs with them, moved us from our relatively comfortable barracks to Nissen huts at Site 4, and converted the chapel into an officer's club. The chaplain complained and was forthwith transferred. Come the early fall of 1944 and Composite Command moved away.

In the late winter or early spring of 1944 the 8th Photo Reconnaissance Wing, under the command of Elliott Roosevelt (son of the President), was established at the base but moved elsewhere in a little while, and for a time there was a Quartermaster Trucking unit whose men were all black and who were quartered and fed away from the rest of us.

In the summer of 1944 the 36th Bomb Squadron and the 406th Bomb Squadron began operations from Cheddington. The former was a radar countermeasure unit that in the Battle of the Bulge is said to have prevented the German tanks from communicating with

Aerial view showing the home of the 36BS "Gremlins". *Courtesy of Frank J. Trovato.*

one another. The 406th was a Night Leaflet Squadron, a propaganda outfit that dropped tons of leaflets, phony ration cards, and the like on the Continent.

Sgt. Frank Trovato, a station photographer later assigned to the 36th Bomb Squadron remembered:

I was assigned to the Photo Unit under Lt. Benjamin Gewirtzman. I had previously been doing photographic work as a civilian and was immediately assigned to performing various base photographic functions such as publicity, progress photos, various activities, medal presentations, aerial photography, combat view in front of aircraft (B24s), training, copy, etc.

Although we had a fair amount of photographic equipment and apparatus, I soon was assigned the responsibility to requisition through military channels additional equipment. This was done by consulting the various Air Force Technical Orders; e.g. K20 (Fairchild) hand held aerial cameras, K17C (Fairchild) long nose vertical camera for aerials (with 12" & 24" focal length lenses) for intelligence and reconnaissance uses; special photographic tanks and related equipment for photo processing; specialized enlargers used for better definition of small images taken from higher altitudes; some photo interpretation equipment; additional ground photographic enlargement equipment, such as 5X7 & and 8X10 view cameras (used mainly for architectural, progress, and equipment photography), 4X5 "Speed Graphics," and GSAP (Gun Sight Aiming Point cameras already there), which were originally intended to be used on fighter aircraft to record effect of armament use upon enemy aircraft.

While the 36th Bomb Squadron was mainly a RCM Group, I was frequently called upon to do some aerial photography for practice missions (in England) in B24 Liberators. On the continent [I] was a Fotog-Gunner member of sortie missions to photograph se-

Airmen of Lt. Landberg's crew wait for the Liberty Run truck. *Courtesy of Lester L. Jones.*

Station 113 aircraft recognition classroom. *Courtesy of Mrs. Harold E. Flynn.*

Station 113 aircraft recognition classroom. Learning "ours" from "theirs". The airmen received aircraft recognition training. When firing .50 caliber machine guns, a mistake could be deadly. *Courtesy of John Madero.*

lected areas, including unfriendly skies in enemy territory. This was also done to evaluate previous mission damage, reconnaissance, rapid action sequence photos, etc. While I never had been given any training on how to use the 50mm machine gun used at the waist gun level, I quickly learned to use it on my first assignment when the pilot instructed me (via throat mike, which I never used before) to be alert for enemy aircraft since he had been informed to expect same. Aerial photography involved the use of K17 and K20 cameras used at various altitudes up to approximately twenty to twenty-five thousand feet. Upon return to the lab in Cheddington, we would quickly develop and make prints of some for transmittal to other units for their evaluation, study, and intelligence purposes.

When I did aerial photography it was on different B24s, therefore I didn't get to know any one crew, although we socialized together. You see, when the crew was not flying, they had freer time than photo personnel since we were doing ground and processing work. Our photo lab was in a larger than average Nissen hut generally away from the other Nissen and billeting huts. I do remember taking many pictures of the entire crews in front of their particular B24 Liberators.

Cheddington offered close proximity to centers of population, Liberty Runs, fairly good movies, an active Aero Club, and a beer garden. For relaxation and entertainment off the base personnel visited the towns of Aylesbury, Tring, Dunstable, Luton, and Leighton Buzzard—in GI parlance "Buzzard Gulch." These were all within a 15 mile radius of the base. London, of course, drew many.[37]

Sgt. Albert Caldwell, an operations clerk, remembered one local pub:

The pub adjacent to the barge canal served as our information bureau. At any time, the owner of the pub could tell you anything that was happening or about-to-be happening on the base. And this

covered a broad range of events including troop movements, bombing runs, base scuttlebutt, or just about any other current event. We never knew whether he was psychic, a professional spy, or just had a hotline base connection.

Sgt. Trovato spoke of the fun on Liberty during those days:

Sgt. Thomas F. Styles and I were buddies, and we went to nearby towns and pubs at night on a pass on the "Military Run" or "Liberty Run." Tom was excellent at shooting darts, since he came from Troy, NY, and they played darts a lot there. Tom broke me in on playing darts, and though I wasn't too bad, I was nowhere as good as he. He was excellent! Well, we would generally play the "Limey's" for a pint of "Mild and Bitters" and generally we won and we generally had a nice sociable evening. The word did get around though about Tom, the "Yank" who was good at darts. One night we went

Station 113 Intelligence Library. *Courtesy of John Madero.*

Aerial photogs Frank Tovato and Tom Styles are all smiles after a successful B24 mission. *Courtesy of Frank J. Trovato.*

Another place for soldier entertainment — the base American Red Cross Aero Club. *Courtesy of Frank J. Trovato.*

on the run to Brentwood. When we got there we played the usual rounds. Finally, when they saw how good Tom was, one of the "Limey's" challenged Tom to a single's dart game. It really looked like they were after Tom. (I think they were laying up for him).Well, I said to Tom, "I'll handle the bets for you," while the Brentwood local man had his sidekick do the same. Well, it went back and forth all night. The betting was a little at first, then the "Limey's" put up much more. The funny part—the more Tom had to drink, the better he got. His opponent was holding up. I'll never forget him. He was a lefty and smoking a cigarette down to the last 1/4 inch. Would you believe at the closing hour, at 10 PM, when the bartender said, "Closing up, Ladies and Gents." Well, the last game—the jig was up. We bet about 20 pounds (about $80, an awful lot for then, but we had been winning and they wanted a chance to recoup before the close). At that point, more "Limey's" were backing up their man. We bet them. The bartender closed the doors. We, the competitors, and the bitters were the only ones there. Tom was SUPER, SUPER!! He got a triple to start off and finished the game shortly while they were all astonished. (A triple is really like a bullseye, almost). So, we won and no longer did they say "Unlucky Sir" as they did when we lost. The man Tom beat was the "Champ of Brentwood." They said they never saw anyone play like Tom—English or American. We almost lost the Liberty Run back to the base, but got it "on the fly"!

The new locale also offered its own set of geographical hazards. West End Hill and South End Hill bordered the area northeast of the aerodrome runways. These rolling hills established an infamous reputation all their own. S/Sgt. Howard "Howie" Nolan, gunner for Lt. Sandberg, spoke of Cheddington and South End Hill:

Right at the end of the runway there were two mountains. To get off, you had to fly right in between those two mountains. It looked like two great big women's breasts. There were spots where people didn't make it, where the planes had piled in and crashed. But even

if you had one of these, they sent you right back up afterwards when you had an accident. They didn't let you stay down.

Sgt. Joseph Danahy, radio operator for Lt. Joseph Hornsby's crew also remembered the hill:

About all I remember of Cheddington is the hill. That hill was a great hazard. We lost a crew to it. They didn't get over it on take off. The railroad ran along that hill. Cheddington was the site of the Great Train Robbery. I remember the hill, walking along a canal to Tring or to buy fish and chips at an inn by a bridge over a canal. Those two things and the weather. Oh, the weather—it was really bad sometimes. Because of the bad weather, we got to spend many a night at some distant base, unable to land at Cheddington. The control tower had big mortars and would fire flares up into the fog or overcast to light up the area with varying degrees of success, none very good. You'd hear the poor devil who was trying to find

Frank Trovato, just to the left of the dartboard, remembered his buddy Thomas F. Styles was "the Yank who was good at darts." *Courtesy of Frank J. Trovato.*

Thomas F. Styles, fourth from left beat "The Champ of Brentwood." *Courtesy of Frank J. Trovato.*

the runway go roaring over. One fellow nearly took the smokestack chimney off the mess hall. You couldn't help but feel glad that you were on the ground.

Lt. Frank Senn of the 18th Weather Squadron remembered it for a special reason:

The one thing I remember about South End Hill was an accident that happened early one morning when a B17, taking off on a mission and loaded to the hilt, did not quite make it and the rear end of the plane hit the hill, knocking off the tail, and the tail gunner fell out on the hill. The B17 circled back and landed, and an ambulance was dispatched to pick up the tail gunner. Luckily the plane landed safely and the tail gunner survived the incident.

There were also other identifying features and manmade obstructions around. Lt. Arthur Bennett, co-pilot for Lt. Sandberg, remembered the smokestacks:

The way we would line up properly with the runway, when we would make a turn onto the final approach, the left wingtip would be on the stack. It looked like a cement plant that was directly in line with our landing pattern. We'd just make a turn around, our wingtip set on the stack. That would line us right up with the runway. We came in by that many times.

On 12 August Major Robert Hambaugh, a Southern gentleman from Birmingham, Alabama, former Commanding Officer of the 858BS, 492BG, and on detached service with the 803rd assumed command of the new 36th Bomb Squadron. Hambaugh trained as a pilot at Randolph Field, Texas, and had already seen plenty of action in the Pacific theater of operations. There as a captain, he was attached to the 27th Bombardment Group in the Philippines. He was there when the Japanese attacked the islands on December 8, 1941—the day after the infamous attack on Pearl Harbor in Hawaii. The 27BG, having no airplanes, fought the enemy with anti-

aircraft guns, machine guns, and even pistols. Hambaugh was one in a group of only 27 men out of the total of 400 to escape capture by making it to Australia. Most of the 400 odd men who were left in the Philippines became prisoners. Of the 27 men who managed to escape, eight were soon killed or missing in action. The remnants of these men, including Hambaugh, went to Java. In February 1942 they fought the Japanese and sank a cruiser and a destroyer. Capt. Hambaugh received the Silver Star for gallantry and for dive bombing the Japanese invasion fleet approaching Java.

The new 36BS now had sixteen crews. By the end of August the strength of the squadron would consist of twelve Field Officers and Captains, nineteen 1st Lieutenants, forty eight 2nd Lieutenants, one Warrant Officer, one Flight Officer and five hundred and fifteen enlisted men. This totaled nearly 600 personnel. The staff officers appointed were Capt. Robert Kinnard as Executive Officer, Capt. Homer Jones, Intelligence Officer, 1st Lt. J.P. Ostler Squadron Navigator, Capt. Jack Beamer as Communications Officer and

Major Robert F. Hambaugh, the new 36BS CO. Squadron photographer Frank Trovato fondly remembered the Commanding Officer: "Major Hambaugh was well known to me and was a swell guy. Everybody liked him." *Courtesy of Dr. Robert F. Hambaugh, Jr.*

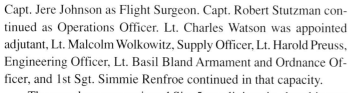

The new 36BS CO had pilot training at Randolph Field, Texas. *Courtesy of Dr. Robert F. Hambaugh, Jr.*

At 6000 ft. over Randolph Field, Texas. *Courtesy of Dr. Robert F. Hambaugh, Jr.*

Capt. Jere Johnson as Flight Surgeon. Capt. Robert Stutzman continued as Operations Officer. Lt. Charles Watson was appointed adjutant, Lt. Malcolm Wolkowitz, Supply Officer, Lt. Harold Preuss, Engineering Officer, Lt. Basil Bland Armament and Ordnance Officer, and 1st Sgt. Simmie Renfroe continued in that capacity.

The squadron was assigned Site 5 as a living site, but this was inadequate due to the present strength of the squadron. The former Personal Equipment School Building in the Tech Site became offices for the Commanding Officer, Operations, Intelligence, Engineering, Communications and Personal Equipment. It was necessary for the 36th to share a briefing room with the 406th Bomb Squadron (H), the Night Leaflet Squadron (NLS). This arrangement was most unsatisfactory due to conflicts in mission briefing

times. The codeword "PICNIC" was given to the 36th as its radio communications identification with flying control. This codeword would not be an entirely appropriate description for the missions that were to follow.

A squadron insignia was designed for the new special outfit. The 36BS insignia depicted a winged radar gremlin whose body and nose consisted of radio tubes and from whose finger tips emitted the radio transmissions which fouled the enemy radar devices. Placed between the wings above the "Gremlin" was the term RAFU, meaning Radar All Fouled Up. This term was related in a way similar to the term "SNAFU". The insignia was designed and drawn by S/Sgt. Stanley L. Walsh, a squadron aerial gunner attached to Lt. Sandberg's crew. Stanley was formerly employed by the Walt Disney Studios.[38]

36th Bomb Squadron (H) RCM Staff
Seated L-R: Capt. Jack B. Beamer, Capt. Jere B. Johnson, Capt. Robert G. Stutzman, Major Robert F. Hambaugh, Major Kinnard, Capt. Homer E. Jones, Capt. James P. Ostler Standing L-R in Middle row: 1st. Lt. Charles H. Watson, 1st Lt. John Latvaitis, 1st Lt. Lloyd S. Ricks, Capt. Thomas R. Graham, 1st Lt. Walt Ludwick, 1st Lt. Edgar A. Everhart, 1st Lt. David D. Merrill, 1st Lt. Basil A. Bland Jr. Standing Rear row: 1st Lt. Robert E. Jackson, 1st Lt. Frederick Mc Intyre, 1st Lt. John F. Kent, 1st Lt. Richard O. Obenschain, 1st Lt. Franklin R. Zatlin. The following Officers are not in picture: Capt. Hubert N. Sturdivant, 1st Lt. Malcolm Wolkowitz, 1st Lt. Clarence Petersen, 1st. Lt. Harold P. Pruess, 1st Lt. David Gould. *Courtesy of Richard O. Obenschain.*

36th Bomb Squadron (H) RCM RAFU insignia. *Courtesy of the USAF Historical Research Agency.*

36th Bomb Squadron RAFU Gremlin sign. RAFU meant "Radar All Fouled Up". *Courtesy of Iredell Hutton.*

Iredell Hutton took note of the squadron move on 14 August:

Today we moved from Oulton to Cheddington. The base is all mixed up. Had much rather stayed at Oulton. Colonel Scott is no longer our CO. Sack brought "Snafu" with him. "Snafu" is the cat.

Co-pilot James Snoddy felt a bit differently about the move for his own reasons. He recalled:

The food at Oulton was horrible. I have always been a breakfast man, but I could not take the powdered eggs which were large lumps of yellow something floating in a sea of green water. The toast was dipped into a vat of some type of grease and was hard to take. We had a lot of Australian corned beef. I would have welcomed Spam, but we never had it. Our barracks were off base on a big farm. We made paths through the farmer's plowed fields to get to the mess hall and to fly. I was happy when we moved to Cheddington. Food was better and although we lived in Nissen huts, we were pretty comfortable.

T/Sgt. Odis Waggoner, flight engineer for Lt. Merlin Vowinkel's crew remembered his transition to a better situation:

We were first assigned to the 492nd Bomb Group, 856th Bomb Squadron at North Pickenham. [The 492nd Bomb Group had just earlier sustained heavier losses than any other B24 group for a

three month period of time].We had eight bombing missions starting July 18, 1944 and ending early August at which time we were transferred to the 36th Bomb Squadron at Cheddington. The plane we flew overseas was taken away from us at Nutts Corner, Ireland and we flew whatever was available at North Pickenham. When we got to Cheddington there was "our" nice new plane we had flown over. Our pilot was able to talk them into assigning it to our crew. We referred to it as "188" [B24, R4-O, nicknamed Lady Jane] which was the last three digits of its serial number.

Missions from Cheddington were depicted by a lightning symbol we painted on our plane. At Cheddington our goal was so many flying hours [normally about 300] instead of so many bombing missions [30] in order to complete our tour of duty.

On this day, Iredell Hutton kept tuned to the war news and also saw another friend from back home North Carolina. He wrote:

Today the Allies made another landing in France. This time it was in the Southern part. From all reports they are doing good. This afternoon while I was laying on the bunk taking a nap, Bill Taylor from High Point came in to see me. He is a gunner on a '17. His crew is one of those that carry propaganda to the conquered countries. We call them "the Paperboys," and they call us "the Milkman."

Lt. Brian Gunderson, attached to the 406th Night Leaflet Squadron, spoke of his days at Station 113 Cheddington:

I was a crew navigator and later squadron navigator in the 406th Bombardment Squadron (H). Although both squadrons were on the same airfield, it was almost as if we didn't know the 36th existed and vice versa. Each squadron had separate sleeping areas, we ate at the same mess, but at separate tables, etc. The key unit was the crew. We worked as a crew, we flew as a crew, we took leave and "Liberty Runs" to nearby towns as a crew. It was not unusual to know very few other people in your own squadron, let alone another crew or people in another squadron, especially when each squadron performed a different mission.

At this time the residents around Cheddington were experiencing Hitler's V1s. Approximately a half a dozen flying bombs dropped within an area of five or six miles of the aerodrome. John Shamp wrote of one hitting nearby on 15 August:

First buzz bomb. We were out near the plane waiting for take off time. We heard the thing go past us and crash in an orchard a mile or so away from us.

The first mission flown from Station 113 was on the night of 16/17 August. Four 36BS aircraft joined with RAF aircraft in putting up a protective MANDREL screen for Bomber Command attacks on Berlin, Stettin, Kiel, Sterkrade, Dortmund, and other targets. On this night Bomber Command lost only fifteen aircraft, which is perhaps good evidence of the effectiveness of the protective screen.

For Iredell Hutton, not only were the V1s crashing nearby, but the night missions were getting longer. On 16 August he wrote:

Tonight we had the longest night mission so far. It lasted 6 hours and 15 minutes. We went up to the Northern tip of Denmark. Not much activity tonight. Just before we took off tonight a buzz bomb landed about ten miles from us. It made a loud noise, and then we saw a large cloud of smoke. London is really getting a pasting these days. It won't be long before we take France, though. We are only thirty miles from Paris now.

Sergeant-Major Henry Woolf in the Adjutant's Office also saw one and said:

I watched from Site 4 one evening a Spitfire pursue and bring down a V1 in an open field south of the base.

Cpl. Charles Todaro, a 36th Bomb Squadron armorer, remembered the V1 bombings:

We were attacked by V1s. We had shelters all around the perimeter. And you'd hear these things chug-chug-chuggin' and you'd just stand there and listen, because if they chugged over you, you were okay. But if the rocket gave out, then it was in the vicinity and you headed for the bomb shelter.

Sometimes the danger was really closer than imagined, as noted in Iredell Hutton's diary on 18 August:

Tonight we had another mission. Our screen covered a raid that was to be on Bremen and the usual Mosquito raid on Berlin. We went up off the coast of Holland. Saw plenty of flak and searchlights. We were far enough away that they didn't cause us any damage. The mission lasted six hours and a few minutes. The missions are much longer now that we are here at Cheddington. When we came in the sirens were sounding off because there was a buzz bomb headed our way. We never saw it, though. The buzz bomb which fell the night before last was only two miles away instead of ten as I had guessed. One of these days, one is going to plaster this base all to hell.

Two aircraft of the 36BS were dispatched the night of 17/18 August and completed their mission without incident. The next night six aircraft were dispatched and successfully completed a MANDREL patrol in support of RAF attacks on Ghent, Bremen, Sterkrade, Holten, Berlin, and other targets.

On 21 August Major Hambaugh, the new 36BS Commanding Officer, wrote to his folks in Alabama:

Dearest Folks, I am getting along fine, plenty to eat and its good food and a nice place for my quarters. I have a good squadron and good boys. We do special work, that's all I can say. [39]

Squadron photographer Frank Trovato fondly remembered Robert Hambaugh:

Major Hambaugh [later Lt. Col.] was well known to me and was a swell guy. Everybody liked him. I think he was kind and considerate. I remember taking some pictures of him, one a nice close-up portrait; also others of him as he was making medal presentations to crew members.

The famous B17 Flying Fortress nicknamed *Swing Shift*. By October 10, 1944 this 406BS B17 had flown 101 missions without a single abort. It was chronicled in the "Stars and Stripes" and numerous hometown newspapers. Five of the B17 airmen were placed on radio doing broadcasts from London and shortwaved to the United States. *Courtesy of Iredell Hutton.*

Hambaugh was also popular with his pilots. Lt. Joe Brookshire for one. Brookshire explained:

Hambaugh and I got along real good. He was a good guy. He used to let me get away with what I thought was murder. My brother was stationed not too far from Bristol. He came over to the field and the colonel let me have an old B24 to take him up and give him the thrill of his lifetime—fly in a '24. I got him up in the air and I let my brother fly.

When we would come home from missions I'd make fighter approaches to landing, where you get a B24 up at some altitude and cut off all four engines and do a hundred and eighty and come in on your final approach that way. He [Lt. Col. Hambaugh] let me do it. I did it two or three times, which is a good way to get killed. That '24 flew like a rock.

Again on the night of 25/26 August six aircraft from the 36th were dispatched. All aircraft operated their MANDREL equipment in positions as required, but were recalled by RAF 100 Group. The

RAF targets were Russelheim, Berlin, Darmstadt, and tactical targets in France.

In his book *A Thousand Shall Fall*, Canadian pilot Murray Peden of RAF 100 Group, 214 Squadron described how the jamming tactics varied and became more and more sophisticated:

To precipitate earlier action on the part of the German controller, we began to simulate breakdowns of the MANDREL screen. A WINDOWing force would form up behind the MANDREL screen, strike off northeast, and fly to Heligoland, 50 miles off the mouth of the Elbe (an operation our crew did on August 25th). While the WINDOWing force was still well on the friendly side of the MANDREL screen, two adjacent MANDREL aircraft would switch off their sets for a prearranged brief period, perhaps 70 seconds.

Through the gap thus created for the benefit, the Freya operators would catch a tantalizing glimpse of a powerful force of bombers heading in the general direction of Heligoland, again posing a threat to Kiel and the Baltic ports from Lubeck to Konigsberg, not to mention several intervening northern targets of great importance which they could attack if they swung south.

Lady Grace of the 406th Bomb Squadron — Night Leaflet crashed on March 14, 1945 at AAF Station 179, Harrington. *Courtesy of Arthur Ledtke.*

Midnite Express of the 406th Bomb Squadron (NL). *Courtesy of Arthur Ledtke.*

This V1 nearly destroyed a local farmer's patch of cabbage. Such was not always to be the case. *Courtesy of Frank J. Trovato.*

Initially the German controller would seize and act upon this valuable piece of information, gratuitously furnished by the malfunction of the enemy's equipment. Again the real bombers of Main force would appear elsewhere later on, when the controller's dispositions favored the attackers and embarrassed him. After two or three feints based on this pattern had conditioned the German controller into being highly suspicious of gift information, provided by what he now realized were contrived breakdowns, Bomber Command would follow the same pattern when the target for the Main Force actually was Bremen or Kiel. This was where audacity was put to the test.

Once again a portion of the MANDREL screen would collapse temporarily; and once again the Freya operators would catch sight briefly of an enormous concentration of aircraft bound for northeastern Germany. Reluctant to be caught again, the German controller would not react strongly, holding back fighters in the central and southern sectors, which he suspected would be the real target area, until the TIs (target indicators) went down and heavy bombing undeniably began, by which time it was too late.[40]

Of course there was no way for Uncle Sam to give a GI the loving touch equal to that of a far away mother or sweetheart. For every GI in every theater of the war a surprise package from home could lift a GI's spirit enormously by providing that special comfort. There was just no way for Uncle Sam to give a GI the loving touch equal to that of a far away mother or sweetheart. Iredell Hutton wrote of how one package gave him comfort on the 25 August mission:

Tonight we had another mission. It lasted six hours and five minutes. Was easier than most. They give us a pack of gum and a Milky Way before we go up now. Tonight we covered a raid on Russelheim, Calais, and German positions in France. Results say they did a good job. I tried the new socks and scarf out tonight [sent from his wife Caroline back home in North Carolina]. They

really came in good. They will help out much better when it gets colder. It was only nine below last night.

The next mission on the night of 26/27 August had seven squadron aircraft dispatched and completing their mission successfully. The RAF sent heavy bombers to Kiel and Konigsberg, and their Mosquitoes attacked Berlin, Hamburg, Dortmund, and other targets.

The mission experiences mixed anxiety, loneliness, and monotony in the cold reality of the air war over Europe and bore deep into the airmen's minds. The airmen counted each mission in minutes and hours to reach the desired 300 hours to complete a tour. S/Sgt. Hutton recorded his tally on 27 August:

Tonight we had another mission. It lasted five hours and 10 minutes. That makes me seventy hours and ten minutes. Didn't see much action except down about London there was a big barrage of fire. It lasted all the while we were there.

The squadron flew again the night of 27/28 August when six aircraft successfully completed their mission without incident. RAF Mosquitoes attacked Mannheim. Two nights later four sorties were flown by squadron aircraft in the protective MANDREL screen. The RAF activity consisted of attacks by Mosquitoes on Essen, Cologne,[41] and other targets. Errors in identifying enemy aircraft plagued many aerial gunners on both sides of night air war over Europe. During this mission the gunners in squadron Liberator #42-51232, R4-J, nicknamed *The Jigs Up* were no exception and nearly made a grave mistake. *The Jigs Up* opened fire on an unidentified twin engine aircraft. No strikes were seen, and the unidentified aircraft flew out of sight. Waist gunner S/Sgt. John Shamp on *The Jigs Up* said of this incident:

Joseph Thome by his navigator's window in the nose of B24 #42-51239, R4-C. *Courtesy of Antoinette Marchello.*

A RAF Mosquito got a little close to us. I called him out on our intercom system at about three o'clock and just about level with us. Hutton turned his turret, but he never saw him. I gave him a short burst of five or six shots. Then he slid under us and away at about nine o'clock and about fifty or sixty feet below us. Herb was on the right waist window, and I held his gun so he could not fire at him because when he passed under us I saw it was a RAF Mosquito. Herb and I were the only ones who saw him.

Pilot Capt. Dick Sackett remembered another snafu during one of his night missions:

In England in '44 and in the prior years they [the British] had a DF [direction finding] network for which the callsign was "Darky." I remember one time we were on a mission screening ahead of the RAF and in some manner my navigator copied the wrong coordinates for our orbiting position. I recall we flew northwest out of our base at Cheddington. We flew and we flew and we flew. It was obvious and evident that we weren't getting anyplace at all because my navigator couldn't seem to get us to where we were supposed to be going. So, finally I asked him about this and he was pretty much obscene about the whole thing. I started to think that maybe the GEE box had been jammed or was being jammed and so forth. It was dark, there was no sign of anything. Now and again you would see a glimmer of light on the ground, but there wasn't anything so I was pretty sure that we were over the North Sea to the Northeast of England. We weren't at our position at the appointed time, so I asked him [the navigator] the reciprocal and we turned around and started back. It seemed that we had been flying for

hours. Finally he was completely aced out as far as a position, so I started to call "Darky" and I got a reply with a request for a long count, which I gave them. They gave me a heading and this procedure continued for some time and we finally ended up at a fighter base called Tangmere in Kent or Sussex. When we got down there they told me I was cleared to land. I could look down and see three circles for these outer circle lights of the aerodrome. They were all interlocked. They started to look like the Olympic logo. I had to ask flying control to switch those on and off. Finally, I got them all turned off except for the one where we were to land.

The last mission for the month was on the night of 30/31 August. Six aircraft were dispatched with all completing their mission without incident. RAF Bomber Command sent heavy bombers to Stettin and Konigsburg. Mosquitoes bombed Berlin, Hamburg, Cologne, and other targets.

Squadron operations for the month of August had eight missions flown from RAF Oulton and the remaining eight from AAF Station 113 at Cheddington. In addition to the MANDREL patrol missions, four search missions were flown by the squadron at the request of ABL-15. These missions contributed materially to the research being carried out in radar countermeasures by the ABL-15 technicians.

Lt. Joseph Thome, navigator for Lt. William Corder's crew, remembered serving at Cheddington as well as working with ABL-15.

We [the 8AF] were doing a lot of different things flying from that same airbase. There were some guys that were ferrying in people

"Some of the work that we were doing there was pretty highly classified." Seen here, the 36BS Communications Maintenance Section Radio Equipment Test Panel. *Courtesy of USAF Historical Research Agency.*

36BS Communications Maintenance Section Status Board and Work Bench. *Courtesy of the USAF Historical Research Agency.*

and going and picking people up close to Germany. I don't think we did much talking among ourselves, because we didn't know what the hell we were doing. We didn't ask any questions.

One of our biggest enemies was because we were so few airplanes flying around, when the main forces were not flying around, that the British were very very careful that they wanted to make sure that nobody was coming in invading their country. We got more shots fired at us by the British than by the Germans just because we weren't on anybody's schedule, going out or coming in.

Some of the work that we were doing there was pretty highly classified. We worked real close with the ABL—the American British Laboratory. They were the ones that were providing the Americans with their electronic knowledge. They were quite a bit ahead of us. We worked together. That's the reason, of course, that we were there. We loaned them the airplanes to put their equipment aboard. And when we weren't flying combat missions we were flying for ABL. We were trying to prove over England what we were going to perhaps do later over on the continent. They [ABL-15] were very very successful in what they were doing. They were so far ahead of us it was terrible. They came out with some pretty good inventions.

We just tried to keep everything way above board. Anything we didn't have to know, why, we weren't told, and we didn't ask any questions. We just went out there and we turned certain switches on and turned them off as they programmed us to do.

Now I had had a special clearance with those people. And even some people on my crew were mad at me because they weren't allowed to go in and out of their own airplane at times. I had to make sure that nobody was fooling around with the radio tubes and that sort of thing. So, it was rather difficult even for me not being able to tell the rest of the crew what the hell I was doing aboard the same airplane they were flying in.

5

Ramp Rooster

September 1944

The 8th Air Force's new 36th Bomb Squadron RCM continued to work under the direction of RAF 100 Group assisting in providing a protective MANDREL screen for RAF night operations. On the evening of 1/2 September four squadron aircraft were dispatched. All completed their mission without incident, jamming between 2100 hours and 2345 hours. Six RAF Sterlings of 199 Squadron were also dispatched. There were seven stations in all, with two aircraft from RAF 199 Squadron flown on each station. Seventy-four RAF aircraft were dispatched on missions over Germany and on other operations without loss. The main attack was a Mosquito attack on Bremen. The screen protected those operations.

The Allied advances were gaining a valuable hold on much of the European continent real estate. On 1 September Iredell Hutton wrote of the good news:

The Captain, who always briefed the General in the afternoon on the latest news, took Sack, John, and myself and gave us the latest poop. I never knew that our armies had eliminated as many Germany divisions as we have.

Hutton later wrote of fun and entertainment on his next liberty:

Sack came over and told us that Bing Crosby was over at Alconbury tonight. So, we took the liberty run over to Alconbury about 7pm. Got there about 7:45. Bing came in about 8:30. He had two of the most beautiful girls with him I have ever seen. He had a comedian with him. His name was Joe De Rise. He was very good. Bing sang a lot of songs. He signed off by singing "White Christmas." He said that he hoped we were all home by then. Bing's hair is about all gone. He is still a good showman.

By 2 September all B17 aircraft were transferred from the squadron. The 36BS now flew B24s exclusively. Yet these were not just typical Liberators. Lt. David Merrill, 36BS Asst. Communications Officer, remembered:

We had antennas bolted to the wings for the jammers we were carrying. They would not normally be put on any B24 except ours.

S/Sgt. Leonard Kottenstette, radioman for Lt. Joseph Brookshire's crew also spoke of the special modifications to the B24s:

You could tell our B24s by the several sabre-like antennas un der each wing. These must have been in the VHF frequency range because of their size. Obviously, they were in the frequency range of whatever the German radar was using those days.

Out on the flightline and in the aircraft hangars the crew chiefs, line chiefs, and mechanics worked tirelessly to keep the planes in

Adolph Menjou performed at a Station 113 "Variety Show". *Courtesy of Mrs. Harold E. Flynn.*

proper flying condition. Often they were out on the line working solicitously through the late hours of the night and at it again during the early hours of the morning. Their work was hastening the successful end of hostilities. Head crew chief T/Sgt. Irl Fife for the B24 #42-50671, R4-F nicknamed *Ramp Rooster* remembered:

MacGillvary and Gulbrandson were my assistants on the "Ramp Rooster" ground crew. Gulbrandson also manned the 50 cal. machine gun which we kept ready at the take-off, and especially as the planes were landing after a mission. This pit was very near where "Ramp Rooster" was moored, so it was our job to man the gun.

My primary concern on duty was to keep the planes in the best mechanical condition possible. We realized men's lives were at stake. The radio equipment in "Ramp Rooster" was really off limits, but I remember listening to the World Series one night.

Another squadron mechanic, Cpl. William Fenster, recalled:

I was fortunate to work with two crew chiefs that were knowledgeable and dedicated to doing their very best work. They were Ross Barkley and "Strawberry" [Emmet] McCombs. They, along with the flight crews, deserve all the credit you can give them. Working as a mechanic was not a glamorous job. We had to work in fog and rain all the time.

The men of the squadron armament section also performed their special work. One squadron armorer, Cpl. Charles Todaro, spoke of his job:

Primarily it was taking care of the turrets, machine guns, ammunition, and that sort of thing; and of course running guard duty. There was a permanent guard at all times, because at the end of a B24 jamming run the equipment was taken out of the airplane and put in a big pit underneath the airplane. An iron grill that was locked was put over it.

The base was off limits, and one night when I was on [guard] duty, I noticed people walking back and forth through this secret base. I asked the English people in town about it. I was told that's a King's pass and it's inviolate. They said sometime in the past— 1300 or 1400, when it was open territory—the land belonged to the King. He gave a pass as a right-of-way to the people who lived in the area. And it goes on forever, so no matter what is built around that pass the citizens have a right to go through it and they use the pass. They can't stop and they can't talk. So, we had these English people wandering through this secret base because of this King's pass.

Another 36BS armorer, Sgt. Kelton Thrower, who had initially served with the 44th Bomb Group, 506th Squadron[42] remembered:

Hoofer Jimmy Cagney visited Station 113. *Courtesy of Frank J. Trovato.*

Comedian Bob Hope drew tons of laughs when he entertained the soldiers on the road. *Courtesy of Joseph A. Bartus.*

Station 113 theater. *Courtesy of John Madero.*

Ramp Rooster, 36BS Liberator #42-50671 R4-F. Note the antennas bolted under the wings.

I was an armament crew chief. I was in charge of five or six airplanes, in charge of the armament on them—the guns, the turrets, and the bomb racks. I had a crew of guys under me. I was probably younger than any of them. I really don't know why they chose me as a crew chief. They did that in the states. That's the funny thing about a war—as big as that war was, it was fought by people that knew no more about fighting, or no more about what they were doing than I did. I certainly didn't know a whole lot. You take an old country boy from Alabama and let us meet in Pueblo, Colorado—and a guy gets up and says, "You're in charge of these five or six airplanes and all the armament on them. We're going to give you a bunch of people. Here's a list of guys that're going to be working with you. You make sure they do the job!" I said, "Well, what is the job?" It's always been amazing to me how a group of young people, they don't do it to be a hero, they just did it because there was a job and they had to do it. Nobody ever complained about it. Everybody was eager to do whatever you asked them to do.

Out on the line, as far as military courtesy, they weren't interested in that. They didn't ask us to salute or stuff like that. It was just a different ball game as far as the Air Force was concerned. If I had an airplane that had something wrong with the guns or the bomb rack, or the turret, or the bombsight or anything—all I had to do is just draw a red line across the flight plan and that plane could not fly. That's a heck of a responsibility. When you go out there and check that thing out and OK it, you've got ten people that are going to risk their lives in that thing for about the next twelve or fourteen hours. That's quite a responsibility, but it didn't bother me and it didn't bother anybody else. They knew that they could do it and they did it. They knew that they could do it before they started and it didn't worry them. I'm sure that all the other factions of the war were the same way, that it was fought and fought well by people who knew no more about what they were doing than I did.

Squadron pilots were required to be familiar with the different aircraft systems and workings of the Liberators they piloted. Capt. Dick Sackett, the pilot of *Ramp Rooster*, recalled:

The engines in the B24 were Pratt and Whitney. The R1830 was a fourteen cylinder radial and developed 1200 horsepower. Inasmuch as our operations were primarily at night, we had on the bottom of the turbo supercharger what they called a flame dampener. It was a contrivance, a box that hung down maybe a foot below the turbo supercharger bucket wheel, which was on the bottom of the nacelle, and it dampened the flame when the supercharger was being used. You had a waste gate in the back of the exhaust pipe that came out at the rear of the nacelle, and as you closed it, it caused the bucket wheel to turn, which would force air into the intake of the engine and give us added power at altitude and so forth, otherwise we couldn't have operated that high. When these things now and again would burn out, I remember one time I had one burn out on number three engine while we were climbing out to position on a night mission ahead of the RAF; it finally burned

A line chief briefs the pilot on the operational status of the aircraft before the mission. *Courtesy of Leonard N. Backer.*

Harold Gulbrandson manning a .50 Cal. machine gun in a trench protecting the *Rooster*.

A ground mechanic changes the spark plugs on a Liberator engine. *Courtesy of George F. Lechner Sr.*

itself out to the point where we had a stream of fire back from that bucket wheel. It must have been ten or twelve feet long. It would be rather foolish to go on a mission like that because you were reveal-

Ground maintenance technician Harold Gulbrandson alongside *Ramp Rooster*. Here, the *Rooster* has 87 missions to its credit. *Courtesy of Quenton (Mac) MacGillivray.*

ing yourself, so we had to call up the spare aircraft which was always standing by for an abort. It didn't happen very often, but it did happen to me once.

The next mission of 5/6 September had four B24 Liberators of the 36th along with six aircraft from 199 Squadron again successfully providing a MANDREL screen jamming from 2115 hours to 0045 hours. The screen was in support of RAF Mosquito operations that bombed Hanover and Steenwijh airfields without loss.

Sometimes the desired results and success were not always obvious in the final outcome. Were the Germans simply learning the Allied tricks? The enemy failed to react to the jamming on the next mission. On the evening of 6/7 September four 36BS B24s and six aircraft from 199 Squadron were again dispatched and successfully completed their jamming from 2100 hours to 2330 hours. The RAF Interceptor/Tactics Report had this to say about the activities on that date: "Associated with attacks on Hamburg and Emden (by RAF 8 Group—a Pathfinder Force of Mosquitoes) was a plan to induce the enemy to react in force, but he declined to do so. Once a MANDREL jamming screen was set up over the North

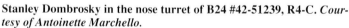

Stanley Dombrosky in the nose turret of B24 #42-51239, R4-C. *Courtesy of Antoinette Marchello.*

Rafael Ramos in the tail turret. *Courtesy of Antoinette Marchello.*

Sea north of 5300N, a WINDOW dropping force flew 150 miles further east, almost to Borkum, in order to simulate a large force making a repeat of the daylight attack on Emden." Bomber Command had attacked Emden with 180 heavies (four engined bombers such as the British Lancaster) in daylight on 6 September. One 36BS aircraft, Liberator #42-50385, R4-H, nicknamed *Beast of Bourbon* was fired on by an unidentified aircraft at 5324N-0242E. No hits were sustained.

Tail gunner S/Sgt. Tony Vaccaro in Lt. Sandberg's crew remembered firing at a very familiar aircraft:

One night coming back from a mission there was a B24 Liberator which was firing at us. I knew it was not our men in that B24 because they were firing blue and green tracers, which I knew were German. I then fired back. I recall the pilot talking to the co-pilot on the intercom, saying, "Tony's firing at someone." Deep in my heart I knew they were Germans in that B24. The next day there was no mention of anyone firing at a friendly plane. I was thus convinced they were Germans.

Two nights later four 36BS Liberators along with eight aircraft from 199 Squadron were dispatched. All aircraft completed their mission without incident, jamming from 0100 hours to 0325 hours. RAF attacks consisted of Mosquito attacks on Nurnburg, Emden, and Steenwijh airfields. The night of 9/10 September four B24s of the 36th were dispatched and completed their mission without incident, jamming from 0115 hours to 0545 hours. Ten Sterlings from 199 Squadron were also dispatched. Fog at Cheddington made a diversionary landing for 36BS aircraft necessary upon return. The screen protected a force of one hundred and twelve Lancasters which attacked Munchen-Gladbach without loss. The next night three 36BS B24s were dispatched. They successfully completed their mission without incident, jamming from 2145 hours to 0001 hours. RAF Mosquitoes bombed Berlin without loss.

On 11 September Major Hambaugh, the new 36BS Commanding Officer, again wrote to his folks in Alabama. His letter said in part:

The top turret gunner, armorer, and engineer Wes Crowther. *Courtesy of Antoinette Marchello.*

Vane Glendening at B17 waist window. *Courtesy of V. Glendening.*

Dearest Folks,

We have been busy, but it makes the time pass faster and that makes it better. The war news is still good, but things seem to have slowed down some, but once in a while they have to.[43]

The 11/12 September mission had five 36BS B24s dispatched and successfully completing their mission, jamming from 2015 to 0030 hours. The RAF had 226 Lancasters bombing Darmstadt. The raid analysis report stated that: "The bombers to Darmstadt followed a route over northern France and were not plotted until they reached the Trier area. At 2327 hours three heavy bomber formations were identified. They were then plotted into the target and on the return route as far as the battle area." On the next night six aircraft were dispatched and successfully completed their mission, jamming from 2040 hours to 2345 hours. This was a moving MANDREL screen. Five of the aircraft experienced intermittent flak over water and enemy occupied territory during these patrols, but no damage occurred. 651 RAF aircraft were dispatched to Frankfurt, Stuttgart, Berlin, Steenwijh airfield, and other targets. Twenty-two of these failed to return, or 3.4%. The enemy raid reaction report stated that the main attacks on Frankfurt and Stuttgart were not plotted until they reached 0600E at 2200 hours. The moving MANDREL screen covered the approach of a WINDOW dropping force which emerged from the screen in the Brussels area. This force was reported as a bomber force. All in all, the enemy was considerably confused and dispatched its night fighters accordingly.

Sgt. Leo Hoffman, a gunner for Lt. Ralph Angstadt, made these notes in his record:

My first mission over France. Saw plenty in the way of excitement—heavy flak.

Again the next night six 36BS Liberators were dispatched and successfully completed their patrols, jamming from 2120 hours to 2359 hours. Two aircraft experienced intermittent light inaccurate flak. The jamming supported RAF Mosquitoes that bombed Berlin and Karlsruhe.

S/Sgt. Hutton experienced new territory during this mission as noted in his diary on 13 September:

Tonight the mission lasted for six hours. First we went over France and then up into Belgium. Saw a lot of fires and flak. Outside of that everything was quiet. First time we have been over the continent.

Two nights later on 15/16 September seven 36BS B24s successfully completed a moving MANDREL patrol, jamming from 2215 hours to 0235 hours. 603 RAF aircraft were dispatched, with seven failing to return for a loss rate of 1.1%. The main attack was Kiel. The raid analysis report stated in part: "To cover the attack on Kiel, the MANDREL screen moved up at 2300 hours from a patrol line extending from 5345N-0320E to 5033N-0250E, to fresh positions from 5505N-0635E to 5318N-0325E. The enemy was thus deprived of early warning, and it may well be that he again antici-

A B24 and B17 parked on the tarmac at Cheddington await servicing. Because of the secret jamming equipment they were placed under armed guard. *Courtesy of John Madero.*

Aerial view of Station 113 Headquarters. One of the many airfields planted on British farmlands and subject to the King's Pass. Note the rows of haystacks at top left. *Courtesy of Frank J. Trovato.*

pated nothing more than a spoof attack, with the result that fighter action was not initiated until after the bombers had crossed the coast." Again the 36BS gremlins were effective!

The next night five 36BS Liberators were dispatched and successfully completed a moving MANDREL patrol. Their jamming was from 2200 hours to 2345 hours and again from 0140 hours to 0230 hours. One aircraft experienced light inaccurate flak over the North Sea. The screen was in support of RAF heavy attacks on airfields in Germany and Holland, and Mosquito attacks on Brunswick and Dortmund. Out of 359 RAF aircraft dispatched, three failed to return.

S/Sgt. Hutton's diary of 17 September, a Sunday, related his heartfelt concern for his brother Norwood, who would participate in Field Marshal Montgomery's vault into Holland to capture the Rhine in Operation Market-Garden—"a bridge too far": He wrote:

Today the news came over the radio that paratroopers and airborne infantry had landed in Holland. This is it for Norwood. I wish so much that I could be there with him. He is a good boy and I hope so much that he comes out OK. The boy has his life ahead of him. I just hope he can make it back home."

Little did Iredell Hutton know that his brother's glider would be blown out of the sky with only three paratroopers escaping the flaming aircraft—luckily, one was Norwood. That evening he would be captured by the enemy while his outfit was attempting to capture one of the bridges in Eindhoven.

The next night of 17/18 September, six B24s were dispatched and completed their MANDREL patrol, successfully jamming from 1945 hours to 2300 hours. RAF attacks were in Holland and on Bremen and Dortmund in Germany. The enemy reaction report from RAF 100 Group states in substance that the enemy's plotting of the night's operations was of a very desultory nature. Only scattered

plots were passed on the bombers over South Holland, where obviously the enemy's plotting systems and communications must have been suffering serious disorganization. There was no evidence of fighter action being initiated.

Favorable results continued after another maximum effort as shown on the mission of 18/19 September when seven 36BS Liberators were dispatched. Six successfully completed a moving MANDREL patrol, jamming from 1830 hours to 2200 hours. One Liberator #42-50385, R4-H *Beast of Bourbon* turned back when it was not possible to operate the special equipment. RAF heavies attacked Bremershaven and Mosquitoes bombed Berlin and Rheine. The MANDREL screen supported these operations. A particularly good enemy raid reaction report from RAF 100 Group this night stated in part: "The aims of the MANDREL screen and the Special WINDOW dropping force were threefold:

(1) To deny the enemy of long range raid information on the force attacking Bremershaven.

(2) To confuse the enemy plotting so that the WINDOW dropping aircraft would appear as a large formation crossing Denmark enroute for a target in East Germany.

(3) To use the WINDOW dropping force to contain enemy night fighters in Southern Denmark until it was too late for them to carry out a successful interception against the main force attacking Bremershaven.

The plan achieved a considerable measure of success. The plotting of the main formation did not commence until 2023 hours at 5400N-0700E. Also, the WINDOW force was plotted as a separate formation from 2053 to 2110 hours in the Westerland area, and because of this threat, aircraft of NJG 3 (German Luftwaffe Night Fighter Group 3) were held in this area until 2110 hours when they were ordered to Westermunde and Wilhelmshaven, ten minutes after the bombing had commenced."

Captured B24 Liberator used by the Germans. *Courtesy of Bruce Edwards.*

An American Yank stands along side the famous RAF Avro Lancaster. This aircraft was capable of carrying a 22,000lb. Grand Slam bomb. RAF pilots gave it great praise because it was very manoeuverable and could endure great punishment. *Courtesy of the Mighty Eighth Air Force Heritage Museum.*

RAF aircraft under maintenance. *Courtesy of Stanley Harris.*

Iredell Hutton recorded another mission on 18 September:

Tonight we had another mission up in the North Sea. Nothing exciting except a little flak from the Frisian Islands. It has been nearly two weeks since they have had any flying bombs here. They started coming again yesterday. As yet you people back in the States haven't heard about the new V2 weapons, but the Germans are using it against this country now.

The next day he saw his competition aircraft up close. He wrote:

This morning we had a flight over to some base to take our Intelligence Officer, who was being transferred there. At the base they had hundreds and hundreds of gliders, bulldozers, and jeeps just waiting for another landing on the continent. It should come in

the future because the boys there said that they couldn't write letters home. So, as yet nothing has happened there. They have hundreds of paratroopers there too just ready to go. With the men we have I can't see why in the heck this thing can't be over before winter sets in. Also while we were there we saw a German ME109, ME110, and JU88. First German planes I have ever seen.

When we were taxiing off the runway our left wing hit a tree and knocked a large part of it off. Didn't stop us from taking off, though. I'm glad nothing happened, because between Sack, Herbie and myself, none of us had our chute with us. Been just too bad if we would have had to bail out.

News over the radio today has it that the Canadian Army has linked up with the airborne army which landed Sunday. That gives Norwood a much better chance of coming out OK.

Hutton boys hit London. L-R Brothers Marion, Norwood, and Iredell out on the town at Trafalgar Square before Norwood jumped into Holland. Absent from this photo was the oldest brother James, an officer off fighting the Japanese somewhere in the Pacific. *Courtesy of Iredell Hutton.*

Captured German ME110 #AX772. Note British markings. *Courtesy of Earl R. Siler.*

Captured German JU88 #HM509. Note British markings. *Courtesy of Earl R. Siler.*

And then there were none—or so it seemed to the Germans after the mission of 22/23 September. Four 36BS Liberators were dispatched in a moving MANDREL patrol, successfully completing their jamming from 2000 hours to 2150 hours. There were no RAF Bomber Command operations on this date, and the screen was in the nature of a spoof to lure the German Luftwaffe fighters into the empty night sky. The next night six 36BS B24s were dispatched and successfully completed their jamming from 1920 hours to 2210 hours with a break at 2100 hours. RAF heavy bombers attacked Neuss, Handorf airfield, and targets in the Munster area. Mosquitoes bombed Bochum and Rheine. The MANDREL screen was put up to protect these forces. Two nights later, on 25/26 September, a flight of three Liberators of the 36th were dispatched and successfully completed a moving MANDREL patrol, jamming from 1930 hours to 2115 hours. No incidents were reported. RAF Mosquitoes attacked Mannheim and Hochst near Frankfurt.

The war news was not good as recorded in Hutton's diary of 25 September:

The news is not so good these days. It has been released that the paratroopers that landed near Arnhem were not all Canadian and Polish, but some were Americans. I hope so much that Norwood isn't among them, because they have been pounded now for 8 days and 7 nights. We are trying to reach them, but as yet haven't got many men over to them. Fresh troopers have been landed, but the Germans are still giving them hell. Within the next several days our troops should be within reach of them.

Marion [who had already completed his missions in the 15th Squadron, flying with the RAF 226 Squadron during 1942] was telling me that the Colonel in charge of him told him he could go back to the states if he wanted to. He told him that since Norwood and I were here, he had rather stay. Was certainly nice of him.

The mission of 26/27 September had four 36BS B24s dispatched. The Liberators successfully completed their mission, jamming from 2225 hours to 0100 hours. The screen was in support of heavy bomber attacks on Karlsruhe and Mosquito attacks on Frankfurt and Homberg.

S/Sgt Hutton remembered the mission of 26 September:

Tonight we went on another mission. It was the most uneventful one we have been on yet. All we did was sit up there and go around in circles. It was all I could do to keep from going to sleep.

He continued to have anxiety and concern for his brother. He wrote:

The news today isn't so good. Our paratroopers, which were mostly Canadian and Polish, had to withdraw from Arnhem. It was the bloodiest battle yet fought on this side. Over 8,000 were landed, and only 2,000 made it back to our lines. For ten days those boys fought like mad. The real truth about the fight will not be known

Asst. Communications Officer Lt. David Merrill remembered the 36BS, "The poker was great!" *Courtesy of Sam Ziff.*

At left James Thompson and his buddies shooting craps. Somebody's got to win ! *Courtesy of J. O. Thompson.*

until the end of the war. I don't think Norwood was in on that, but he could have been.

At the end of the month, everyone looked forward to payday. No matter how little the GI received, payday was always just a bit brighter than any other day. Many GIs ran around collecting debts accumulated during the month. In many corners hastily started crap games were in progress. A general air of exhilaration was in evidence everywhere, and the pubs would always do well that night.

Lt. David Merrill, the Asst. Communications Officer for the squadron, remembered some of the good poker at the 36th:

It was a poker playing squadron. It was like this, see—come payday there was a crap game. And the crap game would last maybe two or three days. And then the money made was in fewer hands, and then everybody started to play poker. The poker went on for about another two weeks or three weeks, and the money then was concentrated in fewer hands. Nobody else had any money because everybody held out a little of it to take a pass. From here on they played gin rummy at a penny a point, which is pretty risky or funny. Everybody who played carried a little book with them. On pay day you'd settle up. You had a little book, and you figured out how much you owed who and who owed you how much. That was a way to make a living. The poker was great !

S/Sgt. Harry Setzer, the radio operator for Lt. Angstadt's crew, was also good at poker. Setzer recalled:

Well, we did play a little cards. We always added a little money. I played a little craps, too! We always played cards at standby [while

The first awards presentation ceremony. South End Hill is in the background. A typical citation read to the airmen: "For meritorious achievement in accomplishing with distinction numerous aerial operational missions over enemy occupied Europe. The courage, coolness, and skill displayed by each of these individuals in the face of determined opposition materially aided in the successful completion of these missions. Their actions reflect great credit upon themselves and the Armed Forces of the United States." *Courtesy of Frank J. Trovato.*

Major Hambaugh presenting awards. Later awards to the airmen would recognize "meritorious achievement while participating in a number of flights against the enemy under hazardous and adverse flying conditions." *Courtesy of Frank J. Trovato.*

waiting before the mission in or around the plane]. I won about twenty-two hundred dollars in craps over there and sent it home. Daddy bought me a car for when I came home. I got a '39 Ford coupe.

The last mission of the month on 28/29 September had five 36BS B24s participating in the protective MANDREL screen operating between 0015 and 0255 hours. They completed their mission without incident. The main Bomber Command attack was again on Karlsruhe, which was attacked without loss.

The first awards presentation ceremony for squadron personnel was held this month. Four Distinguished Flying Crosses, two Oak Leaf Clusters to the Air Medal, and thirty-nine Air Medals were presented by Major Hambaugh. A letter from the Air Officer Commanding RAF 100 Group recognizing work done by certain members of the squadron was also received. (See Appendix F for details.)

September had proven to be a most successful month. The 36BS flew eighty-seven operational sorties with only one abortion, and this was due to the inability to operate certain RCM equipment in the Liberator #42-50385 *Beast of Bourbon.* The abort was not charged to the crew chief. However, the squadron did have its fair share of problems. The need for a briefing room for the squadron continued. It still shared the room with the 406th Bomb Squadron (Night Leaflet)—"The Paperboys." Frequent conflicts remained in scheduling mission briefing times. Another problem concerned getting promotions for ground enlisted men.

In spite of these problems morale was still good—and for good reason. A clipping of "Notes from the Air Force" from the *Stars and Stripes* for 30 September stated: "The Liberator Squadron commanded by Major Robert F. Hambaugh of Birmingham, Ala., has completed 105 sorties without a single abort."[44] Accordingly, in order to celebrate and to escape the mental stress and other rigors of war for much needed rest and relaxation, a number of the men took advantage of furloughs which were recently reopened.

6

Cologne and Woodbridge

October 1944

On the first day of October the 36th Bomb Squadron RCM was relieved from the VIII Air Force Composite Command and assigned to the VIII Fighter Command. During the month the squadron moved from Site 5 to Site 6 at Cheddington. Site 6 was formerly occupied by the Headquarters Squadron of the 8AF Composite Command and was a more desirable site than Site 5. It was now possible to have all the squadron personnel located at one site, whereas before some of the personnel had to be housed away from the squadron area. The overall strength of the squadron during the month was 687. Even though the 36th was authorized a total of twenty-four crews, only sixteen were assigned. Authorized were 114 officers and 426 enlisted men. This figure was exceeded at times due to the assignment and attachment of personnel to the squadron for radar countermeasure training.

The 36BS continued to operate with RAF 100 Group, and along with RAF 199 Squadron were responsible for supplying aircraft for the MANDREL screen. Their support was used in conjunction with WINDOW dropping and spoof forces. The 36BS was called

upon to fill an increasing number of stations in the screen. Raid analysis reports indicated that the countermeasures used were very successful in confusing the enemy's fighter control organization to a considerable degree. Only a few losses sustained during the month were attributed to enemy fighters.

A secret internal memo from Headquarters 8AF identified the equipment status of the thirteen B24 aircraft assigned to the 36BS. It detailed the number of 36BS aircraft fitted with specific jamming and search equipment as follows:

3 B24 6 MANDREL EA (each)

4 B24 6 MANDREL EA PLUS 1 JACKAL EA

1 B24 6 MANDREL 1 SX-2S (Search) RECEIVER

2 B24 3 DINA EA

1 B24 SCR-587, S-27 (Search receiver), APR-1 & PRF MEASURING EQUIPT.

2 B24 DUAL SPOT-JAMMING (Equipment)

It also stated in part:

MANDREL and DINA equipped aircraft are used operationally by RAF 100 Group for screening purposes. The JACKAL

Bartenders of the enlisted men's club. Note the background pin-up girls. *Courtesy of Frank J. Trovato.*

The enlisted men's club served laughter, fun, beer, and cokes. *Courtesy of Frank J. Trovato.*

Lt. John Latvaitis and men of the Radar Shop. Lt. Latvaitis is seen kneeling 4th from left. *Courtesy of John D. Latvaitis.*

equipped aircraft are available for jamming enemy tank communications when required. Signed—DOOLITTLE[45]

Mission activity of late had slowed down for Iredell Hutton, which allowed him time for a breather. He wrote in his diary on 1 October:

We haven't done any flying since last Tuesday night. We have had a stand down every night. Several of the nights I could understand why, but the rest I couldn't. Tonight is one of the most beautiful I have ever seen, and still no planes of the RAF out. All night long planes have been going over here. Most of them looked to me like C47s. They are carrying troops and supplies to our troops. All along the front now things are nearly at a standstill. The reason being that they want to mass men and material for one big push. Yesterday there was a lot of gliders headed east.

This morning the Germans in Calais surrendered after a 24 hour truce yesterday. During that time they evacuated 20,000 civilians.

Three days later Hutton wrote:

The red flags were flying for the first time in eight days. We were up for spare. We were supposed to go to the briefing room for a meeting this afternoon. A British officer explained the work we were doing and how many ships and men they had saved from our work. It must be a good thing, or we wouldn't be doing it.

We were a spare this morning and were only supposed to sit around the plane until all the rest had taken off and then go back to the sack. About 25 till 5 a jeep came out and told us one of the other planes' GEE box was out, so we had to fly. We flew up around Denmark. About eight o'clock John [Shamp] called and asked me if I saw a plane coming in towards the tail. I did and aimed my guns at it. It was a 24, and it played around there for some time. If it had come in any closer we were going to let him have it. He finally went away.

Sick bay. Paint them red and mark them "duty" Doc. *Courtesy of Frank J. Trovato.*

On our way back I saw the first town in the ETO that was lit up. It was Cambridge. It really looked good to see lights on again. When we landed number three engine caught on fire again. It was really bright tonight. One of these nights it is going to blow up.

Photographer Joseph Bartus at work in the darkroom. *Courtesy of Joseph A. Bartus.*

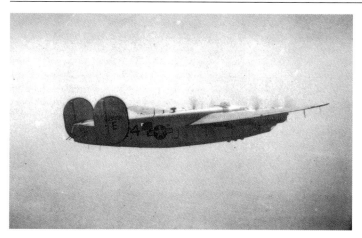

B24 #42-50230, R4-E nicknamed *Rum Dum* was one of two B24's assigned to the 36th during the month. *Courtesy of Leonard C. Backer.*

The next day, 5 October, Hutton wrote:

The crews that are leaving are two of the old ones and two new ones. One of the crews was Lt. Sandberg, and he has been with us ever since we were in Charleston. He has some pretty good boys on his crew, Melita, Walsh, Church, Howie, Amanti, and Vaccaro.

Yes, Lt. Sandberg's crew had moved all right, but not as far away as Hutton had thought. Tail gunner S/Sgt. Tony Vaccaro remembered:

We stayed with a family named Mr. and Mrs. Battlebury. Every time when we came down, back from a mission we used to go over to her house. The whole crew would visit her. She had a lot of rooms. She used to put us up at night. She would treat us like her own, like a son. Her son was in the British Air Force. She really treated us real good. We had tea [after] every mission. We used to go to town, and a lot of guys got drunk having a good time. She waited up for every one of us until we were all home safe. She was really good to us.

The first mission of the month was on the night of 5/6 October when five Liberators were dispatched and successfully completed their mission without incident. The jamming was from 1845 hours to 2100 hours. The MANDREL screen was in support of an attack on Berlin. Nineteen Mosquitoes of RAF 8 Group attacked from 2026 hours to 2048 hours. It was a moving screen, with position "A" being between 5240N-0230E and 5420N-0425E, and position "B" between 5332N-0432E and 5420N-0655E. The Raid Analysis Report by RAF 100 Group indicated the effect of the MANDREL screen on the Enemy Raid Reporting Organization was seen when the first plot on the Mosquitoes attacking Berlin was given at 1940 hours, just off the west coast of Denmark. This provided an illuminating contrast, according to the report with RAF 8 Group raid on the night of the 3/4 October, when without the MANDREL screen, plotting on the formation commenced 20 miles west of Great Yarmouth and continued across the North Sea. There was no indication of enemy fighter action being initiated against this force.

The next mission of 6/7 October produced even more significant results for the jamming gremlins. A flight of seven Liberators were dispatched and successfully completed their mission without incident, jamming from 1815 hours to 2145 hours. The screen was in support of RAF Bomber Command attacks on Dortmund and Bremen. As on the night of 5/6 it was a moving screen, position "A" being from 5232N-0242E and 5430N-0449E and position "B" between 5256N-0332E and 5435N-0640E. The RAF had 484 aircraft attack Dortmund with a loss of 5 aircraft, or 1 per cent. 246 aircraft attacked Bremen incurring a loss of 5 aircraft, or 2 per cent.

An Interception Tactics Report stated that the operations were highly successful. To quote: "To have succeeded in penetrating 120 miles beyond the battle line to the Ruhr and in carrying out a major attack on Bremen, for the loss of 5 aircraft on each was an extraordinarily encouraging outcome. Tactical surprise was evidently achieved in the north by use of a MANDREL screen, a low level approach as far as was possible towards the mouth of the Weser, an unusual approach route and restrictions on signals with the result that fighters were able to get to the target only after the bombing had been in progress for about ten minutes. The raid in the north and its protective screen were intended to lessen the fighter opposition further south, but it appears that even without this there was sufficient confusion in the enemy's control over southwest Germany to prevent any well organized interceptors from coming up."

The noted Asst. Director of British Intelligence, Dr. R.V. Jones, wrote in his book *Most Secret War* :

One of the examples we enjoyed most occurred on 6th October, when we obtained General "Beppo" Schmid's [Commander of the German nightfighter organization] personal reaction to the fact that our losses were only 13 out of 949 aircraft. The night's major

B24 #42-50230, R4-E nicknamed *Rum Dum* with 65 mission symbols. Pilot Lt. Sam Ziff remembered nicknaming his Liberator. *"Rum Dum* was a mutually agreed on logo for our crew. We all selected names of our favorite alcoholic beverage and that was the nickname that was painted on the bird at our position. I was into scotch then and mine was Sam "Vat 69" Ziff. Anyway, it was a fun thing and we all seemed to enjoy it." Lt. Ziff flew 58 jamming missions. *Courtesy of Sam Ziff.*

operations were twin attacks on Dortmund and Bremen. In the latter, our bombers made a low approach under radio silence, while the German early warning radar was jammed by a screen of 100 Group aircraft operating their MANDREL jammers; as a result the nightfighters were only able to attack after our bombers had been over the target for ten minutes. Similarly, the Dortmund force flew low over France and turned north and climbed towards the Ruhr again screened by MANDREL aircraft, while a spoof force of Mosquitoes went on to threaten Mannheim.

The result was confusion to the defenses, and General Schmid reacted with a castigatory diatribe to the whole German nightfighter organization; "I am astonished that in spite of pains, admonitions, and orders throughout the whole year, I have not succeeded in bringing the Jagd Divisionen [fighter divisions] at least to the point of being able to distinguish in what strength and in what direction the enemy is approaching. In my view, there is no excuse whatever for this failure.[46]

Lewis Brandon, DSO & DFC (Distinguished Service Order & Distinguished Flying Cross), a Mosquito Squadron Leader, and top navigator for 157 Squadron of RAF 100 Group in his book titled *Night Flyer* told of the spoofs:

Spoof raids were laid on, often with outstanding success. The Luftwaffe suffered from shortage of aviation fuel and oils—particularly from the end of 1943 onwards. A large number of their aircraft were concerned only with the defense of the Reich, and until things became really desperate a threatened raid would provoke strong reaction from German nightfighters. The more we could persuade the Luftwaffe to launch fighters into the air unnecessarily, the more of their precious oil and petrol was wasted.

There were various forms of spoof raids. The most usual was for as many training aircraft as possible to assemble over Norfolk

The JIGS UP receives necessary modifications by the ground maintenance tech's. L-R is Charles Sanders, Donat Lafond and Henry Hill. Four modified IFF sets were installed with one antenna under each wing and two in the tail. Antennae installation was carried out by the sheet metal men of the engineering department. Further installations to squadron aircraft would conform to the pattern of this Liberator. Courtesy of Casimir Gierlasinski.

Historic Cologne (population 912,000) was a fortress town encircled by fortifications. There were five marshaling yards in Cologne. The industrial part of the city was on the eastern river bank. Cologne was completely devastated. *Courtesy of Dr. Robert F. Hambaugh, Jr.*

and then set off over the North Sea, to simulate a major raid heading for Northern Germany. There might be as many as eighty aircraft involved, and all the jamming and bomber support patrols would be laid on to help the simulation of a really massive raid. Just before reaching the enemy coast, but not before they had been well plotted by the German warning system, the training aircraft would turn back, having carried out a good navigational exercise.

On several occasions spoof raids of this sort brought a reaction of two or three hundred German night fighters and a considerable waste of fuel. Apart from this, some of them were shot down by Bomber Support fighters After one or two of these spoof raids, Bomber Command would probably lay on a major raid on the very same route and catch the German controllers out.

Even when the weather was poor or when Bomber Command was having a night off, 100 Group would usually arrange some activity to keep the Luftwaffe employed. There were very few nights from the end of 1943 until the end of the War when 100 Group had no aircraft over the Reich.[47]

The mission on the night of 7/8 October was indeed a classic electronic warfare jamming spoof—one truly for the record books. There was no offensive by Bomber Command this night, however, six B24s of the 36BS successfully dispatched and completed their mission without incident. The jamming was between 1845 hours to 2200 hours. The screen operated from 5226N-0240E to 5446N-0405E. There was no offensive by Bomber Command this night. The Raid Analysis Report described the operation thus: "Taking advantage of the fact that there was to be no bomber night offensive on this night of 7/8 October, a spoof attack by the MANDREL screen and special WINDOW dropping aircraft, supported by high and low Intruders [RAF Mosquitoes attacking enemy airfields] was planned against Bremen. Following on the attack on that city on the previous night when practically no enemy activity was recorded, it was anticipated that a threat to the same would serve a number of useful purposes. All the evidence so far received shows that the whole operation went according to plan and was an unqualified success. Enemy radar stations plotted the formation as it was anticipated they would, and the enemy controllers, deceived by the spoof, initiated fighter action in accordance with our purpose."

Hutton remembered 7 October for a different reason:

Today the biggest air fleet ever to bomb Germany was sent out from this country and Italy. Over 3,000 bombers with 2,000 fighter planes. Can't see how in the heck they can hold up under it. That is not as big as what is to follow.

We were told tonight that we may have to fly in the morning. If we do that you can bet that big things are about to happen. The last time this squadron flew in the day time was on D-Day. It may be a spoof raid, though.

The next day Hutton wrote of seeing a V1 rocket attack during his furlough in London:

The sirens sounded, meaning that a buzz bomb was coming over. It was just like a bomber—made a heck of a racket. Saw it pass over, the outline against the sky. It had a small light on the bottom which was the exhaust. It looked like a light bulb floating through the air. The noise then cut out all together and everything all around lit up. The light went out and then it landed. The most terrific explosion I have ever heard. The windows shook all around us. It was the first one we had ever seen. We wanted to see it from the beginning to the end. The all clear alarm sounded about 15 minutes later.

On the street I met a paratrooper. He said that he was in a service company and that he handled the casualty list of the troop-

Flight engineer S/Sgt. Thomas Stevens alongside B24 #42-51308, R4-M nicknamed *Modest Maid*. Search equipment and CARPET equipment were installed in this aircraft. *Courtesy of Iredell Hutton.*

ers that landed in Holland. He said that as far as he knew Norwood was still alive. He told me that the airborne landing in Holland was the biggest screwed up affair he had ever heard of. The General is on the carpet about it now. He said that all the troopers were going to move to France. Also said that we had lost about three quarters of our men there. Sure wish that I could hear from Norwood.

The next night's mission on 9/10 October the 36BS had seven Liberators dispatched with six completing their mission as scheduled. One aircraft returned early due to engine trouble. Jamming occurred between 1800 hours and 2200 hours. The screen was formed between 5133N-0205E and 5415N-0317E and was in support of the Bomber Command attack on Bochum by 405 heavies. A one per cent loss was sustained by the attacking aircraft. The effectiveness of the screen as detailed in the Raid Analysis Report said: "The difficulties experienced by the Enemy Raid Reporting Organization in coordinating the estimates of the numbers making the attack were evident. The first plot reported "a large force" a little

Aachen bomb target. The results of precision bombing. Aachen was the first large German city captured by the Americans. One of the biggest battles of the war took place during the siege of this city. *Courtesy of Dr. Robert F. Hambaugh, Jr.*

L-R Weather officers Marshall and Gulliver. Theirs was a most demanding and potentially deadly task — forecasting the horrible weather in Great Britain and Europe. *Courtesy of Arthur W. Gulliver.*

later; 70 four-engined bombers were specified. At 2027 hours, the spearhead of the force was given in the Dusseldorf area and the homeward route was plotted as far as 0530E."

Sgt. George Eberwine, tail gunner for Lt. Norman Landberg's crew, noted the 9 October mission:

4 hours 40 minutes. [location] North Sea. Tough one. One engine out—gas leak. Aborted, but completed our job.

Two days later, S/Sgt. Hutton recorded in his diary:

The red flag is up, so we will have to fly. We went down to briefing and we were going to France. Going near Aachen. General Hodges of the 1st Army gave the German General there an ultimatum to be out by this morning at 10:50, but since he chose not to surrender we are going to have to blast them out. The city has 180,000 people. It is a shame to tear the town up like that. Before briefing was over a boy came in and said that the mission was scrubbed. Every time we get set to go over the continent something happens.

On 12 October he wrote about another mission being scrubbed:

It has been raining nearly all day in this hole. Boy, will we be glad to be out of this country. It is really cold, too. We were sched-

uled again to fly tonight. We were going to France again. It would have been the longest mission this squadron has ever pulled, 8 hours and some minutes. We get out to the ship and all set to take off when they shot the green flares.

The next day Hutton wrote of losses close by:

Last night the 406th Squadron here on the field lost 2 planes. They were lost to flak. One went down in Holland and the other in France. Some of the boys may come out OK.

The 36th flew again on the evening of 14/15 October when seven Liberators were dispatched, completing their mission without incident. The jamming was between 0030 hours to 0345 hours and involved a moving screen, with position "A" being between 5255N-0235E and 5435N-0325E and position "B" being between 5338N-0500E and 5510N-0600E. The main Bomber Command attack was on Duisburg, with 887 heavies attacking that target from 0125 and 0149 hours. Six aircraft were reported missing.

The Enemy Raid Reaction Report from RAF 100 Group stated that no detailed analysis was required to measure the success of the Bomber Command operations on this date. The countermeasures employed were in the form of a MANDREL screen, a Bullseye Force, and two WINDOW raids. This mission was coordinated with the routing and timing of the main forces, and created such a state of hopeless confusion in the Raid Reporting Organization of the enemy that even the most brilliant of ground controller never had a chance to employ night fighters with any degree of success

Lt. Wayne Bailey, navigator for F/O Bert Young, remembered the jamming:

The 36th Squadron flew night radar screening missions for the British RAF. The squadron had electronic jamming equipment in the bomb bays of the airplanes that were used to jam the German coastal radars. We would have a number of picket planes orbiting in individual positions approximately ten miles apart just off the European coast.

The jamming equipment prevented the Germans from seeing through our screen to see what activity was taking place in the air behind the screen. Therefore, the Germans could not plan their defenses until the raiding planes passed through the screen. The English also used it to confuse the Germans as to where the target was going to be. For instance, the English would send a small training group through our screen to the south while the main effort would be moving behind our screen to targets in the north. The training group would turn back short of any encounters. The English had many different tricks of this type to keep the enemy from knowing where the main effort would be heading. We would put the screen up whether there was a raid scheduled or not and regardless of weather conditions.

The evening of 15/16 October had six 36BS B24s dispatched. All successfully completed their mission. They jammed from 1835 hours to 2100 hours between positions 5253N-0312E and 5443N-0523E. The screen was in support of Bomber Command operations, the main attack being on Wilhelmshaven with 480 heavies attacking between 1942-2002 hours. Seven aircraft were lost. The Interceptions Tactics Report stated that the main force was not plotted until it reached at least 0600E. It further stated that the enemy plotting took on the characteristic of a mass conglomeration covering the Frisian-Elbe area. There was no evidence that fighters were sent up to the real target or to any other threatened area until well after the bombing began.

Iredell Hutton wrote of the repeated attacks to Germany's war machine on 17 October:

Cologne has been attacked for about the fifth time in seven days. Since it is our next objective after Aachen, that is the reason. We have encircled Aachen now, so there is no avenue of escape. The Hungarians are debating whether to ask for an armistice or not. I doubt if they do. On the 15th, the RAF dropped more bombs on the German city of Duisburg than the Germans dropped on London during the blitz. Some tonnage.

About the new weapon which the Germans are using against England, it's like a torpedo [the V2]. It travels well over 600 mph and the radar cannot detect it until it is too late to warn the people. It is more dangerous than the buzz bomb.

I hope that I can get the camera and film soon because I want to take some pictures of the damage in London. For a large city it is torn up a lot, but not as bad as one might imagine.

Pilot Capt. Dick Sackett also remembered the missions on Cologne:

A couple of times that we were jamming ahead of the RAF and the target was Cologne. We would get within forty or fifty miles of Cologne and still be there when the bombing started. The light from the explosions was so intense that you could actually see parts of the skyline of the city. Every now and again you would see somebody hit and go down, or an explosion where maybe a couple of airplanes had collided or something. It was one awful thing to see. Of course, we didn't hang around very long once they had started their bombing runs.

The next mission on 19/20 October had seven 36BS Liberators dispatched. All completed their mission without incident. The B24s jammed from 1925 hours to 2245 hours between positions 4820N-0520E and 5040N-0510E. Bomber Command dispatched 907 aircraft, with 860 attacking primary targets, particularly Stuttgart and Murnberg. Eight aircraft, or .8 percent, failed to return. The Raid Analysis Report stated that a preliminary study of evidence available indicated that this night's offensive against the German Night Defense Organization would rank among the major successes of countermeasure operations. The threat to Frankfurt was plotted at 1954 hours at approximately 0555E and accepted by enemy controllers as a major raid. All the fighter action initiated in the early

stages was directed to the Frankfurt-Mainz area, and it was not until after the bombing of Stuttgart that the fighters were sent south in an attempt to intercept the bombers on their return route.

Iredell Hutton remembered this mission in his diary and wrote:

Tonight we had another mission. We went near the German border. We saw some activity, but not much. The RAF sent out the biggest number of planes yet on a single target. We saw one wave of planes going as we came back. Never have I seen so many. They were everywhere. At night they must not fly in formation because they are scattered everywhere. I tried my new heated suit out and it worked fine. They have taken the doors off of the tail, and my back like to froze to death. The RAF target tonight was Stuttgart and Nuremburg. They only lost nine of their aircraft.

On 20 October Hutton continued:

The Americans finished cleaning up Aachen this afternoon at 3:30. The first big German city to come into our hands. The next town to fall will be Cologne. That is really one town that is blown to bits. We have attacked it every day for about two weeks.

Sgt. George Eberwine also noted the 20 October mission:

8 hours 10 minutes. France—South of Troyes. Over 200 miles in. Good mission. Biggest RAF effort of the war. Hit Stuttgart-Nuremberg.

On 21/22 October the 36BS launched eight B24s. One Liberator turned back due to engine trouble. The rest of the squadron aircraft was recalled early by RAF 100 Group due to weather conditions. Iredell Hutton said of this one:

The RAF was going to send up about 1200 aircraft. Briefing was scheduled for 3 o'clock, but a boy came in and said that it had been moved up to 2:30. When we got there they had Stevens and Morin to go on out to the ship and get it ready because they had to take off immediately. We were spare crew, so we had to wait until

Officers Club at Station 113. Note the ceiling light shades. *Courtesy of Earl R. Siler.*

The bar offered good scotch whiskey to calm the nerves after the mission. *Courtesy of Earl R. Siler.*

all the other ships were off the ground before we could leave. They gave us the old crate B-Babes. What a wreck that is. All ships finally got into the air about 4:15. We had to wait 15 minutes before leaving. We came back to the hut and got our mess equipment and started for the mess hall. On the way Capt. [Thomas] Graham drove up in a jeep and told us to get in because we had to take off immediately. When we got to operations Capt. Graham told us two ships aborted, one because the GEE box went out and the other was siphoning gas. The crate we have isn't any better. We got out to the ship and dressed while we were going to position. Our GEE box went completely out, and we couldn't drain the gas out of our Tokyo tanks. We were a way out over the North Sea and discussing whether or not to go back when Sack came in over the interphone telling us that we were called back. The mission had been scrubbed because of the weather.

We got back to the base in a little while and the field had closed in. Every once and a while a break came in the clouds and we could see the field lights. They shot mortars and flares that lit up the field, but we couldn't see anything for the undercast. We circled the field so many times that I was just about sick when we did find an opening and landed. Was really glad to get on the ground again because we were all sweating this mission out. After we landed, since we were the first, they radioed all other ships and told them to go to another field because the overcast was too bad here. We went into interrogation room and got a drink. Herb, Sack, Mac, Morin, and myself really got a glow on. Capt. Graham came in and took the bottle away. He said that the five of us had drank four quarts of whiskey. That was a lie because the boy was feeding as much to the ground crew as we got. We were all looped to the gills.

Pilot Dick Sackett also remembered one particularly tough time trying to land at Cheddington:

I recall coming back to Cheddington one morning, we had been on a late mission and when we got back there the fog was really bad. We had no approach aids there of any kind. About the only way to get down was the large magnesium flares which burned with an unearthly light. You had to do a timed circuit once you did locate the flare. By the time you turned onto the final off the base leg it was pretty dicy as to whether you were going to be lined up at all with the runway. There were people milling around trying to get down. I burned four of those flares getting down, and the last time when I finally did land I wasn't lined up with the runway on the final and I said, "Well, enough of this!" I finally got the airplane lined up on a six thousand foot runway, and I was almost halfway down the runway before I put it on the ground. I'm sure that the nosewheel must have been almost flat before we got stopped because of the brake pressure we had to use.

Radio operator S/Sgt. Joe Danahy of Lt. Joseph Hornsby's crew remembered the bad weather and one of the many diversions into RAF Woodbridge, an airbase on England's east coast:

Woodbridge had cement lined trenches along side the runway. They could release aviation gasoline into them, light it off and the fog would lift [Fog Investigation Dispersal Operation, or FIDO petroleum burners]. Woodbridge was an RAF base which existed for shot up or otherwise distressed aircraft coming back from the continent. It wasn't too far from the channel. The runway was 19,200 ft., not counting the overshoots, which were plowed fields. Supposedly you could land a heavy bomber across it if you had to. If you could get to Woodbridge, you could set anything down, no matter how badly it was shot up, and roll or slide to a stop without hitting anything. Then all you had was fire and other great things to worry about.

We took off on a mission one morning and were unable to get the landing gear all the way up. Then we could get it almost all the way down but couldn't be sure it was locked and wouldn't collapse

The club offered a comfortable setting, a warm fire, but not quite home. *Courtesy of Earl R. Siler.*

on landing. They sent us over to Woodbridge to circle and use up most of our fuel while trying to hand crank the gear the rest of the way down. We finally landed without incident. The trouble was repaired, and we stayed overnight with orders to take off the next morning, timed to meet others over St. Quentin in France. That morning, after spraying the plane with "Kill Frost," we fired it up, only to be unable to start one engine, so we couldn't go that day. This went on every day for nine days. We only had the clothes we started out in and were sleeping in a buzz bombed apartment house, burning woodwork in a fireplace for a little heat.

On the ninth day the trouble, whatever it was that day, was fixed by mid-morning, and as the weather was OK, we made a try for Cheddington. Using the runway from the very beginning, Hornsby was always very careful, we got up to take off speed and nose about fifteen feet into the air when all the engines quit! Down we came, going like the wind, not seeming to slow down at all as we rolled. Joe put the brakes on hard and collapsed the nose wheel, tried again and blew the tires on the main gear. We went off the end of the runway, through a plowed field, and came to a stop just short of a concrete building, a homing station. It seemed to take about a week for the firetrucks and ambulances, etc., to get there. However, we walked away from it. To cap it all off, the necessary repairs were made and we had to take off at about 2 pm and go home. Now all of this led in my case to an advanced case of chickenitis. This plane was the same one that we later had to bail out of with the loss of three lives over France, up near Belgium.

Pilot Joe Brookshire also spoke of Woodbridge:

The weather would be so terrible. All of England would be socked in. Of course all of us, the fighters and bombers, were all trying to land at one field—Woodbridge. It was just like chickens going after a piece of corn. Everyone was just trying to get down at the same place. I don't know how many got hit in collisions in the clouds. But finally we came in. On the final approach at Woodbridge, they were burning gasoline to raise the fog. They raised it about 300 feet. And coming in real low we could see that there would be several ships on the final approach at the same time—bombers and fighters stacked in among them.

Later, after I landed I went back to see how it was going. You could hear those fighters just whistling as they were coming in to land. Some of them would crash, and the Limeys would take their tractors and go out there and throw a hook over the undercarriage of the plane and drag them off this runway—while planes were landing. It took a lot of guts. I never saw any of them get hit by a plane while they were doing it.

While I was there at the [operations] office an American B17 pilot came in and said he had killed his tail gunner. He was coming in real low and there was a small hill or mound in front of him, and he pulled up and just wiped the tail off the ship, and he brought it on in and landed it and reported that he had lost his tail gunner. They sent a search crew out to find the body and they found the guy asleep in a ditch by a road. He had gotten up, walked over the road and reaction had kinda set in, so he had laid down and had gone to sleep.

Iredell Hutton would have to pay the piper for his over indulgence after the last mission. He wrote in his diary on 23 October:

Boy is everyone mad at us for drinking the scotch up the other night. Duke [Calisch] and Krueger are the maddest. The Major took our 48 hour pass, and that is why they are P.O'd. They won't even speak now. The Major told Mac that if Herbie and I screwed up one more time he was going to take our stripes away.

We had a mission tonight over in France somewhere. What a beautiful sight it was up there above the clouds. The moon was half full. When we landed the fog was gathering and we had to circle the field over an hour before we landed. It seems as though the closer to winter it gets the worse the weather gets for flying. Wouldn't be surprised if they don't cancel most of the RAF's flying this winter. Can't see how in the heck Germany can stand such a pounding anyhow.

MANDREL aircraft *Ramp Rooster* in and out of the soup. *Courtesy of Don C. Albinson .*

Not unlike most brothers separated during World War II, Hutton was still thinking about his brother. For this and other reasons, he was losing sleep. On 25 October he wrote:

Still no word from Norwood. Would sure like to get some word of him. Just a single word would do so much good.

This crew [Lt. Boesel's] across from us are really a bunch of night owls. They stay awake nearly all night and keep the rest of the barracks awake with them. Black, Myers, Ends, Bean, Evans, and Roberts. They are either playing cards or just shooting the bull.

The squadron dispatched six aircraft on the night of 23/24 October with one aircraft having to return early due to failure of deicing equipment. Jamming was from 1835 hours to 2045 hours. The screen was a moving one over the continent and in support of the Bomber Command attack on Essen. Essen was attacked by 921 heavies with a loss of eight RAF aircraft. The attack was from 1929 hours to 2002 hours. The Enemy Raid Reaction Report stated that an immediate appreciation of the situation over the Ruhr during the night suggested that a number of aims were achieved. There was no evidence on R/T or W/T that enemy night fighters were active. It was impossible to assess the full value of Bomber Support operations which were carried out. There were very definite indications, however, that some of the spoofing forces still continued to impose a great strain on the Enemy Raid Reporting Organization with the consequent effect of reducing the efficiency of the enemy night fighter controllers.

Sgt. George Eberwine remembered his 23 October mission:

4 hours 50 minutes—France. Climbed to 25,000 ft. Reached 26,000 to get over weather, but it was still up there and we were getting iced-up very much and deicers were not functioning properly. Rough time, but did best thing by turning back. RAF target was Essen.

On the next night six B24s were dispatched and all completed their mission without incident, jamming from 1835 hours to 2015 hours. The screen was again on the continent. RAF Mosquitoes bombed Hanover, Aschaffenburg, and Oberhausen without loss. On the night of 26/27 October again six Liberators were dispatched and five completed their mission. One aircraft failed to complete its mission due to failure of one engine. All aircraft were diverted upon return due to weather conditions. Patrols were otherwise uneventful. Jamming was between 1800 hours to 1945 hours. The screen was from 5622N-0600E to 5425N-0530E. There was little activity by Bomber Command. Sgt. George Eberwine wrote of the 26 October mission:

5 hours 5 minutes—North Sea. RAF pulled spoof raid. Everything went OK. Our field was closed-in on our return. We landed at Foulsham.

Iredell Hutton expressed his sentiments about the cold monotonous routine on the night mission of 27 October:

We were scheduled to fly tonight, but after coming back from chow the white flag was flying so we don't have to. Doesn't make any difference because I hate to fly over the North Sea.

Hutton wrote of having to turn around on the mission the next night:

Briefing was at 10:30 tonight. The British bombed Cologne today with their heaviest attack of the war. We were going to carry out a spoof attack on them. Take off was at 1:02 am. We got as far as the English coast and there we were called back to base. Boy were we mad. The interphone was alive with remarks about returning. The Germans weren't the one that were spoofed tonight, it was us.

Of course, the current news of the day expressed the great exploits of other squadrons as well. Hutton continued:

The RAF sent out a squadron of planes to bomb the German battleship "Tirpitz." A five ton bomb was planted on it. They have tried several times to catch it out of port. It will only be repaired to sail again.

The mission of 30/31 October had seven 36BS Liberators dispatched. All completed their mission, jamming from 2005 hours to 2205 hours. Aircraft in three northern positions on return faced

Crashed B17 Flying fortress. *Courtesy of Iredell Hutton.*

possible collision because they were at conflicting altitude with a returning RAF Bomber stream at 5030N-0400E. The screen was over the continent in support of Bomber Command's attack on Cologne.

Capt. Dick Sackett remembered such hazardous incidents—near misses—when flying his Liberator:

This operation ahead of the RAF of course was with no lights whatever. Nobody used any navigation lights of any kind. Of course you were always ahead of the RAF bomber stream. You always started the return about the time they were nearing the target, which meant that you would have to turn around and head back westward toward the base, and all these aircraft are coming from all over England from various altitudes from 5,000 anywhere up to 15,000 or 18,000 and all headed in the opposite direction. With no lights it furnished a lot of thrills, scary thrills many many times. Coming back west there always seemed to be a light side to the sky and you would see shapes, movement in front of you, and you had to take evasive action quite a few times. It generated what the pilots and the airmen called a "pucker party." It was pretty scary also at night. You kept advising or reminding all of your crew members to keep their eyes open for aircraft because it would be a shadowy apparition to appear in front of you. Many, many times you'd be flying along smoothly, climbing or flying level and all of a sudden the airplane would just bounce and you knew that you had just run through somebody's propwash and nobody had called the sighting of an aircraft because it was so dark, so pitch black all the time. It was pretty hairy a lot of times.

Iredell Hutton also wrote of the same hazard and his good luck on this one:

Tonight we had another mission. This time it was along the battle line in France. The moon was really beautiful. It was so peaceful riding up there among the clouds. The RAF tonight struck at Cologne and Berlin. Can't see how in the heck there is anything left of Cologne. On our way back some RAF planes came flying in at our altitude. We had to dodge to keep from hitting several of them. One of them came so close that Mac told us to shoot them. Not one of us fired a shot. Why should we shoot them when they have been bombing and we are only on a milk run. We were at 16,000 ft. and the clouds were right under us. Why should the RAF fly in the clouds and take a chance of colliding in midair? Don't blame them one bit.

On 31 October Hutton remained concerned about his brother and wrote:

I'm still worried over Norwood. I'm sure that if he was still alive he would get word to Marion and myself in some way. Even if he was in a hospital he would write or have someone else to. Sure hope he is well and safe.

The last mission of the month on 31 October/1 November had seven Liberators dispatched with all completing their mission. The jamming occurred from 1830 hours to 1935 hours and again from 2010 hours to 2135 hours. Three aircraft were fired upon by unidentified aircraft. The screen was again over the continent in support of another RAF attack on Cologne. Aerial gunner Sgt. Leo Hoffman wrote of this night in his mission record:

Flew over France. Cologne was bombed. Saw the bombs and saw aircraft go down—hit by flak.

Tail gunner Sgt. George Eberwine also wrote of this mission:

7 hours 10 minutes—France. Bombing planes hit target. We saw something burning a distance away. Swell show. Good mission.

S/Sgt. Hutton was supposed to fly this mission, but the crew of *The Jigs Up* had to abort. He noted:

We had to fly tonight. The RAF target was again Cologne. Sure making hay out of that place. We put all of our heated equipment on and were warming the engines up when Duke called Mac and told him that the GEE box had gone out. Mac called the tower and they told us to stand by. Several jeeps came out, but no one got in to check the GEE box. Didn't have time to send a new one out, so we couldn't go.

October had proven to be another successful month for the squadron and its missions with RAF 100 Group in providing spoofs and the MANDREL screen. This was in spite of occasional equipment failure and foul weather. German cities such as Cologne, Essen, Bremen, and Frankfurt were suffering dearly from the persistent Allied bombing attacks. So far, the 36th had yet to suffer a combat loss even with the increase in number of stations that they had been required to fill. Such good fortune was certain to end.

Night owls — Sgts. Bean, Ends, Roberts, and Evans of Lt. Boesel's crew. *Courtesy of Iredell Hutton.*

7

Night and Day - I Walk Alone

November brought about major operational changes for the 36th Bomb Squadron. The squadron would now fly not only night missions with the RAF, but would also fly day missions for the 8th Air Force. It operated with RAF 100 Group's 199 and 171 Squadrons by providing a MANDREL screen on eighteen nights of the month in support of RAF Bomber Command bombing operations. Beginning the morning of 25 November a screen was put up by the 36BS supporting 8AF daylight operations. This new screen was different from the RAF screen in that it attempted to deny the enemy the ability to listen in on radio transmissions—the communications during the assembly of 8AF Bomb Divisions. The screen supporting RAF operations continued to work toward countering the German long range radar plotting system. The effectiveness of the screen was based on RAF 100 Group Raid Analysis Reports. The screen was used in conjunction with other countermeasures such as WINDOW patrols, Intruders, and diversionary forces. All must be considered in making an assessment of results. "An Immediate Analysis in a Lighter Vein" from Headquarters RAF 100 Group, which follows, gives a fairly good picture of the spoofery carried out.

An Immediate Analysis in a Lighter Vein
by Y. Smif

Night of 23/24th November, 1944.

Bomber Command had laid on a raid
To be carried out with 100 Group's aid,
But Bomber considered the weather was poor
So Group took a hand at alerting the Ruhr.
They put up a suitably placed MANDREL Screen
Through which, so they hoped, not a thing would be seen.
They sang to the Hun a Serrate[48] serenade
Round the beacons they danced a Perfectos[49] parade.
They intruded up high, they intruded down low
(Just to be beastly they'd put on this show).

Buddies. L-R — Radio Code School Instructor Charles Preston with Iredell and Marion Hutton. *Courtesy of Iredell Hutton.*

The beat goes on. A B17 Flying Fortress delivers its payload. On November 25, 1944 the 36BS began flying daylight missions in support of 8AF bomber operations. *Courtesy of James B. Warner, Lt. Col. USAF (Ret).*

The WINDOW force WINDOWed 100 per cent
And came through the Screen with offensive intent.
The Hun plotted hundreds of heavies around,
But hadn't a hope of control from the ground.
He put up some fighters and led them astray
In a huge mass of blips that faded away.
Our immediate analysis shows in the main
That the poor bloody Hun had been fooled once again.
  L.W. Wells,
  Wing Commander
  Group Intelligence Officer[50]

The first mission of 1/2 November had seven 36BS B24s dispatched. Six completed the mission. One aircraft turned back for mechanical reasons. The position of the screen was between 4916N-0520E and 5103N-0412E. The time of the jamming was from 1925 to 2110 hours. The RAF main attack had 229 heavies over Oberhausen, Germany, from 2026 to 2039 hours. Results indicated that the enemy had taken all possible steps to prepare an efficient defense. Had the enemy controllers been allowed good tracking of the main force, heavy casualties would undoubtedly have resulted. The screen denied him that knowledge until 40 miles just before the target, which was too late for night fighter interception. Eight Bomber Command aircraft were listed as missing.

The next night had seven squadron Liberators dispatched with all completing their mission. The position of the screen was between 5019N-0510E and 5112N-0302E. The time of jamming was from 1815 to 1950 hours. The RAF main attack of 901 heavies was to Dusseldorf from 1903 to 1941 hours. The results indicated that the enemy controllers were not able to secure a real track on the main force until the bombing of the target made the picture clear.

The return route was plotted with considerable care, and the enemy's standing patrol in the vicinity was vectored in for interception. Eighteen RAF aircraft were lost or missing. Surely losses would have been considerably greater had not the screen been there.

S/Sgt. Iredell Hutton wrote in his diary of 2 November:
Tonight our mission took us over France and Belgium. The RAF bombed Dusseldorf last night. From where we were we could see the battle of Flushing going on. The city is in our hands now except for a few snipers. While we were standing around waiting to take off tonight, we saw several squadrons of C47s coming back. They may have had a new landing up in the Walcheren Islands. It was announced tonight that the whole of Belgium is in Allied hands. The greatest fight in the air over the Reich was put on today by the U.S. We sent over 2,000 planes to bomb their synthetic oil plants at Merseburg near Leipzig. Our bombers and fighters shot down a total of 208 German planes.

Two nights later on 4/5 November six squadron B24s were dispatched and all completed their mission. The position of the screen for Station A was between 5140N-0210E and 5322N-0300, and for Station B between 5140N-0347E and 5322N-0337E. The time of the jamming was 1715 to 1930 hours and also from 2000 to 2030 hours. The RAF main attack was 662 heavies on Bochum, Germany, from 1927 to 1953 hours and 163 heavies on Dortmund/Ems Canal at 1919 to 1940 hours.

Unfortunately, the results indicated that the enemy succeeded in securing long range warning. The first plot broadcast was just off the Norfolk coast at 1836 hours. The enemy had patrols operating in the Ruhr which made it impossible to achieve all the aims of the Bomb Support program. Thirty Bomber Command aircraft, or 3%, were reported missing.

Unknown airman on jeep in front of B24 #42-51546, another R4-L which came to be nicknamed *I Walk Alone. Courtesy of Louis J. McCarthy.*

On 6/7 November eight Liberators were dispatched, however, none completed the mission. The MANDREL screen was scheduled to be operated from a position 20 miles west of the Dutch Islands, then curve around in a patrol line north of Brussels and bend southward about 35 miles west of the battle area. The jamming began at 1830 hours and was intended to continue the uncertainty of the situation after the main attacks had finished by jamming until 2215 hours; weather conditions at base, however, necessitated the recall of the screen soon after the conclusion of the main attack. The RAF main attack scheduled from 1928 to 1940 hours included 210 Mosquitoes whose main target was Koblenz.

The results of the evidence indicated that there was considerable confusion in the enemy plotting system which seriously impaired the work of the enemy controllers. Only two RAF aircraft were listed as missing.

Dr. R.V. Jones wrote of the 6 November mission in his book *Most Secret War* :

We now had the advantage of occupying France and Belgium up to the German frontier, so our jamming aircraft could now operate much further forward, and blind the German long-range radars. The Germans had therefore to react very rapidly once they detected a raid approaching, and in the resultant hurry, they inevitably made mistakes, especially when we were encouraging them to do so by means of Spoof raids in which a few Mosquitoes would drop so much WINDOW that they looked like a large force. On 6th November, we made two attacks against Gravenhorst and Koblenz, putting in a Spoof force against Gelsenkirchen. Seven Gruppen were airborne against these raids, with two more at cockpit readiness; of the total of nine, five Gruppen were drawn against the Spoof force.[51]

Tail gunner Sgt. George Eberwine for Lt. Landberg's crew wrote of the 6 November mission:

Crash wreckage of Liberator #42-51226, R4-L in France. There were no pieces of the plane left any larger than gallon cans. It dug a ditch as wide and as deep as a jeep. This B24 would have been nicknamed *I Walk Alone* after the popular Louis Prima song. *Courtesy of the USAF Historical Research Agency.*

Men of Lt. Hornsby's crew examining their Liberator. *Courtesy of Joseph Danahy.*

5hours 25minutes—Belgium (Ghent) A Swell Show. Mission was called back early. My heated suit controls went out and I sure was cold. Both guns failed to operate. Rough situation. I was very cold. It was really rough at low altitude.

Thinking of home, the next day Iredell Hutton wrote:

The boys were listening to the election returns. There was some French brandy here that we had brought back from London with us, so Charles [Preston, a code school instructor] and I drank some of it celebrating the next four years with Roosevelt. We had another mission scheduled for tonight. We got all dressed and had taken off when the message that the mission was scrubbed comes over the radio. Hate to get all dressed and have that happen. We get back to the field and they want just our crew to fly over Bovingdon and check the height of their beam. We did. Got up to around 22,000 feet and the officer Capt. Graham said it didn't work. Personally I think it did.

On Monday morning [November 6] at 10:00 a rocket which the Germans are sending over landed in Luton. Tore about a whole block to hell. They are sending a number of them over now. I guess that's what the Germans call the rockets—V2 . On the radio tonight the Germans said that they had completely demolished Euston Station. What a lie that is, because we just left there yesterday morning.

The next mission was on 9/10 November and marked another 36BS highlight as the gremlins performed their special magic, but the squadron also recorded its first loss. The mission has seven aircraft dispatched with all completing their mission. The position of the screen was between 5017N-0500E & 4902N-0500E at 20,000 ft. The time of the jamming was from 0200-0340 hours. The RAF main attack consisted of a small number of Mosquitoes on miscellaneous targets in Germany. The results indicated that the mission was most effective and the enemy reacted in considerable strength

Wreckage of B24 #42-51219, R4-I. Navigator Lt. Walter S. Lamson and gunner Pfc. Leonard L. Smith were killed in the take-off crash. Sgt. Lester Jones suffered a fractured leg. *Courtesy of Lester L. Jones.*

Official photo of B24 #42-51219, R4-I after the crash. The plane had been redlined that afternoon. Weather conditions were zero zero at the time of the crash. *Courtesy of the USAF Historical Research Agency.*

to the spoof WINDOW force which was put up along with the screen. No RAF aircraft were reported missing. After the mission, a special commendation was received from General Doolittle and Air Vice Marshall Addison for the squadron activities on this night. The commendation read:

HEADQUARTERS
VIII FIGHTER COMMAND
APO 637 AAF STATION F-341
Office of the Commanding General

14 November 1944
SUBJECT : Commendation
TO : Commanding Officer, Station 113, U.S. Army
(Attention : Commanding Officer, 36th Bomb Squadron)

1. This Headquarters has received a confidential message D-67417, dated 13, November 1944, from the Commanding general of the Eighth Air Force. This message is quoted below.

"Attention Commanding Officer 36th Bomb Squadron RCM. Jamming, screening and diversionary efforts of the 36th Bomb Squadron have contributed greatly to the effect of RAF bombing efforts. Mission of 9/10 November was one of the most effective in confusing the GAF [German Air Force] and causing them to assemble in great haste to intercept the bomb stream which was not there, and reflects great credit to the Command and the individuals concerned. Signed Doolittle."

2. This Command forwards this message from General Doolittle with great pleasure and wishes to add its own commendation for a job extremely well done.

By Order of Colonel Webster:
Richard N. Ellis
Lt. Col., Air Corps
Chief of Staff[52]

Another Special Congratulation from the Air Officer Commanding RAF 100 Group Air Vice Marshall Addison stated:
FROM HQ. NO. 100 GROUP.
TO OULTON, NORTH CREAKE, FOULSHAM, GT. MASSINGHAM
SWANNINGTON, 36SQDN. CHEDDINGTON.

THE RESULTS OF LAST NIGHTS SPOOF OPERATION WERE MOST GRATIFYING. OUR AIM WAS AMPLY ACHIEVED IN THAT THE ENEMY WAS INDUCED TO REACT IN A VERY BIG WAY INDEED FIRST IN THE SPOOFED. THE THREATENED AREA UNTIL HE EVENTUALLY BECAME AWARE HE WAS BEING SPOOFED AFTER THE WINDOWERS HAD RETURNED, AND THEN IN THE RUHR AREA WHEN HE BELIEVED A REAL RAID WAS TO FOLLOW THE SPOOF. I KNOW HOW DIFFICULT WERE THE CONDITIONS LAST NIGHT, AND HOW THESE WERE AGGRAVATED BY LAST MINUTE CHANGES IN THE PROGRAMME. THE LATTER HOWEVER WERE MADE TO TAKE ADVANTAGE OF THE BEST POSSIBLE WEATHER CONDITIONS ON A BAD NIGHT AS REVEALED BY THE WEATHER REPORTS. I CONGRATULATE ALL CREWS WHO TOOK PART IN THIS DIFFICULT OPERATION. THEIR DETERMINATION ENABLED THE GROUP TO SCORE A VERY DISTINCT SUCCESS. WELL DONE.[53]

Dr. R.V. Jones also referred to this spoof in his book *Most Secret War*:

Besides providing diversions, Spoof raids could be used to get the German nightfighters up, and so tire them, on nights when we were making no major raids. On 9th/10th November, although the Germans had originally thought that bad weather would prevent us operating, they were deceived into treating a Spoof raid on Mannheim as a major one; and when they had unraveled the deception, they further deceived themselves by concluding that it must be a prelude to a major raid. As a result, aircraft of six Gruppen were airborne for 21/2 hours.[54]

This mission was not without loss. Liberator #42-51226, R4-L, crashed in France while returning from a patrol over Belgium at 0235 hours. The B24 was abandoned in flight when fire broke out in an engine most likely hit by flak. Six members of Lt. Joseph Hornsby's crew bailed out and survived, but three were apparently unable to bail out and were killed in the crash.[55] Radio operator Joe Danahy remembered his function that fateful night:

My particular job [as to the jamming] was to go in the bomb bay and turn on certain switches. They were toggle switches, on, off switches. Turn on certain ones and perhaps turn off certain others. I think the time was probably important. Blind actions. They didn't tell you why you were doing it and I didn't ask.

Danahy continued about the crash of his B24, which would have been nicknamed "I Walk Alone":

Lord God in the mountains, well the thing, it was a miserable airplane. This plane, it was a real loser. We took off about two thirty in the morning. The plane caught fire. Number three engine probably, and we of course had no extinguishers or anything like that. He [Hornsby] tried a shallow dive...tried to blow it out. That didn't do any good. He told me to send a SOS. They had this big liaison

Lt. Joseph Hornsby Official Crew Photo. Standing L-R Sgt. Pete B. Yslava, 2d Lt. Robert H. Casper, 1st Lt. Joseph R. Hornsby, 2d Lt. Fred G.Grey, Sgt. Charles R. Root. Kneeling L-R Sgt. Frank A. Bartho, Sgt. Jack K. Chestnut, Sgt. Raymond G. Mears, Sgt. Joseph P. Danahy. *Courtesy of Dr. Robert F. Hambaugh, Jr.*

transmitter, it was under the table in my little compartment. A big transmitter. I reached down and turned the switch on the light over the table—kind of a spot light to see by. It just went dim direct down and went out. The propeller governors were electric on those planes as opposed to hydraulic on a B17. So the electric system failed for some reason and the other engines ran away. They had no control over them. They were just roaring out of control. I remember seeing the two of them [Hornsby, the pilot, and Robert Casper, the co-pilot] on the controls. They were rustling that plane around trying to keep it flying. He [Hornsby] sent me back to the waist. Ray Mears was back there. He was a waist gunner. He was my assistant radio man. I remember checking him out to make sure his leg straps were alright. I got the trap door open back in the waist. I went out the trap door. He should have come right along, too, but he never did. We assumed he went forward because his buddy was Bartho, [who] was up in the nose with Fred Grey, the navigator. He evidently wanted to see if his buddy was alright or something, (a real fatal mistake to do that). Hornsby hung on to the controls. Casper went out. When Hornsby thought and hoped that everybody was out of there, he let go of things and headed for the bomb bay and jumped out. His chute opened and hit him on the chin. It kind of knocked him out for a minute. He landed alright. There were still three fellows on the plane. I think they were all there up in the nose by that time. Mears, no doubt about it, he went up front to see what was what with his pal Bartho. I tried to get back in the plane. You were supposed to squat down and kind of roll out if you were going to jump out. So, I just sat on the edge and dangled my legs and [I] went out and hung by my hands and changed my mind. I couldn't chin myself back in, so I had to let go! The real hero. The real heroic type action. Oh Jesus, it was a bad time. I must have fallen, well, I should have ended up in China, because I never even thought to pull the damn ripcord. At some point I said, "Now just a minute here, there's a handle you're supposed to pull here." So, I pulled it and it worked like a charm. I remember I was laying, like laying on your stomach in bed, falling in that manner. I said, "Now when that thing opens up it's going to be all fouled up, I'd better turn over." I turned over, just like turning over in bed, then pulled the handle. So it worked like a charm. Well, mostly like a charm, I had one loose leg strap. Part of my anatomy was under that leg strap and when the thing opened, my weight came down on it. It ached for a long time. That was my war wound. I remember seeing the flicker of flames, fire, underneath the layer of clouds, so I hadn't gotten down below them at that point. The thing [the B24] was probably going down at full speed shortly after I got out. It crashed beneath the clouds—at least I could see the reflection of flames. It was some miles away, I couldn't tell you how far. We landed in France near that town, Boucly.

Pilot Joseph Hornsby, recalled:
We lost one engine which blew up, having had a direct hit while crossing over the Rhine river. Then we lost our electrical system

and were losing another engine. We had to come back over that North Sea at night. I decided it was best for us to bail out instead of trying to cross that North Sea in a B24 on two engines. It wasn't too good on a two engine airplane, especially at night. I stayed in the B24 a while. I had the crew out at 8,000 feet. I decided I'd just bail out at 4,000. When I bailed out, I was over Chartres, France. I was the last one out.

The airmen of Lt. Hornsby's crew lost were Lt. Frederick G. Grey (navigator), Sgt. Raymond G. Mears (gunner), and Sgt. Frank A. Bartho (gunner). The crash occurred near Boucly in northern France, and the remains of the bodies which were identified by identification tags were buried in an American cemetery nearby. The other crew members returned to duty on 15 November. The aircraft was destroyed.[56]

Once on the ground in France after the crash of his B24, Sgt. Danahy remembered:

I couldn't see where I was exactly. At one point I remember seeing the moon reflecting on water, a little pond. I thought I saw a concrete highway. I came down and I landed with quite a thump in the middle of a small clearing with tall trees all around it. [If] You don't think that God sits on your shoulders sometimes, why you're very wrong, you know. There I was all ignorance, nice and relaxed because I didn't know if I was going to hit the ground and the chute didn't get tangled and anything. So, I laid there huffing and puffing. I couldn't tell you how long. It was a weird feeling to stand up and say, "Well now, I've got to get outa here. What the devil direction do you go? The moon, I don't know where it had gone. I couldn't see the hand in front of my face. A dog had been barking as I came down, otherwise it had been very quiet. This was after the plane went down. It focused an awful sound. Finally I just started going and I came to the shore of this little pond. Something entered that water on the other side. I said, "Oh God, here comes that dog. He's going to chew me up." Then I got very clever and started whistling "Yankee Doodle." I can't tell you why I did that, but I did. Somebody else began whistling "Yankee Doodle," and it was Jack Chestnut, the engineer. He had landed right on that highway, and so we got together and we laid down by the side of the road. We didn't know where to go anyway. We had these big parkas on and heavy clothes. You know how they say when the chute opens you lose your boots and so on? Well, I still had my big sheepskin boots on and everything. No problem at all. They stayed right with me. So we laid there, and it got to be five o'clock in the morning. At that time the morning bells, the church bells began to ring all over the countryside. After a while somebody came riding a bicycle. He was wearing a cloak. He was coming along that road pretty good on his bicycle in pitch dark. I jumped out in the middle of that road and I said "Nous sommes Americans." He peddled twice as fast. I haven't seen him since. He never stopped or anything. It wasn't long after that a pedestrian came along. We talked to him. I could talk a little high school French. Very little. Chestnut couldn't talk any. Nobody

on the crew could except me. The fellow was a good friendly fellow. He took us to his house, which was like one big room with a loft at the back. His wife was there and a boy, evidently his son. They gave us coffee in a bowl and some eggs and something to eat. Then he took us through the village. By this time there were a lot of people walking around on the street. He took us up to this old man [who] had one of those chromium bicycles they used to have in the thirties there. He was very distinguished looking. People kind of saluting him as they'd go by. Not really saluting but respectfully. I suppose he was the mayor. He turned us over to that man and he took us to his house. There was a maid there, I remember, the guy must be a big shot. After a little delay, maybe he gave us a drink, he took us out to a little barn and opened it up and there was a little car there. It was for all the world like a Model A Ford, only it wasn't. It was similar to that with wire wheels and so on. He put us in the car and drove us off across country. It was all sugar beets fields there, kind of rolling land. He stopped out in the middle of nowhere and told us to get out. I said to Chestnut, "What's he going to do now, shoot us or something?" We didn't have any guns or anything. My .45 cal. was heroically hanging on the bunk back in England. It wasn't too much help at that point. I don't know what I would have done with it anyway!

He took us down the hill and up on top of a knoll that had a big grove of trees on it. Here were these raunchy Americans in there. They had a spotting station for artillery. They had a radio. This fellow [the mayor] knew they were there. They talked on the radio. The radio talking back, it said, "You know how they should get here, they go down a mile or two and they come to an abandoned Sherman tank and and turn left." I thought that was great. Back in the car we followed directions and went to this P47 base. We were joined there. Everybody was walking around with .45s on their hip, all these fly-boy fighter pilots. This was pretty near the front lines, I guess. We knew at that point who had survived and who hadn't. Three were killed. We were all interrogated, but primarily it was Hornsby and Casper that had to answer questions as to what took place. They were just on the verge of sending out the telegrams, "Missing in Action" when they found out what had happened to us. Later, we ended up on a truck and they transported us. I remember going through Valenciennes. We spent one night at a former boy's school. We put up there. I remember being in the latrine, cleaning up in the morning, cleaning myself up. These women were working right in there, cleaning the actual building. They were right in the latrine and nobody thought anything of it. Of course, I wasn't used to that! I found that interesting. Off we went again, and we stayed at a chateau that had been Rommel's headquarters when he was in France. I remember the whole front of the place had been riddled with bullet holes. There was some kind of burned out vehicle in the front yard. We put up there for the night. We ended up at an air base, a former German air base. We got on the DC3, crossed the channel and landed. They sent a plane over from Cheddington to pick us up.

Undoubtedly very glad to be alive after bailing out of his flaming Liberator, Hornsby recalled:

I landed and didn't know exactly where I was. I crawled up in the woods that night. Then I went on. I got picked up and went to a base called A72 [near Amiens] over in France. From there we went to Valenciennes, Belgium. The enemy was still firing rifle and sniper fire. We picked up a plane that flew us back to England. I got back to base about Thanksgiving. I got banged up a little bit and was in the hospital for three or four days.

When asked by the Air Force to go to the crash site, Danahy said:

They wanted us to go out there and identify things. Given the choice, we said "No we wouldn't." The statement was made that there were no pieces of that plane left any larger than gallon cans from the mess hall. It dug a ditch as wide and as deep as a jeep.

There was also trouble for Iredell Hutton on this mission. He wrote in his diary:

This afternoon we were called to brief at 2:15. The RAF wasn't sending any effort up. It was only a spoof raid. The times for take off didn't come in until late so we had time to go to chow before we took off. When we came back from chow we went out to the ship and proceeded to get dressed. No sooner got dressed when a jeep came out and said that the times had changed and we wouldn't take off before 12 a.m. At 12 we went back to the plane and took off at 12:30.

[It] Was freezing from the ground up. The flying was at 15,000 unless we ran into clouds, and then we were to try to climb above it. We got over the channel at around 8,000. I had my scarf and heavy socks on. Guess I would have frozen without them. Never in my life have I been so cold. My feet were so numb, so were my legs and arms. My hands didn't seem to get any heat from the gloves at all. We had to climb up to 24,500 ft. to get above the clouds. It was 47 below up there. We would have certainly been a good target for the enemy because our engines were making vapor trails. This continued all the while we were up. We were over the front tonight. On our way back number one engine caught on fire and we had to come back on three. Have never in my life been as glad to get my feet back on the ground as I was this morning.

When we landed this morning there was one crew missing and up to now they haven't come in. The boys are in my barracks. Sure hope nothing happened to them. There was one boy that we called Irish [Joe Danahy]. Good boy. He is usually laying on my bed listening to the German propaganda programs.

Hutton wrote later that day:

Churchill announced to the Parliament today that the German V2 rockets had landed in England. They have been landing for some time now. It is about time they announced it. Those things really do the damage.

On 10/11 November eight squadron aircraft were dispatched with seven completing the mission. One aircraft turned back early for mechanical reasons. The position of the screen was between 5115N-0350E and 4943N-0500E, and the time of jamming between 1830 to 2125 hours. The RAF main attacks included 63 Mosquitoes on Hanover and other targets in Germany, attacking Hanover from 1957 to 2017 hours and again from 2356 to 0008 hours. The screen was used in conjunction with a spoof WINDOW force. The enemy again reacted in considerable strength. Evidence indicated that elements of at least seven Gruppen were active. Only one British aircraft was reported missing.

The next night the squadron experienced a breather. Iredell Hutton wrote:

There was a stand down tonight. We learned that the plane that went down crashed landed near Abbeville in France. Three were killed. What happened to the rest is not yet known. The tail gunner tried to jump, but his chute got hung up some way and he was killed. It was on this night that John and Herb's guns froze on them and they couldn't fire them if they had needed them.

We were talking around the barracks tonight about the German propaganda programs. They always play the song "Hometown." One fellow said that it made him so homesick at times that if he could find a 45 bullet he would blow his brains out. The object of the program is exactly that. It is funny to most of us. As long as we have to be away, we may as well make the best of it. From the way things look the big push has started in France, Holland, and Italy, and also Russia. There is a big snow in Germany, and that may slow things down for a little while. The biggest snow in 10 years.

Hitler was supposed to make a speech today. It was the annual beer parlor speech that he has made for the last five years. His stooge Himmler made the address. The rumors have it that Hitler is dead or wounded. Some say that he is insane rather than ill or dead.

Yesterday morning the RAF sent 32 Lancasters to bomb the German battleship "Tirpitz." The attack started at 10:30 and was over at 10:45. It sank with (70ft) of mast sticking out of the water. It was 729 ft. long with a crew of 1,600. She was 45,000 tons and sister ship of the "Bismarck."

The Germans are still sending flying bombs and rockets against this country. Most of them are aimed at the London area, but every once in a while one ends up around here somewhere. The sirens sounded here tonight.

The mission the next night of 11/12 November had seven squadron Liberators dispatched. All seven completed their mission. There were two screens this date—the northern screen by two aircraft from 36BS and two aircraft from RAF 199 Squadron. The southern screen had five aircraft of 36BS and six aircraft from the RAF 199 Squadron. The northern screen was positioned between 5406N-0405E and 5420N-0530E, and the southern screen was formed between position 5035N-0520E and 5109N 0345E. The time of the jamming for the northern screen was from 1730 to 1815 hours and for the southern screen from 1720 to 1940 hours. The RAF main attack consisted of 179 heavies on Dortmund between 1858-1912 hours and 218 heavies on Harburg between 1904-1945 hours. Results indicated the screen again effectively denied the enemy long range warning. The first plot was not broadcast until 1837 hours. Seven RAF aircraft were reported missing from those which attacked Harburg.

The prospects of extremely cold weather on the next scheduled mission must have really bothered Iredell Hutton. He wrote on 14 November:

Stand down tonight the same as yesterday. Makes no difference to me if we don't fly any because I hate like heck to fly on these winter nights. I never knew it could be so cold.

On the 15/16 November mission tragedy struck again. Five 36BS B24s were dispatched, but only four completed the mission. Liberator #42-51219, R4-I crashed on take-off. Seven crew members survived, however, two were killed. The position of screen was along a line from 5058N-0350E to 5050N-0500E to 5028N-0510E to 5000N-0442E. The time of the jamming was from 0110 to 0305 hours. The RAF main attack included 48 Mosquitoes on miscellaneous targets in Germany. The screen was again used in conjunction with spoof WINDOW dropping forces. The enemy reacted to the spoof, but not in great strength. One Mosquito failed to return from the attack on Berlin.

Regarding the crash, Lt. Walter S. Lamson (navigator) and Pfc. Leonard L. Smith (gunner) were killed in the crash at 2350 hours, one and one fourth miles from the airfield at Cheddington. Sgt. Lester Jones suffered a fractured leg. All other crew members sur-

Awards Day - Front row L-R — AVM Addison, Air Officer Commanding RAF 100 Gp. Lt. Col. Goodrich, Commanding Officer, AAF Sta. 113, Rear row L-R — Col. Webster, Commanding Officer Fighter Command, 8th Air Force, Aid to AVM Addison, Col. Sullivan, Director of Communications, 8th Air Force, Lt. Col. Hambaugh, Commanding Officer 36BS, 1st Lt. Watson, 36BS Adjutant. *Courtesy of the USAF Historical Research Agency.*

vived. The aircraft was piloted by Lt. Norman Landberg.[57] Landberg remembered the crash very distinctly:

Oh, I can picture it very clearly. The plane had been redlined that afternoon, had flown on a mission and the crew chief told me that they had repaired the vacuum system on number two engine. That was the inboard engine next to the pilot. The units were operated either on number two engine or number three, but number two was considered primary. The vacuum system operated all the flight instruments, the artificial horizon, the needle, and other pieces of equipment. I took off about three to four minutes before midnight. We took off in absolutely zero-zero [ceiling zero, visibility zero, or worst weather] conditions.

The plane had been cleared to fly a second mission on the same day, and I was flying that second mission. I just started to get airborne, my crew chief used to squat between myself and Lloyd Sanderlin, the co-pilot. He used to be on one knee and on take-off, especially on instrument take-off with a flashlight in the event we lost our instrument lights, because in the B24 at that point in time, they were not backlit lights, they were reflective lights. We had little spotlights that would hit the radium dials, so in the event that the little spotlights went out he would have had the flashlight and we would be able to see the instruments. I became airborne and my instruments tumbled, which means that the vacuum system became defective again. And at the same time that that happened all the lights went out and I had no contact, no vision at all of the instrument panel. The crew chief in his zeal to see that I could see the instruments hit me right in the eyes with the beam of the flashlight and I was completely blinded, and at that time my left wing caught [the ground effects] and we started to tumble. How anybody ever walked out of that I'll never know. I literally unsnapped my safety belt and stepped out on the ground. There was no aircraft left around me. I had a bruised knee, but I lost my navigator, Walter Lamson, and [gunner] Leonard Smith. I lost those two men. Sanderlin was my co-pilot. I was able to drag him out. The aircraft never burst into flames even though gasoline was spewing out all over the place.

Tail gunner Sgt. George Eberwine wrote of the crash in his diary:

This had to be the night we had it. Our target was to orbit around Ghent, but [the] plane crashed on take-off. It failed to blow up, thank God. It was tough. Leonard Smith and Lt. Lamson lost their lives, and we'll never know how we all got out, but thank God we did. Lester Jones broke his leg, and it looks like things are over for him. We took off at 11:48 p.m. and crashed a few minutes later. We waited some 40 minutes for help to come. The mission was scrubbed after two other ships took-off.

The injured airman, Sgt. Lester Jones, gunner for Lt. Landberg, spoke of the crash of R4-I:

We had crashed on take off. I was hurt and two were killed. I remember the navigator, Walter Lamson, was killed, he was a real quiet, religious type person. The other, Leonard Smith, was happy-go-lucky. He was a gunner. The night he was killed he was up front. I think that's the reason they were killed. They used the room upstairs with the pilot and co-pilot on take-off, and then after they took off they would crawl down into the crawl space up to the nose part of the plane where the navigator and the nose gunner stayed. They were in the process of doing that when it hit evidently. I rode in the waist as waist gunner, and I stood at the window and it was my job to check the wheels up after take-off with a flashlight because we took off at night. It was real foggy that night and you couldn't see anything. I had just told the pilot the wheels were up. The pilot didn't give any indication to me that there was anything wrong. Everything seemed to be normal. That's the last thing I remember. Of course the plane hit and it threw me forward, and evidently my leg got caught in probably the bomb bay. I remember sliding on along the ground. I knew that we had crashed. I was trying to get my leg out and couldn't. After the plane had stopped, I couldn't get out at all. The crew, George Eberwine and John Witkowski, came around and pulled me out and dragged me away from the plane. The co-pilot Lloyd Sanderlin came along and he was leaning over and covering me up after they got away from the plane in the event there was an explosion. Blood kept dropping in my face. I asked him if he was hurting and he said no, there was nothing wrong with him.

I'm sure that was blood that was dropping in my face. He probably got a bump around his head or face. He didn't seem to be hurting to amount to anything. I didn't know anything about the other two until later. They didn't tell me about what happened to the rest of them. I went on to the hospital.

The official Army Air Force report on the crash of R4-I stated: The crash occurred just after take-off for an operational mission. At the time of the accident the wind at Cheddington was west southwest at 9 mph. Visibility was 1,000 yards in fog. The Liberator took off on runway 8 and climbed normally along the 2,000 foot lane of 8 red hi-lights extending from each side of the end of the runway leading upwind to the L.M.S. Railroad tracks, which are approximately 68 feet higher than the end of runway. Beyond this point there are no lights. The B24 touched ground approximately 3,000 feet east of the railroad tracks slightly to the left of directly on line with the runway, in a field approximately 20 feet lower than the height of the railroad tracks. The aircraft was completely destroyed. An accident investigation board later determined the cause for the accident to be primarily mechanical failure.[58] The bodies of Lt. Lamson and Pfc. Smith were buried in an American cemetery near Oxford.

S/Sgt. Hutton was able to make the mission and wrote on 15 November:

We had a mission scheduled for four o'clock, but it was canceled until 9. We were about the last one to take off. We had a radio operator, Lt. Frey, to fly with us. We were going to France at 16,000

36BS Operations Officer Capt. Stutzman shakes hands with Air Vice Marshal Addison after receiving the British Distinguished Flying Cross. *Courtesy of the USAF Historical Research Agency.*

ft. It was around 1 am when we got into position. We were flying along when I saw a bright light at our same level at 6:30 [position in relation to the 12 hour clock]. I called Stevens and asked him if he saw it. He said yes and was trying to figure out what it was. All of a sudden it took off up into the stars. Never in my life have I seen anything so fast. It must have been one of the German V2 rockets. It wouldn't surprise me if the damn Huns didn't try to send a few over to the states. About 2:50 a message came through for us to return. We were to go to a base called Little Snoring on the east coast. We got there and the field was completely closed in. We circled the field a number of times and we couldn't even see the lights on the ground. Mac kept calling over the VHF trying to locate someone whose field was open.

After flying which seemed for hours a field in Northern England said their field was open. Mac asked Duke the direction to get there. Duke didn't have the coordinates, so Mac asked the field the direction to fly. They said fly 360 degrees for 60 miles. Duke told him that common sense would tell him that if he flew that he would be out in the middle of the North Sea. Mac was getting kinda worried, and so were the rest of us. He called the field which was "Mitis" and told them what Duke said. They told us to fly 300 degrees for thirty miles. In a few minutes Krueger called over the interphone and told us he would do his best to get us down. I'm quite sure that he was going to tell us to jump when he started to descend. When we got to "Mitis" the field was clear. [We] landed without any trouble. It was about seven o'clock when we landed. It was a RAF Polish station. We had chow and then went to bed.

The next day he continued:

Mac called Cheddington and asked them how the weather was. They told him if he could get there by three thirty, he could get in. We got into the plane and were ready to take off. Lt. Boesel took off, but we couldn't get our number one engine started, so we had to hang around to see what was wrong. Couldn't get it started so we had to stay. We met some Mosquito pilots and navigators. All were pretty good fellows. They were Sergeants. They only made 19 pounds a month [one pound equaled about $4 in those days]. Those boys really face the danger, too. We stayed at this base until the 18th. All we had to wear was our heavy flying equipment and boots. People could hear us coming for blocks.

Three days later on 18 November, Hutton learned of the crash of R4-I and said:

Herb, Sack, and myself were at the Sergeants' mess when a call came through for us to go to the plane. We took off about 1pm. Got back to our base about 2:30. For a change the field was open. When we were coming in to land I noticed a wrecked plane on the ground. It was sure torn all to hell. We found out later that it crashed just after take off the other night when we flew. Only the navigator and waist gunner were killed. It seems as though navigators are really catching hell in this squadron.

Hutton finally saw his buddy Joe Danahy, or "Irish," and learned more about the fate of Lt. Hornsby's crew. He continued;

The boys that went down in France came back and told some wild tales about the French. Said their electrical system went out and an engine caught fire. Only three were killed on that crew. This squadron has gone for a long time without losing a ship.

Later he wrote:

It was announced over the radio that we have four armies on German soil now. It looks as if the big push is on.

The next mission of the squadron occurred on the night of 18/19 November when the 36th dispatched five Liberators. All five completed their mission. The position of the screen was from 5050N-0340E to 5049N-0420E to 5008N-0530E. The time of the jamming was from 1815 to 2020 hours. The RAF main attack consisted of 276 Lancasters on Wanne Eickel. Mosquitoes raided Hanover, Wiesbaden, and Erfurt. The Raid Analysis Report stated that the enemy controllers were allowed no clear plotting picture. As far as could be seen, no continuous track was ever formulated on the main bomber force. One RAF aircraft failed to return from Wanne Eickel.

The next day must surely have been one of elation for the 36BS Commanding Officer, for on this day Major Hambaugh was promoted to Lt. Colonel. That evening the squadron faced its next mission when the 36th dispatched five B24s. Again all five completed

their mission. The position of the screen was between 5054N-0425E to 5036N-0450E to 4946N-0513E. The time of the jamming was from 0155 to 0330 hours. This time the RAF main attack of 56 Mosquitoes made two attacks on Hanover at 2243-2310 and 0356-0409 hours. Additionally, 42 Lancasters placed their attack on Koblenz 0258-0359 hours. The results indicated that the plotting on the formations did not commence until the bomber stream was making the final approach into enemy territory. The only evidence of enemy reaction was one Ju88 which took off at 0235 hours. No Bomber Command aircraft were lost during the attacks. The next night, that of 21/22 November, the squadron dispatched six Liberators with all completing their mission. The position of the screen was from 5000N-0530E to 5133N-0325E. The time of the jamming was from 1745 to 2150 hours. This time the RAF main attack consisted of a large force of heavy bombers attacking railway yards, oil plants, and canals in Germany. Mosquitoes bombed Hanover and Stuttgart. No results are available for this mission.

Regarding this mission, Iredell Hutton wrote:

We had a mission tonight over on the continent. We were right along the front in Holland. We were flying along and I happened to see two more of the German rockets speeding up into the heaven. Our forces have taken Metz in France. The French forces have taken Mulhouse and are moving on to the Rhine.

Leaders in RCM — Air Vice Marshal Addison and Lt. Col. Robert F. Hambaugh. *Courtesy of the USAF Historical Research Agency.*

I Walk Alone inflight over the Wash.

On 23/24 November again six squadron B24s were launched with five completing their mission. One aircraft returned early due to an engine fire. The position of the screen was 5000N-0519E to 5114N-0414E. The time of the jamming was from 2030-2120 hours. The RAF main attack consisted of 79 Mosquitoes which attacked Hanover and other targets in Germany. Results indicated that the enemy's plotting system was confused considerably. One RAF aircraft failed to return from Hanover.

On 24 November Hutton reflected on some particularly disturbing news about his brother:

Today I got the letters back which I had written Norwood. On them was written "Missing." Don't guess there is need in writing any more. Would sure love to hear from him.

He also heard some scuttlebutt about his future missions:

Rumors have it that we are going to start flying with the 8th Air Force instead of the RAF. That means that we will start flying in the daytime instead of nights. Will like that much better.

From this time forward S/Sgt. Hutton would no longer write of his missions.

Two nights later the squadron dispatched three Liberators with all completing their mission. The position of the screen was between 5046N-0520E and 4929N-0520E. The time of the jamming was from 1830 to 2040 hours. This time the RAF main attack included 86 Mosquitoes bombing Nuremburg, Hager, Stuttgart, and Erfurt. The results indicated that the presence of the MANDREL screen, followed by a force on a southeasterly course towards the Karlsruhe area, was interpreted as the cover to a major raid proceeding in another direction. One Bomber Command aircraft failed to return from Nuremburg. The next night, 26/27 November, again three squadron B24s were dispatched and all completed their mission. The position of the screen was between 4832N-0533E and 4736N-0614E. The time of the jamming was from 0215 to 0330 hours. This time the RAF main attack consisted of 249 Lancasters raiding Munich and 13 Mosquitoes bombing Karlsruhe and Erfurt. Unfortunately, the results showed there was little reaction by the enemy this date. This time one aircraft failed to return from Munich.

On the night mission of 27/28 November, things were no different. The three B24s were in position to screen in an arc over Belgium. The time of the jamming was from 1900 to 2025 hours. The RAF main attack included a raid by heavies on Freiburg and Neuss. Mosquitoes attacked Berlin, Ludwigshaven, Hallendorf, and Nuremburg. No results became available for this raid and the next three consecutive night missions. The last three nights of the month only two Liberators were dispatched, and all completed their operational missions. On the night of 28/29 November the position of the screen was 5008N-0520E-5112N-0405E. The time of the jamming was from 0440-0545 hours. The RAF main attack included heavies on Essen and Neuss, and Mosquitoes on Nuremburg and Hallendorf. The next night the position of the screen was 5032N-0520E to 5112N-0402E. The time of the jamming was 1940 to 2050 hours. The RAF main attack had Mosquitoes bombing Hanover and Bielefield. The last mission, that of 30 November/1 December, the position of the screen was 5003N-0520E to 5110-0415E. The time of the jamming was from 1904 to 2020 hours. The RAF main attack included approximately 479 heavies attacking Duisburg. Sgt. George Eberwinc logged the 30 November mission:

4hours 15minutes—Orbited at Ghent. As usual, something happened. Everything was going perfectly until we crossed over Ostend on the way back home (Ostend was in Allied hands). It seems a German fighter bomber (perhaps a Ju88) was returning to base from England and was flying near our altitude, and our Allied ground radar picked up our plane and fired a number of bursts of flak at our plane. Fortunately, our plane came out pretty good and made it back to base OK.

The new operations in support of the 8th Air Force began on the morning of 25 November. One morning in particular, the morning of 28 November, heavies of the 8AF did not go out, but three Liberators from the 36th did. They orbited over the regular division assembly area to conduct a new deception. Their operation simulated the 8AF bomber force assembly by reading from a prepared dialogue over VHF (Very High Frequency). A MANDREL screen was also put up. The normal area screened each morning was from approximately 5150N-0230E to 5300N-0300E. Various tactics of an experimental nature were employed. Col. Sullivan, Director of Communications 8AF, stated that the results were very gratifying.

In addition to the operational missions, two important test flights were flown during the month. The first, conducted on 12 November, was for the purpose of testing special SCS-51 equipment (a U.S. instrument landing system) at 25,000 ft. Capt. Graham and a crew ran the first test of the equipment on the Bovingdon range. The beam from the ground station was found to be effective at 25,000 ft. Later similar tests were run by the Lt. Angstadt and the Lt. Vowinkel crews. The 8AF would later use the findings of these tests to good advantage. The beam as detected by the special SCS-51 equipment helped to establish a bomb release line for battlefront bombing through overcast clouds. The second test made on 18 November was for the purpose of determining the distance at which MANDREL and DINA radar jamming equipment would jam VHF communications. This test was made prior to the time the squadron began to operate the MANDREL screen in conjunction with 8AF operations.

Regarding personnel staffing, the overall strength of the squadron decreased during the month. Most of the decrease was due to the transfer to various Bomb Groups radio operators who were originally assigned to the squadron for JOSTLE (the high powered jammer for R/T transmissions and suspected V2 radio control signals)

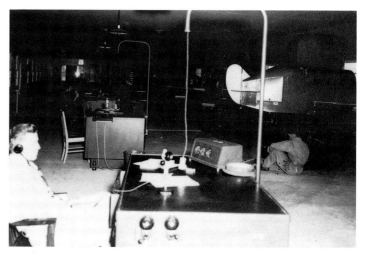

Training was always ongoing. To the right is the Link trainer, the World War II flight simulator for pilots.

training which was now suspended. The total strength of the squadron was 657 as of 30 November, as compared with 687 the month before.

In other areas, pilot training during November continued with routine Link training. Each pilot and co-pilot received approximately four hours of training in the Link. A training film entitled "Resisting Enemy Interrogation" was shown to all the crews. On Sundays instruction and training was given in land mines and booby traps, military courtesy, security, and close order drill.

The squadron still had its share of problems. Difficulty in securing ratings for worthy ground enlisted men offered a real problem. Under the tech order few if any ratings were available. The morale of the squadron continued to be relatively good, although the lack of ratings for ground personnel was a deterring factor. A number of enlisted men took advantage of the seven day furlough privilege. The combat crews were granted seven days leave upon the completion of 200 hours operational time. A completed operational tour consisted of 300 hours.

Two award ceremonies took place during the month, one on 3 November and the other on 16 November, in which one DFC, one British DFC, and twelve Air Medals were presented. (See Appendix F for details.) Surely the hearts of many of the men were elated over receiving these important medals, but at the same time saddened over the loss of five squadron airmen.

8

The Bulge - The JIGS UP

December 1944

The primary mission of the 36th Bomb Squadron during the month of December was again to provide radar countermeasures for the 8th Air Force heavy bombardment operations. Operations continued with the RAF 100 Group, but on a very reduced scale, furnishing only one or two Liberators for the MANDREL screen. Such support was given on nine nights during the month. Persistently poor weather conditions at Cheddington presented a problem from an operational standpoint. Diversions were frequent, and on occasion operations were conducted from other bases. Obviously airmen of the RAF were more accustomed to the English weather than the Americans, but the Yanks were learning fast. RAF ace Johnnie Johnson in his book *Wing Leader* wrote:

The Americans had a very healthy respect for our weather. "When you're lost over Europe," they would say, "all you've got to do is look for the biggest, dirtiest cloud. Fly to it and make your letdown. You'll find that god-damned island below!" [59]

Navigator Joseph Thome remembered:

We flew come hell or high water. We flew every 24 hours—we were up in the sky, no matter what the weather was. They, the Germans, got to understand that something was happening.

Regarding the GEE Box, his aircraft's navigational equipment used for finding his way in foul weather from the base to the missions and back, he said:

Wonderful instrument—you bet! I threw away volumes of star books after I saw that GEE box. It was very very good. One time we lost our antennae for the GEE box and I wasn't able to get to it from the inside of the airplane to the connection where it had snapped off. I just used a pair of dividers—stuck a pair of dividers in there, and I found out that by varying the distance, like you would a pair of rabbit ears on a television set, I was able to bring in signals that I never dreamed possible. And, of course it was just a distance measuring machine, but boy it was good! It was so accurate I could tell whether I was on the right side or the left side of a river. It was very very good. When I used that GEE box for the first time I said, "Man,

this is it. This is the greatest thing that has ever happened for a navigator. I've used that thing all the way in to the heart of Germany. And it wasn't supposed to go that far, but it did.

Mission requirements evolved with new and different types of RCM operations now being employed by the 36BS. Still the most frequently used operation was the MANDREL screen, which was put up for the purpose of screening the Bomb Division assemblies. It had been learned from captured enemy signal documents that the enemy had secured a great amount of valuable information from monitoring the VHF transmissions of 8AF aircraft while they were assembling. The MANDREL screen was put up to deny the enemy this information. The MANDREL screen was put up on twenty-three out of thirty-one days of the month. It was put up on every morning possible, and on many occasions in very unfavorable weather. The aircraft stations of the screen normally covered the area between 5150N-0230E to 5300N-0300E, which roughly parallels the Dutch Coast and was about 60 miles off the coast of East

Navigator Wayne Bailey at his work station with the GEE box. Fellow navigator Joseph Thome remembered the GEE Box: "I threw away volumes of star books after I saw that GEE box. It was very very good." *Courtesy of Wayne Bailey.*

B24 #42-51232, R4-J nicknamed *The JIGS UP. Courtesy of Dr. Robert F. Hambaugh, Jr.*

Capt. Graham poses beside Liberator #42-51239, R4-C, nicknamed *The Uninvited. Courtesy of Richard C. Sackett.*

Anglia over the North Sea. Normally the aircraft would leave the base at 0630 hours, turn on their equipment 30 minutes thereafter, and then proceed to their stations. They patrolled there until 1030, near zero hour, the time the Allied attacking bomber force crossed the English coast. At that time, they would leave their stations for a designated patrol, either to the north and east over the North Sea or to the south and east over Belgium and France, leaving their equipment on until they reached a designated northern or southern point. They then turned off their equipment and returned to base.

Unfortunately, equipment breakdowns persisted. On 5 December Liberator #42-51232, R4-J nicknamed *The Jigs Up* returned prematurely due to an induction coupling blown out on number three engine. The engines on this Liberator would fail again.

The missions of 9, 10, and 18 December had small loose formations of squadron B24s with fighter escort preceding the 8AF bomber stream to the I.P (Initial Point) by a set distance or a set time. The distance was 40 miles for the 9 and 10 December missions, and the time span was 12 minutes ahead of the first force on the 18 December mission. The purpose of this operation was to screen 8AF VHF transmissions. This operation was intended to deny the enemy early warning of the 8AF bombing approach which could be obtained by monitoring VHF transmissions.

On 9 December a six aircraft echelon, staggered three aircraft high, three aircraft low preceded the first bomber force along the bomber route to 4815N-0728E, where they climbed to 20,000 ft. They then proceeded to 4830N-0920E, turned right, turned their jammers off and dropped down to below bomber altitude and returned to base.

Gunner Sgt. Leo Hoffman noted the use of new jamming equipment—JACKAL—and the support by "Little Friends" on this mission:

Had 12 P51 Mustangs for escort. First JACKAL mission. Flight OK. 40 miles in Germany.

On 10 December four aircraft in echelon, two aircraft high and two aircraft low, proceeded 40 miles ahead of first bomber force on

B24 #42-50385, R4-H before the nickname *Beast of Bourbon* was painted on its nose. *Courtesy of Stanley Harris.*

B24 #42-51188, R4-O nicknamed *Lady Jane. Courtesy of Roy W. Stroud.*

JACKAL FAN ANTENNA mounted on B24. *Courtesy of the USAF Historical Research Agency.*

its route climbing to 20,000 ft. at 5025N-0610E. They then proceeded to 4858N-0752E, turned right, turned their jammers off and returned to base. On this mission squadron Liberator #42-51239, R4-C nicknamed *The Uninvited* returned prematurely with number three engine feathered. A broken oil line had caused the oil pressure to drop to zero.

Operations on 11 December had five Liberators fly over France in a southeasterly direction as far as 4800N-0700E. This mission was on the edge of enemy occupied territory. On 12 December *The Uninvited* aborted again. This time the reason was radar equipment failure.

Three days later the pilot brought back early the Liberator #42-50385, R4-H nicknamed *Beast of Bourbon*, due to a fire in number two engine.

Sgt. Lawrence Dickson, tail gunner for Lt. William Sweeney, remembered one similar incident:

Probably the most fear I experienced in my time of flying was one morning we had just taken off and there was a fire behind the left inboard engine. The pilot shut off the engine and we went around, but the fire was in the air, and when he feathered the prop the fire went out. We circled and came back landing on three engines. We found that the gas cap had not been put on. And with the tank full of gas, we had been trailing gas off the wing that was being ignited by the exhaust. I was ready to bail out.

Again on 18 December a small loose formation of five Liberators with fighter escort preceded the bomber stream to the I.P. (Initial Point) by 12 minutes. This was the deepest penetration, to points 5008N-0657E to 4934N-0657E. One Liberator #42-51188, R4-O nicknamed *Lady Jane* returned prematurely with number two engine feathered.

The new deception of spoof dialogue operations that had been tested and tried in November continued in December. On two occasions, first on 1 December and then on 8 December, days on which the Bomb Divisions were grounded, the squadron flew a spoof dialogue mission in conjunction with the MANDREL screen. The purpose of this operation was to simulate the assembly of one of the Air Divisions. The spoof was directed by Lt. Alph Wesley from 417th Signal Battalion at 8AF Headquarters, Pinetree. These spoof dialogue operations consisted of three Liberators orbiting over an area ordinarily used for the assembly of one of the bomber divisions. A prepared script was read by crew members over VHF radio to simulate the actual assembly of a bomber division. The transmitted conversation was recorded by the Signals Section at 8AF Headquarters for study. However, no report was available as to the effectiveness of this type of operation. (See Spoof Plans in App. E)

During the mission of 8 December, the B24 Liberator #42-51232 R4-J, *The Jigs Up* again aborted due to a loose gasoline line on number three engine causing a small fire.

JACKAL equipment mounted in rear waist area of B24. JACKAL had a frequency range from about 17 to 54 MC/S depending upon the tuning head used, with an output of about 1 KW. *Courtesy of the USAF Historical Research Agency.*

A secret internal RCM document dated 10 December from the Radio Research Lab addressed the deceptions and stated in part:

For your information, a VHF combined screen and spoof, plus radar screen is being planned. The purpose is to prevent enemy from intercepting our VHF; to give him impression we assemble when we don't. A possible future expansion is to extend cover up to near the border. The total number of planes for radar screen will be six. They will fly in pairs. The VHF screen will jam our channels with noise modulated but at reduced power. All our bomber frequencies will be covered. On days without operations three planes will simulate assembly. Traffic planes used coming from 36th Squadron. Present operations take care only of VHF screen and Spoof.[60]

Lt Joseph Thome, the navigator for Lt. William Corder's crew, remembered the spoof dialogue missions:

That spoofing accompanied turning on a whole bunch of noise machines. We were trying to camouflage what was behind us. Then we would deliberately let other messages go through. Now when I

Lt. Wilfred Chrisner with B24 #42-50665, R4-K nicknamed *Lady in the Dark. Courtesy of Robert McLean Senn Jr.*

say we, it wasn't only the crew, we were just turning our switches on and off when we were told to as planned by the planners. The planners were the ones that were doing a hell of a bang-up job. And every flight that we came back, why they would have knowledge of how many airplanes were dispatched unnecessarily from various German airbases. They would tell us how many gallons of gas we made them waste. The British were real good at this sort of thing. They just loved that new sort of game. We enjoyed it, too.

We had real recordings of our own [bomber assembly radio transmissions], and there were so many different black boxes in our airplane that we didn't know what in the hell they were doing, but they were labeled set number one, two, three. And we were told to turn set number one, two, three on at such and such a time and to turn it off at such and such a time. That of course was the navigator's job because we put it all in the log. To follow through on what we were told to do, I had to turn my log in. And then they [ABL] would check and see how it matched up with what we were told to do.

S/Sgt. Harry Setzer, the radio operator for Lt. Angstadt, recalled participating in the bomb group assembly simulations:

We went up about a half a dozen times probably an hour to an hour and a half before the squadrons took off for bombing runs and made comments about where we were going [the direction], what we were going to do and what not. I didn't know what we were doing. Three or four of us would be talking like we were the whole squadron, or the whole group. We were laughing and talking and going on and actually we were faking the initial take-off of the whole group. We simulated the talk among the crews.

Lt. Wayne Bailey, the navigator for F/O Young, remembered the bomber assembly spoof scripts, too:

One of the things we did each day was to put up our screen to block radar surveillance, then have a few planes behind the screen where each crew member broadcasted a script over the radio to make it sound as though the 8th was assembling for a raid.

Another new squadron jamming operation undertaken during December was one that directly supported the American ground forces. The gremlin equipment used for these operations was nicknamed JACKAL (AN/ART-3). This equipment was designed for jamming German tank communications. The first JACKAL missions were undertaken on 28 and 31 December during the Battle of the Bulge. The air route to the battle area tracked to southern Belgium where three B24 Liberators were dispatched for the JACKAL operation. (See mission track illustration.) This was the first operation of its kind undertaken in the European theater. The weather over the battle zone was not favorable. On 28 December heavy snow fell, and on 31 December there was dense fog.

Here is how the tank jamming operation request was shown in an internal secret letter excerpt from Headquarters Allied Expeditionary Air Force to the 21st Army Group (under Field Marshal Sir

Liberator #42-50622 R4-N. The nose gun turret was removed and replaced with plexiglass. *Courtesy of Stanley Harris.*

Bernard Montgomery), 12th U.S. Army Group, and First U.S. Army Group (both under Gen. Omar Bradley):

1. JACKAL transmitters suitable for barrage jamming enemy tank R/T are now available for operational use.

2. Method of Operation.

Three Liberator aircraft fitted with JACKAL transmitters will orbit the pin-point selected by the Army Group concerned at a radius of 10 miles and at a height of approximately 20,000 feet.

3. Effect on Enemy Communications.

Results of trials have shown that at no point within the orbit (a circle radius of 10 miles) will the enemy be able to communicate when his transmitter and receiver are as much as three-quarters of a mile apart, while at many points within the orbit, communication will be impossible at a range of 0.3 miles.

Requests for jamming of enemy tank communications were made to the War Room Operations Officer, Allied Expeditionary Air Forces stating the location orbited and the time of operation for the JACKAL equipment.[61]

The following are excerpts prepared and described by Capt. Sturdivant, Squadron Communications Officer, concerning the first JACKAL jamming mission flown by the squadron:

A JACKAL mission flown by this squadron was completed 28 December. Three B-24 aircraft equipped with JACKAL jammers were dispatched to arrive over the target area of St. Hubert, Belgium, at 1000 hours and to orbit within a ten mile radius until 1600 hours. One B-24 aircraft equipped with search receiver (S-27) was dispatched to operate with the jammer aircraft, orbiting around the coordinates, approximately ten to twenty miles outside of the orbiting circle of the jamming aircraft. All aircraft orbited at an altitude of 15,000 to 20,000 feet.

The following JACKAL aircraft were dispatched:

#42-50665, R4-K—*Lady in the Dark*—Flight leader pilot Lt. Ralph Angstadt.

#42-50622, R4-N—*This is It Men*—Pilot Lt. William Neller piloting the search aircraft.

#42-51230, R4-E—*Lil Pudge*—Pilot Lt. Joseph Brookshire
#42-50385, R4-H—*Beast of Bourbon*—Pilot Lt. William Bright

Lil Pudge developed trouble in the JACKAL unit and abandoned operations at 1100 hours, and *Beast of Bourbon* lost number four engine at 1530 hours. Liberators *Lady in the Dark* and *This is It Men* completed the mission. All B24s returned to base safely.

Pilot Lt. Joe Brookshire in *Lil Pudge* remembered this mission differently:

Well first they brought civilians in and they loaded three B24s with all kinds of electronic equipment in the bomb bays—about two tons in each ship. They sent me and two ships, one on each of my wings, out to fly to Bastogne and to circle over Bastogne. Our mission was to jam the communications of the German tank forces. So we got out over the British English Channel and the guy on my right wing said he was losing engines for some reason or other so he turned around and went home. When we got over Bastogne they were shooting junk at us. We made several circles over Bastogne, and the guy on my left wing said he was losing oil pressure, so he went home. I stayed over the damn place for ten hours not even knowing whether we did any good or not. I didn't know if one plane could do it or did it take all three.

Surely General Doolittle at the Headquarters 8AF must have recognized the potential importance of this mission when he wrote in an internal secret message of 19 December:

It is believed imperative that adequate fighter cover be provided missions in which the JACKAL jamming aircraft are employed over enemy territory.

Again, Lt. Brookshire saw it differently. He continued:

When I got back to the base I asked [the powers that be], "Where was my fighter escort?" He said, "You had them." I said, "Well, I never saw them." And I had P38s for escort he told me, and they got a number of German planes, I don't remember how many, that were trying to get at us. But, I never saw them. Once and

Nose art of *This is It Men*, B24 #42-50622, R4-N. *Courtesy of Arthur Ledtke.*

a while we would hear a little shrapnel hit the fuselage from the anti-aircraft. It wasn't bad.

T/Sgt. Ernest Asseln, German speaking operator, operated search receiver (S27) in #42-50622, R4-N, *This is It Men* from 1225 hours to 1500 hours and logged transmissions picked up on certain frequencies, however, he identified no German transmissions. Col. Sullivan, Director of Communications 8AF, complimented the squadron for its successful efforts.

Joe Brookshire, who flew 54 jamming missions, remembered flying Col. Sullivan in the foul weather:

I wasn't what you call a good pilot, but I was a heck of an instrument pilot because I could feel every twist on that B24. The colonel used to have me do a number of things. He had me fly the colonel in charge of communications for the 8th Air Force. The weather was so bad that they had to light a magnesium flare and put it on the runway in front of my plane so I could get lined up on it and make an instrument take-off. The flare burned out and I never saw it. The fog was so dense. So, I'm sitting there trying to figure out where the runway was. Hambaugh drove out in a jeep and rapped on the bomb bay doors and came into the plane and said, "Brookshire, I'm not going to have you fly this mission. It's impossible to get up." I said to Hambaugh, "Well, if the colonel wants to go, I'll take him." See, I was an irascible son-of-a-gun and still am, I guess. Hambaugh said, "Well, it's up to you." So, I tried to line up where I thought the runway was by looking at the blue lights on each side of the runway where I was parked. I tried to make a short field take-off. I got up to about 100 mph and it ran off the runway. When I felt that left wheel run I knew I was going too fast to stop and not fast enough to get off. So I hit my landing gear to unlock it and try to raise it up. And before it could come up the plane came down and hit the taxistrip. The guys on the ground said that my

Nose art of *Li'l Pudge*, B24 #42-51230, R4-E. *Courtesy of Sam Ziff.*

wheels hit on the taxistrip. If they had hit in the mud we never would have made it. But they hit in the taxistrip and I bounced. I bounced high enough that I cleared the railroad embankment that I knew was coming up at the end of the runway. When we got about a couple of hundred feet into the air my legs were shaking so bad I couldn't even push the rudders. When I got up to where I was high enough I told my co-pilot, who was Bob Young, "You've got it." He took over. But we got up, and when the mission was over with I am told that the colonel of the 8th Air Force got a DFC [Distinguished

B24 #42-51230, R4-E nicknamed *Li'l Pudge* on a December mission. *Courtesy of Joseph R. Brookshire.*

Flying Cross] for it, and I got a yellow telegram congratulating me.

The next JACKAL operation was repeated 31 December and was very similar to the first mission. Two JACKAL aircraft and one search aircraft were dispatched and orbited around 5004N-0542E. On this occasion the jammers were switched off while the bombers were at their targets so as to prevent any interference with instrument blind bombing that was being done by 8AF bomb groups. On this mission, one Liberator, #42-51188, R4-O *Lady Jane* aborted due to JACKAL equipment failure.

Lt Joseph Thome remembered these times:
Our success over the Battle of the Bulge was proof of American British Labs successful accomplishments. They did a good job. Our job was doing jamming, for one thing, and we were listening and we were turning our transmitters on at certain times, and it was a very successful operation. The Germans were messed up with just a few of our airplanes.

T/Sgt. Vane Glendening, flight engineer for Lt. Corder remembered:
I was dating a young lady in London and planned to be married in December of 1944. But that was delayed due to the situation of the Battle of the Bulge. Three planes would go out and fly over the battle zone jamming the tank's radio and gunners while our forces were making a desperate thrust to break out of the Bulge. We were over there all day at approximately 10,000 feet. In the morning as we crossed the German lines they would fire at us visually as we jammed their radar. They got pretty close at times, but we received no hits. You could look down and see the enemy moving back. Later in the day cloud cover prevented them from firing at us. As evening drew close cloud cover both above us and below us made things a little difficult. Our navigation equipment went out and we were at a loss to navigate our way home. We turned on our

JACKAL Liberator #42-50385, R4-H nicknamed *Beast of Bourbon* was used in the Battle of the Bulge tank jamming operations. *Courtesy of Iredell Hutton.*

36BS CO Lt. Col. Robert F. Hambaugh flew one of the December missions.

radio compass to BBC and started to follow the course. After a lapse we contacted a ground control named "Colgate." We were told to take certain changes so that they could be sure that it was us and then they directed us to fly the BBC course. After flying the course for a time the needle turned around and we knew we were home.

Lt. Jim Snoddy, co-pilot for Lt. McCarthy, wrote of one of his missions and a diversion during the Bulge:
The missions in conjunction with the Battle of the Bulge were interesting. I believe we flew at eight thousand feet. I remember a night mission during that period. We were flying in and out of the clouds, when I looked out to the left and there was a Black Widow [P61] night fighter tucked under our left wing so close I felt like I could reach out and touch it. I thought at first it was a German because of the hash marks on the side of the fuselage. I called the left waist gunner and asked him if he was asleep. He claimed that his mike cord had gotten tangled up in his gun and he couldn't transmit. The fighter peeled off and disappeared in the soup.

During this period while on a night mission we were diverted to Woodbridge for an emergency landing. The next day we experienced a delay in getting our aircraft repaired, so we decided to pour oil in the bad engine, take-off, feather it after we became airborne, and go back to Cheddington on three engines. It snowed during the night, and the next morning we taxied out with number four engine dripping oil and smoking like a freight train. We pulled out on the runway, opened the turbos and off we went. The runway at Woodbridge was very long, and I think we used it all before finally staggering into the air. I feathered number four, and we climbed out very slowly, I remember a small town right on the coast which we had to fly over, barely clearing some of the chimneys. I was glad when we made it back to Cheddington in one piece.

Navigator Lt. Wayne Bailey for F/O Young flew during this time. Bailey said:

During the Battle of the Bulge, we worked for the 8th Air Force. There was thick ground fog in England and Europe during the beginning of that battle which prevented the use of air support for the ground troops. We flew throughout that period, often using the emergency landing strip at Woodbridge. It had fog burning equipment.

We orbited over the Bulge Battle area and listened for enemy radio communications. When we heard a transmittal, we would jam that frequency. One report we got was a German asking what that airplane was doing flying around up there. Needless to say, we jammed his frequency.

The following is a summary of the various jamming equipment used during the Battle of the Bulge as described in an excerpt from a secret Air Force RCM bulletin:

MANDREL-DINA-JACKAL SCREENING OPERATIONS FOR THE 8TH AIR FORCE

The 36th Bombardment Squadron of the 8th Air Force performed five screening operations from 16-31 December. MANDREL, DINA, and JACKAL RCM equipments were employed on these missions. JACKAL jamming transmitters were first employed on the mission of 28 and 31 December, in which three JACKAL transmitters were used against the German tank communications

Lt. Col. Hambaugh shakes hands with Capt. Graham after the completion of a successful mission in December.

net. Listed below are the screening missions during the period with equipment.

DEC. 16
14 MANDREL
6 DINA
DEC. 23
7 MANDREL
5 DINA
DEC. 28
12 MANDREL
18 DINA
3 JACKAL
1 S-27 SEARCH RECEIVER
DEC. 30
2 MANDREL
4 DINA
4 MANDREL III
DEC. 31
10 MANDREL
14 DINA
2 JACKAL[62]

T/Sgt. Odis Waggonner, the flight engineer for Lt. Vowinkel, wrote of his mission of 18 December:

We started to take a mission to the area around Koblenz, Germany, but lost #2 engine on [B24 Liberator] #188, that was our own plane and had to abort. We flew a mission in J-JIG [The Jigs Up] tonite.

Soon to get his shot at radar jamming was a new arrival to the 36BS, Sgt. Art Ledtke, RCM operator for Lt. Kittle's crew. Lt. Kittle's crew was one of the first new replacement crews to report on board in December. Sgt. Ledtke kept an extensive diary and wrote on Thursday, 19 December:

Arrived in Tring by train and went out to the Cheddington air base by bus. It is an utmost secret base, the only one of its kind. It's an RCM (radar countermeasure) base. It's a new support unit for the 8th Air Force and had been developed by the RAF.

A German battlewagon went all the way up the English Channel to the North Sea undetected in foggy weather. The Germans had used RCM to prevent the British from picking it up with their radar. All the British saw were a few unknown blips on their screens. They could not identify what was happening. Later, when the skies cleared they found out. Through this experience the RAF developed the countermeasure further and formed the RCM unit. They used RAF planes and a few lend-lease American planes. After more American aid was forthcoming the 36th Bomb Squadron (H) was formed under the American 8th Air Force. Their missions are to employ aircraft to deceive or jam enemy radio navigational aids, radar systems, and certain radio and wireless signals. Our missions are not to kill, thank God, but to prevent Allied lives from

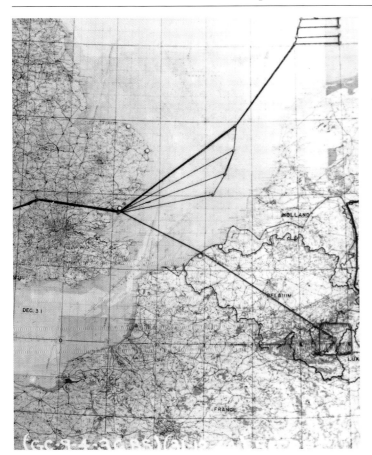

December 31, 1944 JACKAL mission plot. Jamming German tank communications during the Bulge. *Courtesy of the USAF Historical Research Agency.*

being lost. We fly patrol by throwing out a screen of electronic waves through which the German radar and radio waves cannot penetrate. Therefore, they cannot detect when or wherefrom our bombers are coming or how many. So far most of the patrolling is done over friendly or borderline territory. Lately, it is being used to screw up enemy tank communications. There is no limit to the possibility for the unit. Also, it is used to mess up the German radar controlled anti-aircraft guns, which it does effectively.

Also stationed at our base is an outfit called the "propaganda," or "paperboys," who fly all black B24s. They drop propaganda leaflets and chaff over enemy territory to confuse the enemy radar. Both the "paperboys" and our electronic group are called "Heavy" bombardment groups for security reasons.

A few buzz bombs have struck around here in the past few weeks, but none lately. I am learning Morse code. Our crew have been issued heated flying suits today.

The mission of 19 December had seven squadron Liberators providing a VHF screen in support of 8AF bombing operations. Foul weather at Cheddington prevented the aircraft from returning to base. This diversion proved fatal for most of the crew in the B24 #42-51232, nicknamed *The Jigs Up*. The official squadron record stated:

One officer and eight enlisted are missing from the crash of aircraft #42-51232. The crash occurred at about 1810 hours on 22 December, 3 miles northwest of Valley, Wales, over the Irish Sea. Those missing are 2nd Lt. William H. Lehner (navigator), S/Sgt. Arthur R. Clemens (engineer), S/Sgt. Harvey N. Nystrom (radio operator), S/Sgt. Francis J. Lynch (radio operator), and the following gunners: S/Sgt. Andrew Zapotocky, Sgt. Roger F. Gagne, S/

Lt. Harold Boehm Official Crew Photo. Standing L-R S/Sgt. Harvey N. Nystrom, 2d Lt. William H. Lehner, 1st Lt. Harold T. Boehm, 2d Lt. Donald W. Burch, S/Sgt. Andrew Zapotocky. Kneeling L-R Sgt. Charles H. Dautel, S/Sgt. Jaime Fonseca, S/Sgt. Arthur E. Clemens, S/Sgt. Roger F. Gagne. *Courtesy of Dr. Robert F. Hambaugh, Jr.*

Sgt. Jaime Fonseca, and Sgt. Charles H. Dautel. 1st Lt. Harold Boehm, the pilot, and 2nd Lt. Donald Burch, the co-pilot, parachuted to safety on the shore. The aircraft had been diverted to Manston airfield upon its return from an operational mission on 19 December. From Manston it was attempting to return to base. The weather at the base prevented landing, so diversion was again necessary. The aircraft was attempting to land at Valley airfield when its gasoline supply gave out and it became necessary to abandon the aircraft in flight. [63]

After being abandoned, *The Jigs Up* crashed into Mt. Holyhead on the shore by the Irish Sea.

The squadron Liberators had been cleared from Manston to Cheddington to Atcham airfield and then to Valley, and were not on a flight plan. Official records at the time indicated that poor weather was experienced during the whole of the day and that instrument conditions prevailed at Valley during the time of the crash. Also during this time a Brigadier General arrived from Prestwick on an American shuttle after being diverted to Valley owing to the bad weather. The weather at the time of the accident had a broken ceiling at 500 feet with an overcast layer above at 1,500 feet. The horizontal surface visibility was 1,800 yards, restricted by fog.

Lt. Ralph Angstadt, the pilot in the B24 #42-50844, R4-I nicknamed *Miss-B-Haven* said of that fateful night :

The GEE box got us to Valley. This was after flying a mission, being diverted from our own field; taking off again to come back to our field, being diverted again, being sent up to Valley.

Valley did have the low frequency navigational aid, but they wouldn't give us the frequency. So we couldn't orient ourselves. It was a foggy night. I think that the ceiling level was somewhere around 900 feet. The hills up there, some of them are higher. I remember flying around up there that afternoon, we almost landed

Liberator R4-I finally was finally able to land safely. Leo Hoffman remembered "We were flying on fumes. We didn't have enough fuel to light a match to when we got down."

up on a hill, trying to keep contact with the ground and trying to find ourselves. We were at the end of our gas tank. They wouldn't give us the frequency. They wouldn't broadcast it in the clear. No German aircraft had been over the place in a year or so, but nevertheless they wouldn't give the information out in the clear. So, we had to do it. They fired flares up from the field. We could actually see, the clouds lighted up where the flares were. We circled the flares, losing altitude. We were told that we could come on in and land as soon as we saw the field and were in contact with the field. I can still remember. It was a very emotional time. As we broke out of the overcast we were headed in almost the exact opposite of the landing direction and at the bottom of the clouds. My co-pilot and I, I signaled to him that the runway was right down practically beneath us. We had to make really more than a one eighty. We had to turn to the right a little bit in order to be able to make the one eighty back onto the field. We really made a very tight turn. We both knew that we were sucking fumes. There was no second shot at a landing. As we got off to the right a little bit, we of course lost sight of the runway, but then as we turned back to the left we could see the runway again. We were losing altitude. We really wrestled that airplane around. I can remember in order to line up the airplane, we both got on the rudder and just kind of bowed the airplane around.

When we landed, I don't think we had enough gas in the airplane to taxi us. When we got into the operations office we found out that Boehm had crashed. We were told that he had bailed out his crew. So, he spent most of the night looking for them. What we were further told was that the way that they had been able to track the aircraft was such that he was mostly over water when the crew was bailing out. When the last two or three crew members bailed out, they were actually coming over a neck of land before it went into water again. I think the airplane was finally found in water. Two of the crew members managed to parachute onto land. I think they were both picked up.

Lt. Angstadt Official Crew Photo. Standing L-R Sgt. Leo J. Hoffman, 2d Lt. James H. Yeingst, 1st Lt. Ralph T. Angstadt, 2d Lt. Walton A. Dickow, S/Sgt. James V. Marino. Kneeling L-R S/Sgt. Barry Schenberg, S/Sgt. Harry F. Setzer, S/Sgt. Henry S. Berl, S/Sgt. Frederick J. Neiser. *Courtesy of Dr. Robert F. Hambaugh, Jr.*

B24 #42-50844, R4-I nicknamed *Miss-B-Haven*. Courtesy of Jack W. Charlton.

S/Sgt Harry Setzer, Lt. Angstadt's radio operator, said:

I remember someone, a general in the pattern, coming in and he had priority. They had the frequency, we didn't. We were having trouble getting communication with the tower at that time. They kept telling us to hold and circle the flare. I remember that very distinctly. They said we had one other plane in the pattern and he was to land. That was it. I was staying right there and listening to the intercom and the communications.

Sgt. Gordon Heath, the radio operator for Capt. Sackett in the *Ramp Rooster*, also remembered the loss of *The Jigs Up* :

I recall we came back from a mission and we couldn't get into Cheddington because it was fogged in, so we were asked to divert to another base. We went in there. It was a RAF base [Manston] and we were there for one or two days. At the time the British were a little chintzy I believe on the amount of fuel that they would give. I believe our plane would take 2,800 gallons to fill it up. In that case, they would only give us a half a tank for each plane. The planes then took off for Cheddington. We expected that [it] would be clear there, but we couldn't get in because by the time we got there it was fogged in. We were diverted again [to Valley]. I heard on the radio we were all getting low on gas. Everybody was concerned. You could hear the planes talking back and forth. I heard this one crew, the pilot said two engines were out, then one of the crew, probably one of the waist gunners in the back, said, "What are your orders, Sir? What should we do," the guys said, "Bail out?" The pilot said "Yes, bail out!" That was the last I heard of them on the radio. They all bailed out. Eight of them let out in the Irish Sea. The pilot and the copilot landed on shore. There is a big hill close to this airport. It's a funny place for a hill by an airport.

Just as we were about to come in, we looked out the window, and I guess everybody on the plane saw this hill at the same time through the fog and we all yelled. Capt. Sackett rolled that B24 almost over on its back and he turned at the same time and we just

missed the hill. It was pretty nerve wrenching. I recall when we finally got down, we had just enough gas to get down and we ran right up to the end of the runway. All of us got out and just kissed the ground that night. We heard that night and the next morning that air-sea rescue was out looking for all these guys, but they never found any of them except Lt. Boehm and his copilot.

Sgt John Houlick, a gunner for Capt. Sackett, recalled what happened on *Ramp Rooster* :

We were coming back to our field. We couldn't land because it was fogged in. So, they sent us to another field and they were fogged in. So then we had to go to Valley, Wales, and that was getting fogged in. There were three planes left. We had to wait because a general was coming in and we were all low on fuel. They held us up

Capt. Sackett Official Crew Photo. Standing L-R S/Sgt. Gordon Heath, 2d Lt. Frank Scoppa, Capt. Richard C. Sackett, 2d Lt. Earl R. Siler, S/Sgt. Robert Saringer. Kneeling L-R S/Sgt. Joseph Sardo, S/Sgt. John E. Houlick, S/Sgt. Phillip Beeson, S/Sgt. Romulus B. Miller. Said Heath, "All of us got out and just kissed the ground that night. " *Courtesy of Richard C. Sackett.*

to let that general land. That general landed and then we got permission to come in. That's why we held in that pattern for a little while. In the mean time Boehm's crew, he had to be headed out to sea. They had to bail out. We had about ten drops of fuel left. I remember the pilot said there might be water down there. We had to strip off our parachutes and harness. This is a critical time! You're sweating now because you don't know whether to bail out or what and you haven't a chute on and the plane is starting to fall. So we took the chutes off and put our May West on, then put the chutes back on; then I went over by the escape hatch, the back door hatch ready to bail out ,whenever the word said bail out, then I was going to go. I had my hand on the latch ready to open the door. I was first to go and then Miller, he was the other waist gunner, he was going to go and then Joe Sardo, he was our tail gunner, he would have to go behind him. Up front they would bail out through the bomb bay doors. We were cleared to land. He [Sackett] made one pass and made the landing and that was it. That's how come we survived.

Sgt. Leo Hoffman, the Flight engineer for Lt. Angstadt, remembered Valley :

We came back off a mission over the continent and everything was fogged in on the east side of England. They diverted us over there. We were over on the west coast on an emergency landing because there was no place over on the east side that was open, that wasn't fogged in. Lt. Angstadt and Lt. Dickow were both fighting the wheel because of the wind and weather. I was handling the throttles and everything in between them. It wasn't an easy flight down. There were two or three planes that came back and boy, we just had enough gas to get down and that was it, and I mean that was ALL. We were flying on fumes. We didn't have enough fuel to light a match to when we got down. Everybody was out of fuel.

Capt. Dick Sackett in *Ramp Rooster* said:

We had been flying in the Battle of the Bulge and our aircraft were unable to get back to our base at Cheddington, so we were diverted because of weather and we went into Manston, which is an emergency strip out on the coast of England. We sat around there two or three days until we were told the weather was improving at our base. We got what fuel we could from Manston, but we couldn't get filled up.

Our aircraft departed and we were on our way back to Cheddington and we got a message that we could not get in there and they diverted us to another base. Some of the aircraft got down there, but Lt. Angstadt and Boehm and myself were then diverted to Valley, Wales. We had no alternate maps. Well, the weather improved somewhat as we flew over there, but as I remember when we got there I know I was at six thousand feet between a couple of cloud layers and the other guys were up there, too, of course, and we couldn't get any information as to how we could utilize the "Buncher" beacon [homing beacon and radio navigational aid]

there to remain in that area. So, we established a holding pattern on the previous meteorological winds that we had been given quite some hours before. Lt. Boehm was holding. His navigator was holding him, and not knowing this, of course, but apparently one of the legs of the hold was over the Irish Sea. As Lt. Boehm continued his holding pattern, he was running out of fuel. He started to have engines fail on him, so he ordered his crew to bail out. After his crew in the back got out he made a turn which took him inbound over the coast again, then he and the co-pilot bailed out. They landed on the shore, and the other eight fellows went in the sea and drowned. That's what happened.

One of the two *Jigs Up* survivors, Lt. Donald Burch, the co-pilot for Lt. Boehm would forever remember this tragic event. He recalled:

We had been on a flight which went over the continent to a town in the southern part of Germany. We were ahead of the bombing formation. That was the furthest that we ever flew over the continent, the deepest. We went in, came around, and came back according to the flight plan. It was the first time we ever ran in to any flak. It wasn't too bad, really. We came back and our field was socked in. We had to land at a field [Manston] on the southern coast of England. We were socked in to that field. We were lucky to get into it. Finally the home base called us and told us we could take off and come on up and land.

So we took off and on the way up to our base it socked in again. We couldn't land and they told us to keep on going. We had to go up to Wales. We couldn't get in there and that was mountainous country. On the way up we had lost an engine. We started to run out of gas. We ended up losing two engines, and we lost our radar and radio on the way up.

Our navigator did a fantastic job. He brought us in over the base. He said fly two minutes in this direction and make a hundred and eighty degree turn and come around and you'll be right over the base and I think we were. He told us just by wind information

Lts. Boehm and Burch wrestled the controls of *The JIGS UP*, seen here. Courtesy of Melvin A. Remus.

Wingtip of *The JIGS UP* at the edge of Holyhead Mountain and the Irish Sea. *Courtesy of USAF Safety Agency.*

that he had had accumulating on the way up there, wind speed, direction, and all.We could see once in a while a break in the clouds and mountains and some of the planes were lucky to get in there. I remember breaking through clouds and seeing the base for just a few seconds. Then we were in the soup again. The planes were having a hell of a time getting in there. I don't know how they did it, but they did. We never made it. We lost a second engine and the pilot gave the warning signal to get ready to bail out, and then he gave the final signal to bail out. I looked back in through the waist and the rest of the crew apparently didn't wait. They bailed out I think on the first signal because everybody was gone when I looked back there. Then I went. As I broke through the clouds I could see the ocean over here on the one side of me, but I was over land—barely. I landed in a farmer's field. The other guys must have gone into the water and they never found them. They never found them. My pilot was the last one to leave. We were the only ones to survive that thing.

We heard that it [the plane] did crash on the rocks on the shore there. They found parts of the wreckage the next day. But they never found any trace of the crew. They must have gone into the water with their chutes. Our two chutes opened. That was the one and only time I ever bailed out. I had a hard time going, but I went. It was a perfect jump. I think the prop wash flipped me over on my back. These chutes are ones that are on your chest. The prop wash just flipped me on my back and there I was looking at the plane. I disappeared into the clouds, and when that happened, I pulled the string. It was an easy jump. It's a good thing I didn't see the ground. It was at night time. I didn't even know the ground was coming up. I looked down at the ground and everything, then I looked up and was looking around and the next thing I know I was on the ground. It's a good thing cause I was so perfectly relaxed. I just doubled up in a heap. Kind of sprang my ankle a bit. That's all there was to it.

There were six aircraft in the landing pattern at Valley, three of which were from the 36BS. The B24s were #42-50844, nicknamed *Miss-B-Haven*, #42-51232, *The Jigs Up*, and #42-50671, *Ramp Rooster*. The other aircraft were a Wellington, a B17, and a C54. The actual RAF Valley Control Tower log identified all six aircraft in the traffic pattern by specific radio callsigns. The six aircraft were identified as follows:

1. Handful Fox = a British Wellington
2. Lawyer Baker = a B17
3. Messhouse Zebra = a C54 OR Wellington
4. Marker Item = Lt. Angstadt in B24 *Miss-B-Haven*
5. Marker Jig = Lt. Boehm in B24 *The Jigs Up*
6. Marker Fox = Capt. Sackett in B24 *Ramp Rooster*

The actual Valley control tower log with Marker Jig—*The Jigs Up* read:

Extract of Control Tower Log with Marker Jig

Time

1/17 MARKER ITEM—10 miles East of field at 4000 give landing instructions.

TOWER—Are you contact. Are you working high frequency range?

MARKER ITEM—Roger

TOWER—Hold position remain above all clouds for further information.

1718 MARKER JIG—We are behind Marker Item, we will follow him in.

TOWER—How is your gas supply?

MARKER JIG—Between two and three hours.

TOWER—Roger. Stand by.

MARKER FOX—I have two hours gas supply

TOWER—Marker Fox. What is your altitude?

MARKER FOX—6000 feet, on top.

TOWER—Remain there.

1722 TOWER—Marker Jig, give me a call.

HANDUL FOX—Can I land?

TOWER—Can you see the ground?

HANDFUL FOX—Yes.

TOWER—You are #1 and clear to land on runway 32.

HANDFUL FOX—Roger.

TOWER—Marker Jig, can you make an effective let down, how Radio Range?

MARKER JIG—You want us to let down.

TOWER—Stand by.

1725 LAWYER BAKER—I am circling the field.

TOWER—Are you contact?

LAWYER BAKER—Yes.

TOWER—Roger, Runway 32, #2 to land.

LAWYER BAKER—Roger.

TOWER—Marker Jig, hold your position. Will instruct you when to come in.

LAWYER BAKER—Are your lights on on the field?

TOWER—Lights are on the field. You are clear to land.

LAWYER BAKER—Roger.

TOWER—Handful Fox next left, follow the van.

HANDFUL FOX—Wilco.

1729   TOWER—Lawyer Baker, you are #1 to land runway 32. Go to end of runway and turn left.

LAWYER BAKER—Roger. Will you tell control that there is a hole in the clouds? It is good 5 miles North on SW leg.

TOWER—Roger, will inform control.

1732   MARKER ITEM—Tower, Marker Jig would like an immediate let down.

TOWER—Negative

MARKER ITEM—Can you tell me how many ships are down there?

MARKER JIG—Have no information about your range or anything, give info again, will you?

TOWER—(Gave Jig a long call)

TOWER—Marker Item, give message about Marker Jig.

MARKER ITEM—Marker Jig has lost an engine.

TOWER—Roger, will try to get him down as soon as possible.

1735   LAWYER BAKER—Send transportation.

TOWER—Will do.

TOWER—Marker Jig, standyb, will try to get you instructions immediately.

TOWER—Marker Item: can you pass information to Marker Jig?

1737   MARKER JIG—#2 and #4 engines are unserviceable.

TOWER—Roger, standby.

TOWER—Marker Jig, what is your altitude?

1739   MARKER JIG—We are bailing out.

TOWER—Turn on IFF #3 broad, repeat Marker Jig, turn on IFF and #3 broad.

MESSHOUSE ZEBRA—Tower, give me a call.

TOWER—Standby, stay off frequency.

1740   TOWER—Marker Jig, turn on IFF#3 broad, if you read me, turn on IFF#3 broad.

MESSHOUSE ZEBRA—May I take down 2500 feet on 180 degrees?

TOWER—Are you contact?

1743   TOWER—Marker Item, can you estimate position where other aircraft bailed out?

MARKER ITEM—I'm afraid I can't.

1745   TOWER—Marker Item, what is your present altitude?

MARKER ITEM—May I land?

TOWER—Negative, other aircraft over field.

*USAF Safety Agency Headquarters, Norton AFB, CA.

T/Sgt. James Majeur, one air controller that worked *The Jigs Up*, made his official report of the accident. It read:

The tower's first contact (1717) was with "Marker Item," who reported 10 miles East of the field at 4,000 feet and asked if he could be let down through the overcast as he was above the clouds. I asked him if he was working Henpeck Range and he said he was not. He was told to standby and remain at same altitude until further advised.

"Marker Jig" reported in at (1718), stating he was behind "Marker Item" and would follow him in. "Marker Jig" was told to standby. "Marker Fox" reported in shortly after and stated he was at 6,000 feet with about two hours gas supply. "Item" reported he had about two to three hours fuel, as did "Jig."

The tower asked "Marker Item" if it was possible for him to make a Standard Instrument Approach on the East leg of Henpeck Range. He replied he had no knowledge of the range frequency or its letdown procedure. The F.C.O. (Flying Control Officer) informed me he had three aircraft making letdowns on the range at the time.

At 1722 a British Wellington (Handful Fox) called me for landing instructions. He was contact, in sight, and cleared to land No.1 on runway 32. He landed at 1727. At 1725, a B17 (Lawyer Baker), reported contact, requesting permission to land. Landing instructions were given and he landed at 1734.

After "Lawyer Baker" landed, he reported a hole in the clouds 5 miles out on the southwest leg of the Henpeck Range. Information was passed to the British F.C.O.

Shortly after 1730 "Marker Item" called the tower, stating that "Jig" was calling me to the effect that "Jig" had lost #4 engine. Information was passed immediately to the British F.C.O. and the American Operations. A few minutes later (approximately 1736), I established contact with "Jig" and he said that No. 2 motor was also out. I tried to get an altitude and position report from him, which he could not ascertain. At 1739 he said he was bailing out and I was instructed by the British F.C.O. to tell him to put on I.F.F.

MP Roy Tackett overlooks wreckage of the *The JIGS UP* the next morning. *Courtesy of Roy Tackett.*

broad in No. 3 position. I received no "Roger" on this, so I repeated this message several times.

At 1743 I asked "Item" if he could estimate the position of "Jig." He said he could not. James Majeur, T/Sgt., Air Forces

An extract from the certified report by the Senior Flight Officer, Capt. Quintus Feland of the Flying Control Section at RAF Valley, said this:

Seven B24s from Cheddington were unable to land at base, and at 1345 hours Cheddington made arrangements with us to divert the aircraft to Valley if necessary.

At 1600 hours we were informed by the F.C.L.O.(Flying Control Liaison Officer) North West Filter Room, that 5 of Cheddington's B24s were over Atcham, and would probably be coming to Valley. He was warned that our weather would probably clamp down after dark.

At 1655 hours we were informed by Atcham that 3 of Cheddington's aircraft had been diverted to us ETA 1730 hours.

At 1720 hours the F.C.L.O. passed plots on 2 of the B24s (over Menai Straits) and stated that they had 10 minutes endurance. At 1725 hours the two aircraft were over the airfield, one at 4,000', the other at 6,000', and both reported 21/2 hours endurance.

At 1738, the first of these aircraft reported that one engine had cut, and at 1740 reported that he was then flying on two engines. At 1741 he said he was losing height and that they were bailing out.

At 1745, the Coast Guard at South Stack reported having seen an aircraft crash into the sea off South Stack.

Air/Sea Rescue action was taken immediately.

By 1915 hours two of the crew had been found, the Co-pilot near Trearddur Bay and the Pilot near Holyhead.

Search Parties from the 5th Cheshire Regt; 130 Coastal Battery, 307 Holding Battalion, Ty-Croes Practice Camp, Mona, Llandwrog, and Bodorgan assisted the RAF and USAAF volunteers from this station and the Police Force.

Boats under the control of HMS Bee carried out an intensive search, also.

By 2330 hours, information received from the pilot made it appear probable that the other members of the crew (8) had bailed out over the sea. Search parties were recalled, "the search abandoned until daylight."

The Missing Aircrew Report detailed the following in the Remarks of Eyewitness Statements:

Aircraft took off from Manston airfield at approximately 1345 on 22 Dec. 1944 for Cheddington airfield. Upon arriving at Cheddington at about 1430 aircraft was diverted to Atcham and arrived there at 1505 hours. Atcham in turn diverted aircraft to Valley. The aircraft arrived there at about 1729 hours. "GEE" was unserviceable at Atcham and pilot so notified Flying Control. At Valley aircraft 232-J was not able to maintain contact with the control tower. It was necessary to relay messages through 844-I (Lt. Angstadt). At about 1732 hours pilot of 232-J (Lt. Boehm) contacted pilot of 844-I (Lt. Angstadt) and stated that No. 4 engine was

Survivors Donald Burch and Harold Boehm. *Courtesy of Donald Burch.*

out. This message was relayed to the control tower at Valley. At about 1735 hours Lt. Angstadt heard Lt. Boehm state that No. 2 engine was out and that he had given orders to his crew to bail out. Lt. Boehm and Lt. Burch were rescued upon the shore at Holyhead on Holyhead Island. The remaining eight crew members are missing. Wreckage of the aircraft was found on the shore on the morning of Dec. 23.[64]

Near the crash site, not far from Valley, Wales, there were two eyewitness accounts. One was from the South Stack Coast Guard logbook, which read:

Date	Name of Vessel	Position	TIME
22-12-44	USA Liberator	North Stack, Holyhead	1741

Coast Guardsman Peach reported having observed vivid flash, similar explosion north of South Stack. Later confirmed aircraft crashed. Two men bailed out and picked up, eight men previously bailed out, whereabouts unknown. Extensive search combined military police and Coast Guard's concerned Rhoscolyn, Church Bay, and Holyhead, Rhoscolyn & Church Bay patrols, Holyhead patrol, searchlight and there's nothing to report. Eight men missing.[65]

The second eyewitness account of *The Jigs Up* crash was reported by Coast Guardsman Harris, the Assistant Gunner and Officer in Charge at the North Stack Gun Station. He told how it nearly cost him his life. Harris reported to his superior:

At 1740 on 22/12/1944 I saw a 4 engined airplane heading in a dive direct for the gunners' dwellings from the East, when about a 1/4 of a mile away, it canted its port wing upward and headed about west by north, narrowly missing the dwellings and powder magazine. It crashed on the edge of the rocks at high water mark about 50 yards north of the gun shed and immediately burst into flames.

Flashing of the guns of the plane and the danger by fire to the gun shed, I took the fire extinguisher from my dwelling and leaving my wife to phone the authorities, I tried to subdue the flames, and while so doing there was a sudden burst of exploding ammunition. I jumped back and slipped on the oil splattered about and dropped the extinguisher in the wreckage.

At 1922 I was informed by Naval Boat that the crew of the plane had bailed out.

The wreckage of the plane was smoldering at daylight on the next day.[66]

In the end the Accident Investigating Committee offered its opinion regarding *The Jigs Up* accident. It read:

It is the opinion of the Aircraft Investigating Committee that the responsibility for this accident lies in the following three places: First: Flying Control, the flight should have been diverted to Valley immediately after it had become evident that they could not land at Cheddington. Much valuable time had been lost by sending the flight to Atcham, whose weather at the time was uncertain. Second: The pilot should have kept a more accurate check on his fuel supply. At the time the engines were failing the pilot did not realize that he was getting short of fuel, however, during the investigation he readily conceded that this was the only plausible reason for the engine failures. Third: The crew had not been properly briefed on terrain and airport facilities in the area. The pilot had no knowledge whatsoever of the radio range at Valley, nor did he know the position of the mountains in relation to the airdrome. At the time the pilot gave the order to bail out he did not know the airport was situated on an island and the probability of his fellow crew members landing in the sea. They were depending entirely on GEE Box for navigation, and when this went out they had no means of making an exact check on their position.[67]

December would be the last full month the squadron would support RAF Bomber Command. The diary of Iredell Hutton included a newspaper clipping which detailed the 19 December mission called for by Bomber Command. It read:

Stuttgart Bombed Twice in Night—RAF Bomber Command sent more than 1,000 planes to Germany on Thursday night, with Stuttgart and Nuremberg as the main targets. A lighter attack was made on Wiesbaden. Stuttgart had two attacks in 4 1/2 hours, and when the second force of Lancasters arrived just before one o'clock they added to fires still burning from the earlier bombing. Fires and large explosions were seen at Nuremberg. Nine of our aircraft are missing.

December brought eight new replacement crews to the 36BS. Four crews, those piloted by Lts. Senn, Brusila, Wrenn, and Sweeney joined the organization on 1 December. The other four other crews, those piloted by Lts. Kittle, McKibben, Rayner, and Grubisich joined on 17 December.

Lt. Leon Hendrickson, the co-pilot for Lt. Jack Wrenn's replacement crew, who would fly 26 missions with the 36BS, wrote:

Upon arrival at Cheddington we were assigned to our Nissen hut. The local hardware store in Tring was the source of electric heating elements and wire which we jury rigged on the floor around our cots for warmth since heat from the single potbellied coal stove did not radiate very far. The stove tops were handy to prepare toasted cheese sandwiches using local crusty bread and Wisconsin cheese mailed to 1st Lt. Merlin J. Vowinkel, Asst. Ops. Officer, and also to warm and dry our socks which were continually cold and wet. I learned to go to sleep with the lights on since not all crews flew every day and some stayed up late. This never bothered Jack Wrenn, who always slept with his eyes open anyway. Our crew's operational flights were at irregular intervals. We either took our hospitality rations to share with local families, or when several days could be strung together the crew would go by train to London for sightseeing. I was fortunate to become acquainted with one of Winston Churchill's secretaries. So, on occasion I would call at Number 10 Downing Street to pick her up for several days with her family on the south coast at Bournemouth. Flight training and later operational missions precluded long term relationships, and so it was with me.

Newcomer Lt. Wilbur Kruse, co-pilot for Lt. George Grubisich said of these times:

We arrived at Cheddington after a long train ride from Stone, England. We had debarked from the "New Amsterdam," the flagship of the Dutch navy leased to Britain. They brought us to shore in a cattle ferry with crap all over the plank floor.

At Cheddington we were assigned straw biscuits (three separate cushions) and an abandoned RAF Quonset hut for billet or to sleep. This Quonset used to be an officers' mess and club, however, it looked like it was not used since WWI. We took over one bare wing—more like a machine shed for our sleeping quarters. To keep warm we were allowed two coal from the coal yard per day per man. Well, this didn't go far in this old quonset. A couple of the pilots thought they knew something about oil burners, so they conned the flight line out of some used engine oil and some copper tube with a valve for a regulator. They wound this copper tube around this round little coal stove and made an outlet into the fire box.

Two airmen of Lt. Corder's crew very happy to find a most wanted letter from home at the Station 113 Mail Room. *Courtesy of Antoinette Marchello.*

They elevated the oil can up about six feet from the rib of the quonset. The idea was to first heat the oil in the copper tube and let it drip in on the coal fire, thereby giving us both the benefit of heat from coal and no rationed oil. Well, the sad part is that it stunk so bad we couldn't stand it and us rationed ones made them stop it. As a result we slept all through December and January and most of February in our flying sheepskin suits. The straw biscuits are O.K., but you always had two cold rings around you.

At Cheddington we were just a short walk or truck ride to the subway station. I think it was Tring. We would go into London most every week for overnight. I still remember the beds stacked five and six high both side of the underground track with people who had only this place to live during the bombardment of London. The underground in London is a fantastic experience. We could go most anywhere we wanted in the tubes and did.

The general format for going to London was to go from the station and hit a number of pubs before we got to Piccadilly Circus area. This is where the Red Cross run a large Hotel, and the 8th AF pretty much monopolized this hotel. We would make sure we got rooms and often get in on the atmosphere or the environment of Piccadilly Circus, but not purchase, because that was for the mature guys. I just could never believe what I was seeing as to how the pros operated.

We often went to the Grosvenor Palace for dancing, to the best theaters or cinemas, tours, sightseeing, or the parks. I always got my hair cut in London and did what shopping I wanted, including getting a tailor to do my Eisenhower jacket. I was privileged to enjoy such things as deliberate tours of St. Paul's, Westminster Abbey, Tower of London, Madame Tassauds, Phyliss Dixie Theatrical, St. James Park, changing of the guard, and the river Thames.

Lt. John McKibben's crew, one of the new arrivals, would later suffer a dreadful fate. Enroute to Station 113, Lt. Eugene Junkin, navigator for Lt. McKibben's crew, in one of his first letters home to his family in Big Prairie, Ohio, wrote:

December 16, 1944
Dear Folks,

There certainly isn't much to write about, or perhaps I should say that there isn't much I can write about. I have never seen so much fog and rain as I have seen since I got here, but the sun did break through for a while today, so that it isn't always like this I guess.

I am living in a room with the other officers of my crew. Our room is rather small and crowded, but as far as that goes, the quarters are much better that I expected.

The country is rather pretty, but it is so damp now that you can not explore any. Right outside our window we have cows grazing. It almost makes me feel like I am home, although I still know I'm in the army. This country looks a lot like it is around home. Rolling hills, and farm houses with woods scattered around. So far it looks

all right. I'm hoping that I will get to see some castles and some of the sights while I am here. And I probably will be here long enough to see quite a bit.

Once at Cheddington, Lt. Junkin wrote:
December 19, 1944

The quarters here are clean and roomy and plenty of blankets for the bed. The blankets are the main thing, for it is extremely damp and cold this time of year here in England. And since fuel is one of the items which is rationed, it seems hardly likely that we will be able to keep a fire going all of the time.

England is a pretty country—when you can see it. Until yesterday I seldom was able to see more than 10 feet around me. It is remarkable how small their fields are and how, despite the closeness of Christmas, the grass looks as green as in the spring and cabbages grow just like it was summer.

I haven't had much chance to look around, but I have seen very few fences as we know them. Most of the fields are divided by hedges, which are much more picturesque and probably more economical than our wire fences. The cattle are mostly Ayreshire or milking shorthorns, and I presume milk is a scarce commodity, for all I

Christmas V-Mail sent by Major Harold Flynn, the Station 113 Intelligence Officer to his wife. *Courtesy of Mrs. Harold E. Flynn.*

have had is powdered milk or canned milk.

And just two days before Christmas he again wrote home:

Dear Folks,

The weather is still very depressing, and the nearest I will get to seeing snow for Christmas is the white fog that almost continually blankets us. I guess this is just normal weather for the British Isles, though.

We have begun to get our abode fixed up some. We have some small tables with chairs, some shelves, which we built ourselves, and clothes racks which we managed to beg, borrow, and steal from one place or another. We still have some dressers coming, but it may take a while to get them.

I got into London yesterday for the first time. It was mainly to buy some clothes at the Officer's PX. It is impossible to buy any clothes without going into London, and I had to have some as we are required to be dressed in full uniform almost all the time except when we are flying. And with all the mud around here it doesn't take long to get your clothes plenty dirty.

I went about seeing the town. It certainly is a big place. Mac, Stubbs,[68] and I walked all afternoon and saw almost nothing. It was a very dreary day, and I guess that we didn't know exactly where to go. We did get to Piccadilly and some of the other places. There is still a lot of evidence of the bombings, but it is being repaired or in some instances new buildings put up. In the daytime London is just like any other large city with crowds on the street, but at night it is very dark. You just have to almost feel your way along.

In one of his last letters home he said:

December 28, 1944

Dear Folks,

The weather has been much better these last few days. Although it is much colder, I would rather have the cold than the rain and mud which we had before. The ground is covered with frost about an inch thick. It accumulates all over the trees and grass at night, then falls off during the day time. It doesn't melt, but lies there on the ground like snow. I guess that is just about as near snow as I'll see here.[69]

Lt. Wayne Bailey, the navigator in F/O Bert Young's crew who would complete their missions in less than two weeks remembered this Christmas time:

One of the most heart-warming sights I ever saw was at Christmas time. We had been orbiting over the Bulge area and were returning home. It was the first day with good flying weather, and it was crystal clear. All the planes in the area had been primed and were ready to go. Everywhere I looked there were airplanes, not single airplanes, but large groups. They were flying above and below, heavy bombers, light bombers, and fighters. You name it and it was there. There will never ever be an assemblage like that again.

Lt. Robert "Bud" Thomas, the co-pilot for F/O Young, and who flew 42 jamming missions, wrote of his Christmas Day 1944:

A cold morning that started as usual—dark as hell with a 300 foot ceiling! Morgan and I checked the wings for ice. A little frost build-up, but not too bad. The wings and tail section had already been deiced. We taxied out, Chief [F/O Young] was flying instruments, and I as co-pilot was observing visual. Morgan our engineer was standing between us as he usually did on take-off and landings. Just as we got to airspeed and began our lift off, I could see by the runway lights that we were in a bank to the left. About that time Chief shouted that the flight indicator had toppled. When I glanced over and saw it I was positive we were indeed in a steep bank to the left! I screamed to Bert to fly the needle and ball and racked full ailerons and rudder to the right. We fought for the controls for a few seconds until Chief realized that we were in a bank to the left. By then we were in the fog, off course, and were at about stall speed. In what seemed to be a long time, but was really only seconds, we got our heads together and Chief took back the controls. We were then well off course, and I think we both realized we were dangerously low and were heading for the hills to the left of our runway. As we regained air speed, I really sweated and prayed that we would clear that ridge. We shouldn't have, but we did. We cleared out on top of the cloud bank at about 8,000 feet. We headed south southeast out over the channel into a beautiful sunlit morning. Chief and I both agreed that there must have been ice on that left wing. I leaned back and lit a cigarette, then I tuned in Armed Forces Radio. A bunch of British soldiers were singing "God Rest Ye Merry Gentlemen, Let Nothing You Dismay." That has been my favorite Christmas carol to this day.

For Sgt. Art Ledtke of Lt. Kittle's crew, Christmas was a special day for two important reasons. He wrote:

Airmen at Christmas Mass offering up a prayer for strength, an end to the killing, forgiveness, victory, and peace. *Courtesy of Helen J. Vieth.*

December 25, 1944

Christmas and my 28th birthday. We have been loafing around getting familiar with the area, equipment, etc. The day dawned with all the trees and buildings covered with hoar frost, no snow. We were fed extra good chow today, visited a few pubs near the base, had a few beers, felt a little homesickness, and that was Christmas.

At this Christmas time entertainer Bing Crosby, after delivering an especially moving radio broadcast, including the favorite carol "Silent Night," said:

On our fighting front there are no silent nights. But there are plenty of holy nights. I'm sure that all of us are offering up prayers to the gallant gang of American kids to whom anything that has to do with peace still seems very far away.

My own thoughts are a lot humbler than they were last year. I've talked and lived and chowed with these boys—boys whose courage and faith are something that beggar description. Seeing those GIs kneel in a muddy pasture in France brought back to my mind the lines of an old familiar prayer that I'd heard somewhere along the line back home. "God grant unto us an early peace and victory founded on justice and instill into the hearts and the minds of men everywhere a firm purpose to live forever in peace and goodwill toward all.[70]

As 1944 drew to a close Sgt. Ledtke wrote:

December 30, 1944

After dark Pappy Chido and I rode our bikes to a distant hangar to requisition some wood for the legs of a table we were making for our quarters. It was quite dark. We saw a B24 coming in for a landing about 9 p.m. with no landing lights on. It came in perfectly, bounced once, and then flames and sparks flashed up about seven feet and were accompanied by a loud screeching, grinding, scrunching noise. The plane trailed along about 200 yards or so and then ended with a crash following shortly afterwards. Pappy stood there just looking. I said "Come on Pappy, let's get over there to see if we can be of any help." We started off across the field, but on the way a searchlight truck passed us and beat us to the scene, so we did not go any closer. The plane's left wing was crumpled, and the landing gear was ripped off on its left side. There had been only four persons aboard (it had been a test hop or a training hop). All personnel were shook up but OK. One had a bruised leg.

During December the 36BS continued its transition from flying night missions with the RAF to now supporting the 8th Air Force on daylight missions. The overall mission requirements for the squadron changed to VIIIF screens with occasional bomber assembly spoofs. They also began German tank frequency jamming for the Battle of the Bulge. The weather remained foul. The squadron had suffered its greatest loss since its inception the loss of almost a whole crew—eight men for a total of 13 lives during 1944. Many 8AF squadrons had lost plenty more. One such group, "The Bloody Hundredth"—the 8AF's 100 Bomb Group—would lose over 200 aircraft, or about 2,000 airmen lives. Still, for the isolated 36th, the loss was nonetheless deeply felt. In the foxholes, life for the foot soldier was much worse. At this time 72 U.S. infantry soldiers who were prisoners of the Nazis were massacred at Malmedy in Belgium, and thousands of GIs were being killed and wounded during the Battle for the Ardennes. In 1945 more blood would be spilled on the ground and from on high.

9

VHF Screens - Ready n' Able

January 1945

By 3 January 1945 the 36th Bomb Squadron had completed its transition from an occasional support of the RAF to solely supporting 8th Air Force bombing operations with its VHF screens. This shift had begun during November 1944. On the first two nights of January the squadron flew its last missions with RAF 100 Group. For these two missions the squadron dispatched one Liberator to occupy one of the stations in the MANDREL long range warning screen. Both missions were completed successfully and without incident. (See 7 January mission track illustration.)

The main type of operation now employed was the VHF screen. The purpose of the screen was to screen the bomber division assembly. It was designed to prevent the enemy from monitoring VHF radio traffic of the 8AF bombers and also prevent them from gaining valuable information regarding the size of the force, the route to be flown, the bombing altitude, possible bomb targets, and related information.

It had been learned from captured enemy signal personnel and related documents that valuable information regarding 8AF opera-

B17F #425341, nicknamed *Vicious Virgin* from the 427th Squadron of the 303rd Bomb Group. The 36BS would now transition to a full time day job. *Courtesy of Donat E. Lafond Sr.*

tions was gained by the enemy monitoring VHF transmissions during assembly. To prevent this, VHF screen operations were flown on twenty-two of the thirty-one mornings of the month in spite of very severe weather on some occasions. The usual practice for squadron aircraft was for them to arrive at their orbiting stations two hours before zero hour and remain there until zero hour, at which time they would turn their equipment off and return to base. The special screen equipment was turned on normally about thirty minutes after take off. The orbiting stations were set coordinates over the North Sea. The number of aircraft used on each screen ranged from four to eight; the usual number being six. On 26 January it was only possible for three aircraft to take off due to adverse weather. On several occasions part or all of the aircraft in the screen took off from diversionary bases. What can be termed a "split screen" was used on 1 January and 7 January. (See mission track illustration.) A list of the latitude and longitude orbit locations which comprised the standard VHF screens for the missions can be found in Appendix E.

Personnel of the squadron decreased in January. By 31 January there were 599 as compared to 623 on 31 December. Eighteen enlisted men were relieved from assignment and transferred to the Reinforcement Command to serve in the infantry during the Allied push into Europe. Ten of the eighteen men were volunteers.

36BS armorer Sgt. Kelton Thrower remembered the call-up to help out with the ground war, and compared the foot soldier's situation with his:

They asked for volunteers for people from the Air Force to go into the Army to fight in Europe. Out of our squadron they wanted five. One hundred and ten volunteered. All the guys in our outfit were itching to do something. That's the reason so many of them volunteered.

I flew a few missions. Every time that I flew over Europe all I could think about was—well, tonight this is pretty rough, getting over there and getting back with the things we had to put up with, but tonight, if we get back, I'll have a warm dry bed to sleep in, I'll have good food, I'll have a good place to rest, out of danger. All

B24 assembly ship of the 44th Bomb group. The purpose of the the VHF screen was to screen the bomber divisions during their assembly.

those guys down there on the ground, they're here for the duration. They can't do that. They've got to live in it, die in it, and sleep in it.

The total authorized strength of the squadron was 540 officers and enlisted men. On the first of January the 36BS was placed under the 1st Air Division for administration. One new crew piloted by 2d Lt. Arthur Glick joined the squadron on 4 January, giving the squadron 25 crews.

Sgt. Peter Bittner, a waist gunner for Lt. Glick's crew, recalled:

We went over on the "Aquitania." We went to Cheddington and had additional training, but that was mostly for the pilot, co-pilot, and navigator. Most of it was hush-hush. All we knew about was; you go out, and you fly around, and then you come back. Right at the start you had your security lecture. It was re-enforced quite a way through. You always had security. It was so hush-hushed, we were over-impressed probably being new. It was a squadron where actually you didn't mix except for the officers like you did in other squadrons, because mainly you were together as a crew and you functioned as a crew as far as the enlisted men went. You didn't meet too many of the other crews.

During January one waist gunner from each crew was instructed in the operation of RCM equipment. It was planned to have the gunner replace the extra RCM operator now carried in addition to the regular crew. Peter Bittner fulfilled this additional job requirement. He continued:

They were phased out and we took over then part of what they were doing. When they took the radar man away from us, the navigator would come back with instructions and the guys in the waist had to follow the instructions in what to turn on and what to turn off in the bomb bays. He [the navigator] would call back at certain times, according to instructions, and you had your list and you followed it, then reported back to him. You gave him back the list at the end of the flight.

[For Intelligence] You had to keep track of everything you saw in the air and on the ground and report it, and up front they would write it down. And naturally, when you came back they would talk it over and see what you had seen. We did see V2 trails a lot.

Regarding those VHF screens, Bittner recalled:

We went out real early. It was still dark. We had to be in position before the other guys even got to their planes. We had to be out in our area there. Actually, when they passed us, then we could come in. We had to be on station before the other planes took off.

We were often closed in by bad weather after take-off. Our operations were more of a screening nature. When the weather was flyable the Germans knew we would be up. Jamming took many different forms. A lot of the time we would land at a British base. Signing in and getting biscuits [bed mattresses] for our stay was part of "Return Lend-Lease." Some of the time British crews would land at our base. They usually had on their best uniform in case they ended up a P.O.W.

Sgt. Lester Jones of Lt. Landberg's crew, injured at Cheddington during the take-off crash of his B24 in November of 1944, remembered leaving the airbase .

I stayed in the hospital until January when I came back to the states. That was during the time of the Battle of the Bulge. The hospital was loading up. They shipped me out sooner than they intended to because they had to make room for what was coming in from the Battle of the Bulge. When I came back over to the states, they had set my leg (the right femur), but it didn't stay. They had to redo it after I got back over here. That made me stay in the hospital about twice as long as I should have. The second time they went in they put metal pins to hold it in place. I was lucky it didn't hurt anything other than that bone. It stayed in the cast so long. I spent over eighteen months in the hospital all together, but it was mainly because they had to redo it. Of course, shipping me back from England to here made the difference, I think. I finished with about 13 missions. The rest of the crew went on and finished theirs and came back to the states just before the war was over in Japan.

Co-pilot Leon Hendrickson and *Ready N' Able. Courtesy of Leon B. Hendrickson, Jr.*

B24's #42-50476, R4-J with B24 #42-50671, R4-F nicknamed *Ramp Rooster. Courtesy of Arthur Ledtke.*

Lt. Sandberg's *Lady in the Dark* went to a diversionary field. *Courtesy of Art Brusila.*

Crashed British Wellington. Scenes such as this were not uncommon in Great Britain. *Courtesy of John Madero.*

JACKAL equipped Liberator *Ready N Able. Courtesy of Art Brusila.*

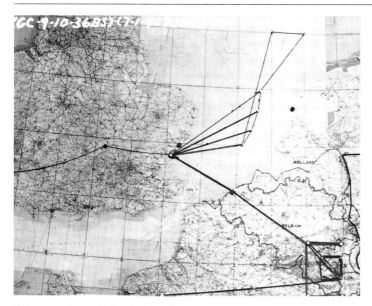

7 January JACKAL mission. *Courtesy of USAF Historical Research Agency.*

Fighters protected the Liberators for the JACKAL missions. Seen here is a P51 Mustang from the 479th Fighter Group. *Courtesy of Art Brusila.*

January had 16 days of snow, and the persistently poor weather conditions continued to be a problem at the airfield, both from an operational and a training standpoint. Aircraft diversions were frequently necessary, and operations were occasionally conducted from other bases.

Lt. Joe Brookshire spoke of one of his great talents—flying in the most horrible and challenging weather conditions:

I had done a lot of instrument flying as a cadet. When I was a cadet in basics my instrument instructor was newly married and wanted to spend time with his bride. So I trained his other cadet students and signed his name to the flight logs. I got so much flying time in basic training on instruments that when I got to advanced I could outfly my instructor. I could lose him on instruments and he'd say, "There's no way you can know where you are!" That training that I got because that instructor was a new groom saved us more than once. I could really fly on instruments. The squadron used me when the weather would be bad. If I could land, then the rest of the ships could try to come in and land. And if I couldn't land we were all diverted to a different field.

The squadron aircrews respected the hard work of the aircraft maintenance men. Bittner remembered:

Our ground crew worked in the open in the bad weather. Sometimes a piece of canvas was all they had as protection. And still they kept our plane flying.

Regarding the weather and his pilot's skills, Bittner continued:

I remember one time we came back and were going around. Our field was closed in. Lt. Glick said, "Do you want to bail out or

Sgt. Henry Suchenski, the tail turret gunner for Lt. Neller's crew shows off his painted flight jacket. They called their Liberator *Lady in the Mood. Courtesy of Joseph A. Bartus.*

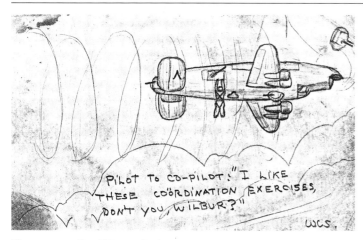

Nose gunner Sgt. Weston Smith remembered, "George Grubisich really loved to fly that B24 and it seemed to me that every time he and Wilbur went out to practice, I was conscripted to fly "spotter". *Courtesy of Weston L. Smith.*

As the nose gunner and "Spotter" Smith recalled, " I made it a point to try and memorize as many geographical features as possible during our travels." *Courtesy of Weston L. Smith.*

do you want to stick with it?" Well, we all stuck with him. He said, "If you see a hole in the clouds, we'll go in." One of the guys spotted a hole there, and he went in it and got us down.

Glick was a very good pilot. They all were. All of our officers were good. In fact, that's one of the reasons I think we were picked for the 36th.

Lt. Victor Gehres, navigator for Lt. Neller, wrote about navigating in the foul English weather:

Due to the adverse weather conditions in which we flew and usually flying over clouds thus being unable to see the ground most of the time, our preflight briefings were very important for the success of our missions. It was critical for us to have the most accurate weather forecast available. In particular the correct direction and velocity of the wind was essential, as we did mostly dead reckoning

navigation. It was sure a big help to have the GEE box as a back up to check our position. The only drawback of the GEE box was it had a limited range, going only part way over France, and occasionally it would malfunction. On one mission we were evidently given the wrong wind direction and velocity, causing us to be off course, and when we returned to the area where the signals for the GEE box would normally be picked up the GEE box failed to function. Shortly before it was time for our ETA [estimated time of arrival] to be up, as I was looking out the window the clouds suddenly disappeared and to my surprise the English coast was below, and I at once recognized our exact location, and shortly was able to give the pilot a correction in course and a new ETA, which brought us back to our base safely.

Lt. Arthur Bennett, co-pilot for Lt. George Sandberg, made many diversionary landings. He recalled:

Sgt. Smith remembered there were "Hundreds of bombers busting their butts to get back home after a mission and into traffic patterns that overlap one another and onto airfields that are spread out all over the place and all look pretty much alike." He continued, " We did this only once." *Courtesy of Weston L. Smith.*

1st Lt. Bert E. Young and crew upon completion of their missions. They were the first crew to complete its tour with the 36BS. Prior to joining the 36BS the crew flew nine combat missions with the 492nd Bomb Group. The crew presented the pilot with a silver plaque inscribed to "Chief", 1st Lt. Bert E. Young - Capable, Courageous, Understanding - from his crew - ETO 1945." 1st Lt. Bert E. Young and Crew. Standing L - R S/Sgt. Donald S. Shore, 2d Lt. Wayne D. Bailey, F/O Bert E. Young, 2d Lt. Robert Thomas, S/Sgt. Robert B. Adams. Kneeling L - R S/Sgt. Douglas G. Mc Comb, T/Sgt. Earl C. Morgan, T/Sgt. Henry W. Parke, S/Sgt. Carey P. Bellard. *Courtesy of the USAF Historical Research Agency.*

After a night mission, we were coming to our field and it was socked in. We couldn't land, and we went to the diversionary field. We came to that field and that was socked in. We circled and lost an engine. The navigator said, "You're right over it now." We looked and we couldn't see anything. He said, "You're right over it. Look underneath!" We looked underneath, and it was like a hand just parted the clouds and we were directly over the field. George Sandberg, being an excellent pilot, just chopped the throttles and

down we went through the hole, and we landed. As we were taxiing, we lost a second engine. So if somebody tells me there's not a BIG MAN upstairs, why I'll tell them they're nuts.

Bennett remembered another diversion:

We were diverted to a fighter base in East Anglia at night. The next day, the next morning when we got up and everything, some B17s were coming back from a mission. We watched as one plane came down without his tail wheel being extended, and the ball turret scraped along the runway and a big sheet of flame went up. We saw ten guys come out of that plane. They went flying out of that thing. It happened so fast, it was amazing!

He remembered the worst thing he ever saw:

When we were at Cheddington, a Lancaster on a night mission landed at our base. We had finished a mission. When we went up to the mess hall we saw the crew just sort of sitting around and just vacant stares on their faces. We found out what happened. A shell had hit the navigator's compartment and put a big hole in it and taken the head off of the navigator, which ended up rolling around in the navigator's compartment there. They couldn't get rid of it. We went down to look at the plane and there was a big damn hole right where the navigator's compartment is. That was the worst thing I ever saw. I could see why these guys were sitting around with vacant stares on their faces. They were in quite some shock when they landed.

During one of their daylight missions the Sandberg crew almost lost a crewman. S/Sgt. Tony Vaccaro remembered:

One time we were on a mission and Stan Walsh opened the latch on the door at the bottom of the plane to take pictures. We had our chutes on and his chute got caught and it opened up and went down. It didn't go all the way down. And as soon as he yelled out, a bunch of us pulled that damn thing right up, otherwise it would have sucked him right out. Well, he was all right. We saved him from going out of the airplane.

Airmen of Lt. Corder's crew having fun in their "sled". *Courtesy of Antoinette Marchello.*

Airmen ready for battle. Ready — aim — fire! *Courtesy of Antoinette Marchello.*

John Shamp passing the time playing solitaire in the barracks. Shamp would complete his tour of duty in February. *Courtesy of John P. Shamp.*

On 2, 5, and 7 January JACKAL tank jamming missions were continued in Belgium over the enemy salient in the Ardennes area. Two JACKAL missions were flown on 2 and 7 January. The gremlin JACKAL transmitters were again tuned to cover the German Tank Communications net. The JACKAL jammer was found to present a problem to 8AF bombers as well. A secret 8AF internal memo detailed one requirement for restricting JACKAL during one mission:

On January 2, 1945, JACKAL operations were carried out for six hours which included in that time, five breaks totaling over two hours which necessitated by air force use of GEE-H [blind bombing through clouds] for bombing. It was estimated that JACKAL interferes with all GEE-H users when JACKAL aircraft are within 100 miles of GEE-H situations.[71]

During these missions two or three aircraft equipped with JACKAL equipment and one equipped with Ferret or search receiver equipment, along with a German speaking operator, were

Left: London furlough. In front of Big Ben. L-R Sgts. Morin, Cuff, Mulligan, and Dickson. *Right*: Out on the town. L-R Sgts. Morin, Cuff, Dickson, and Mulligan posing in front of the Houses of Parliament. *Courtesy of Dick Mulligan.*

dispatched. On the 7 January mission a considerable amount of enemy R/T traffic was monitored. A special operator who flew with the Ferret ship logged several German transmissions during the time JACKAL was operating which indicated that the enemy ground stations were unable to understand each other during this same period. A study of the special operator's log indicated that the jamming equipment disrupted the enemy's tank communication system to a considerable degree. It was also significant that before JACKAL was operated the enemy experienced no difficulties with its inter-communications. It was therefore concluded that JACKAL accomplished its purpose successfully. The special operators used on these missions were Lt. Morris Burakoff and T/Sgt. Ernest Asseln.

Fighter cover was assigned for these missions as the squadron aircraft were to orbit over enemy territory from four to six hours. On two occasions, 5 and 7 January, the equipment was turned off during the period the bombing force was over the target as it was found earlier that the jamming equipment interfered somewhat with the GEE-H instrument bombing equipment. On these occasions the squadron aircraft left the orbiting area during the period their equipment was turned off. All totaled for December and January, there were five JACKAL missions flown during the German counter offensive in the Ardennes salient.

S/Sgt Howard Nolan, waist gunner for Lt. Sandberg, remembered the Bulge jamming:

We jammed communications between tanks in the Bulge. We could see them down there firing at us, these Tiger tanks. Every time we got to a point when we had to turn, you couldn't get out of it, you had to fly this certain pattern, for the radar to be effective. You couldn't go up or down. They seemed to know when you were going to make your turn because they had watched us all day. And every time you went to make a turn they would put up a barrage right there and you would have to fly right through it. Pretty interesting.

Black Liberator #42-51315, R4-U and her black sister ship *Tar Baby* were assigned to the 36BS a month before and had JOSTLE equipment installed. Tests had indicated that JOSTLE was superior to JACKAL for jamming. *Courtesy of Leonard N. Backer.*

The 8th Air Force Headquarters at High Wycombe and the Supreme Headquarters of Allied Expeditionary Forces (SHAEF) wanted answers to their questions concerning the details of the JACKAL missions. Had there been any more JACKAL missions? What was the tactical situation when a mission was called for? Had there been any evaluation of their effectiveness? It was learned that interest in JACKAL had decreased with the breaking up of and disorganization of the salient, and the disappearance of victims. Efforts were being made to determine how much was accomplished. It was found that, from an operational air point of view, two major accomplishments stood out: first, heavy bombers based well in the rear were called up by the ground forces, arrived at their target at the appointed time, stayed for the requested period, and experienced no loss from either fighter or flak; second, operations over the target were successfully controlled by ground stations operating in close coordination near the ground forces.

Playmate **inflight. Beginning in January 1945 the ball turrets were removed from 36BS Liberators to accomodate the jamming equipment.**

B24 #42-51311, R4-T nicknamed *Tar Baby*. Courtesy of Leonard N. Backer.

JACKAL missions were called for by the Army. Mission requests were then relayed by phone and confirmed by teletype to Army Group SHAEF, 8AF. A twelve hour signal was given to forewarn and alert the crews and to ready the planes. A typical JACKAL field order took this form:

1. The field order would be issued at 0400 hours from 8AF Headquarters to 8th Fighter Command, informing the 36th Squadron.

2. The 8AF Fighter Command would dispatch four B24 planes to orbit Bastogne from 1000 hours to 1600 hours, in a 10 mile radius.

3. The 36BS provided three planes which would carry JACKAL and one a monitoring receiver.

4. 8th Fighter Command would provide cover of 4 Thunderbolts [P47s].

5. The operation altitude flown would be between 15,000-18,000 ft.

6. Control over target would be by the 27th Tactical Air Command ground station by use of code words: "Chicago" to start jamming, "New York" to stop, and "Denver" to go home, etc.

7. RCM operators would submit receiver's operator log immediately upon return.[72]

Capt. Dick Sackett recalled:

I flew two of those JACKAL missions. The JACKAL equipment that we carried was used primarily for jamming tank transmissions on the ground. It really messed up the German operations. On those occasions we had an airplane that had a little room built in the bomb bay there for T/Sgt. Ernie Asseln, this German speaking operator, to sit there and monitor the ground transmissions. He could hear them, but on the ground, they were effectively blocked out from each other. Ernie would come back and unload it seemed like reams of paper that he would run through his typewriter, copying these transmissions on the ground. I read some of these reports. Of course he would copy them in English, the German transmissions. It was

quite interesting to read because it really did confuse them down there. The intelligence people would grab those right away, the minute we got on the ground.

During one JACKAL mission squadron Liberators drew enemy flak. Capt. Dick Sackett remembered:

One of the aircraft came back with a hole in the horizontal stabilizer, right ahead of the elevators. They decided it was caused by an anti-aircraft round fused for altitude rather than contact. It went right straight up through the stabilizer and exploded above the aircraft.

Sgt. Henry "Hank" Suchenski, tail gunner for Lt. William Neller in their Liberator nicknamed *Lady in the Mood*, recalled the flak:

We did encounter flak on this mission. An 88mm shell put a hole through the horizontal section of the tail and exploded above our plane. I was in the tail turret at the time. We saw no enemy aircraft on the mission.

Lt. Robert Pepper, co-pilot for the new Lt. Glick crew, wrote of the Bulge:

We usually flew a mission every two or three days, but during the Battle of the Bulge, the pressure was on. We flew eight days straight. I was so exhausted both mentally and physically my eyelids were fluttering and twitching. I knew that if anyone noticed it, I would be grounded, so I would not look at anyone. This was easy because everyone else was having the same trouble and were trying not to look at anyone, either.

For the new replacement crews familiarization training was essential in order to learn and deal with the unique geographic terrain and hazardous weather found in Great Britain. Lt. Wilbur Kruse was the co-pilot for the Lt. Grubisich crew which arrived in December. Kruse, who would fly 21 jamming missions, remembered starting his training at Cheddington:

We learned to approach the landing at Cheddington by orientation of heading at the tall brick flue of a brick yard. If you were headed at 200 degrees southerly and had the brick flue slightly to your left and made your 90 degree left on the base leg just as you passed the flue, then turned on your approach at exactly 30 seconds at 180 mph, you would be fairly close to the alignment with the runway [02-20]. Reducing elevation for landing was by rate of descent. Many times we set in with less than 100 feet visibility.

Lt. Kruse also remembered a special feature available on the squadron Liberators:

Each one of our planes had a destruction button. That was the last thing that we were required to do if we were forced down and faced capture. The last thing the pilot or the co-pilot had to do was to press that destruct button. We had some ultra secret types of radio and radar counter measure equipment and that was supposed to blow that up. That was the last thing you were supposed to do. You had from sixty seconds to three minutes. It was right on the control pedestal.

Lt. Sam Ziff, 36BS pilot, also remembered the destruct button. He recalled that it armed an explosive device that went off on impact. Squadron aircraft instrument specialist S/Sgt. Roy Stroud remembered the aircraft destruct button in the cockpit.

It was a red button. It was illuminated, and all they [the pilots] had to do was push a button. It had a delay so they could get out okay, bail out or escape in any way. At impact it would blow and destroy this equipment. It was just on the radar countermeasures equipment.

New arrival to the 36th RCM operator Sgt. Art Ledtke recorded in his diary on 3 January:

Mel Friedlander, my RO, and I were heading to the post theater when we heard a plane taking off. Mel said, "Gee, they fly in every kind of weather here." It was darker than the ace of spades and foggy. A few minutes later we saw a large red glow flare up on the sky to our west. One more ship gone. It was one of the Paperboys of the 406th from our base. While at the theater, it was announced that all had survived. Later, one Sgt. who had been on the crashed plane said, "After the crash, everyone bailed out as fast as they could as the ship started burning. He said he ran to the edge of the woods, tripped and fell. As he lay there looking at the burning ship, he looked up. There was a large animal standing over him. He thought, "Gee, I got out of the ship okay and now this animal is going to kill me." It was a cow.

Ledtke continued:

The weather has cleared up a little, and every day now we see hundreds of 24s, Forts, and British heavies pass overhead day and night. Usually they are in groups of twenty or so, one continuous flow of planes for hours.

The 36th has for the worst enemy the weather. Honestly, I never believed that planes could fly in such murky, foggy weather. Some times at night we are kept awake by the planes and the shooting up of rockets and flares. We'd hear a ship come in low but unseen, the flares and rockets go popping off. We usually would not see the ship. It seems the weather cannot stop us from doing our job. Even when the bombers are grounded because of ceiling zero, our unit flies the missions.

We had several air raid alerts tonight, but no action. Still no flying time for us. The weather is cold with snow. We are just waiting for the other crews to finish their tour of duty so we can use their planes. We heard a couple of V2 bombs in the distance. Tonight we had quite a time. We all chipped in five bucks to purchase a radio. We heard Axis Sally and her propaganda, which made good entertainment. She also had good American music.

So far in January the heavy bombers flew no missions due to Germany being under heavy cloud cover during the Battle of the Bulge. Our squadron had special priority on new equipment and received our new ship, R4 #42-51685 of the J series. Later, we named the ship "Playmate." Somewhere along the line we lost our bombardier, Jack Campbell, who apparently has been reassigned to another unit

JOSTLE transmitter being loaded in pit prior to being installed in B24. *Courtesy of the USAF Historical Research Agency.*

On 10 January 1st Lt. Bert E. Young and his crew were the first crew to complete their tour of duty with the squadron. Prior to joining the 36BS the crew flew nine combat missions with the 492nd Bomb Group. The crew presented the pilot with a silver plaque inscribed to "Chief, 1st. Lt. Bert E. Young—Capable, Courageous, Understanding—from his crew—ETO 1945."

The three crews piloted by Lts. Boehm, Hornsby, and Landberg were still awaiting replacements for casualties. At this time the squadron had 22 full crews. Five crews with the exception of one or two members of each crew completed their tours during the month. The crews were: Lts. Young, Boesel, Angstadt, Corder, and Vowinkel. Eight men from those five crews did not complete their tour.

T/Sgt. Henry "Hank" Parke was one of the men left behind. He had initially been with Bert Young's crew and remembered this time of transition:

I went over with Bert Young's crew. They were a good crew and I liked them. I was left behind when they went home. Lt. Boehm had lost his crew over the Irish Sea when they bailed out. They all drowned. Boehm took that awful hard, and there was nothing he could do about it. Everything he did was right. He felt responsible for losing them. They were going down, so he bailed his whole crew out and he stayed with the ship until they were all out and then he bailed out. The ones that bailed out first landed in the middle of the Irish Sea. A guy in the lighthouse could see them out there but couldn't do anything for them. That's the story we got. The reason those guys drowned, they didn't have their May West on. Boehm didn't want to fly any more. Me and one other fellow Fred Neiser went to see him. We didn't have a crew and wanted to get going. We talked him into taking us. We got him a whole crew and he flew again. I flew tail gunner for him. He was the greatest guy. When he took us on as a crew, he got a hold of us and he said, "There's only one thing I'm gonna tell you guys," he said, "You're gonna wear your May West. If I ever catch anybody without their May West on in that plane you're done flying with me." He wasn't going to have that happen again. I can't blame him for that.

I tell you that Boehm was some hell of a guy. When we landed at a different base one night, he made them set up a special table at the officer's mess cause he said his crew was going to eat with him. And we all sat together.

T/Sgt. Parke would complete his tour with 47 missions to his credit.

Morale of the squadron continued to be good as the men found fun, rest, and relaxation as forms of release during their off-duty time. The proximity of the station to the London area made it possible for men in the organization to go to London and other adjacent cities on pass frequently. The seven day furlough privilege continued.

Art Ledtke wrote of one such furlough into London:

We managed to obtain 24 hour passes, so Pappy, Bragger, Friedlander, and I left by train for London. We came in at King's Cross Station and went by subway to the west end of London. The subway has several levels. We came in on a low level. At the subway train approach is a concrete landing about three or four feet above the tracks. There we saw the 2x4 chicken wire beds or bunks that were fifteen or twenty feet from the tracks used by the subway trains which run day and night. The London people used them during the air raids. Women, children, and the elderly would spend their nights there, as Germans usually bombed at night. We came up from the subway, wandered around, went through Westminster Abbey, Madam Truseau's Wax Museum, saw the Tower of London (were not allowed in it), and saw Big Ben, etc. Stayed at a USO for the night. The next morning, while having breakfast in the basement restaurant, the building suddenly shook. It seemed like an earthquake but lasted just for seconds. We asked a waitress, "What in the world was that?" She replied, "Just a V2 had landed." When asked if she was scared, she replied, "Not especially. If it misses you, you needn't worry. If it hits you, you got nothing to worry about." Later, after breakfast, we had gone up to ground level and could see in a distance about two whole blocks of buildings were gone. The whole area was blocked off. There was a lot of damage in the West End. I do not know if it was from the air raids, or new damage from the buzz bombs or the V2s.

Once back at the base, he wrote:

We obtained some butter and oranges from the mess hall and then went by bicycles into the countryside. We asked some people where there was something of interest to see, passing out an orange or two and some cigarettes. We were told to take a certain road about one-half hour away to a farm and to see the caretaker there. We did and the caretaker welcomed us and asked us to follow him out to a large barn. There inside was stored a grand gold carriage with plush red velvet interior carvings and decorations. We looked it over carefully and climbed in and sat for a moment, climbed out and asked what it was for. The caretaker informed us that it was a coach for the King and Queen. It had been stored there for safekeeping due to the air raids. Later, we found out that it was the Coronation Coach. The caretaker received the rest of the oranges and butter and was very grateful. So were we. We hadn't expected anything like that.

The next day was most important for Ledtke. He logged his first mission:

We took off blind with the flight indicator caged. It was a rough take-off, and we had difficulty gaining altitude. We had a fellow along by the name of Wall (or Wahl) for a radar instructor. We flew over the North Sea. I got the radar equipment working with no problem. Test fired the guns. We have red colored tracers about every three or four rounds. I got in half an hour of stick time. It was fun, turning, etc., but the pilot certainly has a lot of instruments to watch. He has quite a job. But I found it a hell of a lot of fun. All of the crew members got some stick time eventually. Completed the screening at 10:00 am. Flew back to about where our base should have been. Low ceiling. We couldn't even see the ground at 200 feet. We were diverted to a British base on the northeast coast of England by the North Sea. The weather is almost the same as at our base. However, they had a system there called FIDO. The ends of the runway were edged with a pipeline with perforations in it and fuel oil burning. This made an outline of fire, and the heat burned off the fog a ways above the runways so that they could be seen. When we landed we hit the snow and slush, which flew up and cracked the right waist window. As soon as we got past the pipeline, the fog closed in and we had to follow a Jeep with a large illuminated sign on the rear to our parking area. There was almost a major troop movement there. Eight of our ships, heavy bomb ships of American, Canadian, and British also landed. An hour or so later the field was closed down tight. We had chow and went to a camp movie, ate again and then tried to find a place to sleep. There were about 200 to 300 men, EM [enlisted men], and officers sleeping in one converted mess hall, [on] double bunks about one and one-half feet apart. No room for us. We finally got bunks at 11 pm. in a regular training barracks with the ground personnel. The barracks are better than what we had been used to. The personnel were not too bad of guys. We got along well. They get forty cigarettes rationed a week (we still get seven packs). We got right to bed and asleep. Everyone was pooped out.

S/Sgt. Herman J. Wolters, a radio operator working on a special project and on detached service from the squadron died as a result of electrical shock while performing his duties at Namur, Belgium, on 19 January. No other details about his death are known.[73]

Even though a horrible war was in everyone's daily lives, a number of men in the 36BS found time for love and married English girls. Seven applications for permission to marry were filed with the squadron adjutant.

Sgt./Major Howard Buis, a squadron orderly, was one of many Americans courting an English lass at the time. He wrote:

One evening I decided to visit my wife-to-be. I was in Cheddington and going to Bletchley on bicycle with groceries (everything was rationed in England). I was slipping across the airport runway, against all rules of course, and appearing out of the blue, coming full power down the runway was a B24. The B24 blew a tire about twenty feet from me with my groceries going all over the place. It was scary and I was a little bruised.

L-R Ground maintenance techs Ross Barkley, Hugh Linebaugh, and William Fenster in front of Liberator #42-51315, R4-U. *Courtesy of William Fenster.*

The 36BS had flown 24 missions during January with only one airman lost. Weather had presented the 36th some very challenging and dangerous missions during the Battle of the Bulge. The 36BS had flown missions when the rest of the 8th Air Force's heavy bomb groups stood down. Still mission successes continued as the 36th utilized the JACKAL tank jammers and the VHF jamming equipment for 8AF screening operations.

10

The Uninvited - Beast of Bourbon

February 1945

During February the 36th Bomb Squadron continued to provide its VHF screen for 8th Air Force heavy bombardment operations. This was the only type of operation the 36BS employed during the month. The Operational Research Section of the 8AF determined that squadron Liberators equipped with ORVIL (SCR 522) crystal units that were controlled by a GASTON noise modulator (See GASTON cartoon illustration) would more satisfactorily screen the VHF transmissions than the equipment previously used. Consideration was also being given to using additional aircraft in a separate screen for jamming enemy radar. The British codebreakers, known as the "X" service located at Bletchley Park, learned by monitoring the German control stations that the VHF screen jammed the German long range warning radar devices to a certain extent, although its primary function was to screen 8AF VHF transmissions.

Lt. Robert Pepper, co-pilot for Lt. Arthur Glick's crew, which arrived in January, spoke of the screens:

We flew out alone to coordinates over the North Sea, orbited that point with our jamming devices on until the bomber formations passed through our screen and on into Europe. Then we returned to base. Each of our planes blacked out about 60 miles of the European coast, so we lined up over the channel near the coast to form a screen from the North Sea to France so the enemy could not hear our bombers behind us. Our bomber command would send a decoy force through our screen heading one direction to draw the enemy fighters away from the main force heading in another direction to the main target. It worked quite well. Our greatest fear was to be spotted by an enemy fighter. Even with our 10 fifties blazing away a lone bomber has not a prayer against a fighter.

Sgt. Art Ledtke wrote on the first day of February:
SECOND MISSION
We were awakened at 3 a.m., had breakfast of bread, beans, and dried scrambled eggs and tea. Our ship was gassed up and we

B17 Flying Fortress #338476 letter "P" of the 8AF's 100th BG. "The Bloody Hundredth" lost over 200 aircraft or about 2000 airmen lives. *Courtesy of J. O. Thompson.*

B24 #42-95221, R4-A, nicknamed *Ready N' Able. Courtesy of Erlon C. Curtis.*

36BS B24 R4-A nicknamed *Margie* (also nicknamed *Ready N' Able*) with Orvil antennas. The 36BS official file notes: "ORVILS antennas are seen mounted on underside of wing of B24. There are three antennas, which are regular VHF stubs, mounted on each wing. Each antenna is fed by two of the ORVILS transmitters, the frequencies being properly spaced so that the output of one transmitter does not affect the output of the other. Both transmitters on any one antenna must be operating while tuning to insure proper tuning." *Courtesy of USAF Historical Research Agency.*

found it had a soft nose wheel tire, but we took off anyhow and got above the clouds about 7:15 a.m. It was beautiful and sunny there. We flew off the coast of the Netherlands (still in German hands). Did our screening. We completed our screening at 1 p.m. and were on oxygen because we had to climb to get above an icing condition. We left contrails or vapor trials. No enemy sighted (thank the Lord).

We were above a solid cloud mass all the time. Returned to England. Came in south of London and dropped below a cloud layer. England sure looked good. The snow was all gone. It seemed like coming back to a different country. We picked up with another B24, "The Lady Jane," about 150 miles out and flew beside them for awhile. We passed across the main bomber stream of planes and

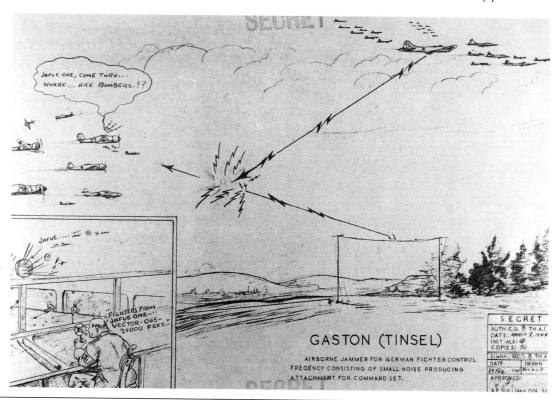

GASTON airborne jammer illustration. Another 36BS radar gremlin. *Courtesy of USAF Historical Research Agency.*

Special men in special aircraft on special missions. Lt. Glick's crew had B24 #44-10609, R4-S which they nicknamed *21 Special*. This B24 was of the first to be equipped with ORVILS. *Courtesy of Peter G. Bittner.*

finally got to see the fellows we were screening for. They were way up above us leaving contrails. Flying below them were fighters, Forts, and Halifaxes which were just above us. We returned to our base in clear weather. While the officers went to debriefing and we were waiting for them, we were served a triple shot of liquor (usually we get one after each mission). Boy, did it go [down] good! Had chow and hit the sack. We had in about eleven hours all told.

Ledtke continued:
THIRD MISSION, February 3, 1945

Took off at 6:30 a.m. and again flew over the North Sea in sight of the Netherlands at times. Passed over several ship convoys, which shot up rockets for identification. We fired a few too to let them know we were friendly. Later on we saw a peculiar column of smoke. It looked like it had circled around up to 10,000 feet and then it disappeared with a large puff at the upper end. We investi-gated, and it was the trail of a V2 bomb launched from German territory. We also saw what we thought was a liferaft on the sea below. We started icing up and then climbed above the icing conditions. Completed our mission and upon return trip we saw many many planes in the sky, and on the sea, convoys. Later we heard that over 2,000 bombers had struck Germany (The formations which had assembled behind our screen). This was said to be one of the largest daylight raids to ever hit Berlin.

The 36BS provided the VHF screen on 24 out of 28 mornings during the month. The usual procedure was for the aircraft to turn on their VHF screen equipment normally thirty minutes after take off, proceed to their orbiting stations two hours before zero hour, and remain there until zero hour, at which time they turned their equipment off and returned to base. Orbiting stations were set coordinates over the North Sea (See Appendix E). The number of

21 Special **nose art.** *Courtesy of Erlon C. Curtis.*

Lt. Mac McCrory's crew celebrate the end of their last mission by buzzing their airfield at Station 113. *Courtesy of Nick F. Senter.*

Crew of B24 #42-51232, R4-J nicknamed *The JIGS UP*. Standing L-R S/Sgt. Thomas F. Stevens, 1st Lt. William M. Mc Crory, 2d Lt. Merril H. Calisch, S/Sgt. Iredell S. Hutton. Kneeling L-R S/Sgt. Norman Morin, 2d Lt. William E. Krueger, S/Sgt. Raymond N. Herbert, S/Sgt. John P. Shamp, S/Sgt. Andrew C. Sturm — Laying down in front. S/Sgt. Hutton flew 54 jamming missions. *Courtesy of Iredell Hutton.*

B24 #42-51239, R4-C nicknamed *The Uninvited* went MIA. The Missing Aircrew Report stated that Lt. McKibben's crew was "last seen at take-off". It was presumed that the Liberator "iced up" and went down in the North Sea. *Courtesy of Charles M. Todaro.*

aircraft used on each screen ranged from six to eight, the usual number being six or seven.

Again this month poor weather conditions offered problems from both an operational and training standpoint. On several occasions missions were flown from diversionary bases. While on operational missions squadron aircraft were controlled by a local ground station, but it was planned that the squadron would soon set up its own ground control station.

At this time modified P38 fighter aircraft nicknamed "Droop Snoots" were scheduled for special operational use in the 36th. Secret RCM memo dated 3 February addressed these upcoming additions:

Lt. John McKibben Official Crew Photo. Standing L-R Sgt. Paul W. Frantz, 2d Lt. Eugene H. Junkin, 2d Lt. John W. McKibben, 2d Lt. Gaylord F. Moulton, Sgt. Max W. Oettl. Kneeling L-R S/Sgt. Raymond P. Brecht, Sgt. Robert G. Brass, Sgt. Harold E. Eckert, Sgt. Bruce E. Gist. *Courtesy of the USAF Historical Research Agency.*

From the Headquarters 8th Air Force, Office of the Commanding General

To: Commanding General, 1st Air Division
SUBJECT: RCM Program for 36th Bomb Sq. (RCM)

The three (3) P-38 aircraft (Droop Snoot) equipped with special radar and search receivers, are to be on detached service with pilots and ground crews from 7th Photo Group.

The P-38s will be flown on investigational radar search missions to known experimental and research establishments or any other points deemed necessary. Information obtained from Prisoners of War and captured documents has indicated the enemy's intention of using radar gun-laying equipment on frequencies not covered by the current employment of CARPET and WINDOW. In order to plan the future gun-laying RCM program, these new frequencies must be determined accurately.

Three officer RCM observers will be place on temporary duty with the 36th Bomb Squadron (RCM) to fly as observers on the P-38 search missions.

By command of Lieutenant General Doolittle.
(signed)
BERT A. ARNOLD
Lt. Col. AGD
Asst. Adj. Gen.[74]

Later on 6 February, in a secret internal memo from Pinetree, it was suggested to increase the 36BS airborne strength and search capability, namely for ELINT (Electrical Intelligence) to counter German control of new fighters, most likely its new jets. The memo stated in part:

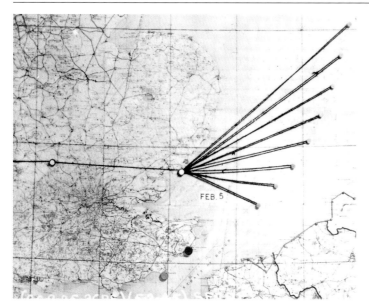

Mission track of February 5, 1945. North Sea graveyard. *Courtesy of the USAF Historical Research Agency.*

Aircraft icing — a deadly airborne hazard. Here it is seen on B24 radio antennas. Navigator Joseph Thome remembered, "We flew come hell or high water. Every 24 hours we were up in the sky, no matter what the weather was." *Courtesy of Art Brusila.*

In view of the probable increased enemy activity during 1945, and the extra burden of monitoring our own countermeasures, it is apparent that one B24 and three P38 aircraft are inadequate for the investigational work assigned.

No provision is made for countermeasures, spoof, or diversions, or for offensive missions involving homing on enemy signals to destroy the source with gunfire or bombs. Indeed it would require perhaps 30 more planes of the light or medium bomb type for this category of operations.

A formidable enemy fighter force will probably challenge our air superiority during the coming year. In addition to the efforts being made to meet this threat with improved fighter escort, it is believed that every effort should be made to disrupt the control of this new fighter force. To some extent the necessary radio and radar links may be jammed or confused by devices carried in the normal operational planes, but a separate specialized unit should be able to accomplish much more effective disruption of the control means.

Additional airborne investigation will be vitally needed during the following year to follow the enemy developments of new radar and communications devices, and to assess the effectiveness of our own countermeasures.[75]

RCM Bulletin No. 19 covering that period gave a breakdown of the 36th Bomb Squadron aircraft with their special equipment:

6 B24 aircraft each equipped with 10 AN/APT-1(DINA) and 1 AN/ART-3 (JACKAL)

4 B24 aircraft each equipped with 10 AN/APT-1(DINA) only

3 B24 aircraft each equipped with 12 AN/ARA-3 (GASTON) modulated SCR-522's (ORVILS)

2 B24 aircraft each equipped with JOSTLE IV

1 B24 aircraft equipped with FERRET equipment

3 P38 aircraft equipped with FERRET equipment [76]

S/Sgt. Hutton, who had finally completed all of his missions—54 in all, wrote in his diary on 1 February:

Since writing last we have completed our tour of duty. I'm glad in some ways that I didn't keep a diary from day to day after we started flying with the 8th Air Force, because there are a lot of things that I don't wish to recall. I've seen ships going down in flames, blown up right beside of us with none of the crews coming out. Several friends of mine that I have made over here have gone down. Some have come back, others haven't. Our plane, "The Jigs Up," went down in the North Sea [the Irish Sea, in fact]. The reason being that there wasn't enough gas to get it to another base. It couldn't return to ours because it was closed in, as it has usually been ever since we moved here.

He continued:

Mother has received a telegram from the WD [War Department] stating that Norwood is a P/W [Prisoner of War] All we can do is hope and pray that they will treat him OK.

On 5 February the squadron suffered its greatest single loss when Lt. John H. McKibben and his entire crew of ten failed to

Waiting outside the airfield Engineering Office the ground crew sweat out the return of "their" airplanes. *Courtesy of Jack W. Charlton.*

Airmen of Lt. Kittle crew outside their barracks called "Section 8". Back row L-R Louis Chido, Cecil Cox, and Norman Brager. Front row L-R Art Ledtke, Melvin Friedlander, and Bob Cortright. *Courtesy of Arthur Ledtke.*

return from their assigned mission. Lt. McKibben and crew were flying in aircraft #42-51239, R4-C, nicknamed *The Uninvited*, and were assigned to station No. 2 at 5246N-0335E. (See mission track illustration.) When nothing was heard from the aircraft it was presumed that it had crashed in the North Sea with all crew members lost. Those missing were: pilot Lt. John W. McKibben; co-pilot Lt. Gaylord Moulton, navigator; Lt. Eugene H. Junkin, engineer; S/Sgt. Raymond P. Brecht; radio operators Sgt. Bruce E. Gist and S/Sgt. Galen A. Brooke; and gunners S/Sgt. Robert G. Brass, Sgt. Max W. Oettle, Sgt. Harold E. Eckert, and Sgt. Paul W. Frantz.[77]

The Missing Aircrew Report stated that the crew was last seen at take-off. The intended destination had been 5246N-0335E (the orbit location for VHF Screen) at time 0550 for an operational RCM mission. The weather had cloud layers up to 27,000 ft., and the visibility unlimited between layers. The crew and their aircraft were believed lost at sea due to icing conditions.[78]

Pilot Lt. Royce Kittle especially remembered Lt. McKibben's crew, and for good reason:

Gaylord Moulton [Lt. McKibben's co-pilot] told me one day that he wanted me to trade co-pilots. He and I were very good friends, and he wanted to co-pilot my plane instead. I said, "Well, you've put me on the spot. I don't feel like I can do that." We dropped it there. They [Lt. McKibben's crew] didn't come back, and that bothered me ever since. If I had traded co-pilots then my co-pilot would have been the one killed.

Some of the airmen of Lt. McKibben's crew huddled around the stove inside "Section 8". February 1945. *Courtesy of Arthur Ledtke.*

HOME, ENGLAND, FEB.1945. Inside Section 8, L-R Bud Brager, Art Ledtke's feet and Cecil Cox. *Courtesy of Arthur Ledtke.*

Movie star Ella Raines, pen pal to William Butler. "She was the only star that answered our fan mail." *Courtesy of William D. Butler.*

Sgt. Marvin Klank, tail gunner for Lt. Roy Rayner's crew, spoke of a similar experience:

A memory sticks with me, too. It seems to me Franz asked me if I would fly that trip for him, and I said "no" to him. We [Lt. Rayner's crew] had flown a couple of days in a row, and I told him we were going on pass. It was to be our first pass in London. I said, "I'd be glad to switch with you, but this is the first time with all the guys [of Lt. Rayner's crew] together." It was that time when they were lost. I think it was a day or two later a liferaft was found with no one in it. That was all that was located.

Capt. Dick Sackett said of the loss:

We had an aircraft that left on a mission and never came back. Nobody heard a word from it. All we could do was just guess as to what happened. Possibly he was climbing toward his orbiting position and possibly on auto-pilot and iced-up, with the weather being what it was most of the time over there. We had a Honeywell auto-pilot in the airplane. It was about a foot square and had as many indicator lights on it as a pinball machine. It took quite sometime to set up. I very very seldom used it. Possibly a man could be in orbit by using the auto-pilot. If he iced up all of a sudden, the thing stalled. You wouldn't have time to get off any sort of a message at

all, because we didn't use voice transmissions, only the wireless key. People figured that possibly that was what had happened.

Sgt. Art Ledtke also felt a very special loss. He wrote:
February 5, 1945

Both crews in our quarters were alerted, but my crew was crossed off the flying list and did not fly, [for] reasons unknown. The other crew, Lt. McKibben's, was billeted with us and we were pretty close to each other. Lt. McKibben, Sgt. Paul Frantz, Lt. Junkin, Lt. Moulton, Sgt. Max Oettle, Sgt. Curley Brecht, Sgt. Bob Brass, Sgt. Harold Eckert, and Sgt. Bruce Gist flew the mission, and by noon had not shown up and were listed as missing. No other word was received all day. At 8 p.m. that evening, we were informed that 4 crewmen survived. That was all we found out about the crew (at that time). Personnel from Headquarters came to our quarters and collected most of their gear and personal property and left. They also said they had no further word on what had happened to the crew (at least that's what they said). Our crew isn't talking very much, but it's easy to see that each of us is wondering who the lucky four are. Death strikes plenty close. After all, we were with this crew from Walla Walla, Washington, all the way through until now. Last night we were kidding that crew before going to bed and they were razzing us. We had been living together, arguing, laughing, and sharing things. Now five are dead, we don't know who.

Sgt. Ledtke continued with his missions and wrote:
FOURTH MISSION, February 7, 1945

Off again over the North Sea. If someone crashed or ditched in the water, there was about fifteen minutes of survival time. It was thick, soupy weather, and we flew several hours blind. At 10 a.m. we received orders to stay out until 12 noon. It's really a strain on the eyes trying to see through the haze and trying to see other aircraft, etc. Every little while, we'd break through into a small clear area. We stayed at a low altitude, 9,000 feet. Boy that was a long drag. Upon return, as soon as we approached the coast of England, the weather cleared up. Large fluffy clouds at 4,000 feet. We clipped through the tops of the clouds, then went below the heavier clouds

A new crew assigned to the 36BS. Men from Lt. Harry Soderstrom's crew pose beside a black B24. *Courtesy of J. O. Thompson.*

above us. We zoomed around and between them. It was a grand feeling. Bud Bragger took the controls for a short time while still over the sea. Bob Cortight (tail gunner) yelled over the intercom, "Wow! Who the hell is flying this?" Apparently when Bud took over, he pulled the wheel down and then over corrected, which bounced the ship quite a bit. We got in about seven hours.

FIFTH MISSION, February 8, 1945

We were seventeen minutes late in getting off the ground. Our regular ship R-Roger broke a starter on one engine, so we transferred to the "Ramp Rooster," F-Freddy. We had trouble with #1 and #4 engines leaking oil on the whole trip. It would blow back on the supercharger and smoke. Bud and I in the waist of the ship kept a sharp look out on it. One generator went out on take-off.

I am now the official radar man. We flew a while at 11,000 or 12,000 feet on oxygen above the clouds. After the clouds lowered we also dropped down a little. Upon the return home we saw a circle of smoke to our right. It was a bomber heading back to land. It was smoking like the dickens. It later either quit smoking or something, anyway we lost sight of it. Off to our left and higher than us were three flights of about twenty-four each. One ship in the center echelon began to smoke, but kept formation. Finally seven chutes blossomed out, and a short time later the ship exploded about fifteen minutes from land. There were no enemy fighters about or any anti-aircraft gunfire. The Air Sea Rescue and boats in the area should take care of the crew. I wonder how they made out? We must have seen seven or eight hundred planes on our way home, plus several convoys on the water below.

One of the crews that had trained with us turned up missing. We worried about them, but later heard they had gotten lost and had landed in France (wrong way Corrigan stuff). Boy, will they ever get a razzing. I hear the pilot was one of those know-it-all

Lt. Louis McCarthy Official Crew Photo. Standing L-R S/Sgt. James C. Griffith, 2d John D. Howarth, 1st Lt. Louis J. McCarthy Jr., 2d Lt. James K. Snoddy, S/Sgt. Robert P. Mc Adam. Kneeling L-R S/Sgt. Howard F. Haley, S/Sgt. Carl E. Lindquist, S/Sgt. Fred K. Becker, S/Sgt. Richard B. Jackson. *Courtesy of Louis J. McCarthy.*

Lt. Victor E. Pregeant III Official Crew Photo. Standing L-R Sgt. Ralph J. Taylor, 2d Lt. David G. Crosby, 2d Lt. Victor E. Pregeant III, F/O Raymond J. Mattoon, Sgt. William J. Lewis. Kneeling L-R Sgt. Kenneth E. Shockley, Sgt. Frank T. Titus, Sgt. Harold J. Broadhead, S/Sgt. Edwin M. Lampson. *Courtesy of the USAF Historical Research Agency.*

guys. Well!! McKibben's crew is officially listed as MIA [missing in action]. Apparently, it was a false rumor that four had survived. All their property has been collected, and the quarters now seem deserted and quiet most of the time. We have plenty of room now. Everytime the radio comes on with "My Guy Comes Back," I get to thinking about them. That was their favorite tune. Bruce Gist never did get to see his daughter who was born while we were enroute to Camp Kilmer by train. I should feel thankful, though, I at least got to see my son. Shucks, I shouldn't think and talk about that—it gets me down in the dumps. I can understand one or two getting killed—saw plenty of death before while on the P.D. [police department] in Saginaw. But to have the ship, six [actually seven] EM and three officers to just disappear, a guy sometimes wonders. No word was heard by radio (radio silence), and no one saw them—one evening they're alive, noisy, etc., and the next day—just gone. But this is war. We have no unbelievers in God, either. This kind of stuff makes a fellow know someone is taking care of him. No luck to it at all. It's too, too, big and too much for just plain luck. It's something bigger than mere man. To be above the clouds looking at the beauty and splendor that can never be seen from the ground seems to bring a guy close to God. It's like we are intruding into a bit of splendor that only the bold, with only the help of God, can see. For if there is a slightest slip up in the chain of mechanical parts, human parts, and the supernatural, well, death is the result for the intrusion. But it's worth the chance to have a glimpse of the awe inspiring sights. It also makes a fellow feel so small and unimportant.

Beast of Bourbon parked out on the tarmac. *Courtesy of Donald Burch.*

SIXTH MISSION, February 10, 1945

A cold front kept us grounded until 8 a.m., but we got in about 5 1/2 hours flight time. We flew our regular ship R-Roger, [nicknamed Playmate]. Saw the enemy coast of the Netherlands again. The whole trip is over the North Sea, 80 miles north of Dunkirk. No incidents. We flew above the clouds at about 10,000 feet and did not see our bombers until on our way in. We were to return at 10:30 a.m. but got an order to stay out until 12 noon. The Germans had tried to jam the message, but our RO Freelander got it right after several repeats.

Sgt. Ledtke spoke of the special modifications of his ship and the equipment operation:

The bomb racks and ball turret were removed from our ship. A plywood floor was installed. The equipment was mounted on plywood and connected to the ship's power supply. It could easily be removed or exchanged. When we were due to fly a mission at briefing we were informed as to which piece of equipment was to be turned on and at what time. When we were aloft, the pilot contacted me by intercom as to the turn-on time. I would then go into the bomb bay and turn on the required sets and check to see if the sets were activated. I would then return to the ship's waist and take up my position as a waist gunner. About every half hour I'd check the equipment to see if it was functioning. Five or six hours later when our mission was over the pilot would give me the turn-off time after the heavy bombers passed our screen. That's all there was to it!

For the next mission he wrote:

SEVENTH MISSION, February 11, 1945

Took off at 6:30 a.m. While on the way to the coast, we saw some large flashes off to the south. Either a town being bombed or German aircraft being fired at. At the coast we passed through a string of 8 searchlights and we had to identify ourself. We turned off the equipment at 8:30 a.m. and headed back, flying between two layers of clouds. At our base the visibility was poor. A short time after we had landed the field was closed in tight.

February 13, 1945

Bomber missions canceled, but ours was not. Our work and our efforts were canceled out the next day. So no mission counted. The field was closed due to the weather, but we took off and flew blind to about 5,000 feet and completed the mission between two cloud layers at 10,000 feet. We were recalled at 8:30 a.m., but the message was not authenticated, so we stayed on our screening orbit for an hour longer. Sometimes Jerry would send out false reports. We flew about without seeing the water or the ground. Finally the navigator George Kimmelman said to drop down to 800 feet, and lo and behold, there was the coastline of England. We had come in right between a pier and a channel buoy. The same place as usual. Right on the nose, perfectly. Boy, George is right on the ball. We then flew about 150 miles to the base at 800 feet, just be-

The men of Station 102 Flying Control. *Courtesy of Don Hope*

low the ceiling. It was 10/10 cloud cover. We arrived at our base at Cheddington right on the nose, too. Soon after we landed the field closed down to a zero ceiling.

Referring to his diet at that time Ledtke wrote:

We are not allowed to eat "gas forming foods," cabbage, beans, etc., while flying high altitude missions. Also, we burned up a lot of calories while on oxygen and were issued high carbohydrate candies to eat while flying. This time when we returned we had a lot left over. We took the candies back to our quarters and then later passed them out to some British kids. Later, we heard that they had gotten sick to the stomach from eating the candy (too rich and they were not used to sweets). Apparently, it upset their stomachs, but the effects soon passed. No more candies for the kids.

In comparison to January the overall strength of the squadron decreased in February from 599 to 581 men. The authorized strength was 534. The decrease was due to the transfer of special radio operators to the various groups and by the transfer of other personnel to the Reinforcement Command, which also drew from the squadron during the previous month. Ten new crews were now assigned to the 36BS.

Lt. David Booker, the navigator for Lt. Harry Stone's crew, in one of the new replacement crews, elaborated on his journey across the Atlantic and his arrival in England on 13 February:

I was a twenty-four year old 2nd Lieutenant in the Army Air Corps in January 1945 when I set sail with Lt. Harry Stone and five other B24 crew members on a tramp steamer for England. There were about 250 Air Corps personnel on the ship in a convoy. We officers were served meals in a dining room complete with table clothed tables. The enlisted men ate cafeteria style. The officers had small cabins with bunk beds for four. The enlisted slept in a dormitory type area.

The trip over was rather uneventful. I remember the beautiful green color of the sea; a submarine alert, the blackouts at night, and an amateur (very amateurish) show put on by members of the

Station 113 flying control tower. *Courtesy of Frank J. Trovato.*

group. We landed at Bournemouth, England, spent two or three nights in tents, and then took a train to our assigned airfield, Cheddington.

When we arrived we discovered we had been assigned to a squadron engaged in radio and radar jamming. This explained why our bombardier had been reassigned before we left the states. Obviously we would be doing no bombing. Our flights were generously uneventful. I had gone through months of training in various locations in the states, including gunnery and navigation schools. None of my training, however, had prepared me for the kind of navigational methods we used in England. Some of it was by using airfields (there were hundreds), railway lines, and forests as checkpoints. (Forests in England are managed in such a way that their outlines change very little over a long period of time.) Most of the time we relied on the GEE box. This was an electronic device similar to LORAN, except faster. It was faster because you could get two lines of position simultaneously, thus having a "fix" of your location in 15 seconds. With LORAN you got one line of position at a time and had to make some adjustment for the distance you had traveled between getting the first and second line of position. We had not used LORAN or GEE box in training, but luckily it took only a few hours' training to become proficient.

When we weren't flying we spent our time playing cards; bridge, poker, and red dog; riding bikes, writing letters home, or drinking beer. Red Dog was a gambling game with high risks. People tended to win big or lose big very quickly.

Sometimes other things interfered with writing the daily letter, so we would write two letters in one day with different dates. Girls or women were always on our mind. I had grown up with one sister and a half dozen girl cousins and no males my age. I married before I was 21, and my wife and I spent a lot of time together. There were lots of females available in Peterborough and other local towns. My interest in them was for companionship and someone to dance with. This wasn't the case for a lot of my colleagues. Sex was

Pilot Victor E. Pregeant III - Known by Roy Rayner as "The OPERA-TOR".

Station 113 Special Staff Officer's on 2/26/45. This photograph was taken the day before the 36BS moved to Alconbury. *Courtesy of Bernard Brodien.*

the major topic of conversation. Some English girls had the belief that if you had sex laying down you were a whore. A lot of sex took place behind buildings in a standing position. There was a saying among the British, especially the British Tommies (soldiers), that the only thing wrong with Americans was, "They're overpaid, over-sexed, and over here." Not only was France invaded, but so was England—by their American allies. (According to many British Tommies.)

One character was not used to being deprived of sex. He was also very cautious about the problems of sexual diseases. Shortly after we arrived in Alconbury he went to London and met a young lady. On the way back to Peterborough, they had sex on the floor of the train compartment. He then installed her in an apartment, sent her to the Air Corps health office for a medical exam, and spent most of his time at the apartment. He also engaged in what sounded like an all day orgy with two young ladies who spent the day in the

enlisted men's room. I was definitely jealous, because I was married and believed in monogamy.

From Cheddington we moved to Alconbury near Peterborough due north of London. This was a much more comfortable field, both for flying and living accommodations. The officers lived in a one story dormitory type building with metal cots (not bunk beds). There were probably twenty of us in one big room. It was difficult to have any privacy, although we tried a variety of ways by moving beds and other furniture around. The enlisted crew members were in smaller rooms in another building, with bunk beds about eight men to a room.

We made occasional trips to London. We stayed at the Red Cross facilities. One night I remember hearing a V1 rocket. They made a ticking noise as they flew overhead. They were relatively slow, and you never knew when they would stop moving forward and head for the ground. The V2s, the next generation of rockets, were silent and probably less scary.

We went to a number of stage shows. Some of them included nude women who had to stay stationary. Apparently if they moved the show would be closed. One play I remember seeing was "Arsenic and Old Lace." Piccadilly Circus was where the professional girls hung out. There was one restriction—they had to keep moving as they solicited for business.

The big purchases my pilot and I made in London were ivory chess sets. They cost around 25 pounds ($100). I still have a few of the pieces. I believe there was always confusion in our minds as to the value of the money we were spending. We would call them pounds, but I believe we thought of them as American dollars. $100 was a lot of money to spend on anything in those days.

We learned that our task was to fly out over the North Sea, form a line with other planes, and turn on our electronic equipment to mask the movements and radio conversations of the bombers forming up over East Anglia. As they would head for Europe, we would head back to our base for breakfast, bridge, poker, and more sleep.

Truck convoy on the road to Station 102 Alconbury. *Courtesy of Charles M. Todaro.*

Moving to Station 102 Alconbury. *Courtesy of Arthur Ledtke.*

We tended to fly regardless of the weather. I believe this was based on the theory that if we flew the Germans would expect the bombers even in weather unsuitable for bombing. Thus, the Germans would waste their resources, including the energy of personnel.

Pilot Lt. Harry Soderstrom's replacement crew arrived on February 13. They faced similar hazards as earlier crews. Soderstrom recalled:

On a couple of occasions I happened to be on a training mission that involved a flight late in the afternoon, so that we returned to base after dark. The RAF flew most of their bombing missions at night, and as we would be returning to base, we would be flying against the flight of the RAF bombers. The problem was that they always flew single plane sorties with no apparent formation or order to the flights. The sky seemed to be full of RAF bombers, and they ALL seemed to be heading at US.

When the crew was assembled I was not only the "old man," I was the senior with regard to chronological age. Everyone else was younger than me. I believe the ages ran from 18-22. Just kids, right?

Art Ledtke's missions continued. He wrote:
EIGHTH MISSION, February 17, 1945

Today we took off flying blind again and got up a couple of thousand feet, then broke clear of the overcast. While out over the sea, we saw a V2 bomb take off from Holland and climb up into the sky and disappear—saw a flash and a streamer of fire and smoke shoot up, then what looked like a comet or meteorite go on up further until it finally disappeared among the stars, headed toward London. The rest of the flight was uneventful, except we crossed under the bomber stream, about 1,500 strong, including fighter escort. Man, I never saw so many planes in the sky. Flights of 50 to 75 planes on each side of us headed toward Germany. The sky was just crowded as far as we could see. We returned to our base and all the way there we never saw the ground. There was a ground fog all the way there. All we could see was the tops of buildings and trees and the white smoke of a train puffing along on the tracks. Apparently the fog was about fifteen feet high above the ground. It was an odd feeling. We were diverted 100 miles or so to Heilis, an emergency base. There the sky was clear and beautiful. We landed, had chow, and then looked over some black colored beat up Forts (battle weary), Navy "Cats"—Amphibians, etc. We left there at 2:50 p.m. to return to our home base. There we had to shoot the field six times before we could land because of the ground fog. The ground personnel shot up flares and rockets so we could locate the field. After we had landed, it did not look too bad from the ground. But the other ships coming in had the same trouble in trying to land.

Lt. William Oldershaw's crew were assigned to the 36BS from the 70th Replacement Depot on February 17. This crew almost didn't

make it across the Atlantic. S/Sgt. Connie Kazak, the flight engineer, wrote about the trip preparation and the good and bad of the flight over:

In Long Island, New York, we picked up a new B24J with very little flying time on it. All it had logged was flying time from the factory, in tests flights, and the flight to Mitchel Field.

The next day we got news that the plane we were going to fly overseas had damaged plexiglass in the nose and that a crew from the factory would be flown in to repair the damage. As it turned out we were delayed eleven days before the repairs were completed.

That was a good deal for me since my buddy on the plane, Carlo Rizzi, had grown up in the Bronx in New York City and had family and friends there. Carlo's sister Mary, whom I had been writing, came to see her brother before he was to leave for overseas. Now this was a great chance for me to meet this lovely young lady in person. And after the war was over Mary would become my wife and loved one.

After eleven days of traveling to New York City and back to Long Island the plexiglass in our plane was replaced with a new one. Our next stop was Bangor, Maine, where we were into a lot of snow and had an overnight stay with -30 degree temperatures. Next we went to Goose Bay, Labrador. When we landed we parked alongside many B24s, B17s, and other Army planes waiting to make the trip across the water. The next day I went out to look over our plane and to check the top of the plane's wings for oil. We had to dilute it so it wouldn't clog up because of the sub-zero temperatures. I told our pilot Bill Oldershaw it would have to be cleaned off before we took our long trip to England. He told me to get the crew and do it. So we got gasoline and towels and at 50 degrees below we cleaned off all the oil. It wasn't an easy job.

Soon we were told to get ready and pack up. All the planes were prepared, and we would leave tonight. The night was again very cold, with the temperature way below 50 degrees. Me and the rest of the crew sat in the cold plane waiting for Bill Oldershaw and John Wilson, the co-pilot, and Ike [Isaac Benghiat] to return

Lt. Paul Pond's crew and buddies with their B24 *Tar Baby. Courtesy of Leonard N. Backer.*

from briefing on the route trip to England. When they came back we started the engines. It was late at night, and the poor men of our crew in the waist section were half frozen because of no heat in the back of the plane. Now we just sat there waiting to move out to taxi into position. There were many B24s and B17s ahead of us, and with the control tower spacing each aircraft's departure by fifteen minutes, I was very worried that we would run out of fuel supply for our electrical auxiliary unit which furnished our electrical power until we got airborne. If we ran out of electrical power we wouldn't have lights or power to open the bomb bay doors and other parts that required electricity.

We finally reached the take-off position. When at last we received our okay for take-off the air traffic controller in the tower told us that if we decided to ditch in the ocean, the water would be so cold we would only live about 45 seconds. The controller also warned us not to try to land in Greenland because at night time and darkness there German submarines were known to transmit erroneous navigation beam information to head us into the high cliffs. So we passed Greenland and our point of no return over water.

Sometime later the pilot called me off my bunk position and asked me to look at the high oil pressure on No.2 engine. He wanted to know what we could do about it. I told him that we couldn't afford to lose No.2 engine or shut it off because our alternator and hydraulic pumps were on No. 2. If we did, we would then lose all the plane's electrical and hydraulic pressure supplies. I told the pilot to slow down the RPM on No.2 engine, to drop the high pressure to near normal, and step up the RPM on No.1 engine to carry the balance of pulling power. We could go along okay that way then. So I began to transfer the fuel from all the tanks to keep the proper level and also to feed No.1 for its higher usage of fuel. I thought we were really in bad shape. We had waited a long time after taxiing before take-off at Goose Bay and we had no extra fuel tanks in our bomb bays. To make things worse, the radio operator couldn't send out a "MAYDAY" or contact anyone to let them know our location. He started to kick the radio set instead of finding the problem and really got worked up. We were now getting dangerously low on fuel. Ike plotted a direct route and double checked it, and I kept transferring the fuel to keep all our engines going. A B24 bomber doesn't have a fuel pump to push the fuel up or down. All the fuel moves by gravity flow, and the big danger is an "air lock," which blocks the flow of fuel travel and ends the fuel transfer cycle. If fuel to the engines stopped, we would all be dead ducks.

It was now getting light outside, and at last we finally got some good news. Ike figured we would be seeing land soon. That we did, and our pilot soon made radio contact with an airbase in Ireland. At last we got the okay to land, and when we sat down safely on the landing runway we were some happy, with cheers from all the crew.

As we taxied off the runway we heard over our earphones that another B24 was coming in. Naturally we all wanted to see, so we all got out to watch. We saw its left landing gear swing in about every direction, but the right gear was down and in its proper land-ing position. Fortunately for all on board the B24 pilot made a great one wheel landing, and after the bomber slowed down it swung to the right and came to a stop in the soft soil. Like us, they too were lucky to have made it down alive.

Art Ledtke continued with his diary:

NINTH MISSION, February 18, 1945

We had a late take-off—7:45 a.m.—climbed up through the haze, lost sight of the ground, and went out to our orbiting position over the North Sea. Completed our screening and then were diverted to the Northern part of Scotland. We could not use the GEE box either all the way. But George's navigation brought us out from the clouds a mile from the base. We were the first ship from our outfit to land. It was a beautiful place on a peninsula. We bought shots of Scotch for one shilling at the Sgt's. Club, slept in a forty bedroom mansion, from 11 p.m. to 2 a.m.

TENTH MISSION, February 19, 1945

Took off, flying blind again. There was a very bad icing condition, but flew 100 or so miles to our orbiting position. We climbed to 16,000 feet on oxygen, completed the mission, but almost ran out of gas. Diverted to Clapton on the East England coast (one of the landmarks on our way back home). It is a Spitfire base. We had chow, and then Bragger and I gassed up the ship. We left there about 3 p.m. Arrived at our base half an hour later.

As previously stated the orbiting stations for the VHF Screens were set coordinates over the North Sea. On 19 February only No.1 station was occupied. Squadron Liberator #42-50385, R4-H, nick-named *Beast of Bourbon*, piloted by Lt. Louis McCarthy and his crew, were assigned to station No. 2. *Beast of Bourbon* crashed on take off, and the other stations were canceled prior to takeoff. The crash was attributed to instrument failure. Of the ten crew members

Crash wreckage of the *Beast of Bourbon.* **Courtesy of USAF Safety Agency.**

aboard, three were killed, two were moderately injured, and five slightly injured. Killed were S/Sgt. Carl Lindquist, Pvt. Fred Becker, and Pvt. Howard Haley. S/Sgt. Robert MacAdam also received moderate injuries and was hospitalized. Aside from the regular McCarthy crew members, Lt. Victor Pregeant and Lt. Foreman, pilot and navigator of the new crews, were on this aircraft. Lt. Pregeant escaped injury, but Lt. Robert Foreman, navigator on Lt. Pregeant's crew suffered a broken hip and was grounded indefinitely. The aircraft was a total loss.[79]

The actual crash report stated that at 0916, the time of the accident the weather had ground fog up to 400 feet, the surface visibility was 30 yards, and the wind was south-southeast at 2mph. The temperature and the dew point were the same at 45 degrees Fahrenheit—perfect weather conditions for England's infamous dense fog. It was determined that the cause for the take-off accident was instrument lag (flight indicator and airspeed indicator) and extremely poor visibility.

The official narrative of the accident read:

The pilot [Lt. Pregeant], after making routine cockpit check, taxied out to marshaling point for take-off. The pilot then checked everything again, including engine run up check. The B24 moved out to end of runway 26 and took off in ground fog with visibility of 30 yards. The aircraft became airborne at approximately 105mph and cleared the end of the runway at 110mph. The pilot was immediately on instruments and held the aircraft in flying attitude to build up airspeed to 135mph. The engines operating at full throttle sounded

normal and gauges indicated 43" and 2500 rpm. At approximately 1/2 mile west of the west end of the runway, slightly to the right, the aircraft touched ground, and the mark of its path indicated that it was in a proper attitude at the time of contact, altimeter reading reached 45 feet and never reduced again. After hitting hedges and trees, the pilot cut throttles and co-pilot cut switches, which possibly delayed fire and explosion, which took place approximately seven minutes after the crash.[80]

Lt. Louis McCarthy, the senior pilot giving Lt. Vic Pregeant the check-ride spoke of the crash of the *Beast*:

It was a terrible morning. Everything happened so fast. The fog was right down to the tops of the grass. They lined us up on the runway with flashlights. We should have never have been allowed to take off. They pushed it, and why they did I don't know. The plane just gave out on take-off. There was no power on any of the engines on take-off for some reason, and that's when we hit. It was a terrible foggy morning. The thing caught fire. I don't know whether gasoline spilled on the hot engines or what. We had to duck because all the ammunition started going off. We got everybody out, including the ones who got killed. I remember looking out through the top of the thing and counting the yellow May Wests, counting numbers to make sure everybody was out. We should never have been sent out that morning, it was so bad.

One of the injured, Lt. Robert Foreman, navigator for Lt. Pregeant, was unable to remember much about the crash. Foreman wrote to fellow crewman Sgt. Harry Broadhead on June 24, 1945:

Cursed was the day of February 19th that I had to leave you boys. From what I remember of Vic's visit, it was some crack-up. One of the boys on leave from the 36th, Lt. Corder, stopped in to see my folks and told them about it. Seems that six of the boys [not so, but three] were killed, including McCarthy, the pilot. Since I don't know too much about the crash, could you write me what you know about it, Harry? Anywho, all I got out of it was a fractured hip. I was in a body cast up to my arm pits till two weeks ago. I'm up on crutches now, and the Doc said that my hip looks good. I should be able to throw the blasted crutches away in a few months.

* Corder himself would be lost in an airplane crash. On August 10, 1959, his T33 jet disappeared after take-off from Naval Air Station Norfolk, VA, enroute to Craig AFB, AL.

Word of the crash spread quickly. S/Sgt. Ed Lampson, engineer, remembered learning of the good luck of his pilot, Vic Pregeant:

The only event I really remember is the feeling the whole crew had when we heard that Vic had crashed on his check ride. This is heady stuff for a bunch of 20 year olds, far removed from home and family, not knowing our future. You can know the relief we felt when Vic walked in with nothing but a BandAid on his head.

Flying Control Officer Capt. Dennis Scanlan at work in Alconbury tower. *Courtesy of Dennis R. Scanlan Jr.*

Another lucky man was Lt. James Snoddy, the regular co-pilot for Lt. McCarthy. He recalled:

I was fortunate to be flying with another crew and was not in that crash. Carl Lindquist was our tail gunner who was killed when our crew crashed on take-off. He was only nineteen. Carl was a good little country boy. He looked like a little elf because he smoked a big yellow crooked stem pipe. He had a girl friend back home, and every night he would come by my hut with a letter to her for me to censor. He didn't mind my reading his personal letters to her. In fact, he would bring letters he had received from her for me to read. He called her his "Little Four Leaf Clover." He mentioned repeatedly that she was his good luck charm. It didn't work out that way.

Tail gunner Hank Parke remembered:

I remember that we heard the crash, and all the sirens went off. We were in the barracks, me and this guy Fred Neiser. We ran right out there and went over to Long Marston and saw it. All the bullets, the ammunition was going off in the flames. We were wandering around the field there looking. You couldn't get too close. We talked to some of the guys that were in it. But what amazed me was those medics we had. We used to make jokes about them, you know. Those guys were something. They were running into that thing, pulling guys out. They were really something. I had a lot more respect for them after that. 'Cause we only knew them before, handing out the whiskey after the missions, you know.

For many the subject of the crash was undoubtedly the main topic of discussion around the airbase. It also led to some debate. Cpl. William Fenster, a squadron mechanic for the Liberator *Beast of Bourbon,* reflected:

I never could figure out how the pilots could see to taxi out to the runways, let alone line up with the runway and take-off. When the "Beast of Bourbon" crashed, the fog was so thick. They never should have been allowed to go.

Navigator Lt. David Booker spoke of the horrible weather that day:

One of the major dangers that we had was the fog. The theory of the upper brass was that if they could put the radar jamming ships up during bad weather when the bombers couldn't go, it would make the Germans think that we were coming and the enemy would waste time and ammunition, etc., in getting prepared for the bombers to come. I remember one flight at Cheddington, we were in line to take off and one of the planes that had taken off ahead of us, they couldn't make radio contact with it and it turned out it had crashed right after take-off. The fog, you couldn't see your hand in front of your face. The top brass at our field and was in the tower. The commander thought well, we better do what we can to get these planes in the air in spite of the fog. I think they probably took an unnecessary risk and lost that plane. There was an embankment near the end of the runway that was higher than the runway itself,

so you always had to be sure to lift off high enough to miss that embankment. And you also had to be concerned about it if you were landing.

Lt. Wilbur Kruse wrote of this time:

The fog was absolutely so bad. There were days in mid winter when you had a hard time walking without hitting something. We learned quickly to make take-offs on instrument headings. You could not see the hooded runway lights until you were exactly at right angles to the lights.

RCM Operator Sgt. Art Ledtke continued logging missions in his diary:

ELEVENTH MISSION, February 21, 1945

A swell, clear flying day. We had started out an hour earlier, flew #4 [position]—an uneventful trip. On February 19, "Beast of Bourbon" aircraft #42-50385 crashed on take-off. Three personnel were killed, all of whom had been in the ship's waist. The ship had cleared the end of the runway, lost altitude, veered off to the right to miss a house, broke through two large trees about eighteen inches in diameter, strewed wreckage all over the field beyond and then burned. A total loss. It was a wonder anyone got out alive.

TWELFTH MISSION, February 22, 1945

We flew #3 and took with us one crew member of the ex-"Beast of Bourbon" who had survived the crash. Apparently, to get his nerves back in shape and also to complete his last mission so he would be entitled to return to the States. This was a very uneventful trip, over the North Sea. We screened for about 1,200 Heavies. Returning, we saw a large portion of them. They flew at 10,000 and had targets spread out all over Germany. Some of the crews in our outfit are P.O.'d because we are getting so many missions in and so much flying time. But we don't care, the sooner we get to go home.

THIRTEENTH MISSION, February 23, 1945

Took off at 5 a.m. and flew #3. Nothing unusual happened. We had the engineer of "Beast of Bourbon" (S/Sgt. Ed Lampson) riding with us (his ship had crashed the other day). Upon return, our base was closed in so we diverted.

FOURTEENTH MISSION, February 24, 1945

Took off at 5:30 a.m., flew the same position. Saw a V2 bomb take off again from the Netherlands. All the crew is pretty well tuckered out. A beautiful day. Saw hundreds of Forts plus some fighters for cover going out.

FIFTEENTH MISSION, February 27, 1945

Prior to going on this mission, our outfit was ordered to move from Cheddington. We packed all of our gear in boxes and had the other crew in our quarters take care of it. Our necessities, we loaded onto our ship and flew the mission. We saw three or four V2 bomb vapor trails. Returned to the Cheddington base and found almost everyone had gone to a new base. The old base was deserted. No lights in our hut. I got off a letter which I wrote in the orderly room which had a Coleman lantern for light. Had a couple of beers at the local pub and went to bed.

On 27 and 28 February the squadron loaded up their aircraft, along with eighty trucks of the 2nd Strategic Air Depot, and moved from Station 113 Cheddington to Army Air Field Station 102 at Alconbury. (See aerodrome map.) It has been noted that the airbase at Cheddington was attacked by German aircraft around the time of the squadron move. Henry Woolf, Sergeant-Major in the Station Headquarters Adjutant's Office, wrote of this time:

Early in 1945, no German planes having been in the area for a good while, our Flight Control men put the airfield lights on one night as our planes were returning from the Continent. There was a sudden burst of gunfire from German planes that had trailed the bombers home; but there were no casualties. We all gave the Flight Control men a good ribbing.

S/Sgt. Erlon Curtis, flight engineer for Lt. Paul "P.J." Pond's crew (a new replacement crew), had just checked into the squadron. Curtis remembered Alconbury and the quick move:

One afternoon we were told to be ready to leave in an hour with our belongings. We were shipped about 60 miles north of London to a small town named Alconbury. We heard the next day the Germans had bombed the runway of the field we had just left.

In Alconbury the Officers were about a mile from the enlisted men. They were in barracks up by the field. We enlisted men were right next to the town, and each man had a room of his own. The disadvantage was the walk of a mile, three times a day, to the mess hall. We had not been there any time when there was a disaster! A crew was taking off on their final mission before going home, they were just above tree level when everything stopped. They tried to land on a roadway, but the trees were too close. A wing was ripped off and the plane blew up. Not a happy beginning for us.

Art Ledtke wrote about his next mission and the squadron move:
SIXTEENTH MISSION, February 28, 1945

Flew with our ship loaded with our personal gear again. During the mission, about 10:30 a.m., our #2 engine started throwing out oil in a steady stream and smoke. After half an hour or more, the Skipper had to feather the prop. RO Freedlander contacted our base, and we had permission to return at 11:30 a.m., half an hour before our mission was to be completed. Upon returning, just before we got in sight of home field, #1 engine started to act the same as #2, but smoking a lot more. We in the waist had buckled on our chest chutes. We shot in for the landing. While taxiing #4 really smoked, strewing out a smoke screen.

We had landed at our new base, Alconbury, England, feeling very lucky. The EM got two rooms for three each as quarters. The officers stayed in a general barracks. For once we get a better deal. Even at chow, for the first time, we had a chinaware to eat out of. The officers have tin trays. The food here is good.

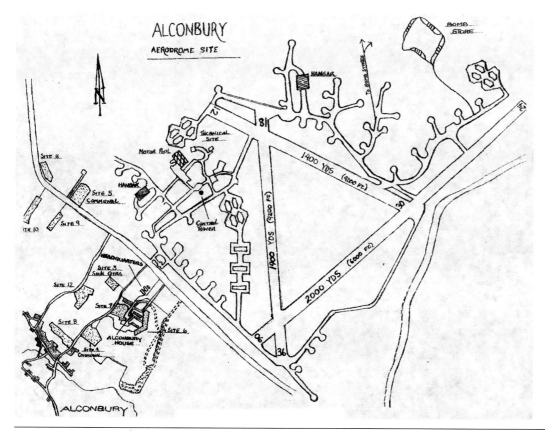

AAF Station 102 Alconbury aerodrome map.

Ledtke's Liberator was nicknamed *Playmate*. Being most proud of her, he wrote:

Our ship, #42-51685, had all the radar screening equipment removed and completely new put in. SCR 522 [VHF command radio], JACKAL transmitters, and CARPET units were installed. We are now fully fitted out with each kind of jamming equipment. Bragger and I learned how to operate them and got familiar with the switches, etc. Our new missions will be over the continent and at 30,000 feet or over.

Even though the squadron had moved to Alconbury, it remained with the 1st Air Division. However, it was now placed under the 482nd Bomb Group—the Pathfinders of the Eighth Air Force. The move brought 97 officers, 450 enlisted men, and seventeen B24 aircraft to Alconbury. Site three was designated as living quarters for the enlisted men, the former WAAF (Women's Army Air Force) site for the flying officers, and the old communal site for the ground officers. The old operations block on the aerodrome was taken over for use as the 36BS headquarters and operations.

The move to Alconbury produced many changes, and problems were inevitable. The morale was naturally affected by the move. The squadron had earlier found a home at Cheddington, and most of the men of the squadron were very reluctant to leave that location. At Alconbury the housing problem was acute, with some available facilities very crowded, sub-standard, or inadequate. However, good meals served in both the officers and enlisted men's messes tended to take the men's minds off such matters.

Other problems existed. Transportation at Alconbury was definitely a problem. This was due to the extensive dispersion of facilities at the field. Still, the GIs found ways to get off base. Several romanced and married English girls. The difficulty in securing rating for worthy ground personnel continued to be a problem. This situation improved slightly when the special radio operators transferred out of the squadron. Unfortunately, the problem of securing necessary RCM equipment still persisted.

Another new replacement crew, led by Lt. James Young, joined the 36th in February about the time of the squadron move. Lt. Young spoke of this time:

Alconbury Mess & Officer's Club. *Courtesy of Art Brusila.*

My crew, along with a whole bunch of other 8th Air Force crews, went to England in January of '45 on the "Ile de France." We docked at Glasgow and were sent to Stone, which was a replacement depot. We had no idea what assignment we were going to draw until we left Stone. After we stayed there for about three days, they put out orders that certain crews were going to certain groups and squadrons. We drew the 36th, which at that time was based at Cheddington. So they sent us down to Cheddington. We were there for several weeks, but we didn't get in any flying time while we were at Cheddington, not even a practice mission. Then they moved the whole outfit up to Alconbury, why I'll never know. They don't tell you anything in the service. Then they gave us a couple of cross country's that they called practice missions before they sent us out operational. And I would say that of all the assignments we could have drawn the only one that would have probably been any easier or any better would have been if we had been on coastal patrol, escorting ships in. Because the last couple of days before we got into Scotland, whenever the ship got within possible range of the B24s, they started escorting us in with about three B24s that just kept circling the ship a mile or two out. They just kept flying circles around it. When they ran out of their time then they would leave and another three would come take over and escort us in.

When we first got to Cheddington the thing they told us that we had to be completely aware of—that [our] operation was absolutely TOP SECRET. We were not to divulge to anyone what kind of work we were in. We couldn't send any word back home about what we were doing. If we ran into some of the other crews that we might have known in training in the states and they asked us what we were doing, to just tell them we were just flying like they were, and not divulge that we were in this counter radar top secret squadron.

Our missions from Alconbury were all [flown] out over the North Sea on single ship missions and [with] no fighter escort. We'd fly out a couple of hours ahead of the bomber stream and turn on these radar sets and would jam German early warning radar whose frequencies had been picked up by our search ship, which flew practically all the time up and down the coast of occupied Europe. They could pick up the frequencies of different radar stations the Germans had there on the coastline. They would bring that back to the base and the radar mechanics would set those frequencies in the jamming equipment. Then the next day they would assign crews to the different planes that were equipped to jam those stations and would send each plane out to its appropriate position that would be within jamming range of that station. They would give the navigators the coordinates of latitude and longitude, and it was up to the navigators to find our proper position. At that time then we started flying an orbit of about fifty miles north and then fifty miles south of our base point and would stay out there until the time was up, whether it was two hours or four hours or whatever it was. We were given a sheet of instructions at each day's briefing that would list the [jammer] set numbers that would be turned on at various times and be turned off at various times. So, we would have to stay out just park the wheel right on the runway light and set your gyro compass to sixty; kick the brakes off, push the throttles up, and when the plane started moving, just hold that gyro compass on sixty degrees until you got your 115 mile an hour airspeed, then lift off, pull the wheels up, and head on out. Coming back most of the time, by the time we got back in around noon or a little after, the fog would have lifted to at least a couple of hundred feet. By using the little radar screen that the navigators had down in the front end of the plane [the GEE box], they could plot the coordinates of the landing runway at Alconbury. They could bring us in where we could just drop right into the traffic pattern. By coordinating that with the automatic direction finder and the sweep second hand on the dash board we could kind of feel our way in like that. We would bring it down to within a hundred feet of the ground. If we weren't able to see the runway lights when you got to a hundred feet, we'd pull out and not try to make it. But if we could get a hundred feet of not really clear but just get some kind of visibility at a hundred feet, we'd come on in. So that was the toughest part of our job; battling that weather.

I'm sure the 36th lost a crew now and then, but we never knew exactly what happened. When I was sent from Stone, the replacement depot, to Cheddington, I think there were either two of three other crews besides mine, so evidently the 36th had either had some planes lost or they had some crews that had stayed over long enough to finish their tour and were being rotated back to the states. They never told us what happened to those planes that were missing.

In the bomber groups, crews had planes that were assigned to them, and they more or less flew the same plane on every mission. Now, we didn't do that. We had about eighteen planes, and the radar mechanics would fix up whatever was called for on the next day's battle order. When they [Operations] put the crew alert out at five o'clock that afternoon, they were going to send out six crews the next day, whatever crew's turn it was to fly got their name on the battle order. The next morning at briefing they assigned crews to the planes that they wanted to fly in certain positions. I don't think that I flew the same plane twice on any operational mission.

Alconbury church. *Courtesy of Art Brusila.*

there until the last set numbers were turned off, and then we would return back to the base at Alconbury.

I found out right quick after we got operational the worst part of it we had to fight was the weather. It was tough taking off in dense fog out of Alconbury because around daylight or shortly before most every morning we took off we had visibility of probably, oh maybe two hundred yards on the better days. [In 1943 8AF Bomber Command prescribed weather limits requiring cloud ceilings of 1,000ft. and surface visibilities of not less than 1 1/4 miles for launching missions.] [81] On a couple of days I took off I could barely see my wingtips, which were just fifty-five feet away. So, all you could do was get out to the runway which was heading of sixty degrees and get lined up with the runway by using the runway light,

After one particular mission Lt. Leon Hammer, the navigator for Lt. Young, recalled a diversion to a base where their crew failed to receive a warm welcome:

There were a number of occasions when our plane almost crashed, partially due to the fog. There was an occasion when, due to fog, we were forced to land at another base, I believe in Scotland. Since our plane carried sensitive secret equipment, we were instructed not to allow anyone, friend or foe, near the plane, which was equipped with submachine guns in order to enforce that order. There was a standoff between the Colonel in charge of that field and us. Eventually he backed down since we had surrounded the plane, refusing to allow him to come near or aboard.

Sgt. Aubrey "Bill" Whitworth of Lt. Soderstrom's crew spoke of how their tail gunner, Sgt. John Fillenger, protected their Liberator.

We often had to pull guard duty overnight protecting our plane. We were advised not to let anyone near the plane unless they knew the password of the day. Johnny was on duty when our crew chief showed up to check out a problem on the aircraft. Johnny, who knew our crew chief, challenged him for the password and the crew chief admitted he hadn't the slightest idea what the word was, which precipitated a fierce verbal barrage. Johnny ordered the crew chief face down on the ramp. [The crew chief] colorfully declined until a warning shot changed his mind. The security officer finally solved the stalemate. Johnny was reprimanded verbally, but as he pointed out, there was nothing said about anyone allowed around the plane who did not know the password.

Having now completed his required number of flying hours, Iredell Hutton prepared to ship back to the States. Hutton wrote on 28 February:

Our armies are still pushing inside Germany. Hope and pray that they keep going. I know that it is taking a lot of Mother's sons away. And it is all useless, but guess it is all necessary if we are to get a suitable peace.

During February word was received from Air Vice Marshal Addison, the Air Officer Commanding RAF 100 Group, that the British Distinguished Flying Cross was to be awarded to Captains Richard Obenschain (Assistant Operations Officer) and James Ostler (Squadron Navigation Officer), both former members of the 803rd Bomb Squadron. Both Capts. Obenschain and Ostler had completed tours in a heavy bombardment group before volunteering for RCM work with both the 8AF and the RAF. (See Appendix F for details.)

Capt. Ostler would soon rotate back to the states, but before he left he related his sentiments about Station 113, Cheddington, in a poem titled:

A Farewell to Cheddington

Sometimes at night when the lights were low,
And the radio playing soft and slow,
I used to dream that I could go
Back to the USA

Back to the land of milk and honey,
Back to the land of decent money,
Back where days are always sunny
Back to the USA

Back to the land of real fresh eggs,
Back to Budweiser beer in kegs,
Back where the girls have pretty legs
Back in the USA

Back to Chicago's skyline tall,
Prettiest pin-up on the barracks wall;
I'm going back, cause I've got the call,
Back to the USA.

Away from England's peasant types,
Back where nobody has any gripes,
But there's no cigarettes, so they all smoke pipes!
Back in the USA.

Away from England's frigid climes,
Where it's not too hot at the best of times,
Back to the source of all these rhymes,
Back to the USA.

Back to the land of ice cream sodas,
Where a case a week is your whisky quota,
Then probably on to Japan's pagodas;
But first—the USA.

Back to the land of porterhouse steak,
Back to my girl, if I get a break;
Don't cancel those orders, for heaven's sake.
I've got a date in the USA.

Alconbury House. *Courtesy of Art Brusila.*

Thatched roof houses along a country lane in Alconbury.

I'm leaving tomorrow, but I won't have you think
That I haven't enjoyed every hour, every wink;
And I'll remember you all as I'm downing my drink
Back in the USA.

So pack my bags, I'm leaving tomorrow,
With a little joy, and a little sorrow;
Anyone got any pounds I can borrow?
To take to the USA?

To all the squadron I'm saying good-bye
From the colonel down to the last G.I.—
I'll be seeing you all in the CBI [China-Burma-India Theater
of Operation] After the USA! [82]

Other awards now came to the 36BS. The squadron was granted battle participation credit for the Normandy Campaign from 6 June 1944 to 14 July 1944 under the authority of 8AF Headquarters. Also, two important awards went to ground crew chiefs. Bronze Star Awards were presented to M/Sgt. Edward Baxley and Sgt. Jack Charlton on 21 February.

As always, payday offered the GIs another reason to celebrate, and this month there was a special dance celebration at the station Aero Club with music by "The Gremlins."

Alconbury — a quaint English village.

On 28 February the squadron's consecutive string of 158 sorties without a single aircraft aborting ended when B24 Liberator #42-51546, R4-L, nicknamed *I Walk Alone* returned to base prematurely due to engine failure in number two and number four engines. Still, most missions had been effective or successful. The 36BS had completed 156 operational sorties on 24 missions supporting the 8AF. Allied bombing was crippling important enemy defenses and also the transportation and industrial means of the Third Reich. Hitler's Nazi war machine was nearing total defeat. And, although death had once again come to the squadron, fortunately these losses were to be the last.

11

Droop Snoots - Miss-B-Haven

March 1945

While at their new base at Alconbury the mission of the 36th Bomb Squadron continued to be that of providing radar and radio countermeasures for 8th Air Force heavy bombardment operations. Squadron operations increased as compared with those during February. The squadron had now moved for a third time, and not all the men were glad to have left Station 113, Sgt. Art. Ledtke remembered feeling uneasy once at the new station:

The night of March 4th, our old base at Cheddington was bombed and strafed by the Germans. A couple were shot down. Looks like we moved out in time. The night of March 5th, we had an alert at our new Alconbury field. One of the 406th PAPERBOYS was shot down over the English coast by a British Mosquito, and one was shot up by the British anti-aircraft guns [killing Col. Earl J. Aber, the 406BS CO]. Apparently the whole area was jittery because of the alerts in affect.

The Germans had developed and used airborne homing devices which were capable of giving a bearing on various RAF's and our plane's jamming transmission locations. The ELINT system was installed in British Mosquitoes and P38s. It was developed to counteract the homing devices and also assisted in trying to upset the V2 bombs the Germans were sending over.

At this time the official function of the 36BS as laid down by 8AF Headquarters required the squadron to:

a. Prevent enemy interception of VHF R/T traffic transmitted by bombers during assembly.

b. Screen bombers during assembly from enemy early warning radar.

c. Jam enemy tank communications.

d. Investigate enemy radar frequencies.

A secret internal report from the office of Lt. Gen. Carl Spaatz, the Commanding General of the Strategic Air Forces in Europe, at Headquarters High Wycombe, to H. H. "Hap" Arnold, the Commanding General of the Army Air Forces at the Pentagon dated 1 March stated the future challenge for the radio countermeasures

program for heavy bombers. The RCM program was to attack three new threats confronting strategic bombing by the Eighth Air Force. The threats were:

a. More effective flak, controlled by new centimeter radar and improved Wurzburg radar.

b. A new German fighter force made up principally of jet planes with extensive and detailed control by radio and radar.

c. Use of proximity fuses in flak ammunition and toss bombs.[83]

In addition to the VHF Screen, a radar screen and search operations were employed in March. The purpose of VHF screen was still to prevent enemy interception of VHF R/T traffic transmitted by the bombers during assembly. The VHF Screen was put up on twenty-seven days out of the thirty-one.

Beginning 16 March an improved type of radar screen designed for the purpose of screening bombers during assembly from enemy early warning radar was flown. These screens were put up on ten days during the month. From seven to nine B-24s equipped with normal and low frequency DINA (APT-1 radar jammer) equipment were used for this purpose. The screen was first flown approximately twenty miles off the coast of East Anglia, roughly parallel-

Alconbury was protected with an air raid shelter offering protection from enemy Intruders — just in case.

The ME262 — the world's first operational jet which flew at a speed of 540 mph. The ME262 flew in combat as bombers, night fighters, and as reconnaissance aircraft. *Courtesy of Barry Rosch.*

ing the coast of Great Britain. Later the screen was put out to about fifty miles from the Dutch coast. No detailed report was received as to the effectiveness of the screen, although tests were conducted.

On 24 March, the date of the 12th Army Group's crossing of the Rhine, the screen was flown for both a morning and an afternoon bombing attack. During this screen the Liberators orbited over fixed coordinates over the North Sea. As many as six B-24s were used for this purpose. The Liberators were equipped with the special ORVIL VHF jammers. ORVILS were SCR-522 transmitters mounted in the B24 bomb-bays that modulated with noise to screen VHF transmissions from enemy monitoring stations. The VHF screen was flown far enough from the source of transmissions so that there was no interference caused, but close enough to the monitoring stations to override any signal that might reach it. From data obtained by the search operators in the B-24 search aircraft, the

coverage of the screen appeared good. Again, the Gremlins were effective.

Search operations were conducted on fourteen days of the thirty-one from a specially equipped Liberator #44-10507, which was recently assigned to the squadron. The primary purpose of the search was to test the effectiveness of the VHF screen. The search aircraft patrolled between the screen and the enemy coast. Search operations were also conducted from specially equipped P-38 aircraft, called "Droop Snoots," on six days during the month. These aircraft (three in number) were brought to the squadron on detached service from the 7th Photographic Reconnaissance Group (7PRG) early in the month and were later assigned to the squadron. Capt. Howard Kasch, liaison officer from the Intelligence Office at Headquarters, High Wycombe, directed the searches. He and Lts. Zeidler, Holt, and Stallcup flew as observers. The pilots on detached ser-

Gravy Train was DINA equipped. *Courtesy of Robert P. King.*

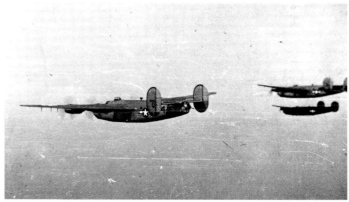

The VHF Screen. Three 36BS B24's. The black B24 was DINA equipped. Two VHF Screens were flown to support 8AF bombing operations on 24 March — the day the 12th Army Group crossed the Rhine.

B24 #44-50502, R4-C nicknamed *Gypsy Jane* joined the 36BS in March. *Courtesy of William D. Butler.*

MANDREL and DINA antennas mounted under the wing of a B24. Each antenna was cut to the required length for the frequency being jammed. Five antennas under each wing were used with ten transmitters located in the bomb bay. *Courtesy of the USAF Historical Research Agency.*

vice from the 7PRG who flew the missions were Lts. Brunell, Riley, Glaza, and Edwards. Mechanics were also sent on detached service from the 7PRG for the purpose of training the squadron engineering personnel in P-38 maintenance. The purpose of the "Droop Snoot" searches was to investigate German radar in Holland and along the front lines. The "Droop Snoots" flew investigational radar search missions to known enemy experimental research establishments plus other points deemed necessary. Information obtained from Prisoners of War and captured documents indicated that the enemy intended to use gun-laying radar equipment on frequencies that were not being covered by the current employment of CARPET and WINDOW, In order to plan the future gun-laying RCM program these new frequencies had to be determined accurately.[44] Similar searches were previously made from RAF Station Foulsham by the same group of men. They were active at RAF Foulsham from approximately 1 September 1944 until the time they were transferred to the 36BS.

Capt. Howard Kasch, the Liaison Officer from the Office of the Director of Intelligence at Pinetree spoke of the "Droop Snoot" P38s and what they did:

In the spring of 1945, as I recall, we had taken the armament out of the P38 and used recording materials [equipment] in place of the armament. We would fly over the English and the Dutch coast looking for the signals that were guiding the V2 rockets to England. We spent a good many months doing this, not realizing that in November of '44, we found out later, that the Germans had changed their guiding signals from the ground to a controlling mechanism inside the V2. [It was] Basically an integrating accelerometer which guided it over a certain part of London, usually on the East side.

P38 pilot Lt. William Zeidler, on detached service from the 7PRG, recalled:

We were flying daylight missions doing radar research for the sites of the V-bombs. The British were flying night missions with Mosquitoes doing the same type of research. We flew up [to] roughly 30,000 feet. 34,000 was about the top altitude for a '38. We were

DINA transmitters mounted in bomb bay. *Courtesy of John D. Latvaitis.*

single airplane, so the only flak you would encounter would be somebody putting up a burst, something of that nature and not a continuous sort of thing. Same thing with enemy intercepts; they made one pass at us, that was it. Of course, all we did was dive and get out of the way. We didn't have any guns or anything of that nature. I did see one of the first 262 Messerschmitts powered by jet. He made a pass one day. It was like lightning. You saw a dot coming and then it was past you. That was one of the first ones that was sighted.

Lt. William Stallcup, another pilot from the 7PRG, said:

I was ordered to report to 3rd Division Headquarters and was asked if I would volunteer to participate in a secret project code named Big Ben. They would tell me nothing of the project, only that it would keep me busy. I agreed to participate and was sent immediately on temporary duty to RAF 192 Squadron at Foulsham, East Anglia. There I joined three other RCM officers, Lt. Thomas Holt, Francis Kunze, William Zeidler, and our commanding officer, Capt. Howard Kasch.

7PRG men on DS to the 36BS. L-R Lt. William Stallcup, Capt. Howard Kasch, Lt. Thomas Holt, Lt. William Zeidler. *Courtesy of William B. Stallcup, Jr.*

Officers of the 7PRG study their maps, planning the next mission. *Courtesy of Richard H. Brunell.*

We were informed that British Intelligence had obtained information as to when the Germans were to be experimenting with the V2 rockets at their laboratories near Peenamunde in the Baltic Sea. They wanted patrols in that area to watch for V2 firings and to monitor frequencies that might be used for control. The British were willing to fly night patrols, but asked that the U.S. provide day patrols. These activities then constituted Big Ben.

We were transferred to the 36th Squadron about the middle of March. We continued to fly missions in both B24s and P38s until the middle of April. My last mission was on April 13 and was the mission to Munich. I remember it well, since it was one of the longer missions I had flown, about 5 hours. We flew from Alconbury to Dresden, south to Munich and then back, and were accompanied by four P51 Mustangs for protection, the only time that protection was provided.

We were provided with four P38 "Droop Snoot" aircraft. All armor had been removed, and special receivers were installed in the snoot. The RCM officer sat in the snoot in a most cramped position, knees under chin. After a four hour mission it was most difficult to walk. Pilots were brought in from Elliott Roosevelt's 7th Photographic Reconnaissance Wing and were rotated after a given number of missions. Since the RCM officer sat well forward of the center of gravity of the plane, maneuvering subjected us to "Gs" much greater than those experienced by the pilot, an experience we could never get them to understand.

Lt. Bruce Edwards, a pilot from the 7PRG, recalled his days with the 36BS:

I was a pilot from the 7PRG, 22nd Squadron assigned temporary duty to the 36th Bomb Squadron to fly the three P38s. It was my only duty to fly them. I had no knowledge of the electronics equipment. I flew two recorded missions, both of not too long a duration. I flew another one not recorded that was nine hours. Either Kasch or Stallcup was the radar operator on that mission. That one flew all the way around Germany. When we flew we would

William Stallcup with his "Droop Snoot" P38. Preparing for a mission. *Courtesy of William B. Stallcup, Jr.*

Lt. Holt with his "Droop Snoot" P38. *Courtesy of William B. Stallcup, Jr.*

go down to one of the fighter squadrons and pick up four P51s, and they would fly along as our escort.

I had no knowledge of the radar observer, what he did, how successful he was, or anything, because that was so classified they wouldn't even tell me. We didn't go above twenty-five thousand. If it was a short flight we would fly down across the border between Germany and Holland, down to the Rhine River down into France and back. My knowledge of electronics since then I know that they [Allied intelligence] could see probably everything from the Dutch coast into the middle of Germany electronically. I'm sure that's what they were doing. They were looking for German radar stations, or the V2 information to see what they could find out. My knowledge of V2s since then, since I'm an aeronautical engineer, those vehicles were not controlled after launch by any radio or radar. They were launched all under internal guidance, therefore they couldn't have found out anything other than if some of them had some telemetry, which may have been. They could maybe pick up telemetry signals, but that would be only during launch.

One of these missions that we made with the "Droop Snoot" was over nine hours in length. We took off and flew [over] the North Sea past Peenemunde to Stettin, down the Oder River to Frankfurt, into Posen, Poland; came back to the Oder, flew down clear to Vienna, and then came back following the Rhine River back on out [and then] to England.

Lt. Edwards spoke of some of the fun times flying his hot P38:

Once on the way back to Alconbury, I was up maybe ten thousand feet and ran across a P51 puttin' along down there, so I decided to give him a thrill. I put it [the P38] into a shallow dive and opened up a little bit to maximum cruise power, and I went by him at about 350 mph. Evidently I had ticked him off 'cause here he came. Right when I got to Alconbury he caught up with me. I didn't know it. I had gone by him and just hadn't paid any attention, but here he came. He had to almost burn the P51 engines out to catch up with me. He caught up with me and so we went into it. We had a simulated dogfight right up above Alconbury for five or ten minutes. Primarily doing just a Lufbery [aerial maneuver] while I was in hard turns, put it in a hard turn up around. In a P51, with torque you can turn pretty good. If you go the other way against this torque, turn to the right, he can't stay with the P38. I played with him first

36BS "Droop Snoots" on the line. *Courtesy of J. O. Thompson.*

to see if he knew about the Lufbery. And well, he turned good and we just sat there and circled each other for a while. Finally, I pulled up and did a real quick end to one, came back down and then went into a Lufbery to the right and promptly caught him. Got right on his tail. I stayed for a while. Then he tried to outdo me and he couldn't shake me. Finally, he gave up and went home. This whole thing went on right up above Alconbury and all the people down there could see it. I came in and landed. I had quite a party of people waiting out there. They thought that was great sport. I didn't know if I was gonna catch it [from the station commander] or what. As long as I won, I thought I was all right.

36BS mechanic M/Sgt. Irl Fife remembered one exciting ride with Lt. Edwards:

Towards the end [of the war in Europe] our squadron got three P38s. I had knowledge of liquid cooled engines, having been on Allison engines during the time I was teaching airplane mechanics. I was taken off "Ramp Rooster" and given the job of flight chief for P38s. I flew on occasion with Lt. Edwards when reporting to Air Force Headquarters at High Wycombe. I would fuel and check the oil and make the plane ready for the return flight. Sometimes fog

would set in making hedge, haystack, and hopping a thrill to descend down through the clouds and watch the altimeter and wondering if it was registering proper. One time Lt. Edwards said on the intercom, "Look at the engine on the left." The engine was feathered and not running. I promptly asked, "Did it quit?" His reply, "Oh, no, just showing you how the plane flies on one engine." If you wanted to be air sick, go up and fly maneuvers with Lt. Edwards. The planes were full of electronic equipment. No armor plate or guns. Speed and maneuverability was the only defense when on a mission. He would spend time every day in the air looping, etc., to keep him conditioned. I've been up with him, and the centrifugal force made it impossible to even move your hand. Fortunately my sickness didn't hit me until after landing.

Sgt. Charles Sanders, another squadron ground mechanic, also remembered the P38s:

When the P38s came in I got my tools and went over to where they were. The P38 pilots were on detached service from the 7th Photo Reconnaissance Group, on loan to us. This group was stationed at Mount Farm near Oxford. These aircraft were what they called "Droop Snoot" P38 Lightnings. They had no guns, but a seat where the guns and ammunition should have been. In the 36th Squadron, one of our observers rode in that seat and operated the ELINT equipment. This was to gather electrical intelligence information on enemy radar in Belgium, Germany, and wherever they needed to. These P38s had two Allison engines with generators and starters, etc., in a much smaller space. This made them harder to work on, however, they had only two engines instead of four like a B17 or a B24. I guess it was not too bad. These P38s had only one mechanic for each plane. By this time we had about twenty B24s with these three P38s.

I remember one day one of these pilots came out to the plane I was crew chief of and invited me to fly to his home base with him. So I did. As we took off, we had not gone very far down the runway

The "Eyes of the Eighth" — One of four 7PRG "Droop Snoot" P38's attached to the 36BS. *Courtesy of William B. Stallcup, Jr.*

"Droop Snoot" P38 interior. The Radar Observer sat in exceedingly cramped quarters. *Courtesy of William B. Stallcup, Jr.*

Bruce Edwards with his "Droop Snoot" P38. *Courtesy of Bruce Edwards.*

"Little Friends". Four P51's of the 479th Fighter Group. P51's escorted the "Droop Snoots". *Courtesy of Art Brusila.*

until I thought I felt the wheels retract. That was not the half of it. We got down the runway and he flipped it upside down. He continued to take off upside down. That was my first and only ride in a P38. I got on the intercom and told him to straighten that thing up, that I had been over there too long to get killed now. That was the only time he turned us upside down, but he did pull some real good "buzz" jobs that day. We got home all in one piece. That trip was quite an experience, but I did not try it again. That was my first and last ride in a P38.

Lt. Wilbur Kruse remembered seeing the V2 rockets that the "Droop Snoots" were looking for:

We were basically moved out of the London area because we flew at the same time the V2 rockets would often be launched and we were continually being caught in the floodlights. I can assure you, even at 10,000 feet these lights darn near knock your eyes out. The British wanted to free the skies. The threat of balloon cables were more numerous in the London area.

On quite a number of missions I counted and located for G3 [Operations] at least eight or nine vertical take-offs of V2s over the Hague. With six planes in position we could to a certain degree of accuracy triangulate the launch area of the Netherlands. I can only say they were spectacular.

S/Sgt. Constanti Kazak also remembered the V2s.

One of our missions was located off the coast of Holland. Flying our pattern in the North Sea near the Hague, we got up at 2:00 a.m. and were in the air early and it was still very dark. We could see the lights coming from the Hague. As the sky started to get light I looked toward Holland and all of a sudden a silver object skyrocketed into the sky and headed toward England. Then another one from another location, and another. I watched as they traveled across the sky. There were a lot of silver streaks. This was our first sightings of V2s.

A P38 in a bank over Alconbury puts on a show. *Courtesy of Art Brusila.*

For relaxation and entertainment Kazak recalled:

We listened to BBC radio a lot. I always made sure I picked the station that played Vera Lynn, the British soldiers' sweetheart and mine. She sure did a lot for my morale.

Sgt. Art Ledtke continued to log his missions in his diary:
SEVENTEENTH MISSION, March 8, 1945

Took off at 8:30 a.m. and used jamming equipment. Uneventful trip, except GEE box went out on the way to the orbiting position. We crossed the bomber stream on the way in. Hundreds of them, I guess the whole 8th Air Force. We flew above the clouds all the way at 9,000 feet. The new equipment is more work and responsibility, but everything went off well. We saw a P38 had crashed at the end of a landing strip.

EIGHTEENTH MISSION, March 14, 1945

Flew J-Jacob, a late flight. Took off about 8 a.m.. While orbiting on autopilot, the Skipper [Lt. Kittle] and co-pilot Blanchard played a game of chess. We used just the jamming equipment. Returning we flew over a squadron of Lancasters with gliders in tow.

NINETEENTH MISSION, March 16, 1945

Took off in our regular ship R-Roger, #42-51685 with all new equipment in place both for jamming and screening. Two screening sets went out and part of the jamming equipment. I located the trouble in a little while. A cannon plug had worked loose. I replaced it and the equipment worked OK. We flew at 15,000 to 17,000 feet. It was 21 degrees below 0 outside. Bragger's heated gloves did not work, and his hands almost got frost bitten. We were on oxygen for about five hours.

Ledtke also noted:

Another crew had damaged our ship while landing. Damaged the nose wheel. But our ground crew and Sgt. Andrew C. Cota [ground crew chief] had repaired it OK. We gave our ground crew our rations just to keep on the good side of them.

For S/Sgt. Iredell Hutton, it was finally time to go home. He wrote:

We got up this morning about five for chow because we are leaving for the boat. They issued us a box of K rations to eat for dinner. We got to Liverpool about 12:30. The town has really taken a beating during the war. The docks have really been blown to hell. It is a very big ship which we are on. The Dutch ship "New Amsterdam." A very beautiful ship. Not quite as big as the "Elizabeth," but much cleaner.

Everyone wanted a ride in the P38 aircraft. Here John Fillenger poses with "Droop Snoot" #43-28479. This aircraft would crash on 6/25/45. *Courtesy of J. O. Thompson.*

Lt. Sweeney Official Crew Photo. Standing L-R Sgt. Francis Preimesberger, Lt. Stanley J. Kardisk, Lt. William J. Sweeney, Lt. John W. Beaty, Sgt. Charles T. Cuff. Kneeling L-R Sgt. Richard G. Mulligan, T/Sgt. Herman P. Schlander, Sgt. Roland A. Morin, Sgt. Kenneth C. Klein, Sgt. Lawrence E. Dickson. *Courtesy of the USAF Historical Research Agency.*

After the crash of *Miss-B-Haven*, S/Sgt. Francis Preimesberger came "out the top hatch and started tossing out the other members of the crew like they were rag dolls." Preimesberger is shown here receiving the Air Medal from Lt. Col. Hambaugh. *Courtesy of Roland A. Morin.*

After a long and reflective voyage across the north Atlantic Hutton arrived in New York. He wrote:

We got into New York harbor today, which is Friday, the 16th. Very beautiful weather all above, but you couldn't see around you at all because of the fog. We had to stop and blow the whistle every few minutes to keep someone from running into us. After it cleared up I took some pictures of New York and also of the Statue of Liberty. A U.S. Army boat came out to welcome us. There was a WAC [Women's Army Corps] band on it. When the band wasn't playing they played some good records. Boy, it really felt good to be back in the good old USA.

I'm very sorry that Norwood can't be with me, but he may be able to before very much longer. [In fact Norwood, now a prisoner of war, would be liberated by the Allies on April 26, 1945.]

For S/Sgt. Art Ledtke, his flying hours and missions continued to multiply. Some missions were eventful, some not. He wrote:

TWENTIETH MISSION, March 17, 1945

Eight hour mission, six hours at high altitude. Saw 6 V2s take off.

TWENTY-FIRST MISSION, March 18, 1945

Five and one-half hour mission. On the way out while above the clouds, we saw a beautiful rainbow on the clouds below. The sun is hidden under the clouds, just kind of a glow coming through. Around it was the rainbow, a complete circle, quite bright. Same jamming. Uneventful trip.

TWENTY-SECOND MISSION, March 19, 1945

Five and one-half hour mission. While on the way out in the dark, we saw an unusual sight. While flying out to the North Sea, the props of the ship, wing edges, and tips were lighted by a phosphorescent glow, St. Elmo's fire. It was a weird, eerie sight.

On March 20, B-24 #42-50844, R4-I nicknamed *Miss-B-Haven*, with Lt. William Sweeney as pilot, crashed on take-off for an operational mission. All crew members escaped serious injury, although the aircraft was a total loss. Sgt. Francis Preimesberger, flight engineer and gunner for the crew, spoke of the crash:

We crashed on take-off on one of our missions. The airplane just seemed to mush in. We couldn't kick extra power to it. She just wouldn't get off the runway very far.

There was a fire in the engine, but they claim that was from dragging along the ground—a friction fire. I think the engine itself must have been defective and not producing enough power. That might be one of the reasons it crashed, rather than a friction fire from running down the runway, because if there was a fire in the engine while taking off, well, it would lose power and naturally it couldn't get off. We all got out all right. We washed it out. It [Miss-B-Haven] never flew again.

Miss-B-Haven was a complete wreck. *Courtesy of Roland A. Morin.*

It could be said that Sgt. Preimesberger was a hero on that day. Radio operator Sgt. Dick Mulligan saw his buddy Preimesberger come to the rescue of the men up front. He spoke of what he saw:

We cracked up and it did catch on fire. Preimesberger was the guy who was the first one out. And he stood on that wing and got us all out of there or we would have been gone. The rest of the plane was really a total loss. The guys came out of the back. They got out pretty good. But in the front which was the pilot, the co-pilot, the navigator, and me, all of us had to get out. We had all our gear on then, our flight jackets and everything else. He [Preimesberger] was the guy that stood up there and got us all out of there. Otherwise, if he had taken off we wouldn't have been able to get out.

Sgt. Lawrence Dickson, tail gunner for Lt. Sweeney, remembered the crash and saw Preimesberger as the hero in the accident:

On March 20, 1945, we walked our plane out to the runway, centering it, getting on board, with the brakes locked and the engines revved into the red, released the brakes, hoping to take off.

We were number two to take off. We were taking off with 2,800 gallons of 100 octane gas in our tanks, and being an experienced hot crew, the pilot pulled the landing gear up immediately and the plane hit a downdraft or air pocket and the plane settled back on the runway at 160mph. We slid for half a mile, smoke and fire shooting back through the plane. When we finally came to a stop the plane was in three sections. Mo [Roland Morin], the ball gunner, was in the tail section with me and was the first to the escape hatch. He was standing on the door trying to open it. I grabbed him with one hand, held him off the door, and opened it with my other hand and threw him out with me right behind him. I started to run toward the cabin or cockpit which was maybe fifty yards from where I was. The fire was bad, but I saw the engineer [Francis Preimesberger] come out the top hatch, and he started tossing out the other members of the crew like they were rag dolls. Their faces were slightly burned and singed, otherwise okay. We were taken to debriefing and to the medics for a check and then back to the flightline and another plane and back into the air before the shock had time to settle in.

Fuselage of *Miss-B-Haven* on hoist. Off to the scrap heap. *Courtesy of Roland A. Morin.*

A checkered truck adapted for use by flying control at Alconbury. Note B17 nose plexiglass for controller to view through. *Courtesy of Leonard N. Backer.*

Playmate bogged down. This B24 was equipped with ORVILS and DINAS. *Courtesy of Arthur Ledtke.*

The official crash report on *Miss-B-Haven* had this to say about the crash: At 1238 hours, the aircraft was taking off for an operational mission. The weather at the time had scattered clouds at 3,000 feet and a broken ceiling at 25,000 feet. The surface visibility was 9 miles and the wind west southwest at 15mph. The pilot taxied out to the runway, received a green light from the tower, pulled out on the runway and took off. The landing gear was immediately retracted, but the Liberator touched down again with gear partially retracted. The aircraft continued down runway 24. Just past the intersection of runways 24 and 30, the aircraft tilted to the left and fire broke out in number one engine, which then blanketed the cockpit. Friction caused the aircraft to catch fire. The aircraft then veered to the left, departed the runway, and ground-looped on the grass a short distance from the runway. All of the crew escaped through the top and bottom hatches. The aircraft was a complete wreck.[85]

Later that day S/Sgt Art Ledtke wrote about the crash in his diary:

TWENTY-THIRD MISSION, March 20, 1945

The morning mission was scrubbed. We slept until 10:30 a.m., missed breakfast, and were just fooling around until noon chow time. A Sgt. came in and said to rush to the briefing room right away. Bragger and I took off for the mess hall, had steaks. The rest of the boys didn't eat until we returned from the mission. We hurried out and warmed up the ship and took off at 12:20 p.m. Very unusual. Someone has messed up somewhere, but we did our job. Upon returning, we saw where I-Ida piled up on take-off. Messed up the whole ship, but no one was injured seriously.

Three days later Ledtke saw trouble for two aircraft at Alconbury, one was his own. He wrote:

MARCH 23, 1945

No mission flown. Scrubbed. After warming up the ship, we were circling around to get on the runway from the perimeter. We crossed over the main runway as the end light indicating the runway was out. We ran off the apron and stopped. By radio, someone ordered us to wheel the ship around. We tried to but bogged down

to the axles of the wheels. Boy, these B24s sure are heavy. We stood around while two gasoline trucks tried to pull us out. They dug around the wheels,etc., but the ship sunk deeper and deeper. They broke off the tail skid by hooking onto it to pull us out. No mission for us. One ship had returned to the field with #1 engine on fire. After landing it was met by the fire trucks and hash wagons. They got the fire out. No casualties.

Ledtke continued:

TWENTY-FOURTH MISSION, March 27, 1945

A five hour mission. I now have 136 hours mission time. We just flew off the English coast and jammed. Trip uneventful.

The squadron was now operating with twenty B24s and three P38s. The P38s were being used for search missions within enemy territory. Ground crews that came along with the P38s terminated their period of temporary duty at Alconbury on 31 March. From then on the 36BS personnel performed all necessary maintenance.

36BS missions increased in March. Art Ledtke recalled, "The missions symbols on *Playmate* had a red lightning slash through a white cloud." Here, *Playmate* proudly displays 35 missions. *Courtesy of Arthur Ledtke.*

Just as in February the problem of securing necessary RCM equipment persisted. Supply channels were such that it was often difficult to get what was needed without considerable delay. This situation was aggravated by frequent equipment changes. Planning operational requirements from a personnel and engineering standpoint presented many problems for a squadron of this type. Operations varied considerably according to the situation, the effectiveness of the equipment employed, enemy countermeasures, and the like.

By now the squadron had become fairly well situated at Alconbury. A number of improvements were made to Site 3 where the enlisted men were housed. Although housing facilities were still very crowded and in some cases inadequate, all the barracks were painted on the inside. Stones were placed along the walks and driveways, and trees and shrubs were planted in the area. Offices and shops were established in several buildings on the airfield.

The morale of the squadron continued to be relatively good. The meals continued to be the chief morale building factor. An increased number of ratings and improvements in housing and grounds also contributed in building morale. Morale seemed to improve as operations increased. This was particularly true of the flying personnel, as they looked forward to the completion of their tour and their return to the Zone of Interior. A period of good weather in March saw a number of soft ball games going on in the field next to Site 3. A number of men also made good use of the volley ball court in Site 3. And again, like February, several men of the squadron married English girls.

Crew chief Irl Fife had found the love of his life. He recalled:

I married a very dear English lady which I met while stationed at Cheddington. We had planned a June wedding but heard the 36th would move, so we moved the date to March 17. We moved around March 1st to Alconbury. Since travel was limited, how would I and my assistants who had a part in the wedding get to Leighton Buzzard? Capt. Sackett said, "We need a practice flight. We will fly

Lt. Senn in the pilot's seat in a newly arrived B24 #42-50576, R4-H nicknamed *Peck's Bad Boys.* Morale seemed to increase as operations increased. Lt. Senn flew 31 operational missions. *Courtesy of Robert McLean Senn, Jr.*

Peck's Bad Boys **nose art.** *Courtesy of Mrs. Emery Turknett.*

you to Cheddington." How many guys flew to their wedding in a Liberator? Capt. Sackett and the crew presented us with a set of silver teaspoons and a card signed by all the men of the crew.

Sgt. Aubrey Whitworth longed for a chance to marry his British sweetheart, but fate dealt him a deadly card. He remembered:

It took a lot red tape, but I was wanting to marry an English gal and I finally got permission. She went into London to find a dress to wear for the wedding, and she was killed by a buzz bomb. That was two weeks before our wedding. That kind of sobered me a little bit.

By the end of March, as the war in Europe was drawing to a close, Lt. Col. Hambaugh wrote to Mrs. Bertha Clemens, the mother of S/Sgt. Arthur Clemens, the flight engineer for Lt. Boehm's crew. Most certainly the other families, the mothers, fathers, wives, and sweethearts of the men lost received a similar message. The squadron commander's letter read:

My dear Mrs. Clemens:

On receiving confirmation of the loss of your son, Staff Sergeant Arthur R. Clemens, 33504740, I was deeply grieved and felt that you might like to know the valiant way in which he served his country.

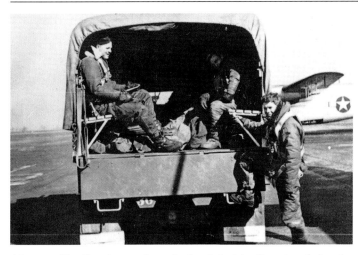

Airmen of Lt. Senn's crew board a truck to take them to mission debriefing. *Courtesy of Robert McLean Senn, Jr.*

While engaged in a flight over England on the 22nd of December 1944, bad weather forced the aircraft in which your son was flying to be diverted to Valley, Wales, England. Flying there, the gasoline supply became exhausted and the crew of which your son was a member were forced to abandon the plane. The aircraft crashed on the beach of the Irish Sea. Two members of the crew, the pilot and co-pilot, were later found uninjured near the wreckage of the plane. The other members of the crew parachuted into the Irish Sea. Every available resource was exhausted in an attempt to discover some trace of the other crew members, but none was found. It is assumed that they perished in the sea and have been declared dead.

Your son was well known to me and the men of my command, and a well liked friend to all. His fine personal habits and American spirit were a constant source of admiration and respect. His service in my command is held in the highest esteem, and his loss has been deeply felt.

Staff Sergeant Clemens knew full well the danger and risks entailed in his duties, but like the true American he was, he accepted the full weight of his grave responsibilities without shirking. In this day of courage and patriotism, your son stands high on the Roll of Honor. You and I have every reason to be proud of him.

However inadequate these words may be, please let them convey a message of deep sorrow and sympathy in your great loss.

ROBERT F. HAMBAUGH,
Lt. Colonel AC,
Commanding[86]

To acknowledge and commend all the airmen of the 8th Air Force for their sacrifice, great success, and heroic achievements, General Dwight D. Eisenhower wrote to Lt. General Carl Spaatz, the Commanding General, U.S. Strategic Air Forces in Europe. His letter read:

Supreme Headquarters Allied Expeditionary Force
Office of the Supreme Commander

Dear General Spaatz,
I have just returned from a visit in the Julich, Duren, Munchen-Gladbach area. As the Allied Armies advance into the former industrialized area of the Rhineland, they are everywhere confronted with striking evidence of the effectiveness of the bombing campaigns carried on for years by Bomber Command and since 1942 by the 8th Air Force. City after city has been systematically shattered. Against these our artillery is often used to blast out pill boxes, snipers and hidden tanks, but it could scarcely add to the completeness of the material destruction. Here and there, possibly because of their relative unimportance as industrial centers, certain towns have been largely spared. These present a remarkable contrast to the ruins of Aachen, Julich, Duren, Cologne and the other Rhineland cities that have been targeted by our big bombers day after day and night after night. The effect on the war economy of Germany has obviously been tremendous; a fact that advancing troops are quick to appreciate and which unfailingly remind them of the heroic work of their comrades in Bomber Command and in the United States Air Forces.

I should like for all your units to know that the sacrifices they have made are today facilitating success on all fronts.

Sincerely,
Dwight D. Eisenhower[87]

This proclamation no doubt started many commendations to filter down to the individual bomb groups. Soon proper recognition to the airmen of the 36BS would be forthcoming for their special support, achievements, and sacrifice.

12

Lightning Strikes

April 1945

April saw the last operational RCM missions for the 36th Bomb Squadron. The missions continued to be that of providing radar and radio countermeasures for the 8th Air Force heavy bombardment operations. Operations had now decreased as compared to March. The March operations were to be the high month for the squadron.

The VHF screen to prevent enemy interception of VHF R/T traffic transmitted by bombers during assembly was put up on eighteen days out of the thirty in the month. On 3 April two such screens were operated. Four Liberators were the usual number employed. Patrols were flown over fixed coordinates over the North Sea, more or less paralleling the coast of England and about fifty miles from the Dutch Coast. No detailed report exists as to the effectiveness of the screen, but the searches conducted by search aircraft indicated that the coverage was good.

Although additional radar equipment was installed in six B24s and partially installed in seven more, with a considerable expenditure of manpower and material, the equipped aircraft were not used operationally. This may be accounted for mainly by the good progress of Allied ground forces and also by the fact that studies

P51 of the 20th Fighter Group, 55th Fighter Squadron parked on a wingtip having a close-up look see. *Courtesy of Earl R. Siler.*

made by monitoring organizations based on the continent indicated that the enemy had been able to "look through and around" the screen sufficiently to secure desired information.

Radar search operations were conducted on three occasions during the month; one by a Liberator over the North Sea area, one by a P-38 over the Baltic seaports, and one by a P-38 over the Munich area. All were accomplished without incident. Squadron search operations terminated on 19 April.

Capt. Howard Kasch, liaison officer from the Intelligence Office at Pinetree on detached service with the 36BS and in charge of the P-38 search program, returned to High Wycombe on 1 April. Until terminated on 19 April the searches were directed by the squadron Communication Section under instructions received from Pinetree. The "Droop Snoot" P38 searches were flown by Lt. Edwards on detached service from the 7th Photographic Reconnaissance Group. Capt. Kasch and Lt. Stallcup acted as RCM observers. The other P-38 pilots, Lts. Brunell, Riley, and Glaza, and their enlisted mechanics, all on detached service, returned to their former group.

Lt. Robert Pepper wanted to fly one of the fast P38 Lightnings but missed out. He recalled:

Near the end of the war in Europe P38s were assigned to our base. Of course, every bomber pilot in the 36th wanted to get checked out to fly P38s. Some of the top brass did indeed get to fly them, but I was too far down the chain of command. The war was over and we shipped out, and I did not even get to sit in one. I did get to drive a jeep around a little on the wrong side of the road—that was exciting.

For Sgt. Art Ledtke, his missions were almost over. The RCM operator wrote:

TWENTY-FIFTH MISSION, April 3, 1945

This mission also uneventful. We had taken off at 4:20 a.m. and started back about 8 a.m. Flew most of the time between two cloud layers, strictly VHF jamming. It looks as if our radar screen

The Sea Isle Motel, Miami, Florida. Franklin Delano Roosevelt draped in black. The nation mourns the loss of the Commander-in-Chief. *Courtesy of Iredell Hutton.*

Taxi accident involving B24 #42-51307 nicknamed *Just Jeanne* before the squadron's last mission. *Courtesy of the USAF Historical Research Agency.*

will not be used this way any longer. No need for it, as the Germans are pretty well beaten down.

[I] received the Air Medal and Cluster today. [It was] presented by the CO, Lt. Col. Hambaugh, and ironically [I] had guard duty at night. The guard duty entailed being on the flight line, keeping an eye on the ships parked there. At one time, I got tired and cold and climbed into the cockpit of a P38 to get out of the wind for a while. From there I could observe the surrounding area.

TWENTY-SIXTH MISSION, April 11, 1945

We took along an extra man, a new navigator, checking him out, his first mission. After a while, Kimmelman let him take over. Kimmelman got into the nose turret and test fired the guns. We scared the new man by telling him tall stories.

Lt. Al Bohne, navigator for Lt. Eugene Eby, recalled seeing what must have looked like the whole 8th Air Force on one of its last spectacular missions:

We were flying our assigned area and switching electronics on and off as prescribed. We were nearing the end of our mission over the channel, and the planes we were protecting joined their formation and set course for the continent targets. This particular raid was one of the famous 1,000 plane raids which were such a sensation in the papers and radio and movie newscasts in America. As this raid was passing us we tried to fathom the immensity of this attack and talked to each other on our intercom and to no one in particular. We jabbered incessantly in excitement as we each wanted the rest to see what we couldn't describe. As far as one could see, from horizon to horizon, the sky was filled with B17s, B24s, P38s, and P51s. This was not a formation—this was a swarm. This con-

L-R George O'Bradovich and Leonard Backer sightseeing London. *Courtesy of Leonard N. Backer.*

centration of aircraft, as spectacular and awesome to us who admired it with pride, also was depressing to me. It had to be as awesome and frightening to the poor enemy civilian as it was inspiring to us. I couldn't fully imagine the horror the enemy civilian would be experiencing. Our amazement was cut short by the hostile approach of a P51. While we were aware that these planes were headed our way, those flyers were not aware that we were there—we were not supposed to be there. Our presence was secret even to them. On his second approach, we became aware that he was seriously considering us a clandestine threat, or perhaps a cripple. The gunners quickly asked if they should return fire if fired upon. Our strategy was to point the guns down, not to follow the fighter, and to stay our course, as our mission was not yet complete. He was apparently convinced that we posed no threat to anyone and returned to his flight.

On April 12, 1945, United States President Franklin Delano Roosevelt died. Squadron personnel joined with personnel of other units on the base in front of the flag pole at the station headquarters to honor the memory of their President and Commander in Chief. Sgt. Joe Danahy remembered listening on his radio that he bought from Iredell Hutton about the death of the beloved American President:

I particularly remember hearing the news of President Roosevelt's death. It came at night in England, and I tuned from one station to another across half the world, or so it seemed. I couldn't understand the words (so many different languages), but suddenly in the midst of a sentence, I would hear "Franklin Delano Roosevelt" and would realize what I was hearing. I heard that news travel across many thousands of miles that night to many, many countries, and I've never forgotten it. I've never forgotten that old radio.

For pilot Lt. James Young that day was indeed a most eventful and dark day in his life. He said:

London's Piccadilly Circus was a favorite draw for all the sights. *Courtesy of Art Brusila.*

Photographer Frank Trovato receives directions from a British Bobby — "Yer coint miss it!" *Courtesy of Frank J. Trovato.*

My toughest day was April 13, 1945, when we made a blind instrument take-off, went out and flew our allotted time on station and came back in. We had one little spot there off the Wash in northeast England that we had to approach the coastline at a very specific altitude, airspeed, and heading, or if not the British anti-aircraft would start taking shots at us. So we had to hit that keyhole just right on the money in all three categories with altitude, speed, and heading. As soon as we got inside then we could just make a left turn and head back to Alconbury. On this particular day I had just gotten back over England and turned to the base and ran into a heavy snowstorm. Well, it didn't really present any problem because I was flying the plane on instruments. The co-pilot was sticking his head out the blister and working the deicer boots to keep the wings from getting covered up with snow and ice, and every once and a while giving the propeller a shot of deicer fluid on the props. I guess I had been in that thing a half an hour or forty-five minutes. I just took a chance and risked a glance up out the front of the plane. Just

St. Johns College at Cambridge. *Courtesy of Art Brusila.*

Kings College Chapel at Cambridge. *Courtesy of James C. Garrett*

as I looked up there a lightning bolt hit us. I mean hit us right on the nose. The two 50 caliber machine guns that were sticking out the nose turret—it fused them and drooped them. The right side of the ship—it broke out all the glass in the navigator's compartment. The right side of the plane looked like we had had a collision with a fighter or something. It just kind of dented it all in. That was the day that we heard that President Roosevelt had died. Of course he died on the 12th of April over here on Thursday. We were six hours ahead over there. By the time the news got over there we were out on a mission.

After this lightning hit, I asked O'Loughlin, my flight engineer, to go back to the bomb bay to check to see if he could find any particular problems, because I knew we had lost a lot of our electronics. [However,] I could still talk to the crew on intercom. He came back five minutes later and said that everything looked all right. He couldn't find any gas leaks or anything. It looked like we were in fairly decent shape. So, we made it on back in to Alconbury and landed.

I went through the usual routine of going through debriefing. I remember Capt. Jones [36th Squadron Intelligence Officer] was taking notes on me, what I had to say. He said, "Well, Young, did anything unusual happen today?" I said, "Nothing unusual Capt. Jones, except that I got hit by lightning coming back." Colonel Hambaugh was standing behind Capt. Jones and he said, "What did you say, Lt. Young?" I said, "I got hit by lightning!" So he turned to Jones and said, "Let's go look at that airplane." So they left and jumped in the Colonel's jeep, took off down the flight line, and found the plane I had flown that day. In the meantime I had finished the debriefing, went on back in the locker room to put up my flight equipment, like the pilot's throat mike, oxygen mask, and parachute harness, all the stuff I would normally use when I was flying. They would always serve us a couple of ounces of either cognac, bourbon, or scotch or something like that after we had returned from each mission. The medics did that. So, I was sitting back there in a chair having my little drink when the Colonel came

stroking in. He walked up to me and put his arm around my shoulder and he said "Lieutenant, every day from now on is borrowed time. You should have died in that plane today." He said that he had never seen anything like that before.

RAFU University education program certificate.

Relieving the tension. Airmen relax by playing baseball. The enlisted men won by 8 to 1.

Lt. Leon Hammer, Lt. Young's navigator, also remembered his bump on that near-tragic occasion:

Our plane was hit by lightning. I was standing facing the front of the plane, because in this particular B24, the navigator's table faced forward rather than backwards. As a result of the lightning strike, I fell backwards, struck my head and was briefly unconscious.

When the plane landed squadron armorer, Cpl. Charles Todaro was in the truck that went to pick up Lt Young's crew. Todaro recalled:

I noticed people were out in front looking at the front turret. What had happened was a lightning bolt had hit the rear turret, the guns, gone through the plane and went out through the .50s in the front turret and melted the barrels. They were just one piece of solid iron. So, that's what they were all looking at. They couldn't believe what happened. When you melt a caliber .50 barrel, you're melting a big piece of iron.

With the war in Europe now about over Sgt. Art Ledtke recorded his last mission for the 36BS:

TWENTY-SEVENTH MISSION, April 18, 1945

Upon take-off, #1 engine was having a bad case of torching. It threw out flames about four or five feet or so. Everyone in the waist had their hands on their chutes, but everything went OK and the flames died down. Anyway, we were too low to bail out if we had to. The rest of the trip was uneventful.

An awards presentation ceremony was held in the briefing room on 3 April. Squadron Commander Lt. Col. Hambaugh presented 46 Air Medals to squadron members. Also at this ceremony Lt. Col. Hambaugh and Major Stutzman, the Squadron Operations Officer, were awarded the Croix de Guerre by the French government as a token of appreciation for the work done by the squadron in assisting in the liberation of France.

Later on 17 April memberships to the Caterpillar Club for men who parachuted to safety were awarded to officers and enlisted men by the Irvin Air Chute Co. of Great Britain, Ltd.

The new members were:

1st Lt. Harold Boehm
2d Lt. Donald Burch
2d Lt. Robert Casper
1st Lt. Joseph Hornsby
T/Sgt. Jack Chestnut
T/Sgt. Joseph Danahy
Sgt. Robert Veliz
Sgt. Pete Yslava

The airmen received the following message from Mr. Irvin: "I am indeed glad that these men were able to save their lives with Irvin chutes, and have much pleasure in welcoming them as members of the club." [88]

On 25 April while taxiing about the perimeter track in preparation to taking off on the squadron's last mission, Liberator #42-51307's nose wheel became cocked at an angle and broke off. The accident caused considerable damage to this aircraft nicknamed "Just Jeanne."

With operations having decreased so sharply, a problem developed as to how best to keep the men occupied. Outside of just relaxing or taking in London, Cambridge, and other sites, some men attended educational classes in German, French, and Spanish languages taught by the Group Education Officer. A number of men also enrolled in other United States Armed Forces Institute (USAFI) courses. Also for fun and entertainment, the enlisted men's soft ball team played its first tournament game against the 685th Material Squadron. The enlisted men won by a score of 8 to 1. For the squadron engineering section a celebration was in order. A 200 mission party was held on 2 April in the former combat officers' mess.

Tying the knot. Father Tomlinson with the newly-weds and friends. Nick Garza married the former Miss Nancy Sears and Howard Buis married Celia Joyce Sanders. The weddings took place at the Catholic Church of St. Thomas Aquinas in Bletchley. Not even war could stop love and marriage. The marriages continue to this day.

For Liberator #42-50750, R4-P and the 36BS — mission accomplished. Would it be off to the Pacific next ? *Courtesy of Leonard N. Backer.*

Sgt. Joe Danahy recalled one way he kept occupied:

At Alconbury, J.O. Thompson and I were all of twenty years old. He used to refer to me as his "Librarian." I had made friends with the mail clerk for the 36th, a fellow named Arnold from Arkansas—good guy—and every month so many boxes of new pocket books were allotted to the squadron. I always got one box for myself, read the books that interested me, and then passed them on to J.O.

And again in April several men married English girls. Two of the men to do so were Sgt. Nick Garza and S/Sgt. Howard Buis from the squadron Orderly Room. Nick Garza married the former Miss Nancy Sears on 6 April, and Howard Buis married Celia Joyce Sanders on 18 April. The ladies were best friends from Bletchley in Buckinghamshire. Both weddings took place at the Catholic Church of St. Thomas Aquinas in Bletchley.

Today, after more than fifty years of marriage, the two couples remain close friends. Howard and Celia Buis now have nine children, which brought them thirty-five grandchildren and four great-grandchildren. Also still married, Nick and Nancy have five children and six grandchildren to their credit.

The scientists and engineers of ABL-15 involved in RCM research and development were now shifting their attention to the war in the Pacific as Dr. John Dyer expressed to Dr. Fred Terman:

In view of the war situation, discussions are in progress with 8th AF concerning revision of [the ABL-15] laboratory program. We are recommending discontinuing most long range laboratory programs and those other programs which in all probability will not be of further importance in the European War. Our intention is to release personnel for intelligence work, for jobs connected with closing of the laboratory, and to soon start sending personnel back to the USA for your use in connection with the Pacific War.[89]

Eighteen days after the death of Franklin Roosevelt, at half past three on the afternoon of April 30, 1945; surrounded by the Russian army and facing certain capture, Adolph Hitler, along with his new bride Eva Braun, committed suicide. Hitler was now dead just ten days after his fifty-sixth birthday. The Fuhrer had been commanding his defeated army from deep within his underground bunker in Berlin since early January 1945.

13

Strictly Victory

May 1945

The last operational mission for the 36th Bomb Squadron was flown on 25 April and the squadron support work ended. The squadron now awaited orders for its future deployment.

The future of ABL-15 was also being discussed. Lt. Gen. Jimmy Doolittle wrote to Gen. Hap Arnold and suggested using the energy and resources of ABL-15 in the Pacific war effort. His secret memo states in part:

The Radio Countermeasures program of the Eighth Air Force has had the active participation of the American-British Laboratory personnel with the facilities available to them for experimentation, limited production of special equipment, and supplies of unusual items.

Since the organization of ABL in the autumn of 1943, work with the Eighth Air Force has accounted for at least two-thirds of the laboratory effort. This has resulted both from the magnitude of the operations of the Eighth Air Force, and from the applicability of RCM to the strategic air war. The full aim of ABL has been to supplement, not replace, the functions of Eighth Air Force personnel in achieving an effective countermeasures program. It has attempted to maintain, here in the field, an organization of specialists in RCM equipment.

The memo went on to describe the different phases of the RCM program in which ABL rendered assistance. General Doolittle closed by stating:

This information on the form and function of ABL assistance in the RCM program is submitted, as it may assist in the establishing of similar civilian technical advice and laboratory facilities in the Pacific.

J. H. DOOLITTLE
Lieutenant General, USA
Commanding[90]

On the morning of 7 May all reveille formations were thrown into an uproar when a broadcast announced the unconditional surrender of Germany. This announcement was later retracted due to its being premature. The next day all organizations stationed at Alconbury formed in their respective sites and were marched by their commanding officers to the athletic field near headquarters. The station commander of Alconbury, Lt. Col. Clement Bird, made the announcement of V-E Day. A prayer of Thanksgiving was offered by Chaplain Willis Brown, and the National Anthem was then

An example of one of the many English haystacks torched in celebration of VE-Day. *Courtesy of Frank J. Trovato.*

The "Blowout". Unwinding after VE-Day. *Courtesy of the USAF Historical Research Agency.*

Let the band play on. *Courtesy of the USAF Historical Research Agency.*

played by the station band. Next the individual unit commanders delivered a short congratulatory and commendatory talk to the men. The program came to a close with the playing of "America" by the station band. Everyone joined in the singing.

An impressive part of the ceremony was a group of aircraft on its way to the continent on the first observation flight scheduled by the 482nd Bomb Group. The aircraft flew over the assembly in a "V" for Victory formation.

This was a most special day for all the men, but unfortunately, all personnel were restricted to the exact limits of the station. All village public houses were considered out of bounds, and all clubs and bars were closed until the usual evening opening time. Other events scheduled that day included a ball game featuring the officers versus enlisted men. Following the ball game, an impromptu "Variety Show" on the athletic field entertained the men. Inevitably the men found ways to celebrate and express their great joy in the victory that all had worked so hard to achieve.

Sgt. Robert King, flight engineer for the Lt. Stanley Studstrup crew, wrote of VE-Day:

On VE-Day Col. Hambaugh announced a victory party to be held in the squadron area. Barrels of English beer were brought in and the party proceeded. The troops were having a great time firing flare pistols and .45 cal. automatic pistols in the air. Some flares landed in the farmer's haystacks and started them on fire. Col. Hambaugh came down the hill to slow down the celebration. To the best of my memory he said, "Gentlemen, I have been standing on the hill watching and listening to you. I have to tell you guys to hold it down." By then all the beer was gone, and some joker had shot himself in the foot with his .45 pistol.

Lt. John Beaty, navigator for Lt. Sweeney's crew, penned a V-Mail letter to his wife Sarah back in Baltimore, Maryland. His V-Mail read:

England
May 7, 1945

Sweetheart,
The big day over here has finally arrived, Germany has officially quit today. In spite of their uniforms and their rank, most of the fellows are just over-grown boys at heart.

Lt. David Crosby's invitation to the 36BS "Blowout". *Courtesy of David G. Crosby, III.*

Lt. Col. Hambaugh at the party with 1st. Sgt. Simmie Renfroe. *Courtesy of George F. Lechner Sr.*

From all indications there won't be much sleeping done tonight. In fact, if you didn't know better you might think this was the 4th of July. There has been a continuous popping of pistols and firing of flares (looks like our Roman Candles red, green, and white). Outside the barracks some of the boys have set fire to the trash cans. Yes! It's quite a hullabaloo—the fire department has just arrived with their engines.

The bonfires can be seen for quite a distance, and they aren't taking any chances. You remember that haystack I told you was right near the field, well, I expect to see that lit up before the night is over. Wish you and the babies and I could get together for a quiet celebration.

All my love,

Johnny[91]

For Lt. Al Bohne, this day was doubly special. He wrote:

My 20th birthday was on May 7, 1945. What a gift when we were informed early that evening that Germany had capitulated. My combat tour had come to an end. A final bash was ordered by the CO to celebrate the end of the European war and the resulting victory. The CO jokingly ordered all officers to the base for the party. I doubt the order would have been necessary. It was a great party. A few over joyous fellows emptied some of the planes of very pistols and flares. They proceeded to light up the night skies. Fires were even started in the streets of our billet area. As the firefighters fought the blaze there, another would be started somewhere else, just to keep the firefighters active. We all bought a couple of haystacks that evening by lighting them afire. I never heard of any disciplinary action as the result of this celebration other than the collection to pay for the hay.

It was the same for Sgt. Art Ledtke, who said:

VE-Day, May 8, 1945

We got word that the war was over. Celebrations started. Officially, we were restricted to the base. Some fellows skipped out and went to London. Our crew was too worried about missing orders for home, so we stayed on base. Most of the GIs did. We had extra rations of food and drinks passed around. After dark rockets, guns, etc., were shot off. Quite a few of the fellows were drunk. I have one vivid scene in mind of the pasture next to our quarters. By the light of the rockets, flares, etc., going off overhead, an old white farm horse which in the past moved very slowly, got scared and started

The glass brick bar at Alconbury. Enjoyed by the 8AF, the RAF, Lt. Col. Hambaugh, and Col. Jimmy Stewart.

Gathering for a "Cook's Tour". *Courtesy of Art Brusila.*

Bridges bombed in Koblenz. Koblenz stood at the junction of the Rhine and Moselle Rivers. It had little industrial activity, but several important marshaling yards. Almost all the damage was done by bombing with a good share of that done by instruments. *Courtesy of Dr. Robert F. Hambaugh, Jr.*

Bomb target Essen. One of the most heavily bombed cities in the world. Home of the Krupp works, the big name German armament industry. *Courtesy of Dr. Robert F. Hambaugh, Jr.*

to run. It ran right through the hedgerow and fence and kept going. It was a couple of days before it was returned to the field.

We partied until the wee hours of the morning. I don't remember too much of the rest. I guess the beer and scotch got to be more than I could handle.

Lt. David Booker, the navigator for Lt. Harry Stone, remembered preparing for the squadron victory bash.

One trip we made by airplane was to an air base in southern England. There was a group of MIT graduate engineers stationed there doing various applied research projects. They had a group of secretaries from New England working for them. We made the mis-

take of inviting some of them back to Alconbury with us to a dance. After we landed, we got caught transporting them off the base to local housing. The punishment was minimum. They went to the dance and were entertained royally. But the next day we were not allowed to take them back to their home base. Another crew got that assignment.

Lt. David Merrill was also very much inclined to participate in the celebration festivities and spoke of his contribution. Little did he realize what it would mean to him further down the road:

Now, the 36th was laying on a big party. We were using British rationed rum, which would take the top of your head right off. We

A most strategic bridge. It was here the first crossing of the Rhine was made. Over it the 1st Army established the first Allied bridgehead. *Courtesy of Dr. Robert F. Hambaugh, Jr.*

The vast devastation of Frankfurt. Frankfurt was one of the main targets of the 8AF. Frankfurt was guarded by more than 250 heavy guns. Population 100,000, this city, founded 794 AD was the center of commercial and financial activities of southwest Germany. The two marshaling yards, one at the North and the other the East of town, bore the brunt of several attacks with small targets scattered about the city sharing in these same attacks. *Courtesy of Dr. Robert F. Hambaugh, Jr.*

Going down low. Flying eye level with the middle of the Eiffel Tower. *Courtesy of Paul J. Pond Jr.*

Koln Cathedral. Koln was a center of trade and political activity in the Rhine, and a chief railway center in the Rhineland. Koln had extensive river harbors, synthetic oil plants, engineering works, and heavy armaments. It was one of the heavier bombed cities. *Courtesy of Paul J. Pond Jr.*

saved the bourbon and rye whiskey, which was a good plan. You didn't get any interference from me.

I had found a little pocket of American girls in Great Malvern, and I naturally had to go over there and consult rather frequently. So, when we had this big party, I undoubtedly went over there and talked to one girl, Rosalind [Kaspar] and her roommate Shirley [Clark] and invited them to the party. We went over in a B24. They said, "Well, how are we gonna get there? I said, "Come back with us in the airplane. I think it will be all right with the pilot." Anyhow, I thought I'd better check with him, and I did. He said, "Why don't we call Hambaugh?" I said, "Good idea!" I called Colonel Hambaugh and he said, "No way!" He said, "No civilians on the airplane! Don't you dare do that!" I was a little bit crestfallen, but said, "Well, all right." And that was it. I went back and found some flying clothes for Roz and Shirl and put them in the back of the airplane. Everybody on the crew was certainly willing to do this. We got back to Alconbury, and I said to the girls, "Now, you stay in the airplane and just be quiet and I'll send somebody out for you." Then I went back to my office and got my driver. His name was Springer, a nice fellow. I sent him out. I told him there was some equipment in the aircraft and that he would know what to do with it when he found it. He was gone for quite awhile, and I wondered where the heck he was. About two hours later, he came back and said, "I took that equipment that you had in the airplane and had it put away." I asked, "Where in the world did you put it?" He said, "Down at the Vicker's house. They got a room there. The Vicker had space and rented the girls a room."

At any rate, the party went on. Well, the girls were the hit of the party. They were the only girls there in formal dresses. And they no sooner had gotten near there that the word was around that there were two American girls on the base, which was a great thing for everybody. Everybody wanted to take a gawk at them, speak to them,

and what not. We went over to dinner at the officer's club and had a steak dinner. We laid on a great party.

After the party we were over at the bar drinking all that good bourbon and rye whiskey. Somehow a little bit later, Roz and I found ourselves sitting on the floor, under the slot machines, with Colonel Hambaugh and the British Territorial Commander, who was in command of the antiaircraft guns at the field. We were singing bonney RAF songs and having a great time, drinking the good whiskey. Hambaugh turned to Roz and said, "How did you girls get here?" Roz replied, "We came in a B24, and it was wonderful!" He turned around and looked at me and he said, "If Lee [that is, the Civil War Confederate General Robert E. Lee] don't inspect us up tomorrow morning, see me in my office, will you?"

I didn't make captain for a couple of months, but that was all right. I can't say he was wrong. I look back on it now with amusement. It was worth the price of admission. These were nice girls. And in five years, Shirl and I were engaged. We've only been married forty-one years.

Flying circles around the Arc de Triumph. *Courtesy of Paul J. Pond Jr.*

Men gathering on, in, and around *Ready N' Able* **for the 36BS photograph.** *Courtesy of Art Brusila.*

However, by no means was it thought that Lt. Col. Hambaugh was a party pooper. It was well known that he got along well with both the enlisted men and the officers. It has even been said that the colonel had a glass brick bar built for the men at Alconbury.

For the ground personnel, observation flights were flown over the Ruhr and Rhineland in Germany. These observation flights, also known as "Cook's Tours," were like a popular travel agency back in the U.S. These flights were done in order for the airmen to show the ground personnel the results of their contributions toward victory, and also to express their appreciation for their tireless work efforts. The flights were made on 8, 10, 11, 12, and 13 May. Three aircraft were dispatched on 8 May and six on each of the other days, making a total of 27 flights. Only skeleton crews were flown, with approximately 10 passengers in each aircraft. All totaled, about 210 ground officers and enlisted men were able to take these flights.

Co-pilot Lt. Robert Pepper flew on one of the observation flights, or "Cook's Tours":

After VE Day the ground people wanted to see the damage done by "us" bombers, so our crew was one assigned to fly low altitude tours over Germany with our waist area full of ground crew people. Unless one could see with his own eyes, he could not imagine how devastated Germany was. Not a bridge standing anywhere, not a railroad, not a highway, not a factory. Frankfurt, for instance, was just a pile of rubble. I was in Frankfurt in 1977. It was easy to distinguish new construction. Looking down the street I could see that about every third building was old, indicating that two-thirds had been completely bombed out.

We lost an engine on one of these tours. We polled our guests to see if they wanted to head for home or fly on down to see Paris. Paris won hands down, so we flew over Paris and around the Eiffel Tower at about 1,000 feet with a dead and feathered engine. We made it back across the channel and landed safely on three engines.

Navigator David Booker steered a "Cook's Tour" and wrote:

After the war ended we were assigned to take maintenance personnel on sightseeing tours of France and Germany. We were amazed at the destruction. In the city of Cologne, it appeared the only building standing was the Cologne Cathedral. We buzzed the French countryside, almost counting the shingles on the roofs of farm houses. We also flew a circle around the Arc de Triumph in France and buzzed the English channel, ending up with water in the bomb bay. One of the most amazing sights were the prisoner of war camps along the Rhine River. There must have been thousands of men under the blazing sun with no trees for shade. One trip we stayed overnight in Paris.

One observation flight after VE-Day was almost a fatal trip for Lt. Leon Hammer:

Three days after the war ended, our crew was on a tour of Europe for the ground crew and other people who did not have a chance to see what they contributed. [We] crossed the continent at Ostend and were fired upon by flak by the British, of all people!

Pioneers in electronic warfare — the 36th Bomb Squadron on May 23, 1945. Some worried that the wings might fall off. *Courtesy of the Joseph P. Danahy.*

Appropriately named Liberator #42-50495, R4-V — *Strictly Victory.*
Courtesy of Wilbur F. Kruse.

Co-pilot Lt. Wilbur Kruse also remembered picking up some flak:

After VE-Day on May 10th we went over Omaha Beach. We encountered flak shortly after we got over the coast. There had always been a pocket of Germans in there that the Allies just lived with. It was those Germans that were throwing up the flak. There were four or five bursts of flak probably 500 yards away. It wasn't life threatening or accurate or anything, but it was a little scary.

On 23 May the entire compliment of men in the 36th Bomb Squadron gathered for a squadron photograph. For this event the men kneeled, sat in chairs, stood on benches, stood under the wings, on the wings, or on the fuselage, and in the cockpit of Liberator R4-A, nicknamed *"Ready N' Able."* Some of the men wondered if the wings would fall off under all the pressure, but luckily this did not happen. The photograph was taken and copies were distributed for all as a memento of their time served in the squadron while in England.

There was much celebration as well back in the United States now that the war in Europe was over. Many church services gave thanks that the killing in Europe had ended, and ceremonies were going on night and day remembering the sacrifice made by our troops. On 27 May a memorial service was held at the Ebenezer United Brethren Church in Lebanon, PA, in memory of S/Sgt. Arthur Clemens. S/Sgt. Clemens had been one of Lt. Harold Boehm's crew that was lost in Wales. The service was conducted by the American Legion Post 158 of Lebanon and included S/Sgt. Clemens' favorite poem. It read:

"BE STRONG"

We are not here to play, to dream, to drift.
We have hard work to do and loads to lift.
Shun not the struggle face it, 'tis God's gift.
Be strong !

Say not the days are evil, who's to blame?
And fold the hands and acquiesce Oh, shame!
Stand up, speak out, and bravely, in God's name,
Be strong !

It matters not how deep entrenched the wrong.
How hard the battle goes, the day how long;
Faint not fight on! Tomorrow comes the song.

By Maltbie D. Babcock[92]

On 30 May the Commanding Officer of the 482nd Bomb Group departed Station 102, Alconbury, for the Zone of Interior. Lt. Col. Hambaugh assumed the duties of station commander.

For Lt. Col. Hambaugh and the men of the 36BS, their time for making this long awaited journey would come soon.

The airmen of Lt. Grubisich's crew were most eager and readying things for their long flight home. Co-pilot Wilbur Kruse would be aiming for his native Kansas. Kruse recalled:

Packing up to go home, [nose gunner] Weston Smith painted "Strictly Victory" on the ship we flew. We washed the plane by hand using aviation fuel, before it left. This gave us better performance, less drag.

14

Liberated from England

June 1945

With the war in Europe now over the adjutants from headquarters, the bomb groups, and the squadrons were burning up their fingertips and busy working on travel orders to send the men on their long awaited trip back home. On 5 June a commendation to the 36th Bomb Squadron finally came down through the chain of command. The commendation from Headquarters 8th Air Force via Headquarters 1st Air Division to the men of the 36th read:

TO : Commanding Officer, 36th Bomb Sq (RCM)

It is with a great deal of pride and personal satisfaction that I transmit this commendation from the Commanding General of the Eighth Air Force to the Officers and Enlisted Men of my Command. Although the job lacked the glory of combat over enemy territory, it was a job which contributed vitally to the success of the operations of our own air and ground forces and also to the operations of our great ally, the Royal Air Force. It is of great satisfaction to know, too, that our operations have undoubtedly saved the lives of many of our comrades. Every man in the organization can feel justly proud for having done his part in accomplishing this vital job. I would like to add my commendation and appreciation for a job extremely well done.

ROBERT F. HAMBAUGH,
Lt. Colonel., AC,
Commanding

HEADQUARTERS EIGHTH AIR FORCE
Office of the Commanding General
23 May 1945

SUBJECT : Letter of Commendation.
To: Commanding Officer, 36th Bombardment Squadron (RCM)
(Thru: Commanding General, 1st Air Div).

1. The advance of the Allied Ground Forces has exposed the effectiveness of air bombardment activities in the destruction of the fighting potentialities of our enemy. The special activities conducted by the 36th Bombardment Squadron (RCM) cannot be over-emphasized in the contribution of the unit to the striking power of this Air Force.

2. Each individual in the organization expended great effort in extensive training in new equipment which you used operationally for the first time on the night of 5/6 June 1944. Cooperating with the RAF, they provided an efficient radar screen of the enemy early warning radar system. Individual activities of every member of your Command combined to effect the greatest possible chance of total success, not only for this operation, but for all operations to follow.

3. The organization, throughout its relatively short but colorful history, has displayed the highest type of initiative and performance. Lacking the glory of combat over enemy territory, your missions were still carried on under the most hazardous of weather conditions. At times, you were successfully carrying out your missions when it was necessary to issue orders standing down all combat operations.

4. Yours was the assignment of catching the enemy at his own game, and in effectively accomplishing this task, the whole nature

Just Jeanne **turns onto the taxiway.** *Courtesy of Leonard N. Backer.*

B24 pilot and squadron leader Col. James Stewart was described as "a very very down to earth, genuine soldier — real dedicated."

and tactics of your missions changed as the enemy scientists devised methods of overcoming our countermeasures. The complexity of your work included jamming of enemy radar, screening of our bomber VHF channels while bombers were assembling, carrying out "spoof" raids, jamming enemy tank communications, and performing special electronic search missions as directed by this Headquarters. The material advantage of these operations may never be adequately assessed, and it is impossible to fully evaluate the number of aircrews, as well as bomber and fighter aircraft, saved when enemy fighters discovered too late the essential interception data.

5. Hard work, exceptional technical ability, and determination to see a job well done enabled the 36th Bombardment Squadron (RCM) to successfully carry out this mission and reflected high credit upon the whole Eighth Air Force.

6. It is my desire that this commendation be disseminated to all members of your Command.

/s/ W.E. Kepner
/t/ W. E. KEPNER
Major General, U S Army
Commanding[93]

The 36BS continued its "Cook's Tours"—observation flights over the Ruhr and Rhineland in Germany for ground personnel—in June. Ten Liberators were dispatched on 16, 19, and 20 June, each plane carrying ten passengers. Seven B24s were dispatched on 23 and 25 June with an average of ten passengers per plane. This made a total of 44 observational flights.

Additionally, the B24s carried passengers from Alconbury and other bases to Paris for 48 hour passes on 8, 14, 20, 26, and 28 June. A total of 134 passengers were transported.

At this time the men of the 36BS found they had a celebrity in their midst. Lt. Leon Hendrickson remembered eating a meal with a Hollywood movie star.

I had dinner one time with Col. Jimmy Stewart while he was stationed at Alconbury. My most lasting memory was of his wiping his mouth on the tablecloth at the end of the meal.

Another 36BS pilot, Royce Kittle, remembered how a youthful hobby kept him away from meeting the famous movie star:

I was always making things out of plexiglass, and I missed flying with Jimmy Stewart one day because I was down at the flight line hunting some broken plexiglass to make a B24 model. I regretted that I never did talk to Jimmy and explain to him what happened. My airplane was written up by him, "A nice airplane, but a little nose heavy." Those were his comments. I was shy of celebrities, and I didn't want him to think I was fawning over him or something. I should have gone to the Officer's Club when he was in there and talked to him about the flight I missed and might have gotten another flight with him. I understand that he had been very considerate of military personnel.

"Droop Snoot" #43-28479 crashed on June 25, 1945 at Alconbury. *Courtesy of Walter Natishyn.*

The Gypsy Jane stripped of her nose guns before returning to the U.S.. Many guns were buried in a ditch at Alconbury. *Courtesy of J. O. Thompson.*

Lt. Pond crew lambing out by their Liberator waiting to go home. *Courtesy of Leonard N. Backer.*

Lt. Col. Robert F. Hambaugh autographed this photograph for his buddy Capt. Dick Sackett before heading home. *Courtesy of Richard C. Sackett.*

Liberated From England ready to go. Co-pilot William Hite smiles out from his window. *Courtesy of Robert P. King.*

Squadron armorer Sgt. Kelton Thrower also spoke highly of the Army Air Force officer and actor. He recalled:

Jimmy was a very very down to earth, genuine soldier, real dedicated. He would go to the briefings. We heard him talk. He was a good person and I admired him.

Lt. Wilbur Kruse spoke of Jimmy Stewart:

Several times Col. Stewart gave me a ride up the hill to the Officer's Club. I always wanted to write and thank him again, but I never knew his address.

Navigator Leon Hammer remembered him, too:

Col. Hambaugh managed somehow to bring together at Alconbury a bar made of glass brick. He sent us all over the place to get this glass brick. We used to fly all over to get liquor. He built this incredible bar that people came from all over the United Kingdom to drink at. The whole RAF used to come there. Jimmy Stewart spent a fair amount of time in that bar there, too. I used to stand next to him and drink.

The last airplane crash of the 36BS occurred after VE-Day on 25 June. Apparently it was all just in fun and no one was hurt. The actual Report of Aircraft Accident stated that the "Droop Snoot" P38, #43-28479, took off from Alconbury on a local check-out flight at 1625 hours. When the P38 tried to land, its landing gear was not locked down and the gear folded. The aircraft belly landed on runway 24. The crash caused damage to the propellers, both engines, the landing gear, the vertical stabilizer, and the underpart of the aircraft fuselage. The Duty Flying Control Officer at Alconbury, Lt. Don Hope, made his official report, which read:

P-38 #479 was coming in for a landing with the right propeller feathered. The landing gear appeared to be down and locked, but as

Airmen Harry Raupp and Everett Worthington with two "girlfriends". The good-byes would not be easy. *Courtesy of Harry Raupp*

An Air-Sea Rescue B17G. The Fortress had a 33ft. Higgins A-1 lifeboat under its belly and sea search radar under the nose used to protect and assist the convoys. *Courtesy of Isaac Benghiat.*

soon as the wheels touched the runway, the landing gear folded and the pilot was forced to make a belly landing. The aircraft was damaged considerably, but the pilot escaped without injury. There were no violations of flying regulations.

The pilot flying the "Droop Snoot" was not attached to the 36BS. He was performing a check-out flight, and even though he had nearly 200 hours flying single engine fighters, he had not flown the P38 before. It was found that the aircraft had run out of gas in the right engine.[94]

With the war in Europe now over, the men of the squadron prepared for the long journey home. The Liberators were dressed down and disarmed in preparation. Sgt. Thrower remembered:

We took out all the guns because we were going to fly back to the states. We took them over to Ordnance to turn the guns in [but] Ordnance had closed. We could not leave Alconbury until we got

rid of those guns. I think we had about eight planes, so that's eighty .50 caliber machine guns.We put them in wooden boxes that we found, took them out in a ditch, got an Englishman with a bulldozer to cover them up, and buried them.

The men had to get rid of their small arms, too. Art Ledtke wrote:

Word came down that all guns and ammo would be confiscated. Several fellows had acquired illegal guns either appropriated or bartered for on the black market. They threw the weapons and ammo into the pasture pond as we left the are to dispose of them.

For most of the men now was the time for saying goodbye, and this did not come easy. Severing the close-knit bond of friendships

Going home. *Courtesy of Ercel Coburn.*

NAME *Carl A. Sayer*
DATE *Nov 1945*

Luxury cruise ship *Queen Mary*. Some took the "slow boat" home.

Resting place of soldiers, sailors, and airmen. *Courtesy of James C. Garrett.*

The American War Memorial Cemetery at Madingley outside Cambridge. *Courtesy of James C. Garrett.*

molded in adversity against a common enemy was surely a painful task. This situation was forced on everyone for them to deal with. The terrific wartime experiences—frozen images; some of pain, horror, suffering, monumental tasks, bewilderment, happiness, and boredom would be locked within the hearts and minds of the men for a lifetime.

Sgt. Dick Mulligan of Lt. Sweeney's crew spoke of the diligent 36BS ground crew getting their B24 in tip-top shape for their trip home:

Col. Hambaugh said "Here is how you're going to get home. You're going to take your plane and you're going to fly it up to Reykjevik, Iceland, and over to Goose Bay [then to the U.S.]. You're going to fly ten other people. It just so happens, that's going to be your ground crew." When I hear that I said, "Wow, we're going to put them on there?" They're going to go out there and be nothing but asses and elbows making sure that plane is in good shape. Well, doggone it, we had engines in there that were just like brand new. They just worked their asses off because they were going to fly on the thing and they didn't want anything wrong with that airplane. So, we went down that runway and this thing just leaped up just so good. Everybody was happy that we had our ground crew on. They were there to make sure it was safe.

Lt. James Hamilton's crew busily prepared their Liberator for the long over-water voyage. Being elated about the prospects of seeing the United States again, the crew painted on the nose of their Liberator *Liberated from England*. These sentiments were surely felt by all the other crews. Lt. Al Bohne, the navigator for Lt. Eby, said:

With the victory celebration behind us, it was now time to concentrate on departing the E.T.O. [European Theater of Operation] and prepare to begin a new tour on the other side of the world. We were trading our elation for concerned apprehension. I, for one did not enjoy the promised prospect of encountering the Japanese.

The day finally came when we were informed that we were about to depart the British Isles. My crew, for some unknown reason, was to fly the CO's plane back to the U.S.. The nose turret had been removed and replaced with plexiglass. Besides our crew, sev-

eral non-flying personnel were to join us on that journey home. We departed Alconbury as a group and arrived at Prestwick, Scotland, just in time for bad weather. This gave us a couple of cold and rainy days to discover Prestwick and its tourist attractions, such as a war would allow.

The weather cleared and we were ordered off. We lined up for takeoff as we had lined up for missions. Only the altitudes were different. The controller in the tower bid farewell to each crew as he OK'd them for takeoff. We listened to each good-bye. One conversation I will always remember:

Controller: "Aircraft Number so and so, you are cleared for takeoff."

Pilot: "Roger, tit-tat and all that, you ole rat."

Controller: "Have a good and safe trip, Yanks. Good-bye, thanks so much, and God Bless you all.

Once airborne and in the navigator's seat Bohne remembered:

The sky was blue, the sun was high, and the plexiglass caused the sun's rays to comfortably warm my little room in the nose. The nose gunner was in the waist section with the other members and our passengers. I was by myself; comfortable, content, and happy. I gave the pilot a heading for Iceland, our first stop, then settled down to enjoy my lot. I was too comfortable and soon fell asleep. I was awakened by the pilot some time later and was asked for our position. I quickly determined that we were considerably off course and gave a corrected course. We were one of the first off Scotland and one of the last into Iceland. For this lack of judgment I was severely censured at great length, for which I had no argument. I believe my self-censure was much more severe, as I have never for-

36th Engineering and Test Squadron insignia. The grandchild of the 36BS. *Courtesy of the 36th Engineering and Test Squadron.*

gotten, nor forgiven myself for that potentially disastrous error. We were not in any immediate danger, had plenty of fuel, great weather, and good radio reception, yet the possibilities frighten me to this day and surpass the embarrassment of that mistake. It was not necessary for me to be reminded that I would not make that same mistake on our final leg to the U.S..

We were given our final course and cautioned to stay a decent distance from the southern tip of Greenland, as it would be in a storm area by the time we would arrive there. We could see the weather long before we arrived in the Greenland area, and I used every navigational art to verify our position. I had consumed many pages of log, plot, and verify. I would not be wrong, and I wasn't.

Bohne found out later that he wasn't the only navigator having difficulty finding the way back to the States. He continued:

After arriving on the North American continent I talked with a navigator from another plane about the Greenland storm. He was not sure of his position in the vicinity of Greenland, and his pilot called for permission to climb to a safer altitude. Their request was denied; however, the crew noticed mountain peaks above the wings and hurriedly climbed without permission.

For most of the squadron men these days also offered time for reflection about their wartime experiences. Sgt. Joe Danahy remembered the challenge of his fleeting youth.

Part of the high price we paid. A statement on the ceiling of the chapel honors the airmen of the United States lost during World War II. "IN PROUD AND GRATEFUL MEMORY OF THOSE MEN OF THE UNITED STATES ARMY AIR FORCE, WHO FROM THESE FRIENDLY ISLES -FLEW THEIR FINAL FLIGHT AND MET THEIR GOD. THEY KNEW NOT THE HOUR, THE DAY, NOR THE MANNER OF THEIR PASSING,WHEN FAR FROM HOME THEY WERE CALLED TO JOIN THAT HEROIC BAND OF AIRMAN WHO HAD GONE BEFORE, MAY THEY REST IN PEACE." On the Wall of the Missing the men of Lt. Boehm's crew and Lt. Mc Kibben's crew join thousands of Americans who were lost including Big Band leader Glenn Miller and Joseph P. Kennedy, the brother of President John F. Kennedy. *Courtesy of James C. Garrett.*

Memorial marker remembering those who served at RAF Oulton, the RAF 100 Group to which the 803rd Bomb Squadron was assigned. *Author's collection.*

8th Air Force Memorial at the entrance of Cheddington Station 113. *Author's collection.*

Everything was so blurred, one mission after another, constant tension—fear, if you will. I remember on days when we didn't fly, a disc jockey on AFN [Armed Forces Network] radio named Bob Sherr, whose theme song was "Opus One" by Tommy Dorsey. I never hear that song now that I don't remember those days.

I was eighteen years of age, not quite nineteen, when I went in the service in April of '43. That's awfully young. It was a pretty scary thing. I had never been away from home at that point. Two and a half years isn't a very long time. It seemed like a long time then. I got it over and done with, and they very graciously allowed me to vote. I had just turned 21 in June, and I was probably home in September or October. We had lots of points.

I chose to come home on the "Queen Mary." I would have walked if they had built a bridge. Hornsby flew home with the Colonel [Hambaugh]. Coming into New York harbor was a never to be forgotten experience. The "Queen Mary" drew a lot of attention. We passed the "Il de France" on the way over. To be in New York harbor and experience all the whistles and boats charging madly around and celebrating—the Statue of Liberty and all was something you will never forget. Really something! Tommy Dorsey [was] playing on the dock as you pulled in. I remember Buddy Rich banging away on those drums. Nearly broke my neck trying to get my head out a porthole to see it all. The first thing they did when you came down the gangplank was hand you a pint of milk.

So what would be the future for the men of the 36th Bomb Squadron? Would they be challenged to perform their RCM functions elsewhere? The Germans had supplied the Japanese military with Wurzburg and Lichtenstein radars, as well as listening receivers for submarines, and anti-shipping bombs. Some of the squadron airmen believed their special work would now be necessary in the Pacific War. One airman, Sgt. Marvin Klank of Lt. Rayner's crew, certainly felt that this would be a strong possibility. He recalled:

I was the tail gunner on Roy Rayner's crew and flew 26 missions to get enough points to go home after the war in Europe ended. We were supposed to go to Kansas for B29 training to fight in the Pacific theater, but they dropped the atomic bomb on the Japanese cities to end that war.

Memorial plaque remembering airmen of the 482nd Bomb Group at the entrance to Alconbury Station 102. *Author's collection.*

Al Bohne expressed a similar belief:

Following the European victory, we were to be sent to the Pacific theatre to continue our secret missions. However, our squadron was divided; some went to Sioux Falls, South Dakota, and the rest to McCord Field, Tacoma, Washington, with headquarters in Tacoma. The war in the Pacific ended while we were on furlough.

Tail gunner George Eberwine remembered preparing for his next assignment.

After we returned from Europe, in my case, I was assigned to Cochran Air Field in Macon, Georgia, and after R & R [rest and recuperation] I was to be assigned to a crew in Sioux City, Iowa, for B29 training for eventual assignment to the Pacific Theater of Operations. Actually all my gear, etc., less personnel items, was shipped to Sioux City and was never recovered by me. I was actually home in Philadelphia on leave in August 1945 when the war ended in Japan and was able to join in the celebration.

The dropping of the atomic bomb on Hiroshima and Nagasaki, the most significant scientific and military event which culminated the end of Second World War precluded the necessity for the 36th Bomb Squadron to transfer its special support function and their RCM gremlins to the Pacific theater of operations.

So what was the important significance of the radar countermeasure operations of the 803rd and 36th Bomb Squadrons during

Welsh divers John MacGwigan, Graham Wright, and Brendan Maguire retrieved a propeller blade of *The JIGS UP* from 40 feet under the Irish Sea. *Courtesy of Brendan Maguire.*

Holyhead, Wales memorial remembering the men of Lt. Boehm's crew. "They shall not grow old as we that are left grow old; Age shall not weary them, nor the years condemn. At the going down of the sun and in the morning We will remember them. We will remember them." — Poem from the service marking the 50th Anniversary of the loss of Lt. Boehm's crew. *Author's collection.*

World War II? Due to the very nature of the work it is difficult to measure exactly. However, as far as the Royal Air Force was concerned, one author, Martin Streetly, wrote in his book, *Confound and Destroy*, that the American contribution was characterized by "a constant willingness to help." He also noted:

The importance of the 803rd/36th Squadron's efforts between June and November 1944 cannot be overstressed. The MANDREL screen was regarded by RAF 100 Group as one of its most effective measures, and during the period in question the American unit shared the operational burden equally with the Group's MANDREL Squadron 199. The equality of effort was continued until the RAF's second MANDREL Squadron, No. 171, was able to take over in October/November 1944.[95]

Another author, Alfred Price, in his book, *History of U.S. Electronic Warfare*, documented the significance of the entire United States RCM program and its contribution in a very specific way. He wrote:

The most significant U.S. contribution to countermeasures during World War II, however, stemmed from the harnessing of the nation's huge electronics industry to mass produce equipment for the Allied forces. Although exact figures are not available on the number of countermeasures equipments produced by other nations, there can be no doubt that during the conflict, U.S. production in this field easily outstripped that of all other nations put together.

In return for all of this effort, what did the U.S. armed forces receive? Taking conservative estimates, radio countermeasures probably saved about 600 Air Force heavy bombers during operations over Europe.[96]

That translates to about 6,000 Allied airmen lives saved! However, does this figure include the number of Allied airmen and soldiers probably saved by the 803rd and 36th Bomb Squadron's deception and jamming support during the Normandy Invasion and the Battle of the Bulge? Most likely not.

George Klemm of ABL-15 summed up the role of the scientists and engineers:

They [the Germans] sat on the continent side and we [ABL-15] sat on the island side and tried to figure out what the other was doing. How closely we were followed or we were leading the Germans in the development of radar and radar countermeasures during World War II, was a hair-breadth difference most of the time. It was rather interesting. We came up with some funny ideas at times. You know, this war was won not by us who were tearing our hair out most of the time, but by the fellows who fought it.

Adjutant Henry Woolf also spoke of the reality of his work when he wrote:

Those of us who worked at base headquarters for two years, from 8:00 am.to 5:00 pm. six days a week, did not romanticize our activities. We griped, of course, especially about the food—I did not taste a drop of fresh milk, for example, in 30 months—and occasionally about some officer's arrogance. (We had three sets of officers during our two years). But I never heard an expression of doubt about the rightness of the war and the need to carry it on until the enemy was defeated.

Navigator Lt. Joseph Thome spoke of the 36BS accomplishments:

I think one of the biggest successes of our whole outfit though was the idea that we were up there every night. We were up there either turning our equipment on or simulating a force coming in from the north, for example, or coming in from the south or coming in from any damn direction that they (the planners) wanted us; to make them [the Germans] think that a big bunch of airplanes were coming.

Airman S/Sgt. Richard Catt, the nose gunner for Lt. Vowinkel, said it best when he spoke of the real price paid—the American sacrifices:

It's a thing that you just took it like they say—you took it one day at a time. It's one of those things, you go up there and you sweat it out and hope that the next one doesn't get you, but it got a lot of guys, you know. There were a lot of losses. It was very depressing at the time because of so many. It seemed like we had an endless supply of people and they just kept putting planes up.

By deceptions, spoofs, and radar jamming missions, the 803rd and the 36th Bomb Squadrons supported America's first great effort into aerial electronic warfare. Their secret work, like the Allied fighter support, had a special place in military air warfare and con-

Airmen of the 36th Bomb Squadron marking 50 years since VE-Day and the end of World War II at the 1995 reunion in North Carolina. Standing L-R Paul Pond, Charles Sanders, Conni Kazak, Wilfred Chrisner, Norman Snider, Iredell Hutton, Art Brusila, Frank Church, Leon Vigdor, Joseph Melita, Royce Kittle, Arthur Bennett, Jack Evans, George Sandberg, Robert Senn, Bill Krueger, Wayne Bailey, George Amos, Norman Olund, William Parks, Jack Kings, Gordon Caulkins, Fred Belcher, John Shamp, Joe O'Loughlin, William Bright. Kneeling L-R Howard Nolan, Fred Greenfield, John Harkins, and Norman Landberg. *Author's collection.*

tributed to the overall success in the campaign for maintaining Allied air superiority. Of course, recognition and credit must be given to all, not only to the squadron airmen, but to the ground support personnel, the mechanics, the medics, the cooks, the flying control, the weather personnel, the photographers, the adjutants, the clerks, those men and women of ABL Division-15, who did the research and development of the jamming equipment to keep the Allies ahead of the enemy scientists. All contributed their time and expertise to see the job done well to its very end, which was victory in Europe.

Airmen of the 803rd and 36th Bomb Squadrons were truly founding fathers in the operational aspects of electronic warfare in World War II. Today the electronic countermeasure program is firmly established in U.S. Air Force doctrine as an important combat support function. Electronic Counter Measures, or ECM as it is known today, continues to save lives. The 36th Bomb Squadron today exists as the 36th Engineering and Test Squadron (36ETS). The new 36th provides the research and development and operational testing of electronic countermeasure equipment for the United States fighter and bomber aircraft. During the United States war with Iraq, even the Stealth F117 fighter bombers were escorted by U.S. jamming aircraft.[97]

Remembering the unique service contribution of the men of the 803rd and 36th Bomb Squadrons, today memorials exist under the peaceful skies of the British Isles. Down a country lane at a crossroads near the old Oulton airfield the 803rd Bomb Squadron is remembered by a monument to honor those who served with

RAF 100 Group. Nearby, at Blickling Hall, an 803rd exhibit makes up part of the RAF Oulton/100 Group display. By the main gate entrance at Cheddington, a marker bearing a marble plaque along with an airfield runway light set in aggregate honors the men of the 8AF. At Alconbury, a bronze plaque at its main gate acknowledges the 482nd Bomb Group, the group to which the 36th Bomb Squadron was last attached. In Wales, at Holyhead's Breakwater Park near North Stack, a memorial bearing a propeller blade from the B24 Liberator *The Jigs Up* remembers the men of the 36th Bomb Squadron, those of Lt. Boehm's crew that were lost to the Irish Sea. Another piece of a propeller blade from *The Jigs Up* accompanies a memorial exhibit at the North Carolina Military History Museum at Fort Fisher, North Carolina. Efforts are ongoing today by Willis S. "Sam" Cole, Jr., the author, and interested individuals near Boucly, France, to erect a memorial honoring the airmen of Lt. Hornsby's crew who were lost on the night of 9/10 November 1944 in the crash of Liberator #42-51226.

During June of 1995 the author hosted a two day reunion in North Carolina for the former men of the 803rd and 36th Bomb Squadrons. The reunion featured guest speakers from the original 36th Bomb Squadron, the 36th Engineering and Test Squadron, the 8th Air Force Historical Society, the U.S. Air Force, and the National Defense University. There was good food, great fellowship, squadron memorabilia, and live big band music. Thirty-one former unit members attended, along with relatives of airmen who had been lost, as well as many wives and family members. A grand and memorable time was had by all.

Appendix A:
803rd/36th Bomb Squadron Mission Record

MISSION RECORD For 803rd Bomb SQ. (H) Prov.

MONTH OF JUNE 1944

Date	Sorties	Effective Sorties Radar Screen	Abortions
JUNE			
3*	1	1	
5/6	4	4	
16/17	6	6	
17/18	5	5	
22/23	6	5	1
27/28	5	3	2
28/29	5	5	
Totals	32	29	3

SUMMARY FOR JUNE 1944
Total Operational Missions 7
Total Sorties 32
Total Effective Sorties 29
Abortions 3
*Special Search Mission 1

MONTH OF JULY 1944

Date	Sorties	Effective Sorties Radar Screen	Abortions
JULY			
4/5	5	5	
7/8	5	4	1
9/10	5	4	1
12/13	5	5	
14/15	5	4	1
17/18	4	4	
18/19	4	4	
20/21	4	4	
21/22	3	3	
23/24	5	5	
24/25	3	3	
25/26	3	3	
28/29	4	3	1
29/30	3	3	
Totals	58	54	4

SUMMARY FOR JULY 1944
Total Operational Missions 14
Total Sorties 58
Total Effective Sorties 54
Abortions 4

SEARCH MISSIONS

DATE	OPERATIONAL TIME
6 July 1944	3:00
10 July 1944	5:40
12 July 1944	6:15
18 July 1944	5:15
19 July 1944	3:50
Total Missions	5
Total Operational Time:	24:00

MONTH OF AUGUST 1944

Date	Sorties	Effective Sorties Radar Screen	Abortions
AUG			
4/5	2	1	1
6/7	5	4	1
7/8	5	4	1
8/9	5	4	1
9/10	4	4	
10/11	4	4	
11/12	4	4	
12/13	5	4	1
13/14	4	3	1
Totals	38	32	6

SUMMARY FOR AUGUST 1944
Total Operational Missions 9
Total Sorties 38
Total Effective Sorties 32
Abortions 6

SUMMARY OF OPERATIONS OF 803RD BOMB SQ. (H) PROV. AT RAF STA. OULTON FOR PERIOD 3 JUNE 44 TO 14 AUG. 44

	Missions	Sorties	Effective Sorties	Abortions
JUNE	7	32	29	3
JULY	14	58	54	4
AUGUST	9	38	32	6
TOTAL	30	128	115	13

MISSION RECORD FOR 36TH BOMB SQ. (H) RCM

MONTH OF AUGUST 1944

Date	Sorties	Effective Sorties Radar Screen	Abortions
AUG			
16/17	4	4	
17/18	2	2	
18/19	6	6	
25/26	6	6	
26/27	7	7	
27/28	6	6	
29/30	4	4	
30/31	6	6	
TOTALS	41	41	

SUMMARY FOR AUGUST 1944
AT CHEDDINGTON
Total Operational Missions........ 8
Total Sorties 41
Total Effective Sorties 41
Abortions 0

MONTH OF SEPTEMBER 1944

Date	Sorties	Effective Sorties	Abortions
SEPT			
1/2	4	4	
5/6	4	4	
6/7	4	4	
8/9	4	4	
9/10	4	4	
10/11	3	3	
11/12	5	5	
12/13	6	6	
13/14	6	6	
15/16	7	7	
16/17	5	5	
17/18	6	6	
18/19	7	6	1
22/23	4	4	
23/24	6	6	
25/26	3	3	
26/27	4	4	
28/29	5	5	
Totals	87	86	1

SUMMARY FOR SEPTEMBER 1944
Total Operational Missions...... 18
Total Sorties 87
Total Effective Sorties 86
Abortions 1

MONTH OF OCTOBER 1944

Date	Sorties	Effective Sorties	Abortions
OCT			
5/6	5	5	
6/7	7	7	
7/8	6	6	
9/10	7	6	1
14/15	7	7	
15/16	6	6	
19/20	7	7	
21/22	8	7	1
23/24	6	5	1
24/25	6	6	
26/27	6	5	1
30/31	7	7	
31/1	7	7	
Totals	85	81	4

SUMMARY FOR OCTOBER 1944
Total Operational Missions...... 13
Total Sorties 85
Total Effective Sorties 81
Abortions 4

MONTH OF NOVEMBER 1944

Date	Sorties	Effective Sorties Radar Screen — RAF	VHF Screen — RAF	AAF Spoof	Abortions
NOV					
1/2	7	6			1
2/3	7	7			
4/5	6	6			
6/7	8	8			
9/10	7	6			1(lost)
10/11	8	8			
11/12	7	7			
15/16	5	4			1(lost)
18/19	6	5			1
20/21	5	5			
21/22	6	6			
23/24	6	5			1
25	6		6		
25/26	3	3			
26	6		6		
26/27	3	3			
27	5		5		
27/28	3	3			
28	8		5	3	
28/29	2	2			
29	7		6		1
29/30	2	2			
30	6	6			
30/31	2	2			
Totals	131	88	34	3	4 / 2 (lost)

SUMMARY FOR NOVEMBER 1944
Total Operational Missions...... 24
Total Sorties 131
Total Effective Sorties 125
Abortions 4
Lost 2

MONTH OF DECEMBER 1944

Date	Sorties	Effective Sorties Radar Screen RAF	Effective Sorties VHF Screen AAF	Spoof	Jackal	Abortions
DEC						
1	7		4	3		
1/2	1	1				
2	6		6			
2/3	2	2				
3	7		7			
4	8		8			
4/5	2	2				
5	9		8			1
6	8		8			
6/7	2	2				
7	8	8				
8	10		6	3		1
9	10		10			
9/10	1	1				
10	8		7			1
11	9		9			
12	8		7			1
12/13	1	1				
13	3		3			
15	6		5			1
16	5		5			
17/18	1	1				
18	9		8			1
18/19	1	1				
19	8		8			
23	2		2			
24	5		5			
25	8		8			
28	9		5		3	1
30	5		5			
30/31	1	1				
31	7		4		2	1
Totals	177	12	146	6	5	8

SUMMARY FOR DECEMBER 1944
Total Operational Missions 32
Total Sorties 177
Total Effective Sorties 169
Abortions 8
Lost .... 1 (non-op.)

SUMMARY OF OPERATIONS OF 36TH BOMB SQ. RCM AT CHEDDINGTON
for period 16 August 44. to 31 Dec. 44.

Month	Missions	Sorties	Effective Sorties	Abortions	Losses
Aug	8	41	41	0	
Sept	18	87	86	1	
Oct	13	85	81	4	
Nov	24	131	125	4	2
Dec	32	177	169	8	1(non-op)
Totals	95	521	502	17	3 1(non-op)

SUMMARY OF OPERATIONS FOR 1944

Station	Missions	Sorties	Effective Sorties	Abortions	Losses
RAF Oulton	30	128	115	13	
Cheddington	95	521	502	17	3
Totals	125	649	617	30	3 1(non-op)

MONTH OF JANUARY 1944

Date	Sorties	Radar Screen RAF	Effective Sorties VHF Screen AAF	Jackal	Abortions
JAN					
1	7		7		
1/2	1	1			
2	7		4	3	
2/3	1	1			
3	4		4		
5	10		5	2	3
6	5		5		
7	7		4	2	1
8	6		5		1
9	5		5		
10	4		4		
13	6		6		
15	6		6		
16	5		5		
17	7		7		
18	7		7		
20	8		8		
21	6		5		1
23	5		5		
24	6		5		1
26	3		3		
28	5		4		1
29	5		5		
31	7		7		
Totals	133	2	116	7	8

SUMMARY FOR JANUARY 1945
Total Operational Missions 24
Total Sorties 133
Total Effective Sorties 125
Total Abortions 8

MONTH OF FEBRUARY 1945

Month	Sorties	Effective Sorties-VHF Screen	Abortions	Losses
FEB				
1	7	7		
2	6	6		
3	7	7		
5	9	8		1
6	8	8		
7	6	6		
8	6	6		
9	6	6		
10	6	6		
11	6	6		
14	7	7		
15	7	7		
16	7	7		
17	6	6		
19	2	1		1
20	7	7		
21	7	7		
22	7	7		
23	7	7		
24	7	7		
25	7	7		
26	6	6		
27	6	6		
28	6	5	1	
Totals	156	153	1	2

SUMMARY FOR FEBRUARY 1945
Total Operational Missions 24
Total Sorties 156
Total Effective Sorties 153
Total Abortions 1
Total Losses 2

MONTH OF MARCH 1945
Effective Sorties

Date MAR	Sorties	VHF-Screen	Radar-Screen	B24 Search	P38 Search	Aborts
1	6	6				
2	5	5				
3	4	3				1
5	2	2				
6	2	2				
7	5	4		1		
8	5	4		1		
9	4	4				
10	5	4		1		
11	5	4		1		
12	5	4		1		
14	5	4				1
15	5	4				1
16	13	3	9	1		
17	14	3	9	1	1	
18	13	2	9	1		1
19	15	3	9	1	1	1 P38
20	11	2	8			1 lost
21	11	3	7	1		
22	4	3		1		
23	12	3	7	1	1	
am24	9	3	6			
pm24	3	3				
25	5	3			2	
26	4	3			1	
27	14	3	9	1	1	
30	13	3	9	1		
31	3	3				
Totals	202	93	82	14	7	5 (1lost)

SUMMARY FOR MARCH 1945
Total Operational Missions 28
Total Sorties 202
Total Effective Sorties 196
Total Abortions 5
Total Losses 1

**SUMMARY OF OPERATIONS OF 36TH BOMB SQ. RCM FROM 1 JAN. TO
31 MAR. AT CHEDDINGTON (THRU 28 FEB) & ALCONBURY FROM 1 MAR.**

	Missions	Sorties	Effective Sorties	Abortions	Losses
Jan.'45	24	133	125	8	0
Feb.'45	24	156	153	1	2
Mar.'45	28	202	196	5	1
Totals	76	491	474	14	3

MISSIONS FOR APRIL 1945
Effective Sorties

Date APR	Sorties	VHF-Screen	B24 Search	P38 Search	Aborts
2	4	4			
3am	5	4	1		
3pm	4	4			
4	4	4			
5	4	4			
6	5	4		1	
7	4	3			1
8	4	4			
10	4	4			
11	4	4			
12	4	4			
13	5	4		1	
16	4	4			
17	4	4			
18	4	4			
19	4	4			
20	4	4			1
23	4	4			
25	3	3			
Totals	78	73	1	2	2

MISSIONS OF THE 803RD & 36TH BOMB SQUADRONS

Here is a review the operations of the 36th Bomb Squadron and its parent organization, the 803rd Bomb Squadron (H) Prov. from the beginning with the first special search mission of 3 June 1944. The next mission occurred the night of the 5/6 June, "D-Day" for the Allied invasion of the continent. During this eleven month period a total of 220 missions were flown with a total of 1218 sorties, 1167 of which were reported as effective. A statistical summary and analysis follows:

Operations from 3 June 1944 to 30 April 1945

SUMMARY
Total Missions 220
Total Sorties 1218
Total Effective Sorties 1167
Total Abortions 46
Losses .... 6 (1 Non - Op)

ANALYSIS OF MISSIONS

TYPE	NUMBER	DATES	EFFECTIVE SORTIES
Special Search	1	3 June 1944	1
RAF Radar Screen	97	5 June 44 to 3 Jan. 45	424
Search Missions	5	6 July 44 to 19 July 44	5
VHF Screen	122	25 Nov 44 to 30 April 45	615
Spoof	3	28 Nov 44 to 8 Dec 45	9
JACKAL	5	28 Dec 44 to 7 Jan 45	12
AAF radar Screen	10	16 Mar 45 to 30 Mar 45	82
B-24 Search	16	7 Mar 45 to 3 April 45	15
P-38 Search	8	17 Mar 45 to 13 April 45	9

Appendix B:
Airmen of the 803rd Bomb Squadron Heavy Provisional

Seen below is a list of men who initially comprised the 803rd Bomb Squadron (H) Provisional. Special Orders Number 156 released these men on detached service (DS) at RAF Sculthorpe with the 803BS to RAF Oulton on 16 May 1944. The men and their original organizations were:

Capt. George E. Paris	306th BG
1st. Lt. Harold P. Preuss	305th BG
S/Sgt. James A. Byrne	311 Sig Co Bomb Div AAF 103
S/Sgt. Stillman R. Dunster	305th BG
S/Sgt. James McFarlane	445 Sub Depot AAF 117
S/Sgt. Wilbert Rider	303rd BG
Sgt. John J. Harkins	92nd BG
Sgt. Charles W. Sanders	92nd BG
Sgt. Arnold Savatsky	384th BG
Cpl. Frank F. Falter	1st Sta Com Sq AAF 121
Cpl. Thomas R. Griffith	303rd BG
Cpl. Thomas D. Hedgecock	379th BG
Cpl. William E. Henry	303rd BG
Cpl. Robert S. Jamieson	92nd BG
Cpl. Donat E. Lafond	303rd BG
Cpl. Charles E. Morton	3rd Sta Com Sq AAF Sta 107
T/5 Jeremiah Pangburn	1119 QM Co AAF 106
Cpl. Harry W. Smith	1st Sta Com Sq AAF 121
Pfc. Herman A. Brown	381st BG
Pfc. Clarence M. Corder	91st BG
Pfc. Elton E. Stone	379th BG
Pvt. Leland W. Todd	351st BG
Pvt. Jack B. Gilbert	303rd BG
Pvt. Vane N.L. Glendening	303rd BG

Special Orders Number 137 of 18 May 1944 stated that the following men were released from assignment from their respective organizations and placed on detached service with 803BS, at RAF Sculthorpe. Those included men from the following bomb groups were:

From 94th BG

1st. Lt. Howard H. Klimetz	T/Sgt. Edward D. Baldwin
T/Sgt. Durand B. Lovelace	S/Sgt. Alvin K. Reynolds
S/Sgt. Benjamin F. Roberts	

From 95th BG

1st. Lt. William C. Gruelich	1st Lt. William P. Overstreet
T/Sgt. Vincent J. Areno	S/Sgt. Harry L. Bumgardner
S/Sgt. Horace L. Flynn	S/Sgt. Raymond A. Battistini
S/Sgt. Edward E. Caldwell	S/Sgt. Alton E. Markley
S/Sgt. Herbert C. Hoover	S/Sgt. Alvin S. Janeczko
S/Sgt. Howard C. Culbertson	S/Sgt. Ira C. Muse

From 96th BG

1st Lt. Charles M. Travis	1st Lt. Leon Vigdor
1st Lt. Kenneth A. Bevan	T/Sgt. Margind Zuckerman
S/Sgt. Nicholas Popadyn	S/Sgt. George E. O'Malley
S/Sgt. John Rovnak	

From 385th BG

Capt. Robert G. Stutzman
1st Lt. Walter B. Slade
1st Lt. William F. Flagler
S/Sgt. James C. Wooden
S/Sgt. Richard R. Long

Capt. Raymond A. Robinson
1st Lt. William R. Hoagland
T/Sgt. Richard J. Davis
S/Sgt. Harold H. Bogart
S/Sgt. Joseph E. Simkins

From 388th BG

1st Lt. Richard O. Obenschain
1st Lt. James P. Ostler
T/Sgt. Garven J. Pinciger
S/Sgt. Robert W. Mier
S/Sgt. Fred H. Belcher

1st Lt. James B. Warner
T/Sgt. John R. Lopes
T/Sgt. George W. Wilson
S/Sgt. Bernard Berg
S/Sgt. Jack C. Kings

From 390th BG

1st Lt. Harvey A. Paul
1st Lt. Warren V. Smith
T/Sgt. Kenneth L. Hagan

1st Lt. Wade L. Birmingham
T/Sgt. George B. Ellison
T/Sgt. Thomas Hennessey

From 447th BG

S/Sgt. Landis L. Pratt
S/Sgt. Roy B. McGraw

From 100th BG

1st Lt. Donald Gilzinger
T/Sgt. Adam E. Rutkowski

The following men were designated as Detachment "A" 858th Bomb Squadron (H) and placed on detached and/or temporary duty at RAF Oulton per Special Order Number 111 from Headquarters AAF Station 113 Cheddington dated 14 July 1944. These men became part of the 803BS. The officers and enlisted men were:

Capt. Jack G. Beamer
Capt. Charles V. Parker
Capt. Robert M. Kinnard
1st. Lt. Eldon R. Bray
1st. Lt. Bernard E. Brodien
1st. Lt. Harold P. Preuss
1st. Lt. Malcolm Wolkowitz
2nd Lt. David F. Gould
2nd Lt. John Latvaitis
2nd Lt. David D. Merrill
2nd Lt. Franklin R. Zatlin
WOJG Robert H. Springer
S/Sgt. James A. Byrne
S/Sgt. Stillman R. Dunster
Sgt. John J. Harkins
Sgt. Densel L. Milem
Sgt. Charles W. Sanders
Sgt. Arnold Savatsky

Cpl Frank F. Falter
Cpl Vane N. L. Glendening
Cpl Thomas R. Griffith
Cpl Thomas D. Hedgecock
Cpl William E. Henry
Cpl Robert S. Jamieson
Cpl Donat E. Lafond
Cpl Charles E. Morton
Cpl Harry W. Smith
Tec 5 Jeremiah Pangburn
Pfc Herman A. Brown
Pfc Clarence M. Corder
Pfc Elton E. Stone
Pvt Jack B. Gilbert
Pvt Leland W. Todd

Appendix C:
36th Bomb Squadron Crews

Shown below in alphabetical order is a roster of 36th Bomb Squadron aircrews and spare gunners as seen in the original history file at the USAF Historical Research Agency, Maxwell AFB. The airmen are named in the order standing or kneeling from left to right. *Note: The official crew photographs for the Lt. Sandberg, Lt. Landberg, Lt. Hornsby, Lt. Boehm, Lt. Angstadt, Capt. Sackett, F/O Young, Lt. McKibben, Lt. McCarthy, Lt. Pregeant, and Lt. Sweeney crews appear earlier in this book.

LT. BOESEL CREW
Standing L-R S/Sgt. James O. Myers, 2d Lt. Ralph H. Weaver, 1st Lt. Albert G. Boesel, 2d Lt. Richard J. Geehern, S/Sgt. Charles A. Ends. Kneeling L-R Sgt. Jack W. Evans, S/Sgt. James A. Roberts, S/Sgt. Richard B. Black, S/Sgt. Ray W. Bean. *Courtesy of the USAF Historical Research Agency.*

LT. BROOKSHIRE CREW
Standing L-R S/Sgt. Leonard Kottenstette, 2d Lt. Oscar F. Van Noy, 1st Lt. Joseph R. Brookshire, 2d Lt. Robert L. Young, S/Sgt. Robert E. Hulne. Kneeling L-R S/Sgt. Joseph A. Johnson, S/Sgt. Jack I. Hope, Sgt. Julian Isgur, S/Sgt. Jack Long. *Courtesy of the USAF Historical Research Agency.*

LT. BRIGHT CREW
Standing L-R Sgt. Louis R. Dallas, 2d Lt. James G. Baker, 2d Lt. William Bright, 2d Lt. Francis A. Geiben, Sgt. Samuel P. Bachner. Kneeling L-R Sgt. Leonard Shrebnick, Sgt. George. C. Amos, Sgt. Henry C. Switzgable, Sgt. Kenneth L. Kennon. *Courtesy of William Bright.*

LT. BRUSILA CREW
Standing L-R Sgt. William Pidgeon, F/O Walter Baker, 2d Lt. Arthur Brusila, 2d Lt. Roy Myers, Sgt. Donald Page. Kneeling L-R Sgt. Wallace Murray, Sgt. John Ballard, Sgt. Gordon Caulkins, Sgt. Eddie Christensen, S/Sgt. George Olliges. *Courtesy of Dr. Robert F. Hambaugh, Jr.*

LT. CORDER CREW
Standing L-R Sgt. Daniel J. Jenks, 2d Lt. Don C. Albinson, 1st Lt. William M. Corder, 2d Lt. Joseph E. Thome, Sgt. Vane Glendening. Kneeling L-R S/Sgt. Jimmie J. Marchello, Sgt. Ralph W. Ramos, Sgt. Stanley J. Dombrosky, S/Sgt. Wesley V. Crowther. *Courtesy of Dr. Robert F. Hambaugh, Jr.*

LT. EBY CREW
Standing L-R Cpl. Frank A. Badum, F/O Alvin F. Bohne, 2d Lt. Eugene J. Eby, 2d Lt. Jacob B. Stuart, T/Sgt. Raymond A. Winslow. Kneeling L-R Cpl. Clarence Poole, Cpl. John C. Dominick, Cpl. Elmer I. Creamer, Cpl. Thomas J. Blanchard. *Courtesy of Alvin Bohne.*

LT. FULLER CREW
Standing L-R S/Sgt. R. J. Witulski, 2d Lt. F. J. Burkhardt, 2d Lt. R. M. Fuller, 2d Lt. G. R. Henson, Sgt. J. E. O'Neill. Kneeling L-R Sgt. Mike Wokich, Sgt. E.C. Dickinson, Sgt. H.V. Evans, Sgt. B.B. Walker. *Courtesy of the USAF Historical Research Agency.*

LT. GLICK CREW
Standing L-R S/Sgt. William F. Landers, 2d Lt. Eugene R. Wise, 1st Lt. Arthur Glick, 2d Lt. Robert A. Pepper, S/Sgt. George Christodulakos. Kneeling L-R Sgt. Charles A. Robinson, Sgt. Marshall Pitts, Sgt. Peter G. Bittner, Sgt. Raymond E. Miller. *Courtesy of Robert Pepper.*

LT. GRUBISICH CREW
Standing L-R Sgt. E.F. Oberlin, Lt. P. Chavez, Lt. G. Grubisich, Lt. Wilbur F. Kruse, Sgt. Walter A. Natishyn. Kneeling L-R Sgt. Weston L. Smith, Sgt. G. E. Kalish, Sgt. Ercel T. Coburn, Sgt. Wayne L. Hatfield. *Courtesy of the USAF Historical Research Agency.*

LT. HAMILTON CREW
Standing L-R S/Sgt. Cecil P. McClure, 1st. Lt. Pietro G. Ferrarese, 1st. Lt. James W. Hamilton Jr., 2d Lt. William H. Hite, S/Sgt. Joseph C. Sivo. Kneeling L-R Sgt. Lloyd C. White, Sgt. Richard H. Smith, Sgt. Allyn H. Wright, Sgt. Emery A. Turknett. *Courtesy of the USAF Historical Research Agency.*

Lt. KITTLE CREW
Standing L-R Sgt. Arthur R. Ledtke, 2d Lt. Wendell Blanchard, 2d Lt. Royce E. Kittle, 2d Lt. George L. Kimmelman, Sgt. Norman H. Brager. Kneeling L-R Sgt. Robert E. Cortright, Sgt. Louis J. Chido, Sgt. Melvin Friedlander, Sgt. Cecil H. Cox. *Courtesy of Dr. Robert F. Hambaugh, Jr.*

LT. MC CRORY CREW
Standing L-R S/Sgt. Thomas F. Stevens, 2d Lt. William E. Krueger, 1st Lt. William M. McCrory, 2d Lt. Merril H. Calisch, S/Sgt. John P. Shamp. Kneeling L-R S/Sgt. Norman Morin, S/Sgt. Iredell S. Hutton, S/Sgt. Raymond Herbert, S/Sgt. Andrew C. Sturm. *Courtesy of Dr. Robert F. Hambaugh, Jr.*

LT. MC KEE CREW
Standing L-R Sgt. Gilbert N. Tatum, F/O Paul Isel, 2d Lt. J. W. McKee, F/O Frank W. Hatscher, Sgt. E.R. Hancock. Kneeling L-R Sgt. Edward W. Czechowski, Sgt. E. J. Waldrop, Sgt. James Buckland, Sgt. L. R. Weiske. *Courtesy of the USAF Historical Research Agency.*

LT. NELLER CREW
Standing L-R 2d Lt. Paul L. Vieth, 1st Lt. William B. Neller, Sgt. Joseph Adams Jr., 2d Lt. Victor W. Gehres, Sgt. Henry Suchenski, Sgt. Sydney Rosener, Sgt. Clarence E. Snell, Sgt. Angelo P. Fazlo, Sgt. Stanley Lewin. *Courtesy of the USAF Historical Research Agency.*

LT. OLDERSHAW CREW
Standing L-R S/Sgt. Vincent A. Grillo, 2d Lt. Isaac Benghiat, 2d Lt. William C. Oldershaw, F/O John A. Wilson, Sgt. John A. Manning. Kneeling L-R S/Sgt. Constanti Kazak, Sgt. Carlo A. Rizzi, Sgt. Harry Raupp, Sgt. Everett L. Worthington. *Courtesy of the USAF Historical Research Agency.*

LT. POND CREW
Standing L-R S/Sgt. Erlon C. Curtis, 2d Lt. James E. Abell, 2d Lt. Paul J. Pond Jr., F/O Bernard E. Hewett, Sgt. Edward W. Kristofeo. Kneeling L-R S/Sgt. Claude W. Gilbo, Sgt. George O'Bradovich, Sgt. William H. Evans Jr., Sgt. Leonard N. Backer. *Courtesy of Dr. Robert F. Hambaugh, Jr.*

LT. RAYNER CREW
Standing L-R Sgt. Damon Thomas, 1st Lt. Forrest Cory, 2d Lt. Roy Rayner, 2d Lt. Arthur Colwell, Sgt. William Brown. Kneeling L-R Sgt. Byron Gordon, Sgt. Dolye Henson, Sgt. Marvin Klank, S/Sgt. George Moore. *Courtesy of the USAF Historical Research Agency.*

LT. RODKEY CREW
Standing L-R S/Sgt. Lewis P. Rylander, F/O Raymond Barta, 1st Lt. Robert M. Rodkey, 1st Lt. George Bickel, S/Sgt. Joseph Cilluffo. Kneeling L-R Sgt. William D. Butler, Sgt. Raymon L. Long, Sgt. Neil M. Leeper, Sgt. Ralph V. Cordell. *Courtesy of the USAF Historical Research Agency.*

LT. SENN CREW
Standing L-R Sgt. Harold Oliver, F/O Wilfred Chrisner, 2d Lt. Robert Senn Jr., 2d Lt. Harry Parker, Sgt. Roy LeTourneau. Kneeling L-R Sgt. Bernard Giza, Sgt. Norman Olund, Sgt. Ed Chowanic, Sgt. Glenwood Poindexter, Sgt. George Johnson. *Courtesy of Robert McLean Senn, Jr.*

LT. SODERSTROM CREW
Standing L-R Sgt. Frank V. Parenti, F/O Robert W. DeWitt, 2d Lt. Harry R. Soderstrom, 2d Lt. John J. Andersen, Sgt. Robert L. Price. Kneeling L-R Sgt. James O. Thompson, Sgt. Aubrey A. Whitworth, Sgt. Laurier J. Bilodeau, Sgt. John B. Fillenger. *Courtesy of the USAF Historical Research Agency.*

LT. STONE CREW
Standing L-R Sgt. Allie L. Gardner, F/O Irvin J. Banta, 2d Lt. Harry J. Stone Jr., 2d Lt. David C. Booker , Sgt. Carmelo w. Goicoechea. Kneeling L-R Sgt. Sidney W. Parrish, S/Sgt. Joseph M. Delongis, Sgt. Charles L. Mangrum, S/Sgt. William H. Selzer. *Courtesy of the USAF Historical Research Agency.*

LT. STUDSTRUP CREW
Standing L-R Sgt. Robert P. King, 2d Lt. Robert S. Ballard, 1st. Lt. Stanley Studstrup, 2d Lt. Eugene K. Soppeland, Cpl. William R. Brooks. Kneeling L-R Cpl. Buford H. Pippin, Cpl. Orlis D. Reed, Cpl. Stuart F. Putney, Cpl. Gardner L. Sundstrom. *Courtesy of the USAF Historical Research Agency.*

LT. VOWINKEL CREW
Standing L-R S/Sgt. Irwin Kirschner, 2d Lt. Frank X. Blechinger, 1st Lt. Merlin J, Vowinkel, 2d Lt. Robert B. Nonemaker, T/Sgt. Odis F. Waggoner. Kneeling L-R S/Sgt. Norvill O. Way, S/Sgt. Richard J. Catt, T/Sgt. Joseph F. Alves, S/Sgt.Sydney J. Brandt. *Courtesy of the USAF Historical Research Agency.*

LT. WRENN CREW
Standing L-R Sgt. Marcel F. Millet, Lt. Moorad Mooradian, Lt. Jack C. Wrenn, Lt. Leon B. Hendrickson, Sgt. George F. Lechner. Kneeling L-R S/Sgt. Charles R. Edwards, Sgt. James H. Cowie, Sgt. James F. Brunson, Sgt. Richard D. Bloomer, Sgt. Jack A. Palm. *Courtesy of Dr. Robert F. Hambaugh, Jr.*

LT. YOUNG CREW
Standing L-R Sgt. Seymour A. Zegas, 2d Lt. James R. Pearigen, 2d Lt. James W. Young, 2d Lt. Leon I. Hammer, Sgt. Joseph F. O'Loughlin. Kneeling L-R Sgt. Everett W. Miller, Sgt. Paul J. Schuchardt, Sgt. Donald E. Upper, Sgt. James C. Garrett. *Courtesy of Dr. Robert F. Hambaugh, Jr.*

LT. ZIFF CREW
Standing L-R Sgt. Elwood Center, 2d Lt. Daniel J. Finn, 1st Lt. Sam Ziff, 2d Lt. Franklyn Gordon, Sgt. William Murray. Kneeling L-R Sgt. Ernest W. Ashby, Sgt. Bernhard P. Jensen, Sgt. James R. Carpenter, Sgt. Warren R. Pechin. *Courtesy of Dr. Robert F. Hambaugh, Jr.*

SPARE GUNNERS
Standing L-R Sgt. Robert Powell, S/Sgt. Warren P. Weilt, Sgt. Robert R. Veliz, S/Sgt. Ulysses S. Beebe. Kneeling L-R Sgt. Frederick D. Greenfield, Sgt. Thomas E. Marron. *Courtesy of the USAF Historical Research Agency.*

Appendix D:
Equipment Descriptions

CARPET I — *APT-2 used to jam Wurzburg radar

CARPET III — APQ-9 and AN/APR-4 transmitter and search receiver for use as a Wurzburg, Ground Control Intercept (GCI) and Gun Laying (GL) radar jammer

CARPET BLINKER — CARPET transmitter and search receiver used in locating and jamming Wurzburg radar frequencies

CHAFF — American term for strips of foil used to most effectively jam enemy radar by creating numerous deceptive echoes.

DINA — APT-1 radar jammer for 95-210 MHz frequency ranges

GASTON — AN/ARA-3 noise modulator for screening of VHF transmissions

GEE — navigational and blind bombing equipment using coordinate and grid information

JACKAL — AN/ART-3 tank communication jammer

JOSTLE — high powered jammer for R/T transmissions & suspected V2 radio control signals

LORAN — long range air navigational equipment

MANDREL — used for jamming of long range early warning radar

MONICA — aircraft tail warning equipment for use against enemy fighter attacks

MOONSHINE — a device used to retransmit Freya radar signals thus creating deceptive returns

ORVIL — Noise modulated SCR-522 transmitter used to prevent ground monitoring of airborne VHF transmissions without interfering with plane-to-plane communications.

S-27 — a Hewlett-Packard audio oscillator or Hallicrafter search receiver

SCR-587 — basic search receiver

SCS-51 — a U.S. instrument landing system

SX28 — communication search receiver

WINDOW — British term for strips of foil used to most effectively jam enemy radar by creating numerous deceptive echoes.

* The different letters were used to designate what type equipment it was. The AN prefix meant the equipment was used by the U.S. Army and the U.S. Navy. The AN prefix was then followed by a slash and the next letter identified the platform or carrier. Letter "A" identified it as an airplane. The second letter identified the type of system. Here "P" meant radar, "R" meant radio, and "Q" meant countermeasures. The third letter meant the purpose: "T" meant transmitter, while "Q" meant special equipment. The number that followed last was the equipment series designator.[1]

[1] Daniel T. Kuehl.*Blinding Radar's Eye: The Air Force and Electronic Countermeasures in World War II* by From Air Power History, The Journal of Air and Space History. Page 18, Vol. 40, No.2, Summer 1993.

Appendix E:
VHF Screen Mission Flight Plan,
& VHF Spoof Program

36th BOMBARDMENT SQUADRON (H) AAF

Office of the Squadron Navigator

STANDARD 3 A/C Screen			STANDARD 4 A/C Screen		
1.	52 54 N	03 38E	1.	52 58N	03 40E
2.	52 24	03 21	2.	52 39	03 30
3.	51 56	02 58	3.	52 20	03 26
			4.	52 02	03 10

STANDARD 5 A/C Screen			STANDARD 6 A/C Screen		
1.	52 54N	03 38E	1.	53 02N	03 42E
2.	52 38	03 31	2.	52 46	03 35
3.	52 24	03 21	3.	52 31	03 27
4.	52 10	03 10	4.	52 17	03 16
5.	51 56	02 58	5.	52 03	03 05
			6.	51 50	02 50

STANDARD 7 A/C Screen			STANDARD 8 A/C Screen		
1.	53 02N	03 42E	1.	53 16N	03 50E
2.	52 46	03 35	2.	53 02	03 42
3.	52 31	03 27	3.	52 46	03 35
4.	52 17	03 16	4.	52 31	03 27
5.	52 03	03 05	5.	52 17	03 16
6.	51 50	02 50	6.	52 03	03 05
7.	51 38	02 35	7.	51 50	02 50
			8.	51 58	02 35

STANDARD 9 A/C Screen			STANDARD 10 A/C Screen		
1.	53 16N	03 50E	1.	53 31N	03 55E
2.	52 02	03 12	2.	53 16	03 50
3.	52 46	03 35	3.	53 02	03 42
4.	52 31	03 24	4.	52 46	03 35
5.	52 17	03 16	5.	52 31	03 27
6.	52 03	03 05	6.	52 17	03 16
7.	51 50	02 50	7.	52 03	03 05
8.	51 38	02 35	8.	51 50	02 50
9.	51 28	02 18	9.	51 38	02 35
			10.	51 28	02 18

VHF Spoof Program

Headquarters Eighth Bomber Command and higher Headquarters had reason to believe that the enemy was able to obtain valuable information relative to the 8AF's bomber's "assembly, route, and possibly the target." So, Major General Frederick L. Anderson, the Deputy Commander for Operations at Headquarters Eighth Bomber Command implemented the VHF Spoof Program so that it "might prove of some assistance to our forces and cause the enemy some confusion."

The secret Headquarters document stated that the effectiveness of a Spoof Program depended largely upon the manner in which it was executed. The plan also made it clear that the same personnel should not be employed repeatedly to read prepared scripts, as their voices might be recognized by the enemey listening stations, therefore disclosing the scheme.

It was understood that the results of the Spoof Program would not be known immediately, however, it was desirable that "every effort should be made to make it as real as possible." Some of the information in the prepared scripts which could be Spoofed were:

a. Bomb load
b. Fuel load
c. Distance to taget
d. Course to be flown
e. Expected time of attack
f. Fighter escort rendezvous, if not present
g. On certain missions even the target

The following Spoof Plans are sample dialogues of Spoof broadcasts with their respective illustrations:

Spoof Plan No. 1

a. "GOONCHILD FROM GOONCHILD BLUE. WHERE ARE YOU? WE ARE UNABLE TO LOCATE YOU." Goonchild would then come back and say, "HELLO GOONCHILD BLUE. THIS IS GOONCHILD. WE ARE FOUR MINUTES BEHIND SCHEDULE AND WILL ASSEMBLE AT CROMER AS BRIEFED."

b. (Angry voice): "WHY DON'T YOU STAY AT 12,000 WHERE YOU BELONG?"

c. "PILOT FROM NAVIGATOR. FLY COURSE 100"

d. "NAVIGATOR FROM PILOT. ARE WE STILL GOING TO BREMEN?"

"PILOT FROM NAVIGATOR. YES, KEEP YOUR SHIRT ON." Another plane in the formation would then come back and say, "GET OFF VHF, GET ON INTERPHONE."

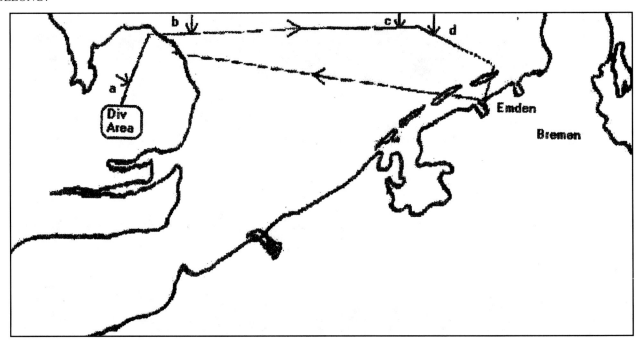

Spoof Plan No. 2

a. "ARE ALL PLANES LEAVING FROM CLACTON?"

b. "GOONCHILD FROM GOONCHILD BLUE. LET'S GO UP TO 21,000 TO GET OUT OF THIS PROP-WASH."

c. "ENGINEER FROM PILOT. YOU CAN TRANSFER THE GAS FROM THE BOMB BAY TANK NOW."

d. "NAVIGATOR FROM PILOT. WHAT IS ETA AT THE TARGET?"

"PILOT FROM NAVIGATOR. ETA IS 1330." (ETA given will be one that will indicate at least an 11- or 12-hour mission.)

e. (Referring to Gydnia) "WE WILL FINISH OFF 60 PER CENT OF THE GERMAN NAVY THIS TRIP."

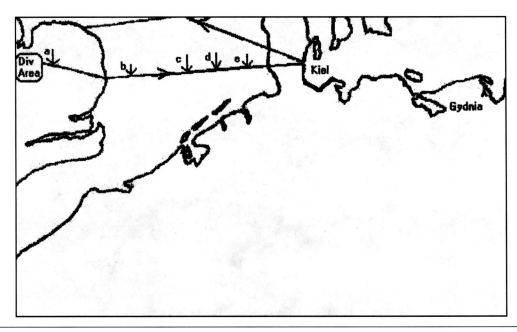

PILOT: RODKEY   SHIP NO: 750-P   27- 3 - 1945

RUNWAY IN USE: 06 - TAXI RIGHT

ORDER OF TAKE-OFF	TIME OF TAKE-OFF	PILOT	PLANE NUMBER	POSITION NUMBER	ALTITUDE
1	0530	BRIGHT	507-D	SEARCH -	12,000
6	0552	SACKETT	502-C	VHF - 1	15,000
12	0604	YOUNG	609-S	" - 2	"
13	0606	WRENN	576-H	" - 3	"
2	0544	FULLER	495-V	SCREEN - 1	9,500
3	0546	SWEENEY	671-F	" - 2	10,500
4	0548	POND	308-M	" - 3	9,500
5	0550	SODERSTROM	546-L	" - 4	10,500
7	0554	OLDERSHAW	230-E	" - 5	9,500
8	0556	RODKEY	750-P	" - 6	10,500
10	0600	BRUSILA	221-A	" - 7	9,500
11	0602	SENN	665-K	" - 8	10,500
9	0558	KITTLE	685-R	" - 9	9,500

CHANNEL 665, SET C WILL NOT BE TURNED ON

EPO HOUR	IN POSITION	EQUIP. ON	EQUIP OFF	LEAVE POSITION
0900	Z - 120 0700 HRS	IN POSITION	Z 0900 HRS	Z 0900 HRS

/S RESCUE - V.H.F. - CHANNEL "D" - COLGATE - CALLSIGN
MAYDAY - EMERGENCY

TIME	COLORS	CHALLENGE	ANSWER	RECN LIGHTS
0100-0700	GRR	X	M	WHITE
0700-1300	RG	Y	S	"
1300-1900	YY	P	C	"
1900-0100				

Appendix F:
Other 803rd/36th Bomb Squadron Honors & Awards

SEPTEMBER 1944

This letter from the Air Officer Commanding RAF 100 Group recognized men of the 803rd Bomb Squadron (H) (Prov.) for their work performed in service to the Royal Air Force.

From: -   Headquarters, No. 100 Group, R.A.F.

To: -   Officer Commanding, 36th Bombardment Sqdn. (H), AAF. Station 113, A.P.O. 639.

Date: -   24th September, 1944.

Ref: -   100G/S.1301/3/1/P.1.   Confidential.

No. 803 (U.S.A.A.F) SQUADRON.
Below is copy of Bomber Command Routine Order No. A139 dated 18th August, 1944, in connection with the above Squadron.

"The Commander-in-Chief wishes to bring notice of all ranks in the Command the excellent contribution made by No. 803 (U.S.A.A.F.) Squadron to the success achieved in recent Bomber operations, and in particular the untiring devotion to duty shown by the Squadron Commander, 0-241067. Lieutenant Colonel Clayton A. Scott and the following captains of aircraft : -

0-798608. Captain Robert G. Stutzman.
0-795831. Captain Raymond A. Robinson.
0-798568. Lieutenant Richard O. Obenschain.

This Squadron initially rendered most valuable service in converting R.A.F. Aircrew and ground personnel from Stirling to Fortress aircraft, and later in undertaking night flying duties.

On completion of this task, the Squadron commenced to undertake operations solely on behalf of Bomber Command, an achievement most worthy of praise as all the crews taking part were tour expired after day bombing operations, and were individuals who were due to return to the U.S.A. for leave. The adaptation of crews of No. 803 Squadron to their role of night bombing was highly commendable.

The above-named Officers by their enthusiasm and inspiration provided a splendid example, and their efforts resulted in a high standard of flying ability and efficiency throughout the Squadron".
(Sigd) A.W. Mylne, Air Vice Marshall, L/C Administration, Bomber Comd.

It is understood from Headquarters, VIIIth Air Force Composite Command that copies of this order have been supplied to personnel of 803 Bomb Squadron, C-B-14 of 24th August, 1944 refers.

A TRUE EXTRACT COPY	/s/ G. Nutkins F/Lt.
	Air Vice-Marshal,
HOMER E. JONES	Air Officer Commanding,
Captain, Air Corps,	No. 100 GROUP, R.A.F.
Intelligence Officer	

OCTOBER 1944

On 11 October word was received that His Majesty the King, on recommendation of the Air Officer Commander in Chief, Bomber Command had approved the immediate award of the Distinguished Flying Cross to Capt. Robert G. Stutzman and the immediate award of the Distinguished Flying Medal to S/Sgt. Herbert C. Hoover. These awards were made to the one officer and enlisted man in the organization as token appreciation for work of the organization in support of Bomber Command Operations. The Original Telegram of notification and congratulatory messages from the Air Officers Commanding, RAF 100 Group and RAF Station Oulton are enclosed.

From: Headquarters, Bomber Command.

To: R.A.F. Station, Oulton. Copies to: Headquarters, No. 100 Group and Air Ministry (S. 10.a.)

Date: 8th October 1944

Ref: Bc/S.2319114/P.

His Majesty the King, on the recommendation of the Air Officer Commanding-in-Chief, has approved the Distinguished Flying Cross to Captain Robert Gordon Stutzman (0-798608) and the Immediate Award of the Distinguished Flying Medal to 38061218 Staff Sergeant Herbert C. Hoover.

Group Captain

A TRUE EXTRACT COPY

C.E. PETERSEN
1st. Lt. Air Corps
Ass't Intelligence Officer

                          EXTRACT

FROM HEADQUARTERS NO. 100 GROUP (THI) 11245A
TO   NO 36 SQUADRON CHEDDINGTON

INFO: COL. SULLIVAN   PINETREE   H.Q.B.C.

QQX BT

A.962 11TH OCTOBER. PERSONAL FOR MAJOR HAMBAUGH FROM AIR VICE-MARSHAL ADDISON.
HAVE JUST LEARNED THAT HIS MAJESTY THE KING ON THE RECOMMENDATION OF THE AIR OFFICER COMMANDING-IN-CHIEF, BOMBER COMMAND, HAS APPROVED THE IMMEDIATE AWARD OF THE DISTINGUISHED FLYING CROSS TO CAPTAIN R.G. STUTZMAN AND IMMEDIATE AWARD OF THE DISTINGUISHED FLYING MEDAL TO STAFF SERGEANT H. C. HOOVER BOTH UNDER YOUR COMMAND.

I WOULD ASK YOU TO CONVEY TO THEM MY SINCEREST CONGRATULATIONS ON THESE AWARDS WHICH ARE A RECOGNITION OF THE FINE WORK THAT THEY HAVE DONE IN 803 SQUADRON AND LATER IN 36 SQUADRON WHILST ENGAGED ON OPERATIONS IN SUPPORT OF BOMBER COMMAND. I WOULD LIKE TO TAKE THIS OPPORTUNITY OF ONCE AGAIN EXPRESSING MY ADMIRATION FOR THE MAGNIFICENT EFFORT WHICH THE UNIT UNDER YOUR COMMAND HAS EXERTED AND IS EXERTING, ON OUR BEHALF. THE WILLING CO-OPERATION AND ENTHUSIASM WITH WHICH YOU JOIN IN OUR ACTIVITIES HAD BEEN THE PRIME FACTOR IN ESTABLISHING THE FINE SPIRIT OF FRIENDLINESS WHICH CHARACTERISES OUR MUTUAL RELATIONS.

BY (THI) 111245A
A TRUE AND EXACT EXTRACT COPY :
   Clarence E. Petersen,
   1st. Lt., Air Corps.

On 12 October an awards presentation ceremony was held in the Briefing Room with Major Robert F. Hambaugh presenting the awards. The award of the Distinguished Flying Cross was made to 1st. Lt. Merlin J. Vowinkel and awards of the Oak Leaf Cluster to the Air Medal were made to S/Sgt. Sidney J. Brandt and S/Sgt. Norvell O. Way for acts of heroism and extraordinary achievement while returning from a mission to France on 18 July 1944. At this time these men were assigned to the 856th BS, 492BG (H). Additionally thirty five Air Medals and twenty four Oak Leaf Clusters to the Air Medal were presented to crew members in the 36BS.

NOVEMBER 1944

On 3 Nov. 1944, Lt. Col. Hambaugh presented the Distinguished Flying Cross (DFC) to Capt. Thomas Graham and Air Medal to Capt. Jere B. Johnson in the Briefing Room. The Air Medal was also presented to twelve officers and enlisted men. The Oak Leaf Cluster was awarded to twenty-four officers and enlisted men. On 16 Nov. Air Vice Marshall presented Capt. Robert G. Stutzman the British DFC in a ceremony in front of the Station 113 Headquarters. Also present was Col. Sullivan, Director. of Communications, 8th AF and Col. Webster, Commanding Officer 8th Fighter Command.

DECEMBER 1944

Awards for the month of December included 26 Air Medals presented to officers and enlisted men. Sixteen men were awarded an Oak Cluster to the Air Medal. Forty seven men were awarded an Oak Leaf Cluster to the Air Medal. A recommendation was made for the award of a Bronze Star Medal to crew chief T/Sgt. Baxley.

JANUARY 1945

By January, a total of 143 Air Medals and 473 Oak Leaf Clusters to the Air Medals had been given to men of the organization. A recommendation was forwarded on 24 January for the award of a Bronze Star Medal to crew chief Sgt. Jack Charlton.

FEBRUARY 1945

On 2 February 1945, under authority of a letter from 8AF Headquarters, subject: Battle Participation Award Normandy Campaign, the 36BS was granted battle participation credit for the Normandy Campaign 6 June 1944 to 14 July 1944. Next, on 16 February word was received from Air Vice Marshal E.B. Addison, Air Officer Commanding RAF 100 Group that the British Distinguished Flying Cross was awarded to Captains Richard Obenschain and James Ostler former members of the squadron. Both Capts. Obenschain and Ostler completed tours in a heavy bombardment group before volunteering for RCM work with both the 8AF and the RAF. The letter from Air Vice Marshal Addison to Lt. Col. Hambaugh is quoted in part: "Capts. Obenschain and Ostler have been awarded the Distinguished Flying Cross in recognition of the valuable work that they did for us whilst your squadron was engaged on Bomber Support operations in this theater. I feel it is a pity that it is not possible to give individual medals to all the personnel of your squadron, but I trust you will regard these awards as denoting our appreciation of the grand work that your unit did for us during the period that you were engaged with our special operations."

MAY 1945

On 1 May the 36BS was awarded battle participation credit for the Germany Campaign. Also on the same day, men of the squadron were authorized medals for the Campaign of Northern France, Campaign for the Rhine, and the Campaign of the Ardennes.

A summary of the 1103 awards made to personnel in the squadron since its activation as an RCM squadron on 13 August 1944 follows:

Distinguished Flying Cross	2
Bronze Star Medal	4
Purple Heart Medal	1
Air Medal	283
Oak Leaf Cluster to AM	813

Appendix G:
803rd & 36th Bomb Squadron Aircraft

On D-Day four war weary Flying Fortress B17 bombers were used for the 803rd Bomb Squadron's first mission in RCM. The B17 aircraft flown by the 803rd were initially used by the 384th, 94th, 95th and 96th Bomb Groups where they had flown a complete operational tour of 25 missions before being sent to RAF Station Oulton. After D-Day some of the B17's (indicated by asterisk*) took part in Project Aphrodite[1]. These B17's flew the ill-fated guided bomber missions against Hitler's dreaded Vengeance weapons and became missing in action. It was Project Aphrodite that took the life of Joseph P. Kennedy Jr., the brother of President John F. Kennedy. The aircraft serial numbers, original bomb group, nickname, and jamming equipment were:

#42-30039, from 384th BG - nicknamed *Liberty Belle* with MANDREL and CARPET* (MIA 10/15/44)
#42-30178, from 95th BG - nicknamed *Darlin' Dolly* (95th BG, 335th SQ) with MANDREL and CARPET* (MIA 1/1/45)
#42-30353, from 95th BG - nicknamed *Ten Knights in the Bar Room* with MANDREL* (MIA 12/5/44)
#42-30066, from 96th BG - nicknamed *Mugwump* with MANDREL and CARPET* (MIA 10/30/44)
#42-37743, from 96th BG - No nickname known with ELINT and MANDREL* (MIA 10/15/44)
#42-30363, from 96th BG - nicknamed *Ruth L III* with MANDREL* (MIA 9/14/44)
#42-3438, from 96th BG - No nickname known with MANDREL* (MIA 10/30/44)
#42-3177, from 96th BG with CARPET and MANDREL
#42-30114 with a JACKAL set (original group unknown)
#42-97691 with JACKAL (original group unknown)
#42-3518 with ELINT (original group unknown)

36TH BOMB SQUADRON B24 LIBERATORS

SERIES	SERIAL #	LETTER	ARRIVED	NICKNAME
B24J	42-50665	K	6/44	*LADY IN THE DARK*
B24J	42-51226	L	6/44	
B24H	42-51219	I	6/44	
B24J	42-51232	J	6/44	*THE JIGS UP*
B24J	42-50622	N	6/44	*THIS IS IT MEN & BAMA BOUND LOVELY LIBBA*
B24H	42-50385	H	7/44	*BEAST OF BOURBON*
B24H	42-51188	O	7/44	*LADY JANE*
B24H	41-29143	B	7/44	
B24H	42-7607	A	7/44	
B24J	42-50671	F	7/44	*RAMP ROOSTER*
B24J	42-51239	C	8/44	*THE UNINVITED*
B24J	42-51308	M	8/44	*MODEST MAID*
B24D	42-40756		9/44	
B24J	42-51230	E	10/44	*LI'L PUDGE & RUM DUM*
B24J	42-50750	P	10/44	
B24J	42-50844	I	11/44	*MISS B HAVEN*
B24J	42-51546	L	11/44	*I WALK ALONE & GRAVY TRAIN*
B24J	42-51685	R	12/44	*PLAYMATE*
B24J	44-10609	S	12/44	*21 SPECIAL*
B24H	42-95221	A	12/44	*MARGIE, READY-N-ABLE*
B24M	44-50576	H	12/44	*PECK'S BAD BOYS*
B24J	42-95507	D	12/44	
B24J	42-51304	B	12/44	
B24J	42-51311	T	1/45	*TAR BABY* (BLACK)
B24J	42-51315	U	1/45	(BLACK)
B24	42-50495	V	2/45	*STRICTLY VICTORY*
B24	42-51307	Q	2/45	*JUST JEANNE*
B24	44-50502	C	3/45	*THE GYPSY JANE*
B24	42-50476	J	3/45	
B24	44-50772		3/45	

UNCONDITIONAL SURRENDER and *Liberated From England* are other 36BS B24 nicknames. The associated aircraft serial numbers and letter assignments for these aircraft are unknown.

*See Communications, Engineering, and Training Section Appendix H for B24 jamming equipment assignment.

36TH BOMB SQUADRON P38 "DROOP SNOOT" AIRCRAFT

During March of 1945 three P38 or F5 "Droop Snoot" aircraft came to the 36th. These aircraft were brought to the squadron on detached service from the 7th Photographic Reconnaissance Group (7PRG) and were later assigned to the squadron. Their purpose was to investigate German radar in Holland and along the front lines. The "Droop Snoot" P38's were:

#44-23156
#43-28479
#44-23501

AIRCRAFT TYPE SPECIFICATIONS

Boeing B17 — Flying Fortress
Powerplants: four Wright R-1820-97 Cyclone 1,200 hp 9 cylinder radial engines.
Dimensions: length 74 ft 9 in.; height 19 ft 1 in.; wing span 103 ft 9 in.
Weight: empty 35,800 lbs; operational 65,600 lbs. excluding jamming equipment.
Performance: maximum speed 287 mph; service ceiling 35,000 ft; range 1,100 miles
Armament: two .50 calibre machine guns in chin, top, ball, and tail turrets; five flexible .50 calibre machine guns. These Fortresses carried no bombs.

Consolidated B24 — Liberator
Powerplants: four Pratt & Whitney R-1830-65 Twin Wasp 1,200 hp 14 cylinder radial engines.
Dimensions: length 67 ft 2 in.; height 18 ft; wing span 110 ft.
Weight: empty 37,000 lbs; operational 65,600 lbs. excluding jamming equipment.
Performance: maximum speed 290 mph; service ceiling 28,000 ft; range 2,200 miles.
Armament: two .50 calibre machine guns in each nose, top, ball, and tail turrets; two .50 calibre machine guns in waist position. These Liberators carried no bombs.

The Lockheed P38 — Lightning
Powerplants: twin Allison V1710-89/91 1,425 hp 12 cylinder inline engines.
Dimensions: length 37 ft 10 in.; height 12 ft 10 in.; wing span 52 ft.
Weight: empty 12,780 lbs; operational 17,500 lbs., excluding search equipment.
Performance: maximum speed 414 mph; service ceiling 44,000 ft; range 2,260 miles.
The "Droop Snoots" flew unarmed.

[1] Roger Freeman, *The Mighty Eighth War Manual*, Page 105 and Individual Aircraft Record Cards from the US AFHRA, Maxwell AFB, Ala.

Appendix H:
Summary of 803rd & 36th Bomb Squadron Reports by the Engineering, Communications, and Training Sections

MARCH 1944 THROUGH JUNE 1945

The primary purpose of the engineering section of the 803BS during its initial period of existence beginning on 20 January 1944 at RAF Station Sculthorpe was the training of the RAF ground crews in the proper care and maintenance of B17 aircraft. The initial number of men assigned the section was twelve airplane mechanics and four armorers. The job called for men to work intimately with Squadron Leader Howard, Chief Technical Officer who gave all manner of cooperation in the performance of the various duties. For a period the men were distributed evenly among the fourteen RAF aircraft. On 25 February a second phase shipment of six airplane mechanics arrived. The American men gave lectures on propellers, engines, electrical, and other aircraft systems. It was said that the audience was in every case very attentive. Lt. Harold Preuss lectured the flying crews on engine operation procedures and related subjects. Factory representatives of Wright Aeronautical Company, Boeing Aircraft Company, Sperry Gyroscope Company, and Minneapolis-Honeywell Company came to Sculthorpe and lectured to the RAF ground and air crews. For a time U.S. airmen took over complete maintenance of several RAF aircraft including two B17C's used for liaison work. The formation of the supply setup was put into the very capable hands of Lt. Henry Bloomer Jr. who did the initial contact work for the procurement of all supplies.

Engineering work began when men of the 803BS ceased to work on RAF aircraft on 21 March and the first B17F and one B17G RCM aircraft arrived. Shortly after this, an additional number of mechanics arrived. A small American technical site which included an armament shop, turret shop, technical supply, was set up. The aircraft were modified for night flying and a program was inaugurated which involved practice night flying, circuits and bumps, as well as cross-country flights. During this period no major difficulties were experienced with the aircraft outside of several engine and oil cooler changes. On 16 May the work terminated at Sculthorpe and the squadron moved to Oulton. The number of aircraft increased to thirteen and the number of mechanics correspondingly increased bringing the total number of engineering personnel to fifty. Various units previously at Sculthorpe — an engine build up department, a small sheet metal and welding shop, and the necessary associated technical supply line were again set up at Oulton.

The six B17's for the 803BS which arrived at Sculthorpe on 1 March came from the 96th Bomb Group. Three B17's were equipped with 9 CARPET and 4 MANDREL. The B17's were #42-30039, #42-30066, and #42-30177. Two more MANDRELS were later added to these aircraft. The three other B17's arrived with 6 MANDREL. They were #42-30363, #42-3438, and #42-37743. B17 #42-37743 was also equipped with ELINT. It should be noted that B17's #42-30363 and #42-3438 were later transferred to Project Aphrodite where both were lost in operations. B17 #42-30353 and #42-30178 arrived at Sculthorpe on 15 May came from the 95th Bomb Group. By 5 June these two B17's were installed with 6 MANDREL. Also during June the 803BS began its gradual transfer from B17 to B24 aircraft. The new B24J aircraft were #42-50665 (R4-K), #42-51226 (R4-L), #42-51232 (R4-J), #42-50622 (R4-N), and the B24H was #42-51219 (R4-I). On 7 June two more MANDRELS were added to aircraft #42-30039, #42-30177, and #42-30066. On 15 June search equipped was transferred from

#42-37743 to #42-3518. On 20 June one JACKAL was installed on #42-51219, #42-51226, #42-51232, #42-50665, all newly assigned B24's. On 22 June CARPET BLINKER was installed in B24 #42-50622.

On the D-Day 6 June mission B-17, #42-30039 returned with #3 propeller feathered. This was due to low oil pressure, which in turn was traced to the fact that the oil tank was empty indicating excessive engine oil consumption. On the 16 June mission, aircraft #42-30363 returned with #1 propeller windmilling. The pilot could not feather the engine and the stationary reduction gear bolts protruded from the nose section.

JULY

July brought the arrival of more new B24H's and B24J's. On 4 July B24H, #42-50385 (R4-H), and #42-51188 (R4-O) arrived each with three DINA having been installed a month before. On 16 July B24H's #41-29143 (R4-B) and #42-7607 (R4-A) arrived. And on 30 July B24J, #42-50671 (R4-F) arrived to the 803rd. July B24 equipment installations included: On 1 July six MANDREL were installed in #41-29143 and #42-7607. On 10 July #42-30039, #42-30066 and #42-30177 were stripped of CARPET and returned to 8AF with the MANDREL equipment given to RAF. On 15 July six MANDREL were installed in #42-51226 and on 25 July six MANDREL were installed in #42-51239.

The first two B24 aircraft equipped with DINA, #42-51188 and #42-50385 were dispatched on the 12 July mission and flew with three B17 aircraft. The 28 July mission had only B24's dispatched with no B17 aircraft sent out.

AUGUST

The operational training activities of the 36BS in August concerned preparing the new crews for night flying. The particular patrols were flown in conjunction with countering the enemy radar installations. Particular stress was laid on navigation training. All crew members had seven hours of instruction at the Mobile Training Unit in operation and maintenance subjects. The pilots and co-pilots received additional training in the Link Trainer. In addition all crew members were given one a hour security lecture and two hours of radar intelligence as well as lectures on tactics and night operations. The navigational training consisted of a local familiarization flight, a day cross country flight with and without GEE; three hours in the GEE trainer, a two hour lecture on GEE and its tactical use, a night cross country, and a lecture in radio and night navigational aids. Night patrols with more experienced navigators were flown by the new navigators. Additionally, the operations section cooperated with the communications section in scheduling CARPET BLINKER training flights. By the end of August, seven crews had received training. Two of these were from the old 856BS and five were new crews from the Combat Crew Replacement Center. The 36BS now had sixteen crews.

The particular type of operations carried out by the squadron called for a large communications section. The section now had a strength of 202 officers and enlisted men including those on temporary duty from other organizations. This included radar observers, radar maintenance officers, radar mechanics, a communications training officer, radio operators, and a special operator. These men received training at both Station 113 Cheddington and at RAF Oulton. Radio operators were trained in JOSTLE, CARPET BLINKER, VISUAL MONICA, and modified IFF. A squadron code school was set up for the purpose of checking out the radio operators each week. A CARPET BLINKER training school was also set up for the training of men there on temporary duty from the Second Bombardment Division.

Two new B24J's arrived during August. They were #42-51239 (R4-C) and #42-51308 (R4-M). The installations of radar countermeasure equipment included six MANDREL to aircraft #42-50665, #42-51232, #42-51219, and #42-50671. Aircraft #42-50671 also had a SX28 receiver installed.

Problems arose in August largely because of the very nature of the work and the equipment being used. From an operational standpoint it was difficult to make plans because of the uncertainty of future requirements. This uncertainty also necessitated frequent changes in the installation of equipment in the aircraft. One piece of equipment that did not present a problem to the squadron was the aircraft bombsight. Because of the nature of operations in which the squadron was engaged there was no use for this type of equipment. The lack of trained maintenance personnel, however, was another problem the squadron faced when it changed from Fortresses to Liberators. This difficulty was overcome by bringing in trained personnel and by giving courses of instruction in the maintenance of B24 aircraft to the old personnel.

From the time of the first mission on 3 June 1944 to 13 August 1944, 123 aircraft were dispatched. There were 8 aborts, or 6.5%. Some of these were due to engineering failures, others were due to failure of radar equipment, and still others to pilot error. Prior to 13 August, 45 aircraft were dispatched without an abort. The overall figures indicated that 168 aircraft were dispatched, of which 8 aborted or 4.7%.

SEPTEMBER

Training for the month of September was confined largely to ground training in the Radar Section. Just as in August flight training for new crews was completed. This was largely navigational training and consisted of a local familiarization flight, a day cross country with and without GEE, three hours in the GEE trainer, a two hour lecture on GEE and its tactical use; a night cross country and a lecture on radio and night navigational aids. Night patrols with more experienced navigators were also flown by the new navigators. Seven crews, five new ones and two from the 856BS received this training. In addition, the Operations Section cooperated with the Communications Section in scheduling CARPET BLINKER training flights. Fourteen CARPET BLINKER training flights were flown during the month.

Radar countermeasure training was carried on at RAF Station Oulton as well as at Cheddington. The AAF Training Detachment at Oulton was under the command of Capt. Hubert Sturdivant, liaison officer with the RAF. Close liaison was received with Squadron Leader Clarkson of the RAF and with excellent cooperation. Radar mechanics completed their training in JOSTLE III, MONICA, and JOSTLE IV (used for Big Ben, the V2 rocket project) during the month. Both officers and enlisted men received this training. M/Sgt. Strong flew two operational missions with the RAF and gave training in the operation of Big Ben equipment. Officers and enlisted men also received other training in JOSTLE provided by Lt. Zatlin. Another phase of training was conducted by Lt. William Coffield on RCM CARPET BLINKER equipment for operators of the Second Bomb Division.

The Communications Section concerned itself with primarily RCM training, the setting up of the JOSTLE Shop, and also installation of MANDREL equipment.

In the engineering department, eight additional sets of MANDREL III were installed in each operational aircraft. Search equipment was transferred from B17 #42-3518 to B24 #42-51308. CARPET equipment was installed in #42-51308. Preparatory to the installation of Modified IFF or MANDREL III ten aircraft of the squadron, #42-50385, #42-50671, #42

51188, #42-51226, #42-7607, #42-51219, #42-29143, #42-51232, #42-51239, #42-50665 had the floors in the right rear section of the bomb bays modified.

Construction work began to enclose rooms in the rear portion of these aircraft bomb bays. Oxygen regulators, heated suit outlets, and overhead lights in the enclosed compartments were installed. Eight additional antennae in the wings and tail for the IFF equipment were installed in these aircraft. On every aircraft of the squadron a light was removed from the bomb bay compartment and installed beneath the radio table to enable the radio operator to tune the liaison transmitter installed on the floor under the table. A modification to enclose the waist windows on #41-29143 and #42-7607 was done.

During the month the squadron flew eighty seven operational sorties with one abortion, this being due to the inability to operate certain RCM equipment in aircraft #42-50385. This abortion was not charged to the crew chief. All B17 aircraft were gradually transferred from the squadron by 2 September.

OCTOBER

During October specialized training in one phase of countermeasures, namely JOSTLE, was suspended temporarily and most of the personnel sent to Cheddington on temporary duty for that training were sent elsewhere. The shop and equipment, however, remained available in case further need for this training arose. Other training on MANDREL III and CARPET BLINKER continued. Upon completion of the CARPET BLINKER (Early warning and gun firing equipment) training, the trainees operated a Wurzburg installation (from the Bruneval raid ?) at the station which was used in connection with the CARPET BLINKER training.

Ground training for flying personnel at this time consisted of training in the Link trainer for pilots and co-pilots, and training by the Mobile Training Unit in various phases of engineering for all crew members, and night vision training for all gunners.

All personnel were given a medical lecture on sex hygiene by Capt. Jere Johnson, the Squadron Flight Surgeon. Three hours of lectures by Lt. Basil Bland were given each week on booby traps and mines.

In the communications department the Radar Shop completed the installation of MANDREL III equipment in three aircraft. The equipment in all aircraft was configured straight MANDREL to a combination of DINA (APT-1) and MANDREL. The prototype of low frequency DINA was placed in one aircraft. The Communications Section changed over equipment from two old aircraft #42-7607 and #41-29143 to new aircraft which were recently assigned to the squadron.

The engineering program of installing rooms in the rear bomb bay compartment continued.

As of 31 October B24 aircraft #42-51188, #42-50671, #41-29143, #42-51232, #42-51308, and #42-51239 had compartments completed.

The program of installing eight Modified IFF (MANDREL III) sets in aircraft #42-51188 and #41-29143 was completed. Three antennae were installed in each wing and two antennae in the tail of each aircraft. On #42-51232, four Modified IFF sets were installed necessitating installing one antenna in each wing and two in the tail. Antennae installation to 36BS aircraft was carried out by the sheet metal men of the engineering department. Further installations would conform to the pattern of #42-51232.

A program to install two MANDREL and four DINA sets in #42-51188, #42-51226, #42-51232, #42-50385, #42-51219, #41-29143, #42-51239, #42-50665, and #42-50671 was completed. General radar and engineering modification work for DINA, MANDREL, and Modified IFF installation began, but was not completed on #42-51230 (R4-M), and #42-50750 (R4-P), two new B24J aircraft.

During the month the squadron completed 81 operational sorties on 13 missions with 4 abortions. Liberator #42-50665 aborted on 7 October and #42-51188 on 23 October due to pilot error. Aircraft #42-7607 aborted on 21 October due to a gas leak in number one engine and #42-50385 aborted on 26 October due to a number one engine failure. Both cases were charged to engineering.

NOVEMBER

November engineering had eight aircraft equipped to jam 8AF VHF frequencies. MANDREL and DINA Class A installations (mounting racks, antennas, and wires, etc.) were made in two aircraft and MANDREL III was also installed in two additional aircraft. The program of installing rooms in the rear bomb-bay compartments continued. By 30 November nine aircraft had these rooms completed. Liberators #42-51230, #42-51239, #42-51188, #42-50671, #42-50385, #42-51232, #42-50750, #42-50844, and #42-50665 had two MANDREL and four DINA sets installed in the rear bomb-bay compartment. Aircraft #42-51230, #42-50671, #42-51188, #42-51232, and #42-50385 had MANDREL III installations completed. Additional VHF sets were installed in aircraft #42-51188, #42-51308, #42-50385, and #42-50622 for spoof missions.

During the month the squadron completed 88 operational screening missions for the RAF; 34 operational screening sorties on six missions for the 8AF; and 3 operational spoof sorties on one mission for the 8AF. On 1 November #41-29143 aborted when two generators failed. On 18 November, Liberator #42-50385, aborted when number three propeller "ran away", due to a faulty governor. On 23 November, aircraft #42-50671, aborted when a small fire was reported on number two engine. This was subsequently traced to an arching generator which burned a hole in the generator cap.

DECEMBER

During December twenty two full crews and three partial crews were assigned to the squadron. Nineteen Liberators were assigned to the squadron, two for maintenance only. December RCM training was again conducted by Lt. William Coffield on CARPET equipment which was used to counter enemy control of flak battery radar. A total of 200 men on temporary duty from Third Division organizations were trained during the month. Three additional instructors and one mechanic were added to the RCM school.

The Radio Code School gave new radio operators training needed to bring them up to a standard of 18 words per minute and to also make them familiar with British-American procedures. Routine ground Link training continued. Each pilot and co-pilot receiving approximately four hours of training during the month. The new navigators were each given five hours in GEE trainers.

Col. Sullivan, 8AF Director of Communications, spoke to the combat crews on 19 December with regard to the nature and effectiveness of the RCM work being done by the squadron in support of 8AF operations. He spoke particularly of the operations of 27 November and 5 December for which graphic charts were prepared and shown.

Eight new crews received indoctrination lectures on security, engineering, ditching, flying control, and UK procedures. A training film on AAF fighters was shown to all crews. Flight training consisted of five day cross country flights and one night cross country. Each pilot shot landings at night. Weather seriously interfered with training activities during the month. The Communications Section now operated its own ground control station at Cheddington for the purpose of transmitting operational messages.

December engineering included the prototype installation of ORVILS for VHF screening in Liberator #42-50622. Nine CARPET (ground fire control jammers) sets were modified for spot jamming. Permanent Class A installations for MANDREL and DINA were installed in aircraft #42-51230, #42-50665, #42-51308, #42-51188, #42-50844, #42-51239, #42-50385, #42-51546, #42-95221, #42-50750, and #42-50671. Permanent Class A installations for MANDREL III (Modified IFF) were installed in aircraft #42-51230, #42-50750, #42-51188, #42-50671, and #42-50385. Permanent Class A installations JACKAL (tank communications jammers) were installed in aircraft #42-51230, #42-51188, #42-50385, #42-50665, and #42-51308. CARPET BLINKER equipment was installed for training purposes to aircraft #42-50622 and #42-51308.

Permanent receiver equipment was installed in aircraft #42-50622 and #42-50671. ORVILS equipment was also installed permanently to aircraft #42-95221. MOONSHINE equipment was permanently installed on aircraft #42-51239. Aircraft #42-50622 had equipment for spoof missions permanently installed. The new aircraft assigned to the squadron during December were B24J's #42-51304 (R4-B), #42-95507 (R4-D), #44-10609 (R4-S), #42-51685 (R4-R), #42-50467 (R4-J) and B24H #42-95221 (R4-A).

Here is a summary of RCM sorties, missions and abortions for the year 1944 as compiled by the Engineering Department, beginning 6 June 1944, the date on which the parent organization, the 803rd Bomb Sq. (H) (Prov) became operational:

Sorties Completed	618	
Missions	121	
Aircraft Lost	3	
Total Abortives	25	Percent ... 3.88
Engineering Abortives	11	Percent ... 1.71
Radar Abortives (GEE and RCM)	9	Percent ... 1.39
Pilot Error Abortives	5	Percent ... 0.77

Data regarding aircraft assigned to the 36BS in December.

TYPE	SERIAL NO.	NAME	LETTER	DISPATCHED	CREW CHIEF	EQUIP
B24J	42-51230	Li'l Pudge	M	30	Quissell	Mandrel III, Dina, Jackal, Mandrel
B24H	42-51188	Lady Jane	O	33	Henry	Mandrel III, Dina, Jackal, Mandrel
B24H	42-50385	Beast of Bourbon	H	31	McCombs	Mandrel III, Dina, Jackal, Mandrel
B24J	42-50750	None	P	34	Pragit	Mandrel III, Dina Mandrel
B24J	42-51315 (black)	None	U	37	Barkley	Visual Monica
B24J	42-50622	This Is It Men/ Bama Bound	N	1	Ingels	Carpet, Jostle Search Receiver, VHF Spoof, Tunable Carpet
B24J	42-50665	Lady in the Dark	K	38	Baxley	Mandrel, Dina, Jackal
B24J	42-50844	Miss-B-Haven	I	35	Charlton	Mandrel, Dina

Appendix H: Summary of 803rd & 36th Bomb Squadron Reports

TYPE	SERIAL NO.	NAME	LETTER	DISPATCHED	CREW CHIEF	EQUIP
B24J	42-51546	I Walk Alone	L	36	Brown	Mandrel, Dina
B24J	42-51685	Playmate	R	39	Cota	None
B24J	44-10609	21 Special	S	39	Gierlasinski	None
B24J	42-50671	Ramp Rooster	F	3	Fife	Mandrel III, Mandrel Dina, Search Receiver
B24J	42-51308	Modest Maid	M	8	Dunster	Mandrel, Dina, Tunable Carpet
B24J	42-51239	Uninvited	C	5	Harkins	Mandrel III, Mandrel, Dina Low Freq Dina
B24H	42-95221	Ready N Able & Margie	A	7	Durand	Mandrel, Dina Orvils
B24J	42-50476	Pecks Bad Boys	J	4	Copestick	None
B24J	42-95507	None	D	9	Bowden	Radio Bomb Release
B24J	42-51304	None	B	9	Sanders	Radio Bomb Release
B24J	42-51311 (black)	Tar Baby	T	30	Linebaugh	Visual Monica, Carpet, Jostle

During December the 36BS completed 12 operational sorties on 8 missions for the RAF and 157 operational sorties on 23 missions for the 8AF totaling 169 sorties on 31 missions.

JANUARY

January training began with one waist gunner from each crew being instructed in the operation of RCM equipment carried in each aircraft. It was planned to have them replace the extra RCM operator now carried in addition to the regular crew. Routine training continued in the Code School. A total of 210 men on temporary duty from various 1st Air Division organizations as well as 25 RCM operators were assigned to the squadron and trained during the month. The CARPET training school conducted by Lt. William Coffield was terminated on 24 January. The school had operated under direct supervision of the RCM Section, Headquarters 8AF.

Indoctrination lectures on security, engineering, ditching, flying control, and UK procedure were given to the one new crew. The training film "Resisting Enemy Interrogation" was shown to nine crews and three dingy drills per week per crew were held. These drills were conducted by the pilot. Also twenty cross-country flights, two per crew were flown. Each of the new crews also shot night landings. Adverse weather again seriously interfered with flight training and caused a delay of thirty days or more in making the new crews operational. Lectures on controlling venereal disease were again given to the men, this time by the Commanding Officer, Lt. Col. Hambaugh.

The Communications Section conducted tests in accordance with a request from the Director of Communications. On 3 January tests were made to determine the effect from airborne ORVILS upon ground reception of R/T transmissions over frequency channels at various ranges. On the same day tests were also made to determine the effect of ORVILS upon plane-to-plane R/T communications over the same channel. Three aircraft were employed. One carrying the jammer was supplied by the squadron. After analyzing the results, it was concluded that ORVILS could be effectively used to prevent ground monitoring of VHF transmissions at ranges tested without seriously interfering with plane-to-plane communications over distances up to forty miles between aircraft. Sixty sets of ORVILS were installed in aircraft.

Five Liberators had rooms installed in the rear bomb bay compartments by the engineering section. A program was formulated to connect the tail turret into the main hydraulic system of the airplane in order to conserve approximately 100 amperes of electrical energy. Kits were procured and the modification work began on aircraft #44-10609. At this time aircraft #42-50622 and #42-50671 had special receiver equipment for RCM operations. Six aircraft, #42-51230, #42-50476, #42-51685, #42-50665, #44-10609, and #42-95221 had Class A JACKAL parts installed for JACKAL operations. MANDREL sets were installed in aircraft #42-50385, #42-50665, #42-51546, #42-50750, #42-50844, and #42-95221. All MAN-DREL III were removed from aircraft. Aircraft having Class A CARPET installations were #42-51230, #42-51311, #42-50665, #42-51308, #44-10609, #42-51315, #42-50622, #42-51685, and #42-50476. Twelve CARPET III sets were installed in four aircraft for spot jamming. Eight DINAs were installed in two aircraft. These two aircraft already contained six sets each, making a total of ten sets per aircraft which was the present program. Aircraft with DINA installations now complete or partially complete were #42-51230, #42-50750, #42-51546, #42-51308, #42-51188, #42-50665, #42-51685, #42-51239, #42-50385, #42-50844, #42-50671, and #42-95221. Liberators #42-51311 (R4-T) and #42-51315 (R4-U), both black B24's were assigned to the squadron during the month. They were installed with JOSTLE equipment and were now available for operations. The 600 lb. JOSTLE transmitter, enclosed in a pressurized tank, was mounted in the ball turret position of the B24. An analysis was made which indicated that JOSTLE was superior to JACKAL and certain aircraft would be used in this capacity. Aircraft #42-51685 and #42-95221 had ORVILS partially complete. Twenty-two LORANS and five radio altimeters were installed. Thirteen B24's had their ball turrets removed.

The squadron faced a problem of securing necessary RCM equipment. Supply channels were such that there was considerable delay in acquiring RCM equipment that was needed for the most effective operational results.

During the month the squadron completed 2 operational sorties on 2 missions for the RAF and 117 operational sorties on 22 missions for the 8AF, totaling 119 sorties on 24 missions. In addition, nine abortions were recorded, of which five were attributable to engineering material failure, two to radar equipment failure, and two to pilot failure.

On 5 January, Liberator #42-50665 aborted due to number two engine failure, #42-51188 aborted due to radar equipment failure, and #42-51239 returned with number four engine failure. On 7 January #42-50385 aborted due to number two engine cutting out at altitude and #42-51188 aborted due to radar equipment failure. On 8 January #42-51188 aborted due to number four engine failure. On 21 January the pilot brought #42-50671 back prematurely claiming a gasoline leak. Later a test hop was made with no gasoline leak in evidence. Decision was pilot error. On 24 January the landing gear refused to retract on #42-50844. However, the pilot had failed to attempt a retraction by depressing the safety solenoid under the instrument panel which would have retracted the landing gear satisfactorily. On 28 January #42-51308 aborted due to number four engine failure.

FEBRUARY

On 4 February the Communications Section conducted an experimental air to ground test at Defford, England to determine the effectiveness of JOSTLE equipment as a spot jammer. In general the test was very satisfactory although no detailed analysis was received from American British

Laboratory. JOSTLE would replace JACKAL as tank communication jamming equipment if and when that type of operation was again required.

At this time four aircraft were equipped with ORVILS equipment. The first two Liberators equipped, #44-10609 and #42-51307 had twelve sets each, whereas the last two #42-95221 and #42-51685 had six sets. On 5 February the crew and aircraft #42-51239 with two MANDREL sets and one low frequency DINA set failed to return from an operational mission.

On 1 February, the RCM School was discontinued and the training school for spot jamming operators was shut down after training approximately 500 spot jamming operators since September 1944. The operators then reported to their bomb groups, which numbered many. Some of the bomb groups gaining these special operators were the 44BG, 93BG, 389BG, 390BG, 392BG, 445BG, 446BG, 448BG, 453BG, 458BG, 466BG, 467BG, and the 491BG.[1] All future training of operators would now be handled at the various Bomb Groups with the aid of Artificial Radar Signal Generators. Lt. Coffield and the instructors assigned to the school on temporary duty returned to their former groups.

During February the Engineering Section connected the tail turret into the main hydraulic system of eight aircraft. Fifteen Liberators had ball turrets removed. Aircraft #42-95221, #44-10609, #42-51685, and #42-51307 had complete ORVIL sets installed by the section.

The squadron completed 151 operational sorties on 24 8AF missions this month. No missions were flown for the RAF. One abortion was recorded when B24 #42-51546 returned prematurely on 28 February due to number two and number four engine failure. On this day the consecutive string of 158 sorties without a single abortion ended.

The problem of securing required RCM equipment persisted. Considerable delay was experienced in securing equipment necessary to achieve the most effective results.

MARCH

In March tests were conducted on seventeen new model ART-3 or JACKAL equipments. These tests for altitude, stability, and endurance were conducted in the Technical Research Engineering Laboratories at Great Malvern by three squadron enlisted men under direct supervision of American British Laboratory technicians. The new sets were found to be superior but still not without defects. These defects were remedied by a slight modification made in the squadron radar shop.

Three P-38's flew a number of search missions against the enemy early warning radar system by patrolling along the coast from Dunkirk to Denmark and also the length of the Ruhr Valley. High frequency (two centimeters) searches were conducted for enemy radar installations. One Ferret B-24 aircraft, #44-10507 was dispatched on several occasions to search the enemy early warning radar. New signals were noticed. To counter this, the DINA or APT-1 was modified to jam these signals. A D/F (direction finder) antenna was also used during the search missions. All the information gathered on these flights was forwarded to Headquarters for final analysis.

The installation program of ORVILS in five Liberators was completed under the supervision of T/Sgt. Payne. ORVIL equipped aircraft were dispatched on numerous occasions. Their mission was to screen all VHF traffic conducted by the Air Divisions. A new installation of twenty-two DINA per aircraft was accomplished in aircraft #42-51311 and #42-51315. The installation of a special British alternator on four B24 aircraft as an extra source of power was completed. The four aircraft were #42-51188, #44-50772, #42-51311, and #42-51315. Work also began in the building and installing of a retractable D/F antenna in one Ferret aircraft.

During the month there were a total of 196 effective sorties flown on 28 missions. The Engineering Section reported that five abortions occurred of which four were attributed to radar malfunctions. The one engineering failure occurring on 18 March resulted from a broken throttle link on number number two engine of aircraft #42-50476. On 20 March Liberator #42-50844 crashed on take off on an operational mission. All members escaped serious injury although the aircraft was a total loss.

The training of all 5 RCM mechanics, who were on flying status as CARPET operators and search receiver operators was accomplished during the month.

The squadron was now operating with twenty B24's and three P38's. The following aircraft were newly assigned: B24's #44-50502 (R4-C), #44-50576 (R4-H), and #44-50772 (R4-?), and P38 #44-23156, #43-28479 and #44-23501. The P38's were used for search missions within enemy territory. Ground crews that came along with these aircraft terminated their period of temporary duty at Alconbury on 31 March. 36BS engineering personnel now performed all maintenance.

No accurate data existed concerning power consumption of all of the various electrical units installed within B24 aircraft. In order to determine the exact figures under actual operating conditions, a test flight was made using Liberator #42-51308. Mr. Paul Robbiano of the American British Laboratories in Great Malvern planned a test and participated in the test flight. This data, when evaluated could prove invaluable for future installations involving power equipment.

The squadron Radar Section needed of two remotely controlled, rotating, retractable antennae to be used in connection with search activities. The success of the project was directly contingent upon how accurately and positively the antenna could be swept through an angle of 270 degrees. T/Sgt. William Fisher, the engineering electrician was given the job. Using components from a turbo-charger regulator, he designed a unit which met these requirements. Preliminary bench test indicated very satisfactory results.

Again the problem of securing necessary RCM equipment persisted. Supply channels were such that it was often difficult to get what was needed without considerable delay. This situation was aggravated by frequent changes in equipment which was necessary.

The problem of planning operational requirements from a personnel and engineering standpoint presented itself. Operations varied considerably according to the situation, the effectiveness of the equipment employed, enemy countermeasures, and the like.

APRIL

In April the Communications Section conducted tests to determine the effectiveness of a retractable direction finding antennae. This was installed in the ball turret position of B24J, #42-50622. Thirteen aircraft were specially equipped for long range radar jamming. Fourteen aircraft were modified to make GEE and LORAN navigational equipment interchangeable. Class A for JACKAL was removed from 6 aircraft . Class A for DINA was removed from 9 aircraft.

Equipment installations involved the following aircraft: Liberator #42-51188 had two Class A for JACKAL installed, thirty-two Class A for DINA installed, Class A for two CARPET, and one CARPET III installed. Aircraft #42-51311 had thirty-two Class A for DINA completed plus thirteen antennas. Aircraft #42-51315 had thirty-two Class A for DINA completed. Aircraft #42-50495 had Class A for thirty-two DINA completed, Class A for two JACKAL completed, Class A for radio altimeter completed, Class A for three CARPET, and one CARPET III completed. Aircraft #42-95507 had Class A for radio altimeter completed. Aircraft #42-51546 had Class A for thirty-two DINA installed, Class A for two JACKAL installed, Class A for three CARPET, and one CARPET III installed. Aircraft #42-50622 had all search equipment removed and Class A for radio altimeter installed. Aircraft #42-50772 had Class A for thirty-two DINA installed, Class A for two JACKAL installed, and thirteen antennas for DINA installed.

During the month a total of 19 missions aggregating 76 effective sorties were flown. The Engineering Section reported two abortions occurred, one of which was due to a failure of the GEE radio equipment on B24M #44-50576 on 7 April, and the other on 20 April on B24J #42-50476 due to a leak in the hydraulic system.

After having completed Class A installations for thirty-two DINA sets in seven Liberators, the entire installation program was canceled. Basic equipment was now installed in aircraft #42-50772, #42-51546, #42-51311, #42-51188, #42-50671, #42-51315, and #42-50495.

[1] US AFHRA, Maxwell AFB, Ala. RCM file.

Notes

1 R.V. Jones, *Most Secret War,* Page 219.
2 Daniel T. Kuehl letter to the author.
3 Alfred Price, *The History of U.S. Electronic Warfare, Vol.1.* Pages 4-5.
4 US AFHRA, Maxwell AFB, Ala. RCM file. From the First Proving Ground Electronic Unit, Eglin field, Florida, Project No. 13 titled COUNTERMEASURES PROGRAM FOR THE STRATEGIC AIR FORCES IN THE EUROPEAN THEATER. Dated Dec. 7, 1943
5 Radio Research Laboratory of Harvard University, Cambridge, Mass. *War in the Ether ,* Press Release dated Nov. 29, 1945.
6 R.V. Jones, *Most Secret War,* Page 387.
7 Daniel T. Kuehl. *Blinding Radar's Eye: The Air Force and Electronic Countermeasures in World War II* by From Air Power History, The Journal of Air and Space History. Vol. 40, No.2, Summer 1993.
8 This daring British raid on the French coast at Bruneval took place on Feb. 27/28 1942. Not only was a German Wurzburg radar captured, but also two prisoners were taken, one of which being a radar operator. The British gained much from this feat in that they learned the Wurzburg was better engineered than their own radar equipment.
9 Daniel T. Kuehl. *Blinding Radar's Eye: The Air Force and Electronic Countermeasures in World War II* by From Air Power History, The Journal of Air and Space History. Vol. 40, No.2, Summer 1993.
10 Alfred Price, *The History of U.S. Electronic Warfare, Vol.1.* Pages 89-90.
11 Stephen L. McFarland and Wesley Phillips Newton, *To Command the Sky.* Pages 52-54 and page 263.
12 J.E. Johnson, *Wing Leader,* Pages 87-88.
13 Alfred Price, *The History of U.S. Electronic Warfare, Vol.1.* Pages 81-82.
14 US AFHRA, Maxwell AFB, Ala. RCM file.
15 US AFHRA, Maxwell AFB, Ala. RCM file.
16 J.E. Johnson, *Wing Leader,* Pages 164.
17 US AFHRA, Maxwell AFB, Ala. 36th Bomb Squadron RCM historical file.
18 US AFHRA, Maxwell AFB, Ala. 36th Bomb Squadron RCM historical file.
19 US AFHRA, Maxwell AFB, Ala. RCM file.
20 US AFHRA, Maxwell AFB, Ala. 36th Bomb Squadron RCM historical file.
21 US AFHRA, Maxwell AFB, Ala. 36th Bomb Squadron RCM historical file.
22 US AFHRA, Maxwell AFB, Ala. RCM document dated 30 May, 1944 from Lt. Col. R.L. Snider, Asst. Signal Comm. Off. for Hq. Air Service Command, US Strategic Air Forces in Europe to Col. Dixon:
23 Headquarters, Bomber Command - RCM for Overlord, from *War in the Ether, Appendix E* via RAF Hendon Museum.
24 Headquarters, Bomber Command - RCM for Overlord, from *War in the Ether, Appendix E* via RAF Hendon Museum.
25 All times given are based on Greenwich Mean Time 24 hour clock.
26 US AFHRA, Maxwell AFB, Ala. 36th Bomb Squadron RCM historical file. This and all subsequent operational mission information found within this file.
27 Previously unpublished RAF document from the William Hoagland collection.
28 Previously unpublished RAF document from the James Warner collection.
29 New York Post, Tuesday, June 6, 1944. Associated Press report. From the Claude O'Brien collection.
30 Via Madeleine Blais.
31 US AFHRA, Maxwell AFB, Ala. RCM historical file. Secret Courier Sheet 0f June 27, 1944 from Signal Communications Officer, Col. George P. Dixon to Director of Operations, Col. Alfred B. Maxwell. Subject: 803rd Squadron, 100th Group.
32 Stephen L. McFarland and Wesley Phillips Newton, *To Command the Sky.* Pages 189 and 190.
33 Denis Richards, *The Hardest Victory; RAF Bomber Command in the Second World War.* Page 321.
34 Murray Peden, *A Thousand Shall Fall.* Pages 414-416.
35 US AFHRA, Maxwell AFB, Ala. RCM file document from Headquarters of U.S. Strategic Air Forces in Europe, Office of Director of Operations, to Col. Alfred R. Maxwell, dated August 1, 1944.
36 US AFHRA, Maxwell AFB, Ala. Station 113 Cheddington file.
37 US AFHRA, Maxwell AFB, Ala. Station 113 Cheddington file.
38 US AFHRA, Maxwell AFB, Ala. 36th Bomb Squadron RCM historical file.
39 Via Dr. Robert F. Hambaugh Jr.
40 Murray Peden, *A Thousand Shall Fall .* Pages 417-418.
41 In February 1942 the head of Bomber Command, the Air Officer Commanding-in-Chief Arthur Harris directed that the four towns of Essen, Cologne, Dusseldorf, and Duisburg be classed as "industrial areas". This new directive placed these four towns as the primary object of area-bombing operations, thereby focusing on the destruction of enemy civilian populations and the morale of the industrial workers. Prior to this time Bomber Command preferred not to specifically target civilian areas, only industrial workplaces. Denis Richards, *The Hardest Victory; RAF Bomber Command in the Second World War.* Pages 146-147.
42 The 44th Bomb Group was nicknamed "The Flying Eightballs" and had many claims to fame. They operated from England longer than any other B24 Group and even though they were able to claim downing more enemy fighters than other B24 Bomb Groups, they sustained the highest missing in action losses. Per Roger Freeman in his book The *Mighty Eighth.* Page 241.
43 Via Dr. Robert F. Hambaugh Jr..
44 US AFHRA, Maxwell AFB, Ala. 36th Bomb Squadron RCM historical file.
45 US AFHRA, Maxwell AFB, Ala. RCM file document.
46 R.V. Jones, *Most Secret War.* Pages 588-589.
47 Lewis Brandon, *Night Flyer .* Page 145.
48 RAF Airborne Intercept radar.
49 RAF Airborne Intercept radar.
50 US AFHRA, Maxwell AFB, Ala. 36th Bomb Squadron RCM historical file.
51 R.V. Jones, *Most Secret War,* Pages 587-588.
52 US AFHRA, Maxwell AFB, Ala. 36th Bomb Squadron RCM historical file.
53 US AFHRA, Maxwell AFB, Ala. 36th Bomb Squadron RCM historical file.
54 R.V. Jones, *Most Secret War,* Page 588.
55 US AFHRA, Maxwell AFB, Ala. 36th Bomb Squadron RCM historical file.
56 US AFHRA, Maxwell AFB, Ala. 36th Bomb Squadron RCM historical file.
57 US AFHRA, Maxwell AFB, Ala. 36th Bomb Squadron RCM historical file.

[58] USAF Safety Agency Headquarters, Norton AFB, CA

[59] J.E. Johnson, *Wing Leader*. Pages 189-190.

[60] US AFHRA, Maxwell AFB, Ala. RCM file document.

[61] US AFHRA, Maxwell AFB, Ala. RCM file document.

[62] US AFHRA, Maxwell AFB, Ala. RCM file document.

[63] US AFHRA, Maxwell AFB, Ala. 36th Bomb Squadron RCM historical file.

[64] Five accident documents via USAF Safety Agency Headquarters, Norton AFB, CA

[65] Coast Guard South Stack Logbook, Holyhead, Wales via Terry Porter.

[66] Coast Guard North Stack Logbook, Holyhead, Wales via Brendan Maguire.

[67] US AFHRA, Maxwell AFB, Ala. RAF Valley file document.

[68] Author believes "Stubbs" to be Lt. Gaylord F. Moulton, the co-pilot for the crew.

[69] Eugene Junkin letters via Ron Junkin

[70] Bing Crosby World War II Armed Forces Live Radio Broadcast Dec.11,1944. On LaserLight Digital #12310. Quote courtesy Kathryn Crosby. Webster's dictionary defines the term "beggar description" as meaning "to exhaust resources".

[71] US AFHRA, Maxwell AFB, Ala. RCM file document.

[72] US AFHRA, Maxwell AFB, Ala. RCM file document.

[73] US AFHRA, Maxwell AFB, Ala. 36th Bomb Squadron RCM historical file.

[74] US AFHRA, Maxwell AFB, Ala. RCM file document.

[75] US AFHRA, Maxwell AFB, Ala. RCM file document.

[76] US AFHRA, Maxwell AFB, Ala. RCM file document.

[77] US AFHRA, Maxwell AFB, Ala. 36th Bomb Squadron RCM historical file.

[78] National Archives, Washington, DC.

[79] US AFHRA, Maxwell AFB, Ala. 36th Bomb Squadron RCM historical file.

[80] USAF Safety Agency Headquarters, Norton AFB, CA

[81] Roger Freeman, *The Mighty Eighth War Manual* . Page 143.

[82] Via Richard C. Sackett

[83] US AFHRA, Maxwell AFB, Ala. RCM file document.

[84] US AFHRA, Maxwell AFB, Ala. RCM file document dated 2/3/45. Subject: RCM Program of the 36th Bomb Squadron

[85] USAF Safety Agency Headquarters, Norton AFB, CA

[86] Via Kathryn Plasterer, sister of Arthur Clemens.

[87] US AFHRA, Maxwell AFB, Ala. 482nd Bomb Group file document.

[88] US AFHRA, Maxwell AFB, Ala. 36th Bomb Squadron RCM historical file.

[89] US AFHRA, Maxwell AFB, Ala. RCM file.

[90] US AFHRA, Maxwell AFB, Ala. RCM file document.

[91] Via Sarah Beaty

[92] Via Kathryn Clemens Plasterer, sister of Arthur Clemens.

[93] US AFHRA, Maxwell AFB, Ala. 36th Bomb Squadron RCM historical file. As seen in this unit history, aircraft of the 36BS did indeed operate over the combat areas over the continent of Europe. Example: The Battle of the Bulge.

[94] USAF Safety Agency Headquarters, Norton AFB, CA

[95] Martin Streetly, *Confound and Destroy* . Page 83.

[96] Alfred Price, *The History of U.S. Electronic Warfare, Vol.1.*, Page 252.

[97] *Journal of Electronic Defense*, October 1996 issue. Page 26. Official Publication of the Association of Old Crows.

Bibliography

BOOKS

Brandon, Lewis. *Night Flyer,* London: Goodall Publications Limited, 1992.
Carty, Pat. *Secret Squadrons of the Eighth*, Stillwater, MN: Specialty Press, 1990.
Freeman, Roger. *The Mighty Eighth War Manual,* Osceola, WI: Motorbooks 1991.
Harris, Sir Arthur. *Bomber Offensive*, Stackpole Books, 1998.
Johnson, J.E. *Wing Leader* , London: Chatto & Windus Ltd. 1956.
Jones, R.V. *Most Secret War.* London: Coronet Books, 1992.
Millar, George. *The Bruneval Raid,* Garden City, New York: Doubleday & Company, Inc. 1975.
Parker, Danny S. *Battle of the Bulge*, Conshohocken, PA: Combined Books, Inc. 1991.
Peden, Murray. *A Thousand Shall Fall,* Stittsville, Canada: Canada's Wings Inc. 1979.
Price, Alfred.*The History of U.S. Electronic Warfare, Vol 1* Westford, MA, Association of Old Crows, 1984.
Richards, Denis. *The Hardest Victory - RAF Bomber Command in the Second World War*, London: Hodder & Stoughton, 1994.
Russell, Francis. *The Secret War ,* Alexandria, Virginia: Time-Life Books Inc., 1977.
Stephen L. McFarland and Wesley Phillips Newton, *To Command the Sky*, Washington: Smithsonian Institution Press, 1991.
Streetly, Martin. *Confound and Destroy,* London: Jane's Publishing Ltd., 1985.

ARTICLES

Hendon, Royal Air Force Museum, *"War in the Ether"*. 1-8. Appendix E.
Kuehl, Daniel T. "Blinding Radar's Eye: The Air Force and Electronic Countermeasures in World War II." *Air Power History,* Vol. 40, No.2, (Summer 1993): 14-24.
Radio Research Laboratory of Harvard University, Cambridge, Mass. Press Release, "War in the Ether", Nov. 29, 1945. 1-10.

USAF Historical Research Agency, Maxwell Air Force Base, Alabama, Microfilm Files:

36th Bomb Squadron (H) RCM	A0548 & A0549
RCM	A5771A
STATION 113	A0470
RAF VALLEY	A0169
COMPOSITE COMMAND	B5118
482nd BOMB GROUP	B0640 & B0641
8th Bomber Command	B5177

Headquarters U.S. Air Force Safety Agency at Norton, CA and Kirtland AFB NM.

PERSONAL DIARIES

Iredell S. Hutton
John Shamp
Arthur R. Ledtke
William F. Flagler

TAPED INTERVIEW

Professor of Electronics Donald Reynolds & the Association of Old Crows in 1982 . From the Association of Old Crows, The AOC Building, 1000 North Payne Street, Alexandria, Virginia 22314-1696.

Acknowledgments

The following individuals helped with this book:

Don C. Albinson
Ralph Angstadt
Richard Ashmore
Mrs. Leonard Backer
Wayne Bailey
Walter Baker
Raymond Barta
Louis Beacock
Fred Belcher
Arthur Bennett
Wade Birmingham
Dick Black
Al Bohne
Eileen Boorman
Bill Bright
Bernard Brodien
Bill Brown Jr.
Art Brusila
Don Burch
Albert Caldwell
James Carpenter
Jack Charlton
Frank Church
Mrs. Dewayne Copestick
Andrew Cota
Kathryn Crosby
Joseph Danahy
Stanley Dombrosky
Jim Dukeman
George Eberwine
John Edwards
Jack Evans
Irl Fife
Bill Flagler
Lt. Col. Damaso Garcia
Victor Gehres
Casimir Gierlasinski
Vane N. L. Glendening
Fred Greenfield
Brian Gunderson
James Hamilton
John Harkins
Frank Hatscher
Leon Hendrickson
Leo Hoffman
Joseph Hornsby
J. Gene Isgur
Ron Junkin
Constanti Kazak
Robert P. King
Royce Kittle
George Klemm
William Krueger

George Amos
Peter Ardizzi
Mrs. Clifford Asquith
Franklin Badum
Jack Baines
Irvin Banta
Joseph Bartus, Jr.
Mrs. John Beaty
Mrs. Issac Benghiat
Laurier Bilodeau
Peter Bittner
Mrs. Aristide Blais
David Booker
William Bordas
Harry Broadhead
Joseph Brookshire
Richard Brunell
Howard Buis
Bill Butler
Phyllis Calisch
Richard Catt
Chris Chrisner
Ercel Coburn
Ralph Cordell
David G. Crosby, III
Erlon Curtis
Lawrence Dickson
Bert Durand
Bruce Edwards
Art Eschbach
William Fenster
Daniel J. Finn
Mrs. Harold Flynn
James Garrett
Mrs. Benjamin Gewirtzman
Donald Gilzinger
Mrs. Robert Green
Art Gulliver
Dr. Robert F. Hambaugh, Jr.
Leon Hammer
Stanley Harris
Gordon Heath
William Hoagland
Don Hope
John Houlick
Lester Jones
Howard Kasch
Mrs. William Keenan
Jack Kings
Marvin Klank
Leonard Kottnestette
Saul Kupferman
Wilbur Kruse
Dr. I. B. Holley

Daniel T. Kuehl
Ed Lampson
Dean and JoAnn Latvaitis
Art Ledtke
John Madero
Mr. & Mrs. Jimmy J. Marchello
Louis McCarthy
Douglas McComb
Quenton MacGillivray
Ray Miller
Norman and Jean Morin
Dick Mulligan
Walt Natishyn
Dick Obenschain
Norman Olund
Frank Paradowski
George Paris
Robert Pepper
Kim Rayner Pike
Glenwood Poindexter
Peter Pragit
Francis Preimesberger
Mrs. Curtis Quissell
Harry Raupp, Jr.
Paul Robbiano
Lewis Rylander
George Sandberg
Mrs. Robert Saringer
Frank Senn
Nick Senter
John Shamp
Earl Siler
Mineard Smith
James Snoddy
Sam & Sarah Sox
William Stallcup
Roy Stroud
Randy Sturm
Mrs. Thomas Styles
Roy Tackett
Joseph Thome
Kelton Thrower
Charles Todaro
Charles Travis
Mrs. Emery Turknett
Anthony Vaccaro
Mrs. Paul Vieth
Odis Waggoner
James Warner
Bill Whitworth
James Wooden
Mrs. Everett Worthington
William Zeidler

Donat Lafond
Norman Landberg
Mrs. George F. Lechner
Raymon Long
Brendan Maguire
James Marino
Cecil McClure
Bill McCrory
David and Shirley Merrill
Marcel Millet
Roland Morin
Mr. & Mrs. James Myers
Howard Nolan
Jim O'Loughlin
James Ostler
Henry Parke
Murray Peden
Anthony Perry
Kathryn Clemens Plasterer
Paul J. Pond, Jr.
Mrs. Victor E. Pregeant III
Stuart Putney
Rafael Ramos
Melvin Remus
Barry Rosch
Dick Sackett
Charles Sanders
Dennis Scanlan
Mr. & Mrs. Robert M. Senn, Jr.
Harry Setzer
Mrs. Donald Shore
James Sloan
Weston Smith
Harry Soderstrom
Leonard Srebnick
Marge Zapotocky Starr
Stanley Studstrup
Robert G. Stutzman
Hank Suchenski
Robert Thomas, Sr.
James O. Thompson
Frank Titus
Arbutus Dautel Topliff
Frank Trovato
Donald Upper
Lawrence Van Noy
Leon Vigdor
Ralph Wahler
Norvell O. Way
Mike Wokich
H. Bosley Woolf
James Young
Sam Ziff